Robert Gebhen

OUR QUEST FOR HAPPINESS

BOOK FOUR

Nihil Obstat:

Reverend JOHN A. McMAHON
Censor Deputatus.

Imprimatur:

✠ SAMUEL ALPHONSUS CARDINAL STRITCH,
Archiepiscopus Chicagiensis

*Feast of the Annunciation
of the Blessed Virgin Mary*

1946

TOWARD THE ETERNAL COMMENCEMENT

OUR QUEST FOR HAPPINESS

The Story of Divine Love

A TEXTBOOK SERIES

FOR

HIGH SCHOOL RELIGION

BOOK FOUR

For the Senior Year

BY

RIGHT REV. MSGR. CLARENCE E. ELWELL, PH.D.

MOST REV. JAMES T. O'DOWD, PH.D., S.T.D.
REV. ANTHONY N. FUERST, S.T.D.
FRANK J. SHEED
VERY REV. JOHN J. VOIGHT, M.A., ED.D.

1957

MENTZER, BUSH & COMPANY
CHICAGO

←
Murillo   *By Ewing Galloway, N. Y.*

THE HOLY FAMILY

EDITORIAL BOARD

LITERARY CONTRIBUTORS TO THE SERIES

Sister Frances Raphael Beaufait, I.H.M., B.A., Monroe, Mich.

Rev. E. W. Carlen, S.M., B.A., Dayton, O.

Sister Mary William Curry, O.S.U., A.B., Cleveland, O.

Sister Regina Clare DeClaire, S.C., M.A., Mt. St. Joseph, O.

Sister Irma Donahue, C.S.J., M.A., Cleveland, O.

Sister Mary St. Therese Dunn, S.N.D., M.A., Cleveland, O.

Brother John Emling, M.A., B.S., Dayton, O.

Sister Mary Agera Gerke, S.N.D., M.A., Cleveland, O.

Sister Mary Pauline Karp, C.S.J., M.A., Cleveland, O.

Sister Mary Florice Keavney, S.N.D., M.A., Cleveland, O.

Sister Mary Celeste Kocab, O.S.F., M.A., Joliet, Ill.

Sister Mary Ambrose Maggini, C.S.J., M.S., Cleveland, O.

Sister St. Ann Murphy, C.S.J., M.A., B.L.S., Cleveland, O.

Sister Mary Rosalia Paulus, O.P., M.A., B.S. in L.S., Akron, O.

Sister Mary Emil Penet, I.H.M., B.A., Monroe, Mich.

Sister Mary Roberta Toomey, O.S.U., M.A., Cleveland, O.

ACKNOWLEDGMENTS

On the completion of this high school religion series with the publication of this the fourth volume, we feel it our duty to express thanks to our Triune God—the source of whatever good there is in man's works—for the honor of having been allowed to act as His instruments in bringing into being anything of value this series may possess. The defects we freely acknowledge to be the results of the imperfections of the weak, human instruments He has deigned to employ.

Under God, we owe a very special word of gratitude to His Excellency the Most Reverend Joseph Schrembs, Archbishop, late Bishop of Cleveland, with whose permission and encouragement work on this series was begun eight years ago; also to his former Auxiliary, Most Reverend James A. McFadden, Bishop of Youngstown.

A full measure of gratitude is likewise due to His Excellency, Most Reverend Edward F. Hoban, Bishop of Cleveland, for having allowed us to bring the task to completion and fruition.

To Mr. Frank Sheed, who has so excellently and so graciously written the second part of the unit on Apologetics, an expression of deep appreciation is a matter of duty and a source of pleasure.

In addition to those to whom we have expressed our indebtedness in former volumes we wish to extend our acknowledgments to all who have contributed in any way to this series. Among many others may we mention Mr. Ernest King for his excellent execution of the art work; Mrs. N. Vajda for her most devoted and intelligent typing of the manuscripts; Miss Patricia McDonough, Miss Florence Skura and former secretaries of the Diocesan School Board Office in Cleveland for loyal, laborious and unselfish cooperation. May He in whose honor it was done reward them.

CONTENTS

UNIT ONE: OUR LIFE, OUR SWEETNESS, AND
OUR HOPE 22

1. THE LIFE OF THE BLESSED VIRGIN MARY 27
2. THE FEASTS OF THE BLESSED VIRGIN 44
3. THE PRIVILEGES OF THE BLESSED VIRGIN 47
4. THE VIRTUES OF THE BLESSED VIRGIN MARY . . . 56
5. OUR LADY, THE INSPIRATION OF TRUE ART . . . 69
6. SHRINES AND PLACES OF PILGRIMAGE 86
7. DEVOTIONS TO THE BLESSED VIRGIN,
MOTHER OF GOD 89

UNIT TWO: A SENIOR LOOKS INTO THE FUTURE   106

1. DEATH—GOING HOME TO GOD 111
2. EXTREME UNCTION, THE SPECIAL SACRAMENT
OF THE DYING 124
3. HELPING SOULS TO HEAVEN 134
4. THE LAST RITES OF THE CHURCH 147
5. MEETING MY MASTER FACE TO FACE 156
6. MY LIFE IN THE OTHER WORLD 158
7. THE GENERAL JUDGMENT 175

UNIT THREE: THE GREAT CHOICE 185

1. MY STATE IN LIFE, WHAT SHALL IT BE 194
2. THE HIGHEST CALLING—SERVING GOD AND MAN
IN RELIGION 198
3. THE UNMARRIED STATE IN THE WORLD 230
4. CAREERS 233
5. THE HOLY STATE OF MATRIMONY (PART ONE) . 242
6. THE HOLY STATE OF MATRIMONY (PART TWO) . 259
7. THE SACRAMENT OF MATRIMONY (CONCLUDED) . 306

UNIT FOUR: BUILDING A BETTER WORLD 328

1. THE VIRTUE OF JUSTICE 335
2. THE SEVENTH AND TENTH COMMANDMENTS . . 348
3. THE EIGHTH COMMANDMENT—THE VIRTUE
OF TRUTHFULNESS 383
4. THE SOCIAL ENCYCLICALS 402
5. A LOGICAL ANALYSIS AND REARRANGEMENT
OF THE *QUADRAGESIMO ANNO*—A REVIEW . . 427

UNIT FIVE: THE REASONABLENESS OF OUR FAITH   447

1. AN INTRODUCTION TO APOLOGETICS 457
2. A. PROVING THE THREE KEY TRUTHS 467
B. CHRIST IS GOD-MADE MAN 488
C. THE CHURCH CHRIST FOUNDED 506

PRAYERS*

In addition to the prayers included in the preceeding three volumes, especially the *Angelus, Regina Coeli,* Hail Holy Queen, *Memorare,* and Mysteries of the Rosary in Book One (p. 9 and p. 463), the seniors could learn the following:

My Queen! my Mother! I give thee all myself, and, to show my devotion to thee, I consecrate to thee my eyes, my ears, my mouth, my heart, my entire self. Wherefore, O loving Mother, as I am thine own, keep me, defend me, as thy property and possession.

(500 days. Plenary indulgence, usual conditions, if repeated every day for month.)

AVE MARIS STELLA

Hail thou star of ocean,
God's own mother blest,
Ever sinless Virgin,
Gate of heavenly rest.

Oh! by Gabriel's Ave,
Uttered long ago,
Eva's name reversing
'Stablish peace below.

Break the captive's fetters,
Light on blindness pour;
All our ills expelling,
Every bliss implore.

Show thyself a Mother;
May the Word divine
Born for us thine Infant,
Hear our prayers through thine.

Virgin all excelling,
Mildest of the mild;
Freed from guilt preserve us
Meek and undefiled.

Keep our life all spotless,
Make our way secure,
Til we find in Jesus,
Joy forevermore.

Through the highest Heaven
To the almighty Three,
Father, Son and Spirit
One same glory be. Amen.

(3 years. Plenary indulgence, usual conditions, if repeated daily for month.)

O Mary, conceived without sin, pray for us who have recourse to thee; O refuge of sinners, Mother of the dying, forsake us not at the hour of our death; obtain for us the grace of perfect sorrow, sincere contrition, the pardon and remission of our sins, a worthy receiving of the holy Viaticum, and the comfort of the Sacrament of Extreme Unction, in order that we may appear with greater security before the throne of the just but merciful Judge, our God and our Redeemer. Amen. (500 days)

A PRAYER FOR CHOOSING A STATE OF LIFE

O my God, Thou art the God of wisdom and good counsel, Thou who readest in my heart a sincere desire to please Thee alone and to direct myself in regard to my choice of a state of life, in conformity with Thy holy will in all things; by the intercession of the most holy Virgin, my Mother, and of my Patron Saints, grant me the grace to know that state of life which I ought to choose, and to embrace it when known, in order that thus I may seek Thy glory and increase it, work out my own salvation and deserve the heavenly reward which Thou hast promised to those who do Thy holy will. Amen. (300 days, once a day.)

*Taken from the *Raccolta,* Official Edition, 1943, with permission of Benziger Brothers, Inc.

A PRAYER TO BE SAID BY CHILDREN IN BEHALF OF THEIR PARENTS

Almighty and everlasting God, who, in the secret counsels of Thine ineffable Providence, has been pleased to call us into life by means of our parents, who thus partake of Thy divine power in our regard, mercifully hear the prayer of filial affection which we offer to Thee in behalf of those to whom Thou hast given a share of Thy fatherly mercy, in order that they might lavish upon us in our journey through life the consoling gift of Thy holy and generous love.

Dear Lord, fill our parents with Thy choicest blessings; enrich their souls with Thy holy grace; grant that they may faithfully and constantly guard that likeness to Thy mystic marriage with Thy Church, which Thou didst imprint upon them on the day of their nuptials. Fill them with the spirit of holy fear, which is the beginning of wisdom, and continually move them to impart the same to their children; in such wise may they ever walk in the way of Thy commandments, and may their children be their joy in this earthly exile and their crown of glory in their home in heaven.

Finally, Lord God, grant that both our father and our mother may attain to extreme old age and enjoy perpetual health in mind and body; may they deserve to sing Thy praises forever in our heavenly country in union with us, their children, giving Thee most hearty thanks that Thou hast bestowed upon them in this valley of tears the great gift of a share in the light of Thy infinite fruitfulness and of Thy divine fatherhood. Amen. (300 days.)

My Mother, my hope. (300 days.)

Holy Mary, deliver us from the pains of hell. (300 days.)

O Virgin Mary, Mother of Jesus, make us saints. (300 days.)

Bless us, Mary Maiden mild, bless us, too, her tender Child. (300 days.)

A Prayer
Before Assembly To Transact Some Public Business

We are come, O God the Holy Ghost, we are come before Thee, hindered indeed by our many and grievous sins, but especially gathered together in Thy Name. Come unto us and be with us; vouchsafe to enter our hearts; teach us what we are to do and whither we ought to tend; show us what we must accomplish, in order that, with Thy help, we may be able to please Thee in all things. Be Thou alone the Author and the Finisher of our judgments, who alone with God the Father and His Son dost possess a glorious Name.

Suffer us not to disturb the order of justice, Thou who lovest equity above all things; let not ignorance draw us into devious paths, nor partiality sway our minds, neither let respect of riches or persons pervert our judgment; but unite us to Thee effectually by the gift of Thine only grace, that we may be one in Thee and may never forsake the truth; insamuch as we are gathered together in Thy Name, so may we in all things hold fast to justice tempered by pity, that so in this life our judgment may in no wise be at variance with Thee and in the life to come we may attain to everlasting rewards for deeds well done. Amen. (3 years.)

A Prayer for the Conversion of Heathens

Have mercy on us, O God of all, and behold us; and send Thy fear upon all the nations that seek not after Thee, that they may know Thee, that there is no God by only Thou, and may tell forth Thy wondrous works. Make the time short, and remember the end, that they may declare Thy wonderful works, and let all the ends of the earth fear Thee.

V. Make a joyful noise unto God, all the earth;

R. Serve the Lord with gladness.

Let us pray

Almighty and everlasting God, who seekest not the death of sinners, but always that they may live; graciously receive our prayer, and deliver the heathen from the worship of idols and gather them into Thy holy Church unto the praise and glory of Thy name. Through Christ our Lord. Amen.

(3 years. Plenary indulgence, usual conditions, if recited daily for month.)

Chart I. CHART SHOWING DIVISION OF SUBJECT MATTER FOR THE FOUR YEARS OF HIGH SCHOOL RELIGION AND CORRELATION OF VARIOUS PARTS

Our Quest for Happiness Is the Story of Divine Love as Revealed in:

A. INSTRUCTIONAL MATTER (Knowledge—Intellect)	The Creative Love of God the Father FRESHMAN YEAR	The Redeeming Love of Christ the Incarnate Son SOPHOMORE YEAR	The Sanctifying Love of The Holy Ghost and the Church JUNIOR YEAR	The Beatifying Love of Our Triune God SENIOR YEAR
1. DOCTRINES (What faith asks and helps us to believe)	CREED: Art. 1, GOD, His existence, nature, attributes; TRINITY, CREATION, Fall, Original Sin, Nature of Man, Purpose of Man's Existence	CREED: Art. 2-7 INCARNATION and REDEMPTION; Grace	CREED: Art. 8-10 1. HOLY GHOST; 2. Grace; 3. The CHURCH: Nature, Attributes, Marks, Growth, Powers; COMMUNION OF SAINTS; 4. FORGIVENESS OF SINS, Indulgences	CREED: Art. 7, 11-12 LAST THINGS; Resurrection of Body, Life Eternal. BLESSED VIRGIN, Angels, Saints
2. SACRAMENTS (First sources of hope of grace and salvation)	In General BAPTISM (Original Sin) CONFIRMATION	HOLY EUCHARIST Doctrinal, Moral, Liturgical and Practical Side	Confirmation (brief review) PENANCE (Receive Holy Ghost) (Holy Orders—with Church)	EXTREME UNCTION—with Last Things HOLY ORDERS MATRIMONY
3. MORALS (What: love of God leads and helps us to do) a) Decalogue	Basic Moral Principles FIRST, SECOND, and THIRD COMMANDMENTS	Principles of Morality THIRD and FOURTH COMMANDMENTS	FIFTH, SIXTH, and NINTH COMMANDMENTS, Capital Sins—Sin	SEVENTH, EIGHTH, and TENTH COMMANDMENTS
b) Precepts		First and Fourth Precepts	Second, Third, Fifth Precepts and other laws of Church	Sixth Precept
4. PRAYER (Other main source of hope of grace and salvation) a) Public (The Liturgy)	Nature and Kind of Prayers. The LITURGICAL YEAR: Nature, Plan, Purpose, Baptism	MASS and Missal, Benedictus, Magnificat, etc.	PENITENTIAL SEASONS: Advent, Lent, Rogation, and Ember Days	BLESSED VIRGIN: Life, Hymns, Poems. Holy Orders, Matrimony, Extreme Unction
b) Private	ACT OF FAITH, Morning and Evening Prayers, Four Creeds, Divine Praises, Collects, etc.	ACT OF HOPE, Spiritual Communion, Pater, Ave, ANGELUS, Meditation, etc.	ACT OF LOVE To Holy Ghost, Litanies, Contrition, Confiteor, Stabat, Miserere, etc.	ROSARY, Angelus, De Profundis, etc.
5. SCRIPTURE	Introduction The OLD TESTAMENT, read in connection with the subject matter	LIFE OF CHRIST—from GOSPELS (with Doctrine and Fourth Commandment)	ACTS OF THE APOSTLES (with Holy Ghost and Church) and Epistles	EPISTLES APOCALYPSE (parts) Life of Blessed-Virgin
6. CHURCH HISTORY	Pertinent points correlated with subject matter	Correlated with other material	SYNOPTIC SURVEY of the History of Christianity	Correlated with other material
7. LIVES OF THE SAINTS	B.V.M. (Faith) St. Thomas, MARTYRS (Witnesses of Faith) Great Missioners	Saints of Missal and Blessed Sacrament B.V.M, John Baptist	APOSTLES, Fathers, and Doctors St. John Nep., Hildebrand, Pius X, Leo I, etc.	BLESSED VIRGIN Saints in all States of Life; Founders of Orders
8. APOLOGETICS: Modern Errors & Objections	Atheism, Materialism, EVOLUTION, Rationalism, Modern Difficulties & Objections and Their Answers	Gnostics, Arians, Luther, Modern Errors	Pelagians, Primacy Church and State NATIONALISM, NATURALISM	APOLOGETICS PROPER; Rationalism, Nestorians, Modern Errors on Morals and Marriage and in Phil. Encyclicals on Education, Marriage, Labor

B. FORMATIONAL MATTER (Character—Will)

9. HABIT FORMATION	To develop INTELLECTUAL habits	To develop habits of WILL	To develop habits to guide IRASCIBLE and CONCUPISCIBLE passions.	To develop all habits
A. VIRTUES				
a) Theological	FAITH—Nature and practice / Hope / Charity	Faith / HOPE / Charity	Faith / Hope / CHARITY	FAITH / HOPE / CHARITY
b) Cardinal	PRUDENCE / Justice / Fortitude / Temperance	Prudence / JUSTICE / Fortitude / Temperance	Prudence / Justice / Fortitude / TEMPERANCE	PRUDENCE / JUSTICE / FORTITUDE / TEMPERANCE
c) Others	HUMILITY, Zeal, Purity, Tact, Studiousness, Piety, Courage, Thoughtfulness, etc.	OBEDIENCE, Religion, Piety, Nobility, Patience, Simplicity, Purity, Courtesy, Politeness, Gratitude, etc.	PURITY, HONESTY, PENANCE, Moderation, Sobriety, Chastity, Neatness, Loyalty, Clemency, Modesty, etc.	TRUTHFULNESS, DETACHMENT, Helpfulness, Liberality, Friendliness, Graciousness, Kindness, Good Manners
d) Gifts of Holy Ghost	Understanding Knowledge / Counsel	Fear of Lord / Piety	Wisdom / Fortitude	Wisdom Knowledge / Understanding Piety
e) Beatitudes	1st and 2nd—Poor in Spirit—Meek	4th and 5th—Hunger for Justice, Merciful	6th and 7th—Clean of Heart, Peacemaker	3rd & 8th—Mourn and Suffer Persecution
f) Fruits of Holy Ghost	Faith, Patience, Long-suffering	Benignity, Goodness, Mildness	Charity, Modesty, Continency, Chastity	Joy, Peace
g) Evangelical Counsels		Obedience	Chastity	Poverty
B. WORKS OF MERCY				
a) Corporal	1. Feed hungry / 2. Give drink to thirsty	3. Clothe naked / 4. Ransom captives	5. Harbor harborless (spiritually and physically—Missions, Orphans, etc.)	6. Visit sick / 7. Bury dead
b) Spiritual	2. Instruct ignorant / 3. Counsel doubtful	5. Bear wrongs patiently / 6. To forgive injuries	1. Admonish sinners	4. Comfort sorrowful / 7. Pray for living and dead
C. VICES				
a) Capital Sins	Pride	Sloth	Lust, Anger, Gluttony	Covetousness, Lust, Envy
b) Others	Profanity, selfishness, etc. / Self-indulgence	Disobedience, Missing Mass, etc.	Intemperance, Quarrelling, Immodesty, Impurity	Religious Indifference, Dishonesty, Back-biting
D. CHRISTIAN PRACTICES Sacramentals	DAILY MASS and COMMUNION Prayer, Thinking with Church Sign of Cross, Holy Water, Grace at Meals, Pictures in Home, etc.	DAILY MASS and COMMUNION Having Mass offered, Visits, Forty Hours, Benediction, First Friday, etc.	DAILY MASS and COMMUNION Mortification of Senses, Loyalty and Obedience to Church, Supporting Church, Confession, Indulgenced Prayer, Candles, Ashes, Palms, Stations, Church Unity, etc.	DAILY MASS and COMMUNION Habits for Life—Control of the Senses; Self-Denial, Christian Burial, Scapulars, May and October devotions, Poor Souls, St. Joseph, etc.
E. ASCETICAL THEOLOGY	Purgative Way: avoidance of sin from incipient love based on faith and fear.	Illuminative Way: practice of virtues, based on growing love and hope.	Unitive Way: perfect love based on divine charity and the gifts.	Union Achieved = The Goal, eternal union in glory
F. CATHOLIC ACTION	Spreading the Faith, Pictures in Home, etc. STUDY	Catholic Citizen Personal Sanctification PRAYER	Mission, Parish, and Diocesan activities ACTION	Catholic Home, Holy Name, Knights, St. Vincent de Paul, N.C.W.C., etc. Catholic Action
10. POSSIBLE CORRELATED ACTIVITIES	Read Scriptures. Dramatize Ceremonies of Baptism, Liturgical Chart of Year (Colored), Pamphlets, Decorate Room for Each Unit Each Year. Observance of Feasts of Martyrs and Great Missioners.	Take daily prayers from the Missal. Change with feast or season. Use New Testament and Missal for activities. Special observance of Feasts of Our Lord.	Holy Ghost in Scriptures. Map Series on Spread of Faith. Read the New Testament; Acts, Epistles, etc. Special observance of Feasts of Apostles.	Read Apocalypse. Dramatize marriage ceremony; preparations, call at rectory to arrange: Marriage, Baptism, sick call, Mass. Observance of Feasts of B.V.M.
11. CORRELATION OF OTHER SUBJECTS WITH RELIGION	Science—Existence of God. Paper on Most Beautiful Thing I Ever Saw, etc. Ancient History, Music	Redemption, focus of history, Engl. A Day in Life of Christ When He was My Age. Songs at Christmas, Easter, etc. Eucharist.	Every school subject can and must be correlated with religion, as the core of the curriculum. Songs to Holy Ghost.	Eccles. Latin: "My Favorite Saint," Vocational Guidance—Scientists, etc., and B.V. in Literature, Architecture, etc.

Chart II

OUR QUEST FOR HAPPINESS

CHART SHOWING UNITS AND SEQUENCE FOR THE FOUR YEARS OF HIGH SCHOOL RELIGION

	FRESHMAN YEAR *Our Goal and Our Guides* God, the Creator	SOPHOMORE YEAR *Through Christ Our Lord* Christ, the Incarnate Redeemer	JUNIOR YEAR *The Ark and the Dove* The Holy Ghost, The Church	SENIOR YEAR *Toward the Eternal Commencement* The Future
UNIT I	OUR GUIDES TO OUR GOAL 7 weeks Desire for Happiness, Guides to it; Reason & Faith; Scriptures and Church	THE PROMISED ONE APPEARS 5 weeks Protoevangelium, Prophecies, etc. Incarnation, Nativity and Early Life	THE DOVE 5 weeks The Holy Ghost and His Mission	OUR LIFE, OUR SWEETNESS, AND OUR HOPE 5 weeks Blessed Virgin, Her life, etc.
UNIT II	OUR ILLUSTRATED GUIDE BOOK 4 weeks The Liturgical Year as a Dramatic Summary of Faith and Morals	IN HIS FOOTSTEPS 4 weeks Principles of Morality Fourth Commandment	THE ARK 8 weeks The Church—2d, 3d, 5th, Precepts	A SENIOR LOOKS INTO THE FUTURE 4 weeks The Last Things and Extreme Unction
UNIT III	OUR SOURCE AND OUR GOAL 5 weeks God, His Nature, Perfections; The Trinity	THE REDEEMER: HIS MESSAGE AND CREDENTIALS 9 weeks Public Life of Christ to Passion (Exclusive)	THE DOVE GUIDES THE ARK THROUGH THE AGES 12 weeks Synopsis of Church History	THE GREAT CHOICE 10 weeks Choice of State in Life; Holy Orders and Matrimony
UNIT IV	LOVE, PRIDE AND THE PROMISE 7 weeks Creation, the Fall and the Protoevangelium	THE PROMISE FULFILLED 8 weeks Passion, Redemption, Grace	THE PLANK IN SHIPWRECK 6 weeks Forgiveness of Sins, Penance	BUILDING A BETTER WORLD 9 weeks Seventh, Eighth, and Tenth Commandments
UNIT V	DIVINE AIDS IN OUR QUEST 6 weeks Sacraments—Baptism, in Particular as the remedy for the Fall; Confirmation	FROM THE RISING OF THE SUN 5 weeks Sacrifice of the Mass, Third Commandment, First Precept	TEMPLES OF THE HOLY GHOST 5 weeks Fifth, Sixth and Ninth Commandments	JUSTIFYING OUR FAITH 8 weeks Synopsis of Apologetics
UNIT VI	RULES FOR A SUCCESSFUL QUEST 7 weeks Basic Principles of Morality and Duties to God (First three Commandments)	THE GIFT OF DIVINE LOVE 5 weeks The Eucharist as a Sacrament Fourth Precept		

LIST OF COLOR ILLUSTRATIONS

TITLE	FACING PAGE
MADONNA OF PEACE	16
SISTINE MADONNA	49
PARADISE	176
TOBIAS AND THE ANGEL	209
HOLY FAMILY	272
ST. JOACHIM AND ST. ANNE	305
ST. ILDEFONSUS	400
BYZANTINE MADONNA	433

Agostino di Duccio　　　　　　*National Gallery of Art, Mellon Collection*

MADONNA AND CHILD

14

FOREWORD TO THE SENIORS

A Look Back

We have arrived, at long last, at the beginning of our final year in high school. Before we cast our eyes ahead let us take a look to see how far we have come.

For three years, in our study of religion, we have been learning the details of the engrossing story of the love of God for the human race.

As freshmen we concentrated on those deeds of love attributed especially to the *Eternal Father*. We learned how God started man on the Quest for Perfect Happiness, equipping him with wondrous gifts: natural, preternatural and supernatural. We saw man reject God's goodness and forfeit supernatural happiness, and we saw God promise to restore that rejected privilege once again to those who would *believe*.

As sophomores we were permitted to learn how Christ the *Incarnate Son*, by His obedience and by His Passion and undying Sacrifice, satisfied divine justice and regained for us the opportunity and the means *to hope* for everlasting bliss.

As juniors the mysterious workings of the *Holy Spirit* in the Church and in individual souls began to unfold before our eyes. We came to realize how the grace of Christ flowed into human lives unto sanctification and salvation. We saw how God enabled us to *love* Him and be loved by Him.

A LOOK INTO THE FUTURE

And now we are seniors, looking ahead to June and to life.

We have just reviewed briefly what our Triune God, Father, Son, and Holy Spirit, has done for us in the past. Let us examine what His love still holds in store for those who love Him in return.

Let us stand, as it were, on a mountain top and look into the misty distances of the future, toward that Eternal Commencement which we hope one day to attain. Three roads lead thither, toward that Gate of Death which opens into eternal peace or woe. We must begin to think about choosing our road, but, before that, let us first see what happens as we pass through the gate and what lies beyond. It will help us choose aright.

As a preparation, however, lest the somberness of such thoughts depress us, let us fill our souls with courage and confidence by looking up to her who is our Life, our Sweetness, and our Hope—Mary, the Mother of God and our Mother.

If we know her, we will love her; and if we love her we already have a pledge of reaching that Eternal Commencement to which all earthly commencements are but a prelude.

THE GLORIOUS UNITY OF OUR HOLY CATHOLIC RELIGION

Our holy religion is like a beautiful diamond whose many gleaming facets reflect into our mind's eye the Light which is God. In the diamond each facet is different, yet all unite to form one, single, glorious whole. In our religion, likewise, although there is the most amazing multiplicity of doctrine and practice, of counsel and precept, all are so closely interrelated, all so intimately interconnected, that if even one of these be disturbed or changed, the full beauty is no longer there.

Our religion is one logical whole. Everything fits. Nothing is out of place. Nothing is superfluous. Have you noticed during your three years of religion that we have taken the basic doctrines of our holy religion in the sequence in which they are found in the Apostles' Creed, which in the main is the sequence found in the Bible and in the liturgical year? We have taken the sacraments, from Baptism to Matrimony, in succession, one or more each

THE MADONNA OF PEACE

year, and each of them has had a natural and logical connection with the doctrines we have studied. We have taken the commandments too, one or more at a time, and have studied them in their usual sequence, and have found that they, too, seem to fit as if God had planned it that way. So it is with every other thing in our religion, although we cannot of ourselves always detect the relationship.

Truly, there is a marvelous unity in the work of God. Studying it gives a person who likes order and logic a deep mental satisfaction, and a slight foretaste of that thrilling joy which we shall experience when we see God. On that happy day my whole being will heave a sigh of happiness at the beauty and perfection of it all; and will say: Truly, God is great. Who is like Him? Now I have everything I need to make me happy forever and ever, for I have found Someone so utterly good and so infinitely perfect that the greatest happiness I can think of will be to be allowed to know Him and love Him, and to be loved by Him for all eternity.

If you are such a person, delighting in straight thinking, if you are one who likes to see how an intricate pattern fits together, then you will get a mental thrill once again from examining with close attention the Chart Showing Division of Subject Matter for High-School Religion, on pages 10 and 11.

CENTRAL THEME FOR THE FOUR YEARS

Surely you remember the central theme which has already been presented in each of the three previous years, each time in a slightly different way. Let us repeat it again: Man was created to give glory to God. This is why man exists. But man finds within himself an insatiable yearning for happiness. How do these two purposes unite —glory to God and happiness to self? Quite easily; for he who pours out his entire self in an absolutely unselfish way in the task of increasing the glory of God, will find incomparable happiness. *God is Love*. But *love means giving,* not receiving, and they who give, as God gives, they who imitate the outpouring of the Creative Love of God the Father, the wholly unselfish Redemptive Love of God the Incarnate Son, and the divinizing, sanctifying Love of God the Holy Ghost—those who know how the *Three Persons* of the Blessed Trinity beatify themselves as well as us by the infinite love they bestow on one another— they who know these things *and do them*—they will find that Love, the possession of which will bring to its fruition *Our Quest for Happiness*.

OBJECTIVES FOR THE FOUR YEARS

To Love
1. Our chief objective, then, throughout these years has been and will be again this year, *to help us habitually to love God.*

Through Hope
2. Our second objective has been to aid in *forming* those *habits* of mind and will and body which will make us more sure, more steady and more firm in our *confidence in God and His promises.*

And Faith
3. Our third objective is to help us to *know our religion* by *believing* all that God has revealed, that we may live our faith, *spread God's love* and bring happiness to ourselves and to others.

OUTLINE OF SUBJECT MATTER FOR THE SENIOR YEAR

This year we shall study the material listed in the fourth column of the Chart on page 12. It includes the following topics:
1. Articles 7, 11, and 12 of the Apostles' Creed.
2. The Blessed Virgin.
3. The Angels and Saints.
4. Extreme Unction, Holy Orders, Matrimony, and Vocation.
5. The Seventh, Eighth, and Tenth Commandments and the **Sixth** Precept of the Church.
6. The Epistles and the Apocalypse.
7. The Encyclicals on Marriage, Education, and Labor.
8. Apologetics.
9. Correlated points in Church History.

10. The saints, prayers, errors and objections, etc., having connection with this subject matter.
11. The virtues, practices, habits, attitudes, etc., which should be developed or the vices which should be combated in connection with this material or with the present or future needs of the students.

ARRANGEMENT OF SUBJECT MATTER IN UNITS

The subject matter for this senior year has been arranged in the following five units.

		Suggested Time Allotments
UNIT I.	OUR LIFE, OUR SWEETNESS, AND OUR HOPE (Mary, the Mother of God and Our Mother)	5 weeks
UNIT II.	A SENIOR LOOKS INTO THE FUTURE (The Last Things)	4 weeks
UNIT III.	THE GREAT CHOICE (Vocation, Holy Orders, Matrimony)	10 weeks
UNIT IV.	BUILDING A BETTER WORLD (Seventh, Eighth, Tenth Commandments)	9 weeks
UNIT V.	THE REASONABLENESS OF OUR FAITH (Apologetics)	8 weeks

CENTRAL THEME FOR THE SENIOR YEAR

Mary is my Mother. I must go to her for help, for courage, for guidance, for all grace. She will lead me to the right choice. She will help me give glory to God. She will show me how to find happiness. *Ad Jesum per Mariam!*

OBJECTIVES FOR THE SENIOR YEAR

1. To take a calm, clear look into the future; to begin planning our lives; to acquire that knowledge and to form those habits and attitudes needed for a holy, happy, useful life on earth and for an eternity of happiness and of glory to God in heaven.
2. To learn to know and love the Blessed Virgin.
3. To cultivate the virtue of justice as a foundation of a better world.

VIRTUES FOR THE YEAR

This year, in imitation of our Blessed Mother we shall attempt to practice all virtues, as perfectly as possible, placing an accent on love of God and on justice.

GENERAL STUDENT BIBLIOGRAPHY

I. SCRIPTURE AND LITURGY

Holy Bible.
St. Andrew Daily Missal.
Gueranger, *The Liturgical Year* (15 Vols.) Burns, Oates.
Thompson and Stock, *Concordance to the Bible,* Herder.
Vaughan, *Divine Armory of Holy Scripture,* Herder.

II. GENERAL REFERENCE

American Catholic Who's Who, Romig.
Attwater, *Catholic Dictionary,* Macmillan.
Brown, *Catalogue of Novels and Tales by Catholic Authors,* Burns, Oates, etc.
Butler, *Lives of the Saints,* Kenedy.
Catholic Encyclopedia.
Catholic Periodical Index.
Conway, *Library List,* Catholic Unity League, New York. (10,000 recommended books and pamphlets.)
Guide to Catholic Literature, Romig.
Jane Frances, Sister, *Saints for Modern Readers,* (A bibliography), Catholic Library Assn.
Martin, *Catholic Religion,* Herder.
National Catholic Almanac, St. Anthony Guild.
Official Catholic Yearbook, Kenedy.
O'Rourke, *Library Handbook for Catholic Students,* Bruce.
Schuster, *Living Catholic Authors of Past and Present,* St. Louis.
Willging, *Index to American Catholic Pamphlets,* Catholic Library Assn., Scranton.
Booklist of the Marian Library, U. of Dayton. (Also supplement.)

III. OTHER RELIGION TEXTBOOKS

Baltimore Catechism.

Campion, *Catholic Action Series,* Sadlier.

Cassilly, *Religion: Doctrine and Practice,* Loyola.

Christian Brothers, *Manual of Christian Doctrine,* La Salle Bureau, New York.

Deharbe, *Complete Catechism of the Catholic Religion,* Herder.

Falque, *Catholic Truth in Survey,* 2 vols., Benziger.

Gasparri, *Catholic Catechism,* Sheed and Ward.

Gaume, *Catechism of Perseverance,* 4 vols., Gill, Dublin; Benziger, New York.

Graham, *Faith for Life,* Bruce.

Kirsch-Brendan, *Catholic Faith,* Book Three, Kenedy.

Laux, *Course in Religion for Catholic High Schools,* Benziger.

Noll, *Religion and Life,* 4 vols., Sunday Visitor.

Russell, *Your Religion,* Herder.

Weger, Hilary, and Others, *Studies in Religion,* 4 vols., Sadlier.

IV. MAGAZINES AND PERIODICALS

Altar and Home
America
Ave Maria
Catholic Action
Catholic Digest
Catholic Family
Catholic Mind
Catholic Missions
Catholic World
Catholic Youth
Christian Family Monthly
Columbia
Commonweal
Extension
Field Afar
Liturgical Arts
Magnificat
Marianist
Messenger of the Sacred Heart
Orate Fratres
Queen's Work
St. Anthony Messenger
Shield
Sign
Tabernacle and Purgatory
Thought
Torch
Truth

V. DIOCESAN AND WEEKLY NEWSPAPERS

The *Register, Sunday Visitor,* Baltimore *Catholic Review,* Boston *Pilot,* Brooklyn *Tablet, Catholic Action of the South,* Chicago *New World,* Cleveland *Universe Bulletin,* Dubuque *Witness,* London *Tablet,* Los Angeles *Tidings, Michigan Catholic,* Milwaukee *Herald Citizen,* New York *Catholic News,* Philadelphia *Standard and Times, San Francisco Monitor.*

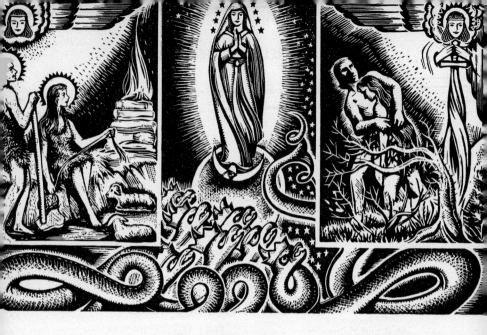

UNIT ONE

Our Life, Our Sweetness, and Our Hope

Mary, Virgin Mother of God, and Our Mother

PART ONE: INTRODUCTION

Saving our souls is no easy task. The road to eternal life is difficult and beset with dangers, and when we stray from the true path, bitterness and discouragement are our lot; but God in His goodness and love, of which we have seen so many examples these past years, has given us special help and grace. He has made us children of the most beautiful, the most glorious, and the most powerful creature that has ever or ever will come forth from His hand. He has given us *Mary*, our *Mother*, to be *Our Life, Our Sweetness, and Our Hope*. In this unit we shall learn many things about her that we did not know before. May they lead us to love her, and to love and imitate her Son as she did.

DIAGNOSTIC EXPLORATION OF WHAT YOU ALREADY KNOW ABOUT THE BLESSED VIRGIN

1. What facts of the Blessed Virgin Mary's life can you recount?
2. Name the feasts of our Blessed Mother.
3. What privileges did God confer on Mary? Why?
4. What is Mary's place in the scheme of Redemption?
5. What virtues did our Blessed Lady practice?
6. Name some ways in which art has glorified her name.
7. What devotions to Mary do you know or practice?
   a. Public Devotions.
   b. Private Devotions

SOME OF THE OBJECTIVES OF THIS UNIT

1. To become better acquainted with our Blessed Mother, her glory, her privileges, her importance to us.
2. To learn about her feasts and to celebrate them in a fitting manner.
3. To make habitual the regular practice of several devotions to the Blessed Virgin and thus to promote personal holiness.
4. To foster great confidence in and a tender love for Christ's Mother and mine.

After deciding whether any of the following or similar assignments will help us learn or apply the material in this unit, we can begin with Part Two on page 27. The *Parallel Readings* and *Related Readings* which follow may also be of assistance.

SUGGESTED ASSIGNMENTS AND ACTIVITIES

A. GROUP ASSIGNMENTS

1. Use some poems on the Blessed Virgin for choral speaking or individual recitation. For example, those found in Thomas Walsh's *Catholic Anthology* (Macmillan, 1928) on pages 43, 97, 111, 113, 268, 274, 308, 454, 456, 458, 466.
2. Write a symposium or radio program on the Blessed Virgin, using her hymns, poems, etc., telling of her virtues and showing her influence for good in the history of the world.
3. Learn to sing one or more of the Latin hymns or canticles to the Blessed Mother:

   a. Magnificat
   b. Alma Redemptoris
   c. Ave Regina Coelorum
   d. Regina Coeli
   e. Salve Regina
   f. O Sanctissima
   g. Stabat Mater
   h. Ave Maris Stella

4. Have individuals or groups collect and decorate the room with the pictures of:

   a. Famous Madonnas
   b. Marian cathedrals
   c. Symbols of our Lady
   d. Shrines and pilgrimages
   e. Any other subject referring to our Blessed Mother

5. Have groups or individuals learn to sing the various famous Ave Marias (Palestrina, Schubert, Bach-Gounod, etc.)

6. Learn and sing the better-known English hymns to Mary.

7. Have representatives of different language groups sing famous hymns to Mary in their own language or in English translations.

8. Arrange to begin this year with a special celebration of the feast of the Birth of the Blessed Virgin (Sept. 8), of the most Holy Name of Mary (Sept. 12), of the Divine Maternity (Oct. 11) and the Immaculate Conception (Dec. 8). Plan also to observe all the feasts of our Blessed Lady.

B. OTHER ASSIGNMENTS

1. Report on the life and work of famous painters of Madonnas: Giotto, Murillo, Raphael, Fra Angelico, etc.

2. Make a list of the shrines or places of pilgrimage to the Blessed Virgin and learn the story of at least three of them.

3. Make a class report on the story of La Salette, Bernadette and Lourdes, Fatima, Guadalupe or any other famous Marian shrine.

4. On the feasts or vigils of feasts of the Blessed Virgin, read the Proper of the Mass for the feast.

5. Report on the history of the Miraculous Medal, the Seven Dolors, the Scapular, the Sodality of the Blessed Virgin or Legion of Mary, the Little Office of the Blessed Virgin, the Litany of the Blessed Virgin, or the Rosary.

6. Translate a hymn to Mary from Latin or any other language.

7. List Madonnas, hymns or poems to the Blessed Virgin, etc., in the order of your preference, giving the reasons for your selections.

8. Write a composition on:

   a. Mary as a Girl
   b. Mary in the Temple
   c. Mary at the Annunciation
   d. The Blessed Virgin and St. Joseph
   e. Mary in her Home at Nazareth
   f. Mary's Influence on Art (or Literature), etc.
   g. Mary, My Model
   h. All Grace Through Mary
   i. The Purity (or any other virtue) of Mary
   j. Devotion to the Immaculate Heart of Mary
   k. Mary's Privileges
   l. My Duties to Mary, My Mother

9. Paraphrase or write about the *Magnificat* or the Hail Mary.
10. Have a box in the room for questions or problems of the students and each Friday, or as needed, spend fifteen minutes discussing and answering them.
11. Read and make a report on any book about the Blessed Virgin.
12. To learn the contributions of Mary to America read some book like Daniel Sargent's *Our Land and Our Lady* or the article "Mary and Columbus" in *St. Anthony Messenger*, Oct. 1942.
13. Report on: the indulgences on the Rosary; or indulgenced prayer and practices in honor of Mary (cf. The Raccolta); or Mary and Our Country (cf. Sargent, *Our Land and Our Lady*).
14. Make a card index or give an illustrated lecture on the books and pamphlets or on the pictures of the Blessed Virgin in your library.
15. If you can think of any other good assignment for this unit on which you would like to work, submit your ideas to the teacher for approval.

RELATED READING IN BOOKS AND PAMPHLETS

Books: *The Mary Book*, National Shrine, Washington, D. C.
Barrett, *Our Lady in the Liturgy*, Herder.
Croarkin, *Our Lady in Poetry*, Chicago, J. Maher.
Eleanore, Sister M., *Mary*, Bruce.
Fuerst, *This Rosary*, Bruce.
Gerbet, *Lily of Israel*, Kenedy.
Haugg, *The Rosary and the Soul of Woman*, Pustet.
Haffert, *Mary in Her Scapular Promise*, Carmelite Fathers, New York.
Hurll, *The Madonna in Art*, Page & Co.
Kelly, *Mary the Mother*, Encyclopedia Press, N. Y.
Lord, *Our Lady in the Modern World*, Queen's Work.
Loyola, Mother M., *Hail, Full of Grace*, Sands & Co., London.
St. Alphonsus Ligouri, *Glories of Mary*, Kenedy.
McElhone, *Feasts of Our Lady*, Bruce (Meditations on 30 feasts).
McNabb, *Mary of Nazareth*, Kenedy.
Martindale, *Our Blessed Lady*, Sheed & Ward.
Paula, Sister M., *The Virgin Mother*, Benziger.
Plus, *Mary in Our Soul Life*, Pustet.
Resch, *Our Blessed Mother*, Bruce.
Robertson, *Famous Italian Pictures and their Story*, Robertson.

Rohner, *Veneration of the Blessed Virgin,* Benziger.
Ryan, *Our Lady of Fatima,* Herder.
Sargent, *Our Land and Our Lady,* Longmans, Green.
Snyder, *Salve Regina,* St. Anthony Guild.
Vassall-Phillips, *Mary, the Mother of God,* Macmillan.
Willam, *The Life of Mary, the Mother of God,* Herder.

Pamphlets (See Willging, E., *Index to Catholic Pamphlets*) :
Devotion to Mary, B.C.P.A., Clyde, Mo.
Our Lady's Feasts, Paulist.
Rosary Novenas to the Blessed Virgin, Paulist.
Burke, *Our Lady's Month,* Paulist.
De Montfort, *True Devotion to the Blessed Virgin,* O. S. Vis.
D'Orazio, *Our Lady of Perpetual Help,* Mt. St. Alphonsus.
Husslein, *All Grace Through Mary,* America.
Husslein, *The Blessed Virgin,* America.
Lord, *A Novena to Mary Immaculate,* Q.W.
Lovasik, *Novena and Triduums for all Feasts of the Blessed Virgin Mary,* B.C.P.A., Clyde, Mo.
Moran, *Love Your Rosary,* Paulist.
Pius XI, *Encyclical on Rosary,* N.C.W.C.
Sheehan, *Mary, the Mother of God,* Paulist.
Tanco, *Our Lady of Guadalupe,* Paulist.
Devotion to the Blessed Virgin, Sunday Visitor.
Mary Immaculate, America.
The Rosary, My Treasure, Benedictine Convent, Clyde, Mo.

PARALLEL READINGS IN OTHER HIGH SCHOOL RELIGION TEXTS

	Campion	Cassilly	Falque	Gaume	Laux	Manual of Chr. Doctr.
Mary	I, 91 II, 252; 298	81; 193; 406	I, 179 II, 32; 42; 198		I, 105 III, 70	73
Feasts of Our Lady	I, 87; 88; 91	81; 193; 326; 384; 428	II, 33; 36; 198	IV, 26; 31; 39; 40; 47; 48	I, 87; 106	553
Devotions	I, 297	193; 513	II, 205	IV, 40		79

Given in volumes and pages, except Gaume, which shows volume and chapter.

Our Life, Our Sweetness, and Our Hope

PART TWO

"And a great sign appeared in heaven: a woman clothed with **the** sun, and the moon was under her feet, and upon her head a crown **of** twelve stars." Apocalypse 12, 1.

SECTION ONE: THE LIFE OF THE BLESSED VIRGIN MARY

A. THE EARLY LIFE OF MARY
  1. HER PARENTS
  2. THE IMMACULATE CONCEPTION—MARY'S FIRST PRIVILEGE
     a. The Church Proclaims the Doctrine
     b. Mary Proclaims the Doctrine
     c. The Immaculate Conception in Christian Art
  3. THE BIRTH OF THE BLESSED VIRGIN
  4. MARY IS PRESENTED TO GOD
  5. MARY MAKES A VOW OF VIRGINITY
  6. THE BLESSED VIRGIN IS ESPOUSED TO AND MARRIES ST. JOSEPH

B. MARY IN THE GOSPELS
  1. THE ANNUNCIATION AND INCARNATION
  2. THE VISITATION AND NATIVITY
  3. THE HIDDEN LIFE OF MARY IN NAZARETH
     a. How Mary Merited the Highest Place in Heaven
  4. CHRIST LOST IN THE TEMPLE
  5. THE BLESSED VIRGIN IN THE PUBLIC LIFE OF OUR LORD
  6. MARY DURING THE PASSION
  7. MARY AFTER THE RESURRECTION
  8. THE ASSUMPTION
  9. APPLICATION

The life of the Blessed Virgin Mary was a life of utter humility, of seraphic charity, and of absolutely selfless service of God. As a result, it was a life of supreme virtue and unparalleled happiness. It gives us an example of how we should lose our own desires in the one supreme ambition to glorify God. It shows us how we must strive to imitate the virtues of Jesus Christ if we wish to attain the Goal of our Quest—*The Eternal Commencement* with Jesus and Mary. Study this life well then; study it prayerfully, that you may be attracted by its beauty, and learn its secrets.

A. THE EARLY LIFE OF MARY

The Gospels tell us nothing of the early life of our Blessed Mother. What we know is based on legends and traditions that have come down to us from the past.

1. HER PARENTS

According to these sources, the parents of Mary were St. Joachim and the good St. Anne. We cannot be wrong in surmising that they were both persons of deep sanctity, for God would hardly have let the lives of the parents of her who was to be the Mother of His Divine Son, cast any shadow of opprobrium on her or on Him. You might look up the stories about them in various sources, for example, the *Catholic Encyclopedia.*

The Church celebrates the feast of St. Joachim on the day after the feast of the Assumption, that is, on August 16; while the feast of St. Anne is in the previous month, July 26.

We owe much to these two saints. They gave us *Mary,* who is the joy and pride of the human race, for she is the human being who, after her Divine Son, will occupy the highest place in heaven. They gave us Mary who gave the world the Redeemer it so sorely needed and so anxiously sought. Their training reflects itself both in Mary and in Christ. Many good Catholics render them thanks by doing something special in their honor on their feast days.

We are told that St. Anne, like St. Elizabeth later, was advanced in age and had not yet been blessed by God with the grace of having a child, although she had prayed long and fervently that God would so bless her and remove from her the disgrace that every Jewish woman felt at being childless.

Philip Gendreau, N. Y.

LOURDES

Here our Blessed Mother appeared to little Bernadette Soubirous, in 1858, and announced: "I am the Immaculate Conception." The grotto and niche appear beneath the basilica, somewhat to the right of the center of the edifice.

2. THE IMMACULATE CONCEPTION—MARY'S FIRST PRIVILEGE

God finally answered the prayers of St. Joachim and St. Anne, and there took place within the womb of St. Anne, the miracle of grace which we call the Immaculate Conception.

Every human being since the sin of Adam is conceived with the soul in the state of original sin, that is, deprived of sanctifying grace and the friendship of God. In the case of the Blessed Virgin Mary, however, because she was to be the Mother of God, and in anticipation of the merits of her Son, at the moment her soul was infused into her body, it was preserved free from original sin. This is what is known as the *Immaculate Conception.* It took place at the first moment of Mary's life beneath the heart of her mother, St. Anne, and it is the first and one of the greatest privileges of the Blessed Virgin.

As a result of the Immaculate Conception, Mary was saved from being under the domination of Satan, and was full of grace from the first moment of her existence on earth. Our Lord granted St. John the Baptist the privilege of being cleansed from original sin before he was born; but the Blessed Virgin Mary never had original sin touch her soul. In the first moment of her life, her soul was preserved immaculate.

a. The Church Proclaims the Doctrine

The only proof needed by a Catholic that the Blessed Virgin was preserved from original sin at the first moment of her conception, is the official, infallible definition of the doctrine of the Immaculate Conception by Pope Pius IX, on December 8, 1854.

"The Blessed Virgin Mary was, in the first instant of her conception, by a singular grace and privilege granted to her by Almighty God, through the merits of Christ Jesus, the Saviour of mankind, preserved from all stain of original sin."

Of course, the Church had always taught and held the doctrine. Some theologians may have given arguments against it at various times, but Pope Pius IX in the proclamation of the doctrine showed both from Holy Scripture and Tradition that it had always been the teaching and belief of the Church. The Franciscans and the Spaniards had a special love for this doctrine. An old Spanish salutation upon meeting a person was to say, "*Ave Maria purissima*" (Hail, Mary most pure), to which the person would answer, "*Sin peccado concepida*" (Conceived without sin).

b. Mary Proclaims the Doctrine

In 1858, four years after the solemn proclamation of the doctrine, our Blessed Mother herself announced it to the world from a small mountain village in southern France, within sight of the Spanish border—Lourdes.

From Ewing Galloway, New York

THE GROTTO AT LOURDES

The statue of the Blessed Virgin stands in the niche in which our Blessed Mother appeared to Bernadette. The halo around her head and the inscription beneath her feet both contain the words of our Lady: "I am the Immaculate Conception"—the former in French, the latter in the local dialect of the region about Lourdes.

Notice the woman on the left praying her rosary with outstretched arms which have dropped a bit as they grew tired. It is a penance offered to the Blessed Virgin.

Notice also the *brancardier* (volunteer litter bearer) talking to the boy. The strap on his shoulder is a sign of his office, and aids in carrying the litter with the sick person. Is he perhaps asking the young man if he wishes to offer his services to the sick in honor of Mary?

It was here that our Blessed Lady appeared repeatedly to little Bernadette Soubirous, now St. Bernadette, and during one apparition said: *"I am the Immaculate Conception."*

c. *The Immaculate Conception in Christian Art*

In Christian art the Immaculate Conception usually shows Mary as a beautiful, modest young girl, "clothed with the sun, and with the moon under her feet, and upon her head a crown of twelve stars." Apoc. 12, 1. Her robe is spotless white, her mantle blue, and at her feet often there is an apple, while under her foot is the crushed head of the serpent, in fulfillment of the first promise of a Redeemer made to Adam: "She shall crush thy head, and thou shalt lie in wait for her heel." Gen. 3, 15.

Murillo, the famous Spanish painter, painted the Immaculate Conception at least twenty-five different times, each time in a slightly different way. The most famous of these many pictures is in the Louvre Gallery in Paris. It is one of the most glorious pictures in the world.

The feast of the Immaculate Conception is celebrated on December 8. Americans have a special reason for making it a day of great joy, because our Blessed Lady, under the title of the *Immaculate Conception,* has been chosen the *Patroness of the United States.* What are some of the things one might do to celebrate this feast?

3. THE BIRTH OF THE BLESSED VIRGIN

Nine months after the Immaculate Conception, when the time had elapsed which God in His wisdom has established should normally pass between conception and birth, Mary was born, probably in Jerusalem. The Church accordingly has placed this feast of the *Nativity of the Blessed Virgin* on September 8.

Four days later, on September 12, occurs the feast of the *Most Holy Name of Mary.* According to the custom of the Jews, the ceremony of giving a child its name usually took place on the eighth day after birth. St. Jerome tells us that, under the inspiration of God, St. Joachim and St. Anne gave her the name *Mary.*

4. MARY IS PRESENTED TO GOD

A tradition founded on a story in one of the apocryphal gospels says that when Mary was three years old she was presented in the Temple, and that she lived there for some time. There are scholars who doubt that Mary, or Jewish girls in general, actually lived at the Temple, but at any rate, her parents presented our Lady to God, and the Church celebrates the feast of the *Presentation* on November 21.

The Ceremony of Presentation

The ceremony of Presentation took place in the Temple, in the Women's Gallery. It began by offering a sacrifice. The priests and levites assembled in the inner inclosure and received the victim for the sacrifice from the hands of Joachim. They were dressed in the costume worn only by the priests of the Temple: a round turban or mitre, made of very thick linen cloth, a long white tunic somewhat like an alb, and a cincture of blue.

One of the priests took the lamb, presented by Joachim, said a short invocation and killed it; then catching the blood in a brass vase he sprinkled the blood around the Temple.

A portion of the lamb, wrapped in fat, covered with incense and sprinkled with salt, was next placed on a golden dish. Then the priest barefooted ascended the platform in front of the brazen altar and placed the offering on the logs which fed the fire.

The rest of the victim, except the breast and the right shoulder, which belonged to the priest, was given to Joachim, to be used at the usual banquet for relatives and friends who had gathered for the celebration.

A trumpet was sounded, the priest went to the Court of the Women, and St. Anne, veiled, followed by St. Joachim, and carrying Mary in her arms, approached the priest, and said: "I come to offer you the gift which God gave me." The priest accepted the gift in the name of God and, extending his hands over the assembly, prayed. A canticle of thanksgiving accompanied by harps of the priests terminated the Presentation of the Virgin. (Cf. Lev. 12, 5-8.)

5. MARY MAKES A VOW OF VIRGINITY

Some time during her life, and probably while she was very young, Mary made a vow to remain a virgin. She had firmly resolved to keep this vow all during her life, because when the angel appeared to her, and she was already espoused to St. Joseph at the time, she reminded the angel that she had made the vow.

6. THE BLESSED VIRGIN IS ESPOUSED TO AND MARRIES ST. JOSEPH

The arrangements for the espousal and marriage of Mary and St. Joseph were probably made in the usual manner of that time, in fact, in the manner which was customary in most of the world until modern times in the United States.

There was no courtship, Mary's husband being selected for her, though not probably without her previous assent, by her father or guardian. One legend relates that there were many suitors and that each left a staff and that in the morning one staff had flowered—it was the staff of St. Joseph and accordingly he was chosen.

An Espousal in the East

The *espousal* of Mary and Joseph was most likely celebrated with the customary simplicity of ancient times. Often the husband to be, in the presence of the guardians and a few witnesses, presented his intended wife with a piece of silver, saying to her, "If thou consentest to be my bride, accept this pledge." By accepting it she became solemnly engaged. The scribes thereupon drew up the contract.

The intended husband promised to honor his wife, to provide for her support, her food, her clothing according to the custom of Hebrew husbands, and settled upon her a dowry. Then he signed the contract, to which the woman, also, added her signature. A short benediction terminated this ceremony, which preceded the marriage by several months.

$\longrightarrow$

Richard King   *Courtesy of the Catechetical Guild*

THE ANNUNCIATION

The highest privilege of the Blessed Virgin Mary consists in the fact that God honored her above all men and angels by making her the Mother of God. It was at the Annunciation that Mary received this honor. At her humble words: "Behold the handmaid of the Lord," the Incarnation took place. The Word of God, Son of the Eternal Father, united the Divinity of the Second Person of the Trinity to a human nature and "became flesh and dwelt amongst us."

An Oriental Wedding

The wedding ceremony also was probably the same as that usual in the Orient; the friends of the bride came to congratulate her and helped her prepare and adorn herself with jewels and a crown and a bridal veil which covered her modestly from head to foot and concealed her face. When she was ready all proceeded to the house of the groom, walking under a canopy. There he and his friends joined the procession, waving palms and playing cymbals and flutes and harps.

His friends sang parts of the Canticle of Canticles of Solomon and the younger men began a beautiful, restrained religious dance, such as the one David danced in joy before the Ark.

Upon arriving at the future home of the newlyweds, the friends of the couple sang to them. The groom placed a ring on the bride's finger. A cup of wine was poured, both drank some of it and the groom then spilled the rest on the ground as a symbol of generosity. Wheat was also thrown, as a symbol of abundance, and then the wedding banquet took place and the ceremony was complete.

B. MARY IN THE GOSPELS

Mary's life as recorded in the Gospels, is already known from the study of the life of Christ in the sophomore year. Let us go through the story briefly again, or if you prefer more detail, refer to some book or to the article in the Catholic Encyclopedia under "Virgin" or to other sources.

1. THE ANNUNCIATION AND INCARNATION

Mary first appears in the Gospels at the *Annunciation* when the great event occurred for which all her life was a preparation, namely the *Incarnation*. At that time she conceived the Son of God by the power of the Holy Ghost and became the Mother of God. You remember the story: Gabriel's greeting, "Hail, full of grace"; Mary's fright; Gabriel's reassuring words and his message that Mary should give birth to a Son; Mary's ready faith and her difficulty. The angel's answer: "The Holy Spirit shall come upon thee and the power of the Most High shall overshadow thee"; and the beautiful humility and obe-

dience of Mary's answer: "Behold the handmaid of the
Lord, be it done to me according to thy word." Luke
1, 26-38.

Prayerful consideration of and meditation on this beautiful scene of the Annunciation and Incarnation reveal
Mary's character and virtues.

After the espousal and the Annunciation, but before the
wedding ceremony already described, St. Joseph came to
know that Mary had conceived a child. Not knowing
the mystery of God which Mary in her trusting humility
left to God to reveal as He saw fit, but knowing the absolute purity and sanctity of Mary, St. Joseph was tempted
to put her away secretly. It was then that God sent an
angel to tell him of Mary's dignity.

2. THE VISITATION AND NATIVITY

The *Visitation* of Mary to Elizabeth took place shortly
after the Incarnation. On that occasion you may recall
Mary sang her *Magnificat*. She stayed with Elizabeth
three months and then returned home. Some months afterwards came the trip to Bethlehem and the birth of Christ.
The Circumcision, the Presentation of our Lord in the
Temple, and the Purification of Mary on the fortieth
day, the Adoration of the Magi, the Flight into Egypt, and
the Return to Galilee, followed in succession. Mary took
part in all these events.

It is not necessary to go into detail concerning them
again, although it would be of value to you to ponder
over them once more, on your knees in chapel or church.
You will learn more of the life and virtues of the Blessed
Virgin in that way than in any other.

3. THE HIDDEN LIFE OF MARY IN NAZARETH

It would be well, however, for us to give special consideration to the years of the *Hidden Life of Mary* with
Jesus and St. Joseph. There are mysteries and lessons in

ADORATION OF THE MAGI

What were our Blessed Lady's reactions to the honor paid both to her Son and to her by the Magi? Did she permit it to puff her up with pride? Or did she accept it as another unmerited gift of God, and bowing herself down yet more humbly, resolve to serve Him with even greater singleness of purpose and purity of intention?

her hidden life that are often missed. Do you know what some of these lessons are?

The Blessed Virgin Mary gained for herself, with the assistance of God's grace, the highest place in heaven. Not only is she above all other members of the human race in glory, but she is also above even the highest of pure spirits, above Gabriel and Raphael and Michael, those great archangels; and above all Cherubim and Seraphim.

38

Mary merited this tremendous happiness and honor by a life, the greater part of which was spent washing dishes, sweeping the house, preparing meals, washing and mending clothes, carrying water, caring for her Child and performing a hundred other humble tasks. And many people, in their foolish ignorance and pride, consider such tasks menial and degrading!

Not only did these things not demean the Blessed Mother, but they gained for her the zenith of glory for eternity. For it is not the intrinsic dignity of what we do that counts so much; it is how we do it and the intention which guides us that matters. Mary did everything for the glory of God; she did it with exquisite perfection and with never a thought of self. Her intention turned everything to gold, or should we rather say, her intention turned everything to God?

4. CHRIST LOST IN THE TEMPLE

The only break in the silence of thirty years of the Hidden Life was the trip to Jerusalem when Jesus was twelve years of age. You remember Mary's sorrow on that occasion, when she lost Jesus, and her amazement when she found him. You will also recall St. Luke saying that when Jesus had told Mary that He must be about His Father's business, Mary and Joseph did not understand the word He spoke to them, but that Mary kept all these words in her heart. Luke 2, 42-52.

5. THE BLESSED VIRGIN IN THE PUBLIC LIFE OF OUR LORD

After the death of St. Joseph, and when Mary was approximately forty-five years of age, our Lord began His Public Life. His first act was a miracle worked at the word of His Blessed Mother—the changing of water to wine at the wedding feast in *Cana*. There is much food for thought here! Mary likes to see us happy. Mary likes to prevent our being embarrassed. She wants us to be fed.

ST. MARY MAJOR

Santa Maria Maggiore, in Rome is the most honored of all the Marian cathedrals in the world, and one of the oldest and most magnificent churches in all Christendom. It is also referred to as Our Lady of the Snows from the miracle which took place here in the fourth century. Do you know the story of the incident? It led to the building of the basilica. The feast of the dedication of this church is celebrated each year on August 5th, the day the miraculous fall of snow occurred in 352.

She will ask her Son to perform miracles for her friends if the case calls for it—physical favors as well as spiritual. Do you remember Lourdes?

After this incident at Cana, Mary almost disappears from the Gospels until we find her at the foot of the Cross on Calvary. St. Mark records an incident when "His Mother and His brethren came . . . calling Him." Mark 3, 31. On that occasion Jesus told the multitudes, "whoever does the will of God, he is My brother and sister and mother." Mark 3, 35. Mary is not mentioned by name in this scene and disappears again until good Friday.

6. MARY DURING THE PASSION

In the Stations of the Cross, the fourth station commemorates the meeting of Christ and His Sorrowful Mother on the way to Calvary, but Scripture does not mention the incident. It is from tradition that we know of it. Neither do the Gospels mention Mary at any other time during the Passion, previous to the last scene on Calvary. However, Mary most certainly was in Jerusalem for the Passover celebration, as St. Luke states that our Lord's parents "were wont to go every year to Jerusalem at the Feast of the Passover." Luke 2, 41. We can presume that Mary continued to do so even after the death of St. Joseph and the departure of our Lord from the home in Nazareth.

The writers of the synoptic Gospels do not tell us that Mary was at the foot of the Cross. St. Matthew merely says that "many women were there . . . . among them . . . Mary Magdalen, and Mary the mother of James and Joseph, and the mother of the sons of Zebedee." Matt. 27, 55. St. Mark says about the same thing. St. Luke remarks: "All His acquaintances, and the women who had followed Him from Galilee, were standing at a distance looking on." Luke 23, 49. He does not mention Mary by name.

It is St. John who tells us: "Now there were standing by the cross of Jesus His Mother and His mother's sister, Mary of Cleophas, and Mary Magdalen." John 19, 25. When Jesus saw St. John and His Mother, He said to her: "Woman, behold thy son"; and to St. John: "Behold thy Mother." The Gospel concludes the scene by saying that "from that hour the disciple took her into his home." John 19, 27. So we know that from then on St. John took care of our Blessed Lady.

7. MARY AFTER THE RESURRECTION

We next meet our Blessed Mother after the Resurrection, in the Upper Room with the Apostles and disciples (Acts 1, 14), making the first great Pentecost novena after the Ascension, and although we are not told directly that she was there when the Holy Ghost came, all tradition assures us that she was.

Once the Church had been established, and the Mystical Body of Christ was on earth to carry on the work of her Divine Son, Mary disappears from the scene. Tradition tells us that she lived at Jerusalem or at Ephesus with St. John, and that she died, most probably at Jerusalem, on Mount Sion where the Benedictine Abbey of the Dormition, that is, the Falling Asleep of Mary, is shown to the Christian pilgrims today as near the place where our Lady slept in the Lord. An early church in the Garden of Gethsemane is also said to mark the place of her burial and *Assumption.*

8. THE ASSUMPTION

After her death and burial, Mary's body, before it began to suffer corruption, was reunited with her soul and was then assumed into heaven.

There is a tradition or a legend that all the Apostles except St. Thomas were present when Mary died. St. Thomas arrived late; he wished to see the body, and when the tomb was opened the body was gone. Thus, says the story, did the Apostles come to know of the Assumption.

Many painters have chosen the death and the Assumption of the Virgin Mary as a subject for pictures.

The feast of the Assumption is one of the oldest in honor of our Lady. It is celebrated on August 15.

9. APPLICATION

Mary's life is one of utmost simplicity, without display. All who hope to do great things for God, for the Church, for their country and their fellowmen should learn from it that hidden sanctity, service to others, humility, self-

THE ASSUMPTION

Shortly after the death of the Blessed Virgin, her body was assumed into heaven and there reunited for eternity with her spotless soul.

effacement, and the martyrdom of faithfulness in the performance of unsung tasks, are of great value in the sight of God. By means of them Mary attained the highest place in heaven.

REVIEW OF SECTION ONE.

SECTION TWO: THE FEASTS OF THE BLESSED VIRGIN

The accompanying list gives the seven greater feasts and many of the lesser feasts in honor of the Blessed Virgin which are celebrated during the year. They are in the order in which they occur, starting at the beginning of the liturgical year.

As it will be impossible to tell the story connected with each of these feasts we shall choose the first two of the lesser feasts, leaving the others to your own initiative and love of Mary.

THE FEASTS OF THE BLESSED VIRGIN MARY

GREATER FEASTS		LESSER FEASTS
Immaculate Conception	Dec. 8	
	Dec. 10	Translation of the House of Loreto
	Dec. 12	O.L. of Guadalupe
	Jan. 23	Espousal of St. Joseph
Purification	Feb. 2	
	Feb. 11	O.L. of Lourdes
	Friday after Passion Sunday	Seven Dolors
Annunciation	Mar. 25	
	Apr. 26	O.L. of Good Counsel
	May 24	O.L. Help of Christians
	May 31	Mediatrix of all Graces
	Saturday after Sacred Heart	Immaculate Heart of Mary
	June 27	O.L. of Perpetual Help
Visitation	July 2	
	July 16	O.L. of Mt. Carmel
	July 17	Humility of the B.V.M.
	Aug. 5	O.L. of the Snows
	Aug. 13	O.L. Refuge of Sinners
Assumption	Aug. 15	
Birth of B.V.M.	Sept. 8	
	Sept. 12	Holy Name of Mary
	Sept. 15	Seven Sorrows
	Sept. 24	O.L. of Ransom
	Oct. 7	O.L. of the Rosary
	Oct. 11	Maternity of the B.V.M.
	Oct. 16	Purity of the B.V.M.
Presentation of the B.V.M.	Nov. 21	
	Nov. 27	O.L. of Miraculous Medal

The feast of the *Translation of the House of Loreto* is based on devotion to the Holy House of Nazareth. It commemorates the story that angels took the home of the Holy Family in Nazareth and translated or carried it to Loreto, a town on the east coast of Italy. Whether this is indeed the Holy House or not, is hard to determine, as you will agree if you read the article about the *Santa Casa* in the *Catholic Encyclopedia;* but at any rate, veneration of the house in which the Holy Family lived is commendable, whether this be the real Holy House or not.

The feast of *Our Lady of Guadalupe* commemorates the apparition of our Blessed Mother on Saturday, December 9, and Tuesday, December 12, 1531, just outside of Mexico City to Juan Diego, an Indian who had but recently been baptized and was on his way to Mass. The Blessed Virgin sent Juan to Bishop Zumarraga to request that a church be built where she stood. The Bishop asked a sign to prove it was really the Mother of God who had asked it, and on Tuesday, as Juan was running to get the priest for his sick uncle, he was again met by the Blessed Mother who told him that the uncle would not die and once more bade him go to the bishop. When Juan asked for a sign, Mary told him to go up to the rocks and pick some roses—remember it was December 12. Juan went, found and gathered the roses, placing them in his cloak. Our Blessed Mother rearranged them and told Juan to take them untouched and concealed in his cloak to the bishop. When he opened the cloak before the bishop and his attendants, the roses fell out, and on the cloak there appeared a life-size image of the Blessed Virgin, just as Juan had said she appeared. The picture may still be seen on the cloak in the shrine at the beautiful basilica of Guadalupe near Mexico City. It is the most famous shrine to our Lady in North America. (See pages 87 and 293.)

There are beautiful stories connected with the other feasts of our Blessed Mother, for instance, Our Lady of

GUADALUPE

The shrine to our Lady at Guadalupe, just outside Mexico City is not only the most ancient and most venerable of all Marian shrines in the Western Hemisphere, but it marks the site of the only officially recognized apparition of the Blessed Virgin Mary in the Western World. We Americans should hold it in high honor. We should recognize in it a sign of Mary's love for the country in which it is located and a pledge of her protection of the race to whom she has thus showed her favor.

Lourdes, Our Lady of the Snows, Our Lady of Ransom, Our Lady of the Miraculous Medal. You may already know them or can look them up.

A real lover of Mary learns about her feasts and the stories connected with them, and he delights in showing Mary special honor on these, her festal days, by prayer, by penance, by devotions, by practices of mercy, and especially by assisting at Mass and receiving Holy Communion, and by imitating some virtue of Mary's life in her honor.

SECTION THREE: THE PRIVILEGES OF THE BLESSED VIRGIN

A. THE GREATEST PRIVILEGE—MOTHER OF GOD
1. THE DIVINE MATERNITY IN THE SCRIPTURES
2. THE DIVINE MATERNITY INFALLIBLY DEFINED
3. THE DIVINE MATERNITY IN THE LITURGY

B. EIGHT OTHER GREAT PRIVILEGES
1. THE IMMACULATE CONCEPTION
2. PERPETUAL VIRGINITY
3. ABSOLUTE SINLESSNESS
4. MARY'S BODY PRESERVED FROM CORRUPTION
5. "FULL OF GRACE"
6. MEDIATRIX OF ALL GRACES
7. SPIRITUAL MOTHERHOOD OF ALL MEN
8. QUEEN OF ANGELS AND OF SAINTS

Lauren Ford   *Courtesy of Liturgical Arts*

Almighty God has made the Blessed Virgin Mary the most glorious of all His creatures. He has bestowed on her the most magnificent privileges.

A. THE GREATEST PRIVILEGE—MOTHER OF GOD

The greatest privilege of Mary is her selection to be the Mother of God, or, as it is also called, the *Divine Maternity*.

1. THE DIVINE MATERNITY IN THE SCRIPTURES

The Divine Maternity was already foreshadowed in the prophecy of Isaias: "Behold a virgin shall conceive and bear a son, and His name shall be called Emmanuel." Is. 7, 14. Emmanuel means "God with us." Therefore this prophecy means that a virgin shall be the Mother of God.

The Divine Motherhood is more clearly indicated at the Incarnation when Gabriel tells Mary that the Child who shall be born of her "shall be called the Son of the Most High." Luke 1, 31. It is recognized by Elizabeth when she greets Mary as "the Mother of my Lord." Luke 1, 43.

2. THE DIVINE MATERNITY INFALLIBLY DEFINED

You most likely recall that it was because of Nestorianism that the Church clearly defined this doctrine of the Divine Motherhood of the Blessed Virgin. Nestorius, the patriarch and bishop of Constantinople, had objected to calling Mary *Theotokos* (i.e., the God-bearer). He claimed that Mary was only the mother of Christ—a mere man, and therefore, he said, she could not be called the Mother of God.

The whole Christian world was outraged by this heretical blasphemy, and at the famous Council of Ephesus in Asia Minor in 431—the Third Ecumenical Council—under the leadership of that courageous and learned Greek Doctor, St. Cyril of Alexandria, the heresy was condemned and the true doctrine which the Church had always taught was proclaimed, to the tumultuous joy of the people. The Council declared: "If anyone confess not that Emmanuel is God in strict truth and that there-

Raphael (1483-1520)
(Raffaelo Sanzio)

THE SISTINE MADONNA

fore the Blessed Virgin is *Mother of God,* let him be anathema."

3. THE DIVINE MATERNITY IN THE LITURGY

The Church's belief in the Divine Maternity is everywhere visible; in the liturgy of Advent and Christmas, in the Creed which says that Christ, the Son of God, was born of the Virgin Mary, in the Hail Mary, and the invocations of the Litany of Loreto: "Holy Mother of God, Mother of Christ," and in the Angelus.

The Feast of the Divine Maternity, celebrated on October 11, was made a feast of the first class for the Universal Church in 1932.

The Divine Motherhood is a popular theme in art how often the Madonna has drawn the attention of famous painters—in music, and in poetry.

Mary's office as Mother of God is not only the highest of her privileges, it is the reason for all the other honors and privileges showered so freely upon her by God. We shall now examine the most important of these.

B. EIGHT OTHER GREAT PRIVILEGES

It was because Mary had been selected to be the Mother of the divine Son that God gave our Blessed Lady her four great *negative* privileges: freedom from original sin (the Immaculate Conception) ; freedom from any violation of her virginal integrity and purity (perpetual virginity) ; freedom from all personal or actual sin (absolute sinlessness) ; and freedom from the corruption of the body in the grave by being assumed into heaven.

It was because Mary was to be Mother of God that she was also given four *positive* privileges: perfect holiness (fullness of grace) ; the office of Mediatrix of All Graces; the Spiritual Motherhood of all men; and the title of Queen of Angels and of Men.

Lauren Ford   *Courtesy of Liturgical Arts*

THE NATIVITY

1. THE IMMACULATE CONCEPTION

The first of Mary's privileges in order of time is the
Immaculate Conception, which has already been ex-

plained in Section One. It was the initial step taken by God in preparing a worthy Mother from whom Christ was to take His own flesh and blood.

This preservation of Mary from original sin consisted in this, that sanctifying grace was infused into her soul at the moment of its creation and union with her body.

2. PERPETUAL VIRGINITY

The Perpetual Virginity of our Blessed Mother means that she was ever a virgin—before the birth of Christ, at the birth of Christ, and after the birth of Christ. She was a virgin in body and in soul. That is, she was unsullied by even the slightest violation of the most perfect virginal chastity, whether in body, in thought, or in desire.

The Perpetual Virginity is a doctrine of faith, the official teaching of the Church clearing up any doubt that might have been occasioned by the reference to our Lord as the "firstborn," (Luke 2, 7), and by the other reference to the "brethren" and "sisters" of Jesus. Matt. 13, 55-57.

Christ is called the "firstborn," not because our Blessed Mother had any other children after Him, but because the firstborn belonged to God and also enjoyed special privileges. As for the terms "brethren" and "sisters," the reference in St. Matthew shows clearly enough that by them is meant what all orientals mean even today when they speak of their "brothers" or "sisters," namely all relatives. Thus Abraham says that he and Lot are "brethren" when they were actually cousins. Gen. 13, 8.

3. ABSOLUTE SINLESSNESS

Our Blessed Mother was preserved by God from actual sin as well as from original sin, and not only from all mortal sin but also from deliberate venial sin. Indeed not a single semi-deliberate venial sin ever cast its shadow over the snowy whiteness of her pure soul. She was absolutely and completely sinless.

4. MARY'S BODY WAS PRESERVED FROM CORRUPTION

The fourth of the negative privileges of Mary is enshrined in the doctrine of the *Assumption* of the body of the Blessed Virgin Mary into heaven. This doctrine, which has recently been solemnly defined and declared a dogma of Faith, has already been studied in the life of our Blessed Mother. It means that Mary's body did not corrupt in the tomb and wait in dust for the general resurrection on Judgment Day. By a special privilege it was assumed into heaven and rejoined with her spotless soul shortly after her death.

5. "FULL OF GRACE"

What the doctrine of absolute sinlessness presents in a negative way, this doctrine completes in a positive manner. Not only was Mary's soul free from all sins and imperfections, but it was also ever adorned with that gift of God which bestows supernatural life and beauty on the human soul, namely, sanctifying grace. Mary's soul was always in the state of grace. More than that, Mary's soul was always *filled to the limits of its capacity with grace*. Did not the angel say, "Hail, full of grace"?

Mary cooperated perfectly with every grace God gave her during her entire life. Therefore she increased constantly, by leaps and bounds, in her capacity for grace; yet her soul was ever "full of grace." What then must be the over-powering and entrancing spiritual beauty of this most glorious of God's creatures.

6. MEDIATRIX OF ALL GRACES

Not only is our Immaculate Mother full of grace but she is the Mediatrix of All Graces. This doctrine has a direct relation to us. All grace comes from God through the merits of the God-Man, Jesus Christ. It is distributed by the Church. Now it was Mary who gave Christ to the world—she is His Mother. She is also the Mother of His

Mystical Body, the Church. So all the graces of redemption flow to the world through Mary. Christ is the Mediator, and Mary, under Him, and through His Mystical Body, the Church, is the Mediatrix of All Graces.

Does this not show how necessary for our salvation it is that we be devoted children of Mary? St. Antoninus warns: "Whoever asks anything without her intercession endeavors to fly without wings." And St. Bernardine of Siena exclaims: "O Lady, thou art the dispenser of all graces, our salvation is in thy hands." Let us be convinced then, of this: We shall never reach the Eternal Commencement without Mary, and with her we shall not fail.

7. SPIRITUAL MOTHERHOOD OF ALL MEN

The privilege of being the Spiritual Mother of all men was conferred upon Mary at the moment of the Incarnation. In giving us Christ, Mary gave us life—divine life; thus she is the spiritual mother of all. In conceiving our Blessed Lord, the head of the Mystical Body, Mary also conceived us, because we are members of this body, the head and the members of which form but a single whole.

At the time of our Lord's death He confirmed and gave public notice to this spiritual motherhood of Mary, when, turning to St. John, He said, "Behold thy Mother." John 19, 27.

In this scene St. John was acting, not as a private individual, but as the representative of the Church and its members. In telling John, therefore to behold his Mother, Christ is telling all members of His Church to look on and to accept Mary as their Mother.

The initial grace of supernatural life which was conferred upon us at Baptism was thus obtained for us by the Blessed Virgin, our spiritual Mother. So are all other graces. She who is the Mediatrix is also our Mother. What a consoling bit of knowledge!

If you would like to learn more about this privilege of Mary, you could do nothing better than to read the Encyclical of Pope Pius X, *Ad Diem Illum* (Fcb. 2, 1904).

8. QUEEN OF ANGELS AND OF MEN

The last privilege of Mary which we shall mention is that she is Queen of Angels and of Men.

Christ is King of the Universe, and Mary, His Mother, is its Queen. All the angels acknowledge her as their sovereign. To comprehend what this means you must recall what you know about the angels. Being pure spirits, they possess angelic natures with perfections completely above those of human nature. Yet in Mary, by God's grace, our feeble human nature has been raised above the angels, and they, in ecstatic joy, freely and happily acknowledge her to be their queen.

All human beings should extol her as great, for she is also Queen of Patriarchs, Queen of Prophets, Queen of Apostles, Queen of Martyrs, Queen of Confessors, Queen of Virgins, Queen of All Saints. Yes, she is queen of all men—Queen of Heaven and Earth.

These are the great privileges of the Blessed Virgin Mary. In such manner has God exalted her above every other creature in the universe. It might be well for us now to take a look at the virtues which are the secret of this greatness.

REVIEW OF SECTIONS TWO AND THREE

←

THE CATHEDRAL OF CHARTRES

This Cathedral of Notre Dame in Chartres, France, is considered by many art critics as the most beautiful church in the world. Like our Lady, its beauty is not easily appreciated at first sight, nor from a distance. One must come close; one must enter to fall under the spell of its charms. The interior is made a resplendent jewel by the sparkling beauty of its mediaeval stained glass windows, the most exquisite stained glass in the world—and the most beautiful of all is the Blue Madonna Window.

SECTION FOUR: THE VIRTUES OF THE BLESSED VIRGIN MARY

A. MARY PERFECT IN ALL VIRTUES

B. THE FOUNDATION VIRTUE—HUMILITY

C. THE THEOLOGICAL VIRTUES IN MARY
1. CHARITY
2. FAITH
3. HOPE

D. THE MORAL VIRTUES IN MARY
1. CHASTITY
2. POVERTY
3. OBEDIENCE
4. PATIENCE
5. PRAYER—THE VIRTUE OF RELIGION

Lauren Ford   *Courtesy of Liturgical Arts*

A. MARY PERFECT IN ALL VIRTUES

One of our chief tasks during this senior year will be to attempt to form in ourselves that superb Christian character which is the result of the balanced practice of all the virtues of Christ our Guide and Master. It is by imitation of the virtues of Mary that we can best hope to achieve this goal. Let us look then at Mary's virtues.

St. Alphonsus Ligouri, who had a very special love for the Blessed Virgin and who wrote a book on *The Glories of Mary* which all should read, gives therein the following ten as the principal virtues of the Blessed Mother of God: humility, love of God, love of neighbor, faith, hope, chastity, poverty, obedience, patience, and prayer. Then to show that these are only the outstanding virtues, he quotes St. Thomas Aquinas who says that "whereas other saints excelled, each in some particular virtue, the one in chastity, another in humility, another in mercy; the Blessed Virgin excelled in all and is given as a model in all."

B. THE FOUNDATION VIRTUE—HUMILITY

Humility is the virtue which serves as the foundation of all other virtues. It leads a person to estimate himself at his real worth before God, and to refer all good qualities or powers he possesses, or any good he may have done, to their true source, that is, to God. Without humility no other virtue can thrive; it is the deep and hidden foundation. When it goes, all other virtues feel the loss; as it increases, so do other virtues grow in us. Humility has a lowly opinion of self, except as aided by God's grace; humility conceals heavenly gifts, refuses praise, serves others, is retiring, does not shun contempt.

The humility of Mary was so great that many saints, themselves eminent in the practice of this virtue could only stand in amazement at the profundity of the humility of our Lady. It was the Blessed Virgin's humility which drew God to her; He "regarded the lowliness of His hand-

Wisd.7.26

Ecclus.50,6

Cant.2,1

Ecclus.24,24

Luke 1,28

Luke 1,28

Luke 2,35

Gen.3,15

John.19,27

Ex.3,2

Ecclus.24,18

SR

Cant.2,2

Num.17,8

Num.10,33

Cant.7,4

maid." What facts or incidents in Mary's life show that she possessed deep humility?

Mary knew the greatness of the graces and privileges heaped on her by Almighty God, yet she never preferred herself to any other person. She knew how great God is; she realized her own nothingness, and she acknowledged that everything she had, as great as it made her, was an unmerited favor from God. Mary was humble. True clients of Mary are humble too.

C. THE THEOLOGICAL VIRTUES IN MARY

1. CHARITY

The second virtue of Mary was charity, that is, love of God and love of neighbor for the sake of God. If humility was the foundation of Mary's virtues, charity was the keystone, the crown, the soul. Mary in her humility had no room in her heart for undue love of self, but only for love of God, and because of God, love of all His creatures, especially those created in His image.

There are two great commandments which contain all that is laid down in the Mosaic Law and the Prophets, yes and all that is contained in the Christian additions to that law. These two commandments, given us by God Himself, are these:

FIRST: "Thou shalt love the Lord thy God
with thy whole heart,
and with thy whole soul,
and with thy whole mind."

SECOND: "Thou shalt love thy neighbor as
thyself." Matt. 22, 37-39.

Mary kept these two commandments perfectly. No earthly love, no love of created things ever captivated

←

THE VIRTUES OF THE BLESSED VIRGIN MARY

Can you give an explanation of each of the symbols?

her heart; every moment of her life she was wrapped in love of God. Even in sleep, Saint Ambrose says, "her soul watched."

Mary was constantly aware of the presence of God, unceasingly offering her Son to Him for man's salvation. Thus, in this great love was included love of all that God has created; so, at the same time Mary was engaged in a constant act of love of neighbor. Indeed her life was one of complete unselfishness and heroic devotion and service to all of God's creatures.

This thought should spur us to more frequent acts of love of God; it should rebuke our inconstancy, our love of self or of creatures contrary to the will of God.

2. FAITH

You may remember some of the evidences of Mary's faith which were mentioned when we studied our Blessed Lady as an example of the virtue of faith in our freshman year. Mary's entire life, indeed, was one single act of faith, but there are two occasions in her life in which faith stands out most clearly. The first is at the Annunciation when the angel assured her that she could be the Mother of God, and yet remain a virgin. Mary believed the angel and spoke the words which made possible the Incarnation of our Redeemer. The second great occasion on which Mary's faith stood out clearly was on Good Friday and that first Holy Saturday, when, after the death of her Son, her faith in His divinity and in His mission as Messias stood unshakably firm. When all others lost hope and found their faith wavering, Mary was firm in her belief of her Son's divinity.

3. HOPE

Mary is our Life, our Sweetness, and our Hope. She is our Life, for she gave us spiritual life. She is our Sweetness, for in the bitterness of the sufferings which God

SIENA CATHEDRAL

This striking church, dedicated to our Lady, under the title of the Assumption,
has one of the richest and most interesting exteriors of the Italian cathedrals. It is
in the Italian Gothic style.

permitted her and her Divine Son to endure for us, the bitterness of our lives has been swallowed up and sweetness has been left to us. She is our Hope, for her confidence in God was unbounded and constant at all times: in the trials at Bethlehem when Christ was born; on the flight into Egypt; at the wedding feast at Cana; at the foot of the Cross. Mary's hope was as great as her faith and her love.

C. THE MORAL VIRTUES IN MARY

1. CHASTITY

As a result of the sin of Adam, all our bodily senses with their appetites and urges tend to seek pleasure just for the sake of pleasure. They rise up against the command of right reason, as well as against the dictates of the natural and positive divine law. These tendencies are usually most urgent in relation to the pleasure arising from the attraction which God has created between man and woman. The virtue which controls these tendencies and regulates the enjoyment of these pleasures according to reason and divine command is the beautiful virtue of *purity* or *chastity*.

This great virtue, and all the subordinate virtues related to it—modesty, continence, and so forth—shine forth with virginal freshness in the life of the Blessed Mother. So great was our Lady's love of virginity, and of the allied virtue of chastity or purity that we are told she would have foregone the tremendous privilege of being the Mother of God if it meant she would have been obliged to sacrifice this virtue. She knew how dear it was to God.

The greatness of Mary's purity can also be appreciated by the fact that God's grace preserved her from all internal temptations against this virtue, as well as from every inordinate motion of all the other sense appetites. Mary was free from concupiscence. She is the "lily among thorns" (Cant. 2, 2), and her virginal beauty inspires others to purity.

2. POVERTY

One of the greatest causes of the universal unrest of the world in recent times is the wild and uncontrolled desire for earthly possessions. It causes tension in the individual, between individuals and groups, and among nations. The only virtue which can control this tendency is the virtue of *poverty* with its attendant *spirit of detachment*. Mary has given us the highest example of these, at Bethlehem, in Egypt, at Nazareth.

The material goods of the world were created so that they might assist men to reach and possess God who alone can engender real happiness. But men get pleasure from these attractive creatures of God, and are dazzled by them, so that they no longer see the True God. It is only by giving to these created things the value that they have in God's eyes, that is, by considering them as instruments to be used in working out our salvation, that we can find contentment and happiness. The virtue of poverty and the spirit of detachment from earthly goods permit us to do this. They help us look on created things as objects loaned to us by God, as objects to which our hearts must never become unduly attached.

There are two phases to poverty: poverty in spirit, which means *detachment* from earthly possessions, whether we are blessed with riches, or not; and secondly, poverty in actuality, by which we add to poverty in spirit by distributing our goods, especially to those who have greater need of them than we have. Mary was both poor in spirit and poor in actuality, and as a proof of this, St. Alphonsus reminds us that at the Purification, Mary and Joseph presented only the offering of the poor.

3. OBEDIENCE

The next virtue of the Blessed Virgin which we shall call to mind is in some ways even greater than the virtues

of poverty and chastity, for it entails not only detachment from worldly goods and carnal desires, but even more, detachment from our own will. It is the great virtue of obedience.

Obedience is the virtue by which one person submits to and carries out the will of another with the intention of complying with the command, as coming from a representative of God. In other words, it is not only an external act of the body, but it is especially an internal act of submission on the part of the will. Now, Mary was obedient. She obeyed and respected all lawfully constituted authority, in the home, in the State, in the Church. Above all, she obeyed God. In fact, she never followed her own will and wishes, but every action of her entire life was dictated by what she knew to be the will of God. Her obedience was prompt, willing, and complete. She obeyed her parents, she obeyed the decree of Cæsar Augustus, she obeyed the decisions of her husband, St. Joseph. She obeyed all the prescriptions of the Mosaic Law, and her readiness to obey God is beautifully illustrated in those humble words: "Behold the handmaid of the Lord." Luke 1, 38.

Have you noticed that the three virtues just studied are the three evangelical counsels which comprise the basic vows of religion? They who would follow Christ closely must give up the indulging of their bodies, their possessions, and their own wills.

4. PATIENCE

Mary's patience is also another remarkable virtue. Meditation on it can teach us much. Never in her whole life is there a word of complaint, or a sign of impatience. No matter how unreasonable a thing may seem to be, Mary is patient. Recall the census with its strange prescription that each person had to go to the city of his

---

ancestors; the sudden flight into Egypt in the middle of the night; our Lord's reply at the wedding at Cana. Under all circumstances Mary was patient: during all of her Seven Dolors, during the Passion, and especially as she stood at the foot of the Cross, where her compassion made her a "martyr of patience."

In close connection with this virtue of patience, which word comes from a Latin word meaning "to suffer," we must also remember Mary's practice of the virtues of *penance* and *mortification*. Mary's penances were a mortification not only for her body but even more for her mind and for her will. By them she made of herself a constant victim of love of God.

5. PRAYER—THE VIRTUE OF RELIGION

Lastly—for we could not recount all of Mary's virtues— let us conclude this section by referring to her practice of the basic *virtue of religion*. Religion is a moral virtue inclining the will to give to God the honor and worship which is due to Him as the source and goal of all things. The acts by which it is exercised are especially these six: adoration, prayer, the offering of sacrifice, the making of vows, the fulfillment of lawful oaths, and the sanctification of specified times and days. Let us take only the *practice of prayer*.

Christ said to His disciples, that they must always pray. Luke 18, 1. St. Paul tells the Thessalonians: "Pray without ceasing." 1 Thess. 5, 17. Mary fulfilled this injunction, for Mary's life was a constant prayer. Every act that she performed, every thought she had, was a raising of her mind and heart to God. She was constantly recollected, constantly aware of the presence of God. Even in the occupations of her active life, her soul was ever absorbed in the deepest contemplation of God; for Mary's prayer, like the flight of an eagle, was not restricted to the feeble oral prayer and meditation which we know, nor even to the sublime contemplation of the saints; no, it was more like the prayer of an angel, for Mary, in the silence of her soul was constantly making a never-ending act of pure love of God.

As we shall not treat of the other virtues of Mary, let us merely remind ourselves here of something we learned in our freshman year. *All* the *virtues* needed in a *Christian life* can be reduced to *seven:* faith, hope, and charity, the supernatural theological virtues; and prudence, justice, fortitude, and temperance, the supernatural moral virtues. Any other virtue is but a subdivision of these. Mary practiced all these virtues in all their aspects and parts; and in each she gave us a perfect example of that virtue.

If you would be a *child of Mary,* if you would gain for yourself her maternal love and powerful protection, honor her by imitating her in the practice of these virtues, even as she imitated Christ, her Son and her God. There are many ways of doing this but none better than by joining her in daily uniting yourself to Christ in His Adorable Sacrifice, by attending Mass and receiving Holy Communion.

REVIEW OF SECTION FOUR.

ACT OF CONSECRATION
TO THE IMMACULATE HEART OF THE BLESSED VIRGIN MARY*

O Mary, Virgin most powerful and Mother of mercy, Queen of Heaven and Refuge of sinners, we consecrate ourselves to thine immaculate heart.

We consecrate to thee our very being and our whole life; all that we have, all that we love, all that we are. To thee we give our bodies, our hearts and our souls; to thee we give our homes, our families, our country. We desire that all that is in us and around us may belong to thee, and may share in the benefits of thy motherly benediction. And that this act of consecration may be truly efficacious and lasting, we renew this day at thy feet the promises of our Baptism and our first Holy Communion. We pledge ourselves to profess courageously and at all times the truths of our holy Faith, and to live as befits Catholics who are duly submissive to all the directions of the Pope and the Bishops in communion with him. We pledge ourselves to keep the commandments of God and His Church, in particular to keep holy the Lord's Day. We likewise pledge ourselves to make the consoling practices of the Christian religion, and above all, Holy Communion, an integral part of our lives, in so far as we shall be able to do so. Finally, we promise thee, O glorious Mother of God and loving Mother of men, to devote ourselves wholeheartedly to the service of thy blessed cult, in order to hasten and assure, through the sovereignty of thine Immaculate Heart, the coming of the kingdom of the Sacred Heart of thine adorable Son, in our own hearts and in those of all men, in our country and in all the world, as in heaven, so on earth. Amen.

*An indulgence of 3 years. A plenary indulgence, on the usual conditions, if this Act of Consecration is repeated daily for a month (S.C. Ind., Feb. 21, 1907; S.P. Ap., April 29, 1933). Quoted with permission of Benziger Brothers, Inc., from *The Raccolta* (1943), p. 265-6.

SECTION FIVE: OUR LADY, THE INSPIRATION OF TRUE ART

INTRODUCTION: THE HIGHEST ART—THE ART OF
CHRISTIAN LIVING

A. OUR LADY, THE INSPIRATION OF TRUE LITERATURE

B. OUR LADY, THE INSPIRATION OF BEAUTY IN MUSIC
1. PLAIN CHANT
2. POLYPHONIC MUSIC
3. MODERN CLASSICAL MUSIC
4. THE FOUR MARIAN ANTIPHONS
5. THE HYMN WHICH MARY COMPOSED
6. OTHER MARIAN HYMNS IN LATIN
7. VERNACULAR HYMNS TO OUR BLESSED LADY

C. OUR LADY IN OIL, FRESCO AND PASTEL
1. MARIAN ART DOWN THE AGES
a. The Oldest Picture of Our Lady?
b. In the Age of the Iconoclasts
c. Modern Painting Begins
d. The Age of the Masters

D. MAGNIFICATS IN STONE AND GLASS

OUR LADY, THE INSPIRATION OF TRUE ART

After having learned the glorious privileges and virtues of the Blessed Virgin, let us now see how Mary has been the inspiration of the arts: literature, music, painting, architecture.

THE HIGHEST ART—THE ART OF CHRISTIAN LIVING

In introducing the topic of Mary and the arts, it would not be fitting to omit the important fact that, besides being the inspiration of all lesser art, our Lady has also been and still is the inspiration of the highest of all arts—*the art of Christian Living;* the art of forming Christ in ourselves and in others. If you were to ask for the masterpieces of her influence in this field, we should have to point to the saints of heaven, every one of whom was a true disciple of Mary.

←

MADONNA AND CHILD

This beautiful picture captures some of the modest loveliness which we associate with the Virgin Mother of God. We know instinctively that she was shy and sensitive in the public eye; but we also know that beneath that maidenly delicacy and mildness there was a moral courage and power to put the bravest men to shame. Mary possessed all virtues in an eminent degree. She practiced them more perfectly than any other son or daughter of Eve.

She in her own life fashioned the original and the most perfect masterpiece, modeled on the life of Christ. The saints are copies, none as beautiful as she, who is the *first Madonna,* but each, in a particular way, reflecting the various beauties of which she is the most perfect purely human replica. It would be an interesting project to read the biographies of saints who were outstanding for their love of Mary, to see how they honored and followed her in her imitation of Christ.

A. OUR LADY, THE INSPIRATION OF TRUE LITERATURE

But now, let us turn to our topic, and see how the influence of Mary has created beauty in the various arts, and first in literature.

What is literature if not man trying to portray and to capture in words, truth, and beauty, and blessedness. What is literature if not an imaginative record of man's yearning for happiness. Too often, it is a story of man, looking for heaven in the corruptible pleasures of earth, but in the *Marian Art* and *Literature,* it is fallen man looking up and grasping for a star.

It is particularly in that higher branch of literature called *poetry* that the influence of Christianity and the spell of Mary has been felt; and the hymns of the Christian poets are frequently poems and prayers in one. Nor must it surprise us that sinful men have written beautiful things of Mary, nor that non-Catholic writers have, at times, outdone those of the household of the Faith. Beauty, be it spiritual or physical, intellectual or moral, attracts all men, saints and sinners alike; and Mary was beautiful in body, in mind, in will. Accordingly, none of those who know her escape the magnetism of her perfection.

The list of names and titles of Poems in Honor of the Blessed Virgin on pages 72-73 will show how Catholics and non-Catholics alike have vied with one another in paying tribute to Mary in verse. From this long list you

THE MARY ALTAR

National Shrine of the Immaculate Conception,
Catholic University, Washington, D. C.

This altar stands in the basement church of the shrine. It is hoped that the edifice, when completed, will give America a shrine not unworthy of our Immaculate Mother, Patroness of the United States.

see how often the beautiful character of our Lady has enticed the poets to create gems of literary beauty. From among these or from other collections you will be able to find one which you especially like; or perhaps, some beautiful stanzas, like those glorious lines of Wordsworth's "The Virgin":

> "Our tainted nature's solitary boast;
> Purer than foam on central ocean tost!"

POEMS IN HONOR OF THE BLESSED VIRGIN

Those marked with an asterisk are recommended for memorization

The Mary Book (Shrine of the Immaculate Conception, Washington, D. C.):

TITLE	AUTHOR	Page
O Mary Mother	Dante G. Rosetti	35
Mater Immaculata	William Wordsworth	50
The Mother's Hymn	William C. Bryant	54
The Poet's Ideal of Woman	Percy B. Shelley	55
The Immaculate Conception	Robert Southey	57
Sir Lancelot, Serf of Mary	Alfred Tennyson	59
Ave Maria	George Byron	63
The Annunciation	Mrs. Hemans	63
A Virgin Shall Conceive	Alexander Pope	64
Hymn to the Virgin	Edgar Allen Poe	66
Hymn Before Action	Rudyard Kipling	66
Madonna Dell' Acqua	John Ruskin	70
Mother Out of Sight	John Keble	72
Mary	Oliver Wendell Holmes	74
Our Lady of the Rocks	Dante G. Rossetti	86
Mother of Mercies	Father Faber	295
Virgin Immaculate	Eleanor Donnelly	324
The First Christmas	John Milton	337
A Christmas Carol	Aubrey de Vere	343
Mater Dei	Catherine Tynan	347
Thou Blessed Babe	Phoebe Cary	350
Mary in Egypt	Mrs. Hemans	353
Cathedral of Chartres	James Russell Lowell	439

The Catholic Anthology by Thomas Walsh (Macmillan Co.)

CATHOLIC AUTHORS:

The Gaelic Litany to Our Lady	Eighth Century	36
Irish Hymn to Mary	Anonymous (Ninth Century)	43
From the Mariale	Bernard of Morlas	52
Stabat Mater Speciosa	Jacopone da Todi	73
Lady of Heaven	G. d'Arrezo	79
To the Virgin Mary	F. Petrarch	92
The Queen of the Angels	G. Boccaccio	94
Song to the Virgin Mary	Pero Lopez de Ayala	97
A Prayer to the Blessed Virgin	G. Chaucer	101
Mother Most Powerful	G. Dominici	102
Rosa Mystica	Old English Hymn	102
To the Virgin	John Lydgate	104
Hymn to the Blessed Virgin	Anonymous	105
Hymn to Mary	Zerea Jacob	109
To Our Lady	Robert Henryson	110

TITLE	AUTHOR	Page
His Mother's Service to Our Lady	Francois Villon	111
The Benedictine *Ultima*	(Learn to sing for next unit)	113
Ballad to Our Lady	William Dunbar	130
Star of the Sea	Alexander Barclay	135
Prayer to the Blessed Virgin	R. de Padron	135
Carol to Our Lady	Old English	141
The Marigold	William Forrest	147
To Our Blessed Lady	Henry Constable	177
Our Lady's Lullaby	R. Verstegan	180
The Assumption	Sir John Beaumont	183
Quaerit Jesum Suum Maria	Richard Crashaw	202
Song of Praise to Mary	Angelus Silesius	209
Kolendy for Christmas	From Polish	236
Our Lady in the Middle Ages	Frederick W. Faber	260
Raphael's San Sisto Madonna	George H. Miles	268
Our Madonna at Home	Rafael Pombo	274
He Would Have His Lady Sing	Digby M. Dolben	306
Mary Immaculate	Eleanor C. Donnelly	308
Vigil of the Immaculate Conception	Maurice F. Egan	311
Ave Maria Gratia Plena	Oscar Wilde	313
On the Annunciation of Fra Angelico	Manuel Machado	395
Communion	Caroline Giltinan	413
The Mother	Kathryn W. Ryan	413
Mary's Baby	Shaemas O'Sheel	423

NON-CATHOLIC AUTHORS:

*The Virgin	William Wordsworth	*454
*Aspiration	Charles Lamb	*456
Hymn of the Angelus	Edgar Allen Poe	458
Mary's Girlhood	Dante Gabriel Rossetti	461
Prayer to the Virgin of Chartres	Henry Adams	466
Our Lady	Mary Coleridge	471
*To the Lighted Lady Window	Marguerite Wilkinson	*477
The Madonna's Lamp	Prince Wilhelm	478

Catholic Flowers from Protestant Gardens by Treacy (Kenedy)

The Angelus	Bret Harte	3
A Chant to the Blessed Virgin	James Hilhouse	76
The Angel Gabriel and the Blessed Virgin	Henry W. Longfellow	83
Ave Maria	Sir Walter Scott	111
The Blessed Lady's Land	Henry W. Longfellow	270

Or those other lines of yearning in Lamb's "Aspiration":

> "Lady most perfect, when thy sinless face
> Men look upon, they wish to be
> A Catholic, Madonna fair, to worship thee."

It may be that the class will want to divide all the poems among its different members in an effort to find the ones they like best. It may also be that you will want to choose and memorize one poem in honor of Mary as your *Class Poem to Our Lady*. It may even be that you, too, will feel the urge to try your poet's wings to honor her. If so, spread them and see if you can fly, for all these things will help you to love Mary more, to know her better, and think of her oftener.

B. OUR LADY, THE INSPIRATION OF BEAUTY IN MUSIC

Music owes more to Mary and to the Church than most people know. The music of the masters has its roots in the chant and polyphony which the Church developed from the music of the Greeks; and songs in praise of Mary can be traced back to the dawn of Christianity.

1. PLAIN CHANT

The beauty and strength and moderation of the official music of the Church, the Plain Chant or Gregorian Chant as it is called, shows clearly that the influence of Mary is on it and in it. Like her, it is mild, calm, gentle, prudent, chaste, virginal. It takes a long and deep acquaintance with the chant of the Church to come really to understand and like it, for it is purposely different from the music of the world. It is intended to purify the imagination and to awaken in the mind thoughts which will raise our hearts to heaven, to Christ, and to Mary; not to drag them down to earth by exciting the passions. Even in a physical way, when sung as the Church would have it sung, the Plain Chant soothes us, mind and body. It rests and refreshes us.

It was from the unharmonized Plain Chant of the Church, which developed under the guidance of regulations made by Pope St. Gregory the Great (590-604), that the inspiring polyphonic church music has sprung.

2. POLYPHONIC MUSIC

In plain chant all sing in unison. In polyphonic music many parts are blended together in rich harmony.

Giovanni Pierluigi da *Palestrina,* the greatest of the composers of polyphonic music felt Mary's influence. He is said to have been given his musical training by the choirmasters of the principal church dedicated to Mary —St. Mary Major in Rome. He wrote hymns in her honor, an "Ave Maria," a beautiful "Stabat Mater" for a double chorus, litanies of the Blessed Virgin, and what is one of his greatest productions, the Mass: "Assumpta Est Maria." He lived in the sixteenth century.

3. MODERN CLASSICAL MUSIC

The music of the Church has influenced many composers who are eminent for classical, symphonic, and operatic music. Some of them wrote "Masses" which are more operatic than liturgical, more worldly than religious. Among them are Haydn, Beethoven, Mozart, Gounod, Verdi and others. Gounod also wrote a famous *Ave Maria.* He took a beautiful flowing prelude of Johann Sebastian Bach, and transcribed and adapted it to the words of the *Ave.* Gounod's, however, is not quite so well known as that of Franz Schubert whose *Ave* is acknowledged to be the best known song in the world. Many other composers have attempted to set the Ave Maria to music. Frequently, however, these pieces, while beautiful, are not appropriate for Church use. Why not?

4. THE FOUR MARIAN ANTIPHONS

To return now to purely liturgical music, there are four great hymns, antiphons, or anthems, in honor of Mary. They are said or sung at the end of the Divine Office according to the time of the year. The first "Alma Redemptoris Mater," is sung from Advent until the feast of the Purification. It is followed by the "Ave Regina Coelorum," which is used from the Purification to Easter and

THE MADONNA OF THE HARPIES

therefore principally during Lent. The third you should already know—The "Regina Coeli," "O Queen of Heaven Rejoice." It is used during the Paschal Season, that is, from Easter to Pentecost. During that time it also replaces the Angelus. Do you know it by heart?

The fourth and final Marian anthem, the "Salve Regina," "Hail Holy Queen," is well known to all Catholics, being said after every Low Mass with the other prescribed prayers for Russia. The title for this unit, as you may have noticed, is taken from the Salve Regina. The whole first part of the *Glories of Mary*, by St. Alphonsus, to which we have referred before, is devoted to an explanation of this beautiful prayer and hymn, invocation by invocation. It would be profitable and enjoyable reading for anyone.

5. THE HYMN WHICH MARY COMPOSED

In our sophomore year, we became acquainted with the *Magnificat*—the hymn which our Blessed Mother composed at the Visitation in response to the greeting of Elizabeth. Now that we are older and understand things better, we would do well to go through the Magnificat again, analyzing and interpreting it word by word, and phrase by phrase, and then learning it by heart. It is a glorious song of praise, honoring God and our Blessed Mother at one and the same time. It would certainly please the Blessed Virgin if we learned to sing it in the beautiful cadences of the plain song of the Church.

6. OTHER MARIAN HYMNS IN LATIN

There is another favorite hymn to our Blessed Lady called the *Ave Maris Stella*. Its English translation is, "Hail Thou Star of Ocean, God's Own Mother Blest." The pilgrims to Lourdes love to sing the fourth verse: "Monstra te esse matrem . . ." "Show thyself a Mother." This hymn is used at Vespers of the feasts of the Blessed Virgin Mary. It has several musical settings.

The *O Sanctissima* is another beloved hymn to Mary; it has a melody, beautiful in its simplicity. The students of a certain school in Europe, when they went mountain-climbing, would sing it, with bared heads, as they stood on the peak they had just climbed. It was a sign of honor to Mary, and both a "Thank You" for her protection, and a "Please" for a safe descent. A lovely custom, was it not? Do we have any like it? Could we adopt this one, or inaugurate others like it?

The *Stabat Mater* (At the Cross her Station Keeping), is a plaintive hymn to our Sorrowing Mother. It has twenty stanzas, many of which are a plea to Mary to help us commiserate with her and her Son. It is used as the Sequence for the Mass of the two feasts of the Seven Dolors and is very appropriate for the Way of the Cross. Palestrina set it to music in a magnificent composition for double chorus. Rossini also composed a Stabat Mater, but many think it wholly inappropriate, the music being too unrestrained for so sacred a topic. Do you know other musical compositions or settings for hymns which are not in keeping with the Church's standards for liturgical or other sacred music?

The last Latin hymn to Mary which we will mention is a prayer for a happy death known as the Benedictine *Ultima*. It would be a good hymn to learn for the next unit on the Last Things. A reference to it can be found in the list of poems on page 73.

7. VERNACULAR HYMNS TO OUR BLESSED LADY

When we come to the vernacular hymns to Mary we find them in the English language in such numbers and variety that it is impossible to make a choice. You must make your own, using this for a criterion: Which would Mary herself like?

As regards the many beautiful hymns to Mary in the various foreign languages: French, Italian, German,

Spanish, the Slavic tongues, and so forth, it might not be amiss, if there are students who can sing such hymns, to have them sung for or by the class to show how every nation under the sun has vied with one another in paying our Lady tribute in song and verse. The famous Lourdes Hymn: *"Ave, Ave, Ave, Maria"* could be sung very appropriately.

C. OUR LADY IN OIL, FRESCO, AND PASTEL

1. MARIAN ART DOWN THE AGES

Christian artists have striven from early days to portray to the world the face, which, as Dante so beautifully expressed it:

> .... unto Christ
> Has most resemblance, for its brightness only
> Is able to prepare thee to see Christ. *Paradise,* Canto 32.

How successfully they have been can be ascertained from the fact that most of the famous paintings of the world are the various Madonnas of the great masters.

a. The Oldest Picture of Our Lady?

It is difficult to trace pictures of the Blessed Virgin to a date earlier than the fifth century, but then, as a result of the Nestorian heresy, which, as you may recall, denied Mary the title of Mother of God, a strong interest in the Blessed Mother was aroused. Thus does God draw good from evil. The Empress Eudoxia, on a pilgrimage to the Holy Places in Palestine at that time, sent to her sister-in-law, Pulcheria, a supposedly authentic picture of the Blessed Virgin. Pulcheria placed it in a church in Constantinople. What became of it later is not known, but a legend says it was brought to Venice and placed in the beautiful Church of St. Mark, where today a picture of the Blessed Virgin of great antiquity is still venerated. The legend claims St. Luke as the one who painted the picture.

b. In the Age of the Iconoclasts

In the eighth and ninth centuries the heretical Iconoclasts (*icon*—image; *clas-* —break) or Image Breakers opposed the use of statues and pictures as being idolatrous. As a result of their wild destruction, many ancient pictures were lost, yet the veneration of the faithful, who knew the proper use of images, only increased, and in the ninth century, Mary began to appear on coins and in the austere paintings of Byzantine artists.

c. Modern Painting Begins

In the thirteenth century painting veered away from the straight, ascetical lines of Byzantine art and added a touch of mildness in the eyes, in the smile, in the general treatment of the Madonna. An Italian named Cimabue has been given much credit for the change, but read the article about him in the *Catholic Encyclopedia* and decide for yourself.

The flatness of Byzantine art also gradually gave way to greater fidelity to life with the addition of the effect of depth and the third dimension. Backgrounds and perspective also were introduced, with the passage of time.

The real founder of the Italian school of painting was Giotto who began working toward the end of the thirteenth century at Assisi and Florence.

In the fourteenth and fifteenth centuries came Fra Angelico, literally "Brother Angelic." This was the name the people gave to Guido da Vicchio after he became a Dominican and started painting his lovely, charming, colorful angels and Madonnas.

Other artists preceded and succeeded him, giving the

→

Richard King   *Courtesy of the Catechetical Guild*

THE CORONATION

On her Assumption into heaven the Blessed Virgin Mary was crowned as Queen of Heaven, and as Queen of Angels and Men.

world a rich treasury of religious paintings, in which scenes from the life of the Blessed Virgin Mary and especially pictures of the Madonna and Child were a most prominent part.

Christian art also has created countless artistic symbols of Mary; the lily, the rose of Sharon, the fleur-de-lis, the moon and stars, and monograms of many designs.

d. The Age of the Masters

The sixteenth century brought into existence some of the most famous pictures in the world—most of them Madonnas; yet one must in Christian truthfulness say that many of these are less art for Mary's sake, than art for its own exuberant indulgence in color and line and beauty.

Greatest of all are those of *Raphael* (Raffaele Santi) who painted the *Sistine Madonna,* the *Madonna of the Chair,* the *Madonna of the Grand Duke,* and countless other Madonnas as well as other topics. Of the Sistine Madonna—which, like most great masterpieces, cannot be fully appreciated in any copy—Gillet has said that it is: ". . . the most beautiful devotional picture in existence." It hangs in a gallery in Dresden. The Madonna of the Chair, which the same critic says is "the best liked by women," is in Florence, as is the Madonna of the Grand Duke.

We have no space for detailed description here; in fact, it might be better if each one would choose his own favorite Madonna, learn its story and its excellence, relate what he has learned to the class, and make the resolution that, some day, as fine a copy of it as Christian moderation will allow shall adorn his home.

Of the other great Madonna painters we must next mention him whose Madonnas are often preferred to those of Raphael — Bartolome Esteban *Murillo,* the Spanish painter whose pure and happy life is reflected in his beautiful pictures. His *Madonna and Child* in the Pitti Palace in Florence is remarkable for the exquisite beauty of the face, especially of the eyes of Mother and Child.

Among the other masters there are Botticelli, Andrea del Sarto, Correggio (Antonio Allegri), and Titian (Tiziano Vecellio), each of whom has painted some lovely Madonnas.

D. MAGNIFICATS IN STONE AND GLASS

Beauty of a completely different type has found its inspiration in the love of the Blessed Virgin Mary—beauty in stone and glass, the majestic beauty of the great Marian cathedrals.

First and foremost there is that of *Notre Dame of Chartres,* in France, southwest of Paris. No picture has ever done it justice. One must see it to fall under the spell of its lofty, delicate, Gothic stateliness. One must enter it and drink in the heart-stirring beauty of its world-famous mediæval stained glass windows, especially the exquisite window of the south transept, the lovely Blue Madonna of Chartres. It was built in the twelfth century, and stands as a tribute to the engineering skill and artistic sense, as well as to the love and devotion of its builders who worked on it in silence and in prayer. Like all Marian art it proves that love of Mary produces beauty, physical as well as spiritual.

There were Marian churches earlier than that of Chartres. There was one at Ephesus where the Nestorian heresy was condemned in 431, another at Alexandria, another in Gaul, but the mother church of them all, in dignity at least if not in antiquity, is the great basilica of *St. Mary Major* in Rome. It was built in the fourth century by Pope Liberius and therefore is also known as the Liberian Basilica. Unlike the soaring Gothic of most of the French cathedrals, St. Mary Major is in the style of the Roman architecture, with the round arch, the flat

By Burton Holmes   From Ewing Galloway

NOTRE DAME DE PARIS

This well known church to our Lady, the Cathedral of Notre Dame de Paris, is a gem of the Gothic style of architecture, and a proof of the great devotion of the French nation during the Middle Ages. People who could give so much of their time and means as to build such a lovely monument to the honor of the Mother of God certainly must have loved her deeply.

paneled ceiling, and rows of columns separating the middle nave from the side aisles.

According to tradition, an old Roman couple had decided to leave their wealth to the Church. Our Blessed Mother appeared to them, telling them to erect a church in her honor on the spot on the Esquiline Hill where snow would fall the following morning, August 5. The snow fell, and Pope Liberius erected the church, which is often called *St. Mary of the Snow*. There is a feast to celebrate the tradition and the dedication of the Church on August 5 each year. St. Mary Major ranks third in dignity among the churches of the world, being preceded only by St. John Lateran, and by St. Peter's on the Vatican Hill. We might tell many interesting facts about this grand basilica, one of the richest shrines in the world, but we must leave them to you to find out.

In Florence, there is the gorgeous cathedral called the *Duomo* and dedicated to *Our Lady of the Flower* (Florence is the city of flowers). Its entire exterior is of exquisite beauty, being faced with varicolored, light marble. The ornate cathedral of *Siena* has also an exterior of colored marble, laid in the most fascinating striped design and highly ornamented with statues. It is dedicated to the Assumption.

The cathedral of *Rheims,* with its fine graceful sturdiness and its magnificent rose window, is one of the best known churches in the world. Its triple portal is loved everywhere. Hardly less famous is *Notre Dame de Paris,* the cathedral of Paris, and scene of many a varied event in the course of history.

The cathedral of *Speyer* in Germany, a noble specimen of the massive, Romanesque style, is a church of our Lady. It was intended as a mausoleum for the emperors of the Holy Roman Empire.

All the cathedrals of Portugal are dedicated to Mary.

Spain, too, has its Marian churches. The cathedral of *Seville,* one of the three largest churches in the world is dedicated to Nuestra Señora de la Sede—Our Lady of the See; while that of *Toledo* is in honor of the Assumption. Both of these are enormous edifices, but even in the smallest detail they are perfection. Mary was perfect, so her churches must not lack perfection, and her clients have ornamented these churches with works of art, from front to rear, from side to side, from bottom to top, inside and out. Every detail is a tribute to Mary, and to God.

REVIEW OF SECTION FIVE.

SECTION SIX: SHRINES AND PLACES OF PILGRIMAGE

Let us now turn our attention to the great shrines and places of pilgrimage where Mary is honored throughout the world. The best known is that at *Lourdes,* where our Blessed Lady appeared eighteen times to Bernadette Soubirous from February 11, 1858, to the feast of Our Lady of Mt. Carmel, July 16, of that same year. You remember the story: the beautiful lady in white and blue and gold with the Rosary; Bernadette sprinkling holy water at the apparition; our Lady saying: *"I wish to see many people here;" "Pray for poor sinners! Pray for the sick world!" "I have a secret to entrust to you." "Penance! Penance! Penance!"* You remember the miraculous spring; Mary's request for a shrine; and, in the sixteenth apparition on March 25, the feast of the Annunciation, Mary's revelation of her name with the words: *"I am the Immaculate Conception."* You know also the unceasing stream of miracles wrought at this shrine ever since.

But Lourdes is not the only shrine or place of pilgrimage in Mary's honor. If you would know some of them, look through the long list in the article on pilgrimages in the *Catholic Encyclopedia.* Let us mention a few. France also has *Chartres.* Spain has *Montserrat* in the serrated mountains, outside of Barcelona; and *Our Lady of the Pillar* at *Saragossa.* At this latter place is venerated an ancient statue which tradition says goes back to the day on which our Blessed Lady appeared to the Apostle St. James (Santiago), encouraging him in his apostolic labors on the Iberian Peninsula. In Italy, there is *Loreto* with the *Holy House,* scene of many miracles; there is the miraculous picture of Our Lady of Perpetual Help in the church

───────⟶

OUR LADY OF GUADALUPE

This is the picture of our Lady which she, herself, miraculously imprinted on the cloak of the Indian convert, Juan Diego in 1531. It stands, today, above the high altar of the basilica of Guadalupe. (See page 293.)

of St. Alphonsus in Rome. In Switzerland there is *Einsiedeln* with the miraculous statue brought by St. Meinrad in the ninth century.

The Polish people have *Czestochowa,* a rich shrine with a miraculous picture painted on a piece of cypress wood, reputedly by St. Luke. In the early Middle Ages it was one of the best known shrines in Europe. *Our Lady of Walsingham* was England's most popular shrine until King Henry VIII destroyed it. The national shrine of *Our Lady of Fatima* in Portugal is dedicated to the Immaculate Heart of our Lady of the Rosary. It was founded in the twentieth century and already has gained great popularity.

Here in the Americas there is, first and foremost, the miraculous picture of Our Lady of *Guadalupe,* near Mexico City. In the United States there have been no recorded apparitions of our heavenly Mother, but every sector of the country has its churches and chapels with venerated pictures and shrines in honor of famous shrines in other lands, as for instance, those of Lourdes and Czestochowa, and also pictures of Our Lady of Perpetual Help, Our Lady of the Miraculous Medal, Our Sorrowful Mother. Then there is the shrine of Our Lady of Victory, built by Father Baker, at Lackawanna, just outside of Buffalo, and other churches to which pilgrimages are made.

Certainly there are some in or near your own home, or in your diocese. You might pay Mary the honor of visiting them.

SECTION SEVEN: DEVOTIONS TO THE BLESSED VIRGIN, MOTHER OF GOD

A. OUR NEED OF MARY
   1. HOW MARY HAS HELPED

B. SAINTS WHO HAVE LOVED MARY

C. MARIAN DEVOTIONS
   1. THE MONTHS WITH MARY
   2. MARY'S DAY
   3. THE ROSARY
   4. OTHER PRAYERS TO MARY
   5. DEVOUT PRACTICES IN HONOR OF MARY
     a. Sacramentals
     b. Devotion to the Seven Sorrows
     c. The Little Office of the Blessed Virgin
     d. Pilgrimages, Penance

D. MARIAN SOCIETIES

DEVOTIONS TO THE BLESSED VIRGIN, MOTHER OF GOD
A. OUR NEED OF MARY

It is impossible to save our souls without the help of the Blessed Mother of God. She is Mediatrix of all Graces; if she does not intercede, we do not receive. But Mary helps all who come to her in the spirit of her Son. Devotion to Mary, consequently, is a necessity and an assurance of her assistance.

1. HOW MARY HAS HELPED

Every century and every age has its stories of how the Blessed Virgin came to the aid of those who have invoked her powerful patronage.

In the thirteenth century, when the Albigensian heresy was threatening to engulf Christian civilization it was devotion to our Blessed Lady, preached by St. Dominic, that turned the tide and saved Europe.

At the naval battle of Lepanto, in 1571, the threat from Mohammedan domination of the continent was repelled with the assistance of the Queen of the Rosary.

In our own day our Blessed Lady of Fatima, while

asking for prayers for sinners and reparation to her Immaculate Heart, has promised to defend our modern world against the scourge of atheistic communism by bringing about the conversion of Russia.

It behooves us then, as individuals, as a nation, yes, as a world, to have deep devotion to the Mother of our Redeemer. Just in what this devotion consists may perhaps be learned best by studying the lives of some of Mary's most devoted clients.

B. SAINTS WHO HAVE LOVED MARY

All saints necessarily have deep devotion to the Blessed Mother. Some, however, have been particularly notable for the beauty of their devotion to her.

Among these we must mention, St. John the Evangelist, St. John Baptist, St. Cyril, St. John Damascene, St. Dominic, St. Bernard, St. Alphonsus Liguori, St. Simon Stock, St. Ildephonsus. We have already mentioned St. Alphonsus as author of the *Glories of Mary;* St. Dominic, as organizer of the great devotions to Mary which preserved Europe from the Albigensian heresy and St. Cyril as the valiant defender of the Mother of God against Nestorianism. St. Simon Stock we will meet in connection with the scapular. St. Bernard is noted for the tenderness and intensity of his devotion to Mary and for the burning eloquence of his sermons on our Lady. St. John Damascene, like St. Cyril, defended our Blessed Lady's title of Mother of God against the heretical Nestorians. He wrote a prayer to the Blessed Virgin in which he beseeches her to "receive tenderly the supplication of a sinner who loves thee tenderly, honors thee in a special manner, and places in thee the whole hope of his salvation."

What other saints do you know who were devoted servants of Mary?

C. MARIAN DEVOTIONS

We have learned much about our Blessed Mother thus far in this unit, but we really have learned nothing about her unless we know and adopt some of the devotions and practices which her clients have always loved to use.

1. THE MONTHS WITH MARY

All good Catholics know that there are special periods of time devoted to Mary. First there is *the month of May*. The origin of the use of this month as one of special devotion to Mary is not clear, but it is a practice of relatively modern times. There is no set formula of prayers and exercises for May devotions, although the ceremony of crowning our Blessed Lady enjoys a wide popularity in this country, as does the construction and decoration of May altars in churches, schools, and homes.

Then, there is *the month of October* which is dedicated to the devotion of the Holy Rosary, due to the fact that the feast of the Most Holy Rosary falls in that month. This feast can be traced back to 1571, when the threatening advances of Islam were checked by the signal victory of a Christian fleet under Don Juan of Austria, over the Mohammedan fleet, at the Battle of Lepanto.

The battle was fought on Sunday, October 7, as the whole Christian world, at the request of Pope Saint Pius V, was praying the Rosary to our Lady of Victory. Each side had about 250 boats in the battle and when it was over, the Turks had lost 192 of theirs, fifteen having been sunk and the rest captured. Somewhere in your English course you have certainly read Chesterton's stirring poem about the battle, entitled "Lepanto."

In gratitude for the victory the pope ordered a commemoration of the Rosary on that day, and before long a special feast was established.

2. MARY'S DAY—SATURDAY

The Saturday of every week is devoted in a very special way to the Blessed Virgin. In fact, whenever the Saturday has no special feast or only a feast of simple rank, the Church allows the votive Mass in honor of our Lady to be said, and prescribes the recitation of the Office of the Blessed Virgin by those obliged to say the breviary. *Saturday,* you learned in your freshman year, is *Mary's Day* because she proved her faith and hope and love on that *first* dreary *Holy Saturday.* She proved her love of us by never wavering; we, too, must prove the steadiness of our love for her. The practice of receiving Communion on the first Saturday of each month in reparation to the Immaculate Heart of Mary was recommended by our Blessed Mother in one of her apparitions at Fatima. This has led to the development of the five first Saturdays in reparation to the Immaculate Heart, to parallel the first Fridays to the Sacred Heart.

3. THE ROSARY

The most popular and best loved of all devotions to Mary is the *Rosary.* No one should be allowed to graduate from a Catholic high school unless he has proved individually that he knows how to pray the Rosary, and has learned the three sets of mysteries by heart.

Lest there be a single one who lacks that ability, let us here set down the three groups of mysteries, and a description of the manner of saying the Rosary.

THE MYSTERIES OF THE ROSARY

THE JOYFUL MYSTERIES

1. The Annunciation
2. The Visitation
3. The Birth of Christ
4. The Presentation of Our Lord
5. The Finding of the Child Jesus in the Temple

THE SORROWFUL MYSTERIES

1. The Agony in the Garden
2. The Scourging at the Pillar
3. The Crowning with Thorns
4. The Carrying of the Cross
5. The Crucifixion

THE GLORIOUS MYSTERIES

1. The Resurrection
2. The Ascension
3. The Descent of the Holy Ghost upon the Apostles
4. The Assumption of the Blessed Virgin Mary
5. The Coronation of the Blessed Virgin Mary

How to Say the Rosary

The Rosary begins with the Sign of the Cross; many people, after signing themselves, reverently press the cross to their lips. Then the Apostles' Creed is said on the crucifix, an Our Father on the first large bead, a Hail Mary on each of the next three small beads, concluding with the Gloria. Following this, the first mystery of the series to be said is announced or called to mind, and an Our Father and ten Hail Marys follow on the one large and the ten small beads. While reciting these prayers, at least to gain certain indulgences, we are supposed to *meditate* on the mystery of that particular decade. Then the decade is concluded with the Glory be to the Father, etc., and the second mystery is begun, and so on to the end of the fifth mystery, meditating all the while on the mystery being said.

Various indulgences, Brigittine, Crozier, Dominican and Papal may be attached to a rosary by having it blessed by a priest who has the necessary faculties. What these indulgences are would be an informative and practical topic for a careful report. For recitation of the beads in the presence of the Blessed Sacrament one can gain a plenary indulgence.

The Rosary is a powerful prayer. He who says it well and says it faithfully all during his life will have little to fear at the hour of death.

4. OTHER PRAYERS TO MARY

The second prayer which we shall mention is already included in the Rosary. It is the favorite prayer to the Blessed Virgin, the *Hail Mary*. You already know the sources from which we received it. It should be said often, for at the sound of Mary's name, hell quakes and the devil flees.

The third and fourth prayers to Mary are the *Angelus,* and its Paschal substitute, the *Regina Coeli*. They, too, must be known by heart so that we recite them with fluency. If we stumble in saying them it proves we do not use them.

Fifth comes the *Hail Holy Queen*. It should be reviewed to insure a complete understanding of its terms, as should the sixth prayer every faithful servant of Mary knows —the *Memorare*.

In addition to these it would be commendable to learn by heart the words of the *Magnificat,* and as some have done, the invocations of the *Litany of the Blessed Virgin*.

Finally we should know and form the habit of frequently using short indulgenced *ejaculations,* such as "Mary, conceived without sin, pray for us who have recourse to thee." "Sweet Heart of Jesus, be my love; sweet Heart of Mary, be my salvation." There are many other indulgenced prayers and ejaculations in honor of the Blessed Virgin listed in *The Raccolta*. A report on these would be very instructive. Indulgenced devotions and practices are also listed. Let us examine a few.

Courtesy of the Cleveland Museum of Art, J. H. Wade Fund

OUR LADY OF THE ROSARY

This illustration of our Lady surrounded by the fifteen mysteries of the rosary is an example of a most remarkable art technique. The picture was painted on glass, from the reverse side, with a needle for a brush. The process, named for its inventor, is called *Verre Eglomisé,* that is, Glass, Eglomised. The actual size of the picture is 3½ x 2¾ inches.

5. DEVOUT PRACTICES IN HONOR OF MARY

a. Sacramentals

In addition to the saying of prayers, the true child of Mary adopts certain devotional practices to honor his Mother. First he wears the *Scapular* of Our Lady of Mount Carmel, or carries or wears a scapular medal.

A scapular is part of the habit worn by some religious orders. There are many different scapulars, but the best known and most widely used is that of the Carmelites or the Scapular of Our Lady of Mt. Carmel—a highly prized and richly indulgenced sacramental. A credible tradition says that our Blessed Mother herself gave this scapular to St. Simon Stock, a holy Carmelite monk in the thirteenth century, and promised that all who died wearing it would be saved. As knowledge of the promise spread, devotion to the scapular developed; the growth being particularly marked since the sixteenth century.

In addition to the scapular, the true child of Mary wears or carries some *medal* of the *Blessed Virgin,* for example, the Miraculous Medal.

What would you think of the suggestion that instead of buying quickly discarded rings or pins or the like as a sign of one's school allegiance, Catholic high school students spend the same money to buy really nice pins or medals of the Blessed Virgin that anyone would be proud to wear for a lifetime. The school initials and the year could still find a place on them.

In his home, the true client of our Blessed Mother secs to it that the walls of every room have a picture of Mary or something else that would please her, for example, a crucifix or a picture of the Sacred Heart.

There are lovers of Mary who have a little shrine of the Blessed Mother in their bedroom—a picture or a statue, a vigil light, a vase for some flowers, with perhaps a place to kneel and a card containing some prayers to Mary. This is especially fitting at Christmas, and in May and October. There are others who secure or collect a series of pictures of Mary, usually the more devotional Madonnas of the masters, and have a frame or easel in which to put them, one at a time, changing them to fit the mood of the season.

b. Devotion to the Seven Sorrows

The client of our Blessed Mother has devotion to the *Seven Sorrows* of Mary: 1) Simeon's Prophecy, 2) The Flight into Egypt, 3) Losing Christ in the Temple, 4) Meeting Her Son on the Way to Calvary, 5) Standing at the Foot of the Cross, 6) Taking Christ down from the Cross, 7) The Burial of Christ.

c. The Little Office of the Blessed Virgin

Many priests and members of religious communities, particularly of women, and not a few of the laity daily recite the Little Office of the Blessed Virgin. This Little Office is patterned on the Divine Office which the priest says every day. It is highly indulgenced, and its different hours take perhaps a total of twenty-five minutes to say.

d. Pilgrimages, Penance

One who loves Mary visits her images, makes novenas to her, joins *processions* in her honor and with regularity makes pilgrimages to shrines dedicated to her. Finally, a real lover of Mary undertakes many *acts of mortification* for her, fasting and giving alms and performing works of mercy in her honor.

D. MARIAN SOCIETIES

In addition to the prayers and devotional practices which honor Mary, there are certain religious orders or pious *organizations* dedicated to her which one can join or to which one can become affiliated.

The Carmelites (O. Carm.) are a mendicant order dedicated to Mary under the title of Our Lady of Mount Carmel. They include communities both of men and of women with rules of varying degrees of strictness. There is also a third order for the laity.

The *Servites*, or Servants of Mary (O.S.M.), another religious mendicant order of men, have for one of their special purposes the spreading of devotion to Mary, particularly to her sorrows. There is also a third order of Servites for the laity, as well as a Confraternity of the Seven Dolors which may be erected in any church.

The Marists (Society of Mary, S.M.) are also dedicated to Mary; so are the Marianists (Society of Mary, S.M.). The latter community is a teaching order of priests and brothers. The Oblates of Mary Immaculate (O.M.I.) are similarly dedicated to her, as are many other religious communities of men. The motherhouse of the Catholic Foreign Mission Society of America has been named Maryknoll, and its members are usually referred to as Maryknollers. It hardly needs to be said that every religious order of men honors and serves Mary.

Corresponding to these religious orders of men, there are hundreds of various communities of women dedicated to the honor and service of the Blessed Virgin. Indeed most nuns show their special devotion to Mary by including her name in their new name in religion.

Confraternities and *sodalities* for the laity supply the means whereby the majority of Mary's subjects may honor her in an organization. Most common and prominent among these are the Confraternity of the Holy Rosary,

---

←

Fides Foto

THE QUEEN OF THE WORLD

This statue, in the church of Our Lady Queen of the World, the Cathedral of Port Said, Egypt, represents our Blessed Mother as she appeared to Blessed Catherine Labouré.

the Confraternity of the Scapular of Mount Carmel, or any other scapular, the Sodalities of the Blessed Virgin and the Legion of Mary. But there are many others. To join these and faithfully perform the services in honor of Mary which they impose is a joy and an honor to the Mother of God.

REVIEW OF SECTIONS SIX AND SEVEN.

CONCLUSION

I have *three mothers:* my natural mother, my Holy Mother the Church, and Mary, my heavenly Mother. All of them love me. If I am a worthy son or daughter, I must love them, for they have conferred great benefits on me.

Through my heavenly Mother I am a brother of Jesus Christ. Through her hands all graces that I have received have come to me. Through those hands all graces yet to be given to me must come. Therefore, *I need Mary. My quest for happiness*—my journey *toward the eternal commencement* can never succeed except by and through her and the grace her Son distributes through her hands. Accordingly, I must be devoted to her; otherwise I cannot save my soul. She is *our Life, our Sweetness, and our Hope.*

To honor her, therefore, let each of us hereby make and keep the following seven resolutions:

1. I will, in honor of Mary's purity, control all the passions and tendencies of my body.
2. I will, in honor of Mary's courage and patience, cheerfully accept the trials God sends my way.
3. I will, in honor of Mary's poverty, detachment, justice, and obedience, be absolutely just and respect the rights of all men.

←

Murillo   *Philip D. Gendreau, N. Y.*

VIRGIN AND CHILD

This is one of the best known and most loved of the Madonna masterpieces.

4. I will, in honor of Mary's Christian prudence, listen to the whisperings of her Spouse, the Holy Spirit.

5. I will, in honor of Mary's faith, believe everything God's Church asks me to believe.

6. I will, in honor of Mary's confidence in God, trust His eternal Providence and mercy.

7. I will, in honor of Mary's great charity, love my God in a truly Christian manner; I will love all my brothers in Christ, and my own immortal soul because of God.

There are many ways in which this unit might be brought to a conclusion. One which would certainly please our Blessed Mother would be for us as individuals or better, as a group, to go to a church or chapel to spend a half hour honoring her in prayer, meditation, and song. The program might include:

The *Rosary*, with "We fly to thy patronage"
The *Ave Maria*, said or sung
The *Angelus*
The *Hail Holy Queen*
The *Memorare*
The *Magnificat* (chanted or recited)
The *Litany of Loreto* (chanted in Latin or recited)
An *Act of Consecration to the Immaculate Heart of Mary*
Blessing and Reception of a Medal of the Blessed Virgin
Enrollment in the Scapular
Enrollment in the Sodality or Legion of Mary
Benediction (if possible)

REVIEW OF UNIT ONE

1. Summarize the main outline of the three previous years of our religion course.

2. What is the central theme of our course; what are the central objectives?

3. Who were the parents of Mary?

4. What does the Immaculate Conception mean?

5. How long has this doctrine been taught by the Church? How long has it been officially defined as a doctrine of faith?

6. Has Mary ever encouraged devotion to the Immaculate Conception?

7. When is the feast of the Immaculate Conception?

8. Did Mary take a vow of virginity? Was it temporary or permanent?

9. When does Mary first appear in the Gospels?

10. Describe the Annunciation.

11. Describe the Visitation.

12. Describe the hidden life of Mary at Nazareth.

13. Describe a day in the "career" that gained Mary the highest place in heaven.

14. Enumerate the Blessed Virgin's appearances during the Public Life of Christ.

15. Follow the Blessed Mother from Good Friday morning until the descent of the Holy Spirit.

16. Tell of Mary's life after the first Pentecost until her death.

17. Enumerate and give the date of the seven major feasts of the Blessed Mother.

18. Tell the story of: the Holy House, Guadalupe, Lourdes, Our Lady of the Snows, etc.

19. Enumerate five of the nine great privileges of the Blessed Virgin. Which is the greatest?

20. Refute the objection that Mary was not a virgin because Scripture refers to Christ's "brothers" and "sisters."

21. What was the privilege of absolute sinlessness?

22. What does the Assumption mean? What privilege did it include?

23. Explain what it means when we say that Mary was "full of grace"?

24. What does the privilege of Mediatrix mean? What practical conclusion and resolution should it lead us to form?

25. Why is Mary justly called our Spiritual Mother?

26. What are five of the ten principal virtues of Mary listed by St. Alphonsus? Do you like the sequence in which he places the virtues? Would you list them differently? Why? Describe incidents or facts which prove that Mary possessed and practiced each of these virtues.

27. Prove that Mary has been a tremendous cultural influence in the world.

28. Show her influence in the highest art and science—that of Christian living.

29. Show her influence in: literature (quote to prove your point), music, painting, architecture.

30. Name the four great Marian antiphons.

31. Recite the Regina Coeli, the Magnificat.

32. Which do you consider the most beautiful hymn to Mary?

33. Name as many great Madonnas or painters of Madonnas as you can.
34. Name as many Marian cathedrals as you can. Describe one of them. Which do you like best? Why?
35. How many famous shrines of Mary do you know? Tell the story connected with any of them.
36. Tell of Mary's help in certain great moments in history.
37. Name some saints who loved Mary in a very special manner. Quote incidents or facts to prove your point.
38. Name as many devotions in honor of Mary as you can recall.
39. Why did October become the month of the Rosary?
40. Why is Saturday "Mary's Day"?
41. Tell how to say the rosary so as to gain the indulgences.
42. Name the fifteen mysteries in proper order.
43. Name as many prayers to Mary as you know by heart. How many others can you name? Recite the Angelus, the Memorare.
44. How many indulgenced ejaculations to Mary do you know perfectly?
45. Mention some practices which honor the Blessed Virgin.
46. Mention some orders of men and women founded or named for Mary.
47. What is the value of confraternities or sodalities in honor of our Lady?
48. What has this unit taught you about the Mother of God?
49. In what way does God's goodness to Mary prove His great love of us?
50. What different resolutions might a person make as a result of any of the things learned in this unit?
51. Frame or find five additional good questions on this unit.

GAL. 5, 21

GO FORTH O CHRISTIAN SOUL

PS. 23, 3-4

UNIT TWO

A Senior Looks into the Future

The Four Last Things; Extreme Unction

PART ONE: PLANNING THE UNIT

INTRODUCTION

Encouraged and strengthened by the knowledge that
Mary is our Mother and also the Mediatrix of all graces,
we now turn to some doctrines which to a true Christian
are indeed serious and sombre, but never depressing. They
will act as a necessary preparation for our study of The
Great Choice in Unit Three.

These truths deal with the four last things: death, judgment, heaven, hell, and with other facts which God has
made known to men in order to guide them so to live as

to pass from the mortal life of this world to the happy life of immortality in the next. But let us first see what you already know about these topics.

DIAGNOSTIC EXPLORATION OF EXISTING KNOWLEDGE OF THE FOUR LAST THINGS

1. What happens to the body at death? What to the soul?
2. How many judgments are there?
3. Who will judge us?
4. What are the possible verdicts?
5. Prove that there is a hell.
6. Prove that there is a purgatory.
7. What would you do if a person were seriously injured?
8. Which are the last sacraments? Who can receive them?
9. When should they be received?
10. What are some of the joys of heaven?
11. In what do the torments of hell consist?

SOME OF THE OBJECTIVES OF THIS UNIT

1. To come to a deep realization of the transitory nature of all things here below and to foster a spirit of detachment from earthly goods and pleasures.
2. To inspire a fear of eternal damnation and a desire for everlasting happiness.
3. To learn how to assist the dying, Catholics as well as non-Catholics.
4. To map a plan of life.

CENTRAL THEME OF THE UNIT

Everything depends on the moment of death.

After determining whether or not the assignment of any activities or readings such as those listed below will be helpful in mastering the matter in this unit, we can turn to Part Two, on page 111 and begin our study of the unit.

SUGGESTED ASSIGNMENTS AND ACTIVITIES

1. Read a book or pamphlet dealing with death, heaven, eternal punishment or some other topic treated in this unit. Write a report on it or a "blurb" to be used to attract readers to the book.
2. Find an article on the Poor Souls in any Catholic magazine. Clip it for bulletin board display. Read it and give a report on it to the class.

3. Read Gray's *Elegy in a Country Churchyard* and memorize certain stanzas as directed by the teacher; or, as a group project, assign parts to each of four or five students to be recited to the class and interpreted.

4. Read *The Dream of Gerontius* and prepare reports in which Newman's treatment of the following points is discussed:

    a. The dying Christian, his hopes and his fears.
    b. Consolation afforded by the Church in her last rites and prayers for the dying.
    c. First meeting with the Judge after death.
    d. The judgment of the soul.
    e. The soul's entrance into purgatory.

5. Paraphrase or write an essay on the *Dies Irae* or quote passages that refer to the following:

    a. The end of the world.
    b. Final Judgment.
    c. Christ, the just Judge.
    d. Christ, the merciful Judge.

6. Study the Preface of the Mass for the Dead and compare it with the Preface of the Cross. What is the keynote of each? What consolation does the former afford?

7. Make a study of the Epistle and the Gospel of the Mass for the day of burial. Are the same Epistle and Gospel used in the other Masses for the Dead?

8. Prepare a dialogue between yourself and a sick person who does not wish to see a priest; or between yourself and a relative of this sick person. The relative holds that information regarding the real condition of the sick person may be too disturbing if revealed to him.

9. Prepare an outline for a mental prayer on the following subjects:

    a. "Death Comes as a Thief in the Night."
    b. Christ the Conqueror of Death the Conqueror.
    c. How a Christian Dies.
    d. The Torments of Hell.
    e. November and the Poor Souls.
    f. The Joys of Heaven.

10. Report on prayers, ejaculations, and practices indulgenced for the benefit of the Poor Souls. (Cf. *Raccolta*, Official Edition, p. 444 ff.

11. Find common objections to the doctrines of hell and of purgatory and locate answers to each.

*12. Prepare a radio script entitled "Interviews with the Past," in which the following or other persons express their views on death and dying:

St. Paul	Henry VIII
St. Agnes	Father Campion
St. Lawrence	Cromwell
Julian the Apostate	St. Blanche, Mother of St. Louis
Cardinal Wolsey	Oliver Wendell Holmes
St. Thomas More	The Little Flower

13. Draw up a Plan of Life. Put it into permanent form for use perhaps as a marker in your prayer book. Resolve to reread it on the tenth anniversary of your graduation from high school. Have a class discussion on a good plan of life. Determine what habits and virtues are necessary if an individual is to lead a happy, successful life of service to God and to man.

*14. In class, or even as a game at a party, ask everyone to check his person to see if he is carrying any object that could identify him as a Catholic. Ask the members of your family and your friends to make a similar check.

15. Dramatize the entire procedure of sending for and receiving a priest, and for the administration of the last sacraments to a person who has suddenly been taken ill in your home.

16. Make arrangements for a Question Box in which to deposit the problems and questions of the class. Take fifteen minutes on Friday to discuss or answer them.

*17. Illustrate any part of this unit in a poster, pictogram or picture.

*18. Read a portion of Dante's *Il Purgatorio* and report on it.

*19. Locate Scripture texts which prove that there is a hell.

*20. Gather arguments which will tend to help a non-Catholic see that the eternal punishment of hell is necessary and just.

*21. Gather arguments to help a non-Catholic friend understand the doctrine of purgatory and agree to it.

*22. Answer the objection that the doctrine of purgatory is an invention of priests foisted on the people for the sake of money.

23. Locate or give a description of some famous picture connected with death, the Last Sacraments, heaven, hell, purgatory, the Last Judgment etc., e. g. Raphael's Last Judgment in the Sistine Chapel; Fra Angelico's The Elect, etc.

*24. If you have an original idea for an assignment on which you would like to work, submit it to your teacher for approval.

RELATED READINGS IN BOOKS AND PAMPHLETS

Books: Arendzen, *The Church Triumphant,* Macmillan.

Arendzen, *Eternal Punishment,* Macmillan.

Arendzen, *Extreme Unction* (T.F.S.), Macmillan.

Conway, *The Question Box,* Paulist.

DeZuluetta, *Letters on Christian Doctrine,* Vol. 3, Benziger.

Hammer, *God, Christ and the Church,* Benziger.

Hill, *The Catholic's Ready Answer,* Benziger.

Kelley, *When the Veil is Rent,* Kenedy.

Mac Eachen, *Dogmatic Series, Vol.* 5, Catholic Book Co., Wheeling, W. Va.

McLaughlin, *Purgatory, or the Church Suffering,* Macmillan.

McNeil and Aaron, *The Means of Grace,* St. Anthony Guild.

Scott, *Answer Wisely,* Loyola.

Scott, *Things Catholics are Asked,* Kenedy.

Sheed, *A Map of Life,* Sheed & Ward.

Spirago and Clark, *The Catechism Explained,* Benziger.

Sullivan, *The Fundamentals of Catholic Belief,* Kenedy.

Vonier, *Death and Judgment* (T.F.S.), Macmillan.

Pamphlets:

Baker, *Heaven,* Paulist.

Daly, *The Souls in Purgatory,* Queen's Work.

Dooley, *God's Guests of Tomorrow,* Mission.

Elliott, *Eternal Punishment,* Paulist.

Jaggar, *Extreme Unction,* Paulist.

Kerby, *The Judgment of God; The Sense of Duty,* O.S.V.

Lonergan, *The "Myth" of Hell,* America.

Lord, *Everybody's Talking About Heaven,* Queen's Work.

Lord, *Death Isn't Terrible,* Queen's Work.

Lord, *Forever and Forever,* Queen's Work.

McSorley, *Do the Dead Live?* Paulist.

Morris, *The Heroic Acts of Charity,* I.C.T.S.

Noll, *After Death—What?* O.S.V.

O'Brien, *Why Do We Pray for the Dead?* O.S.V.

Rumble and Carty, *Hell,* Radio Replies Press.

Welfle, *Our Precious Bodies,* Queen's Work.

PARALLEL READINGS IN OTHER HIGH SCHOOL
RELIGION TEXTS

	Cam-pion	Cassilly	Falque	Gaume	Graham	Laux	Manual of Chr. Doctr
7, 11, and 12th Articles of Creed	I, 253	431; 493 499		II, 21-23 26-27			107,139,141
Death	I, 253	493	I, 24; 77			I, 133 IV, 21	142
St. Joseph	II, 299	407, 420					74, 82
Extreme Unction	I, 248	284	II, 301	II, 43	217	II, 144	474
Rites of Church	I, 257			IV, 52		III, 86	561
Hell	I, 283	502	II, 373	II, 19	337	I, 166	148
Purgatory	I, 258; 286	506	II, 372	II, 20	335	I, 162	145
Heaven	I, 281	499	II, 371	IV, 54	338	I, 159	146
Judgment	I, 279	431	II, 367	II, 21	328	I, 170	143

Given in volumes and pages, except Gaume which shows volume and chapter.

PART TWO

From thence He shall come to judge the living and the dead.
. . . I believe . . . in the resurrection of the body, and life everlasting.
Amen.

SECTION ONE: DEATH—GOING HOME TO GOD

A. DEATH AND MY SOUL
   1. IMPORTANCE OF THE LAST MOMENT

B DEATH—GOING HOME TO GOD, OR . . . ?
   1. ITS NATURE
   2. DEATH AND THE BODY
   3. DEATH AND THE SOUL
   4. DEATH—A CONSEQUENCE OF ORIGINAL SIN
   5. THE CERTAINTY AND UNCERTAINTY OF DEATH
   6. PREPARATION FOR A HAPPY DEATH
      a. Remote
        1) A VIRTUOUS LIFE
        2) PRAYER TO THE BLESSED VIRGIN
        3) DEVOTION TO ST. JOSEPH
        4) THE LIFE OF ST. JOSEPH
      b. Immediate
        1) A GOOD CONFESSION
        2) RECEPTION OF VIATICUM
        3) EXTREME UNCTION

A. DEATH AND MY SOUL

1. IMPORTANCE OF THE LAST MOMENT

As a punishment for original sin, God in His wisdom has decreed that all human beings must pass through the gate of death—"It is appointed unto men to die." Heb. 9, 27. He has also seen fit to arrange that each person's eternity shall depend on the state of his soul at that tremendous moment.

Since this is so, Christian wisdom suggests that we consider what death is and what will be at stake for us when we reach its portals.

B. DEATH—GOING HOME TO GOD, OR . . .?

1. ITS NATURE

Man is a creature in whom a material, mortal, corruptible body has been given life and made human and rational by being united by God in the unity of a human nature, to a spiritual, and therefore, an incorruptible and naturally immortal soul. Death is the dissolution of this union. It is the separation of body and soul.

2. DEATH AND THE BODY

Death therefore means that the material, corruptible element in man, the body, loses the principle which gives it life and consequently breaks down into the elements that compose it. In other words it begins naturally to decompose. It returns to the dust from which it was made, according to the word of God, "Dust thou art, and into dust thou shalt return." Gen. 3, 19.

Faggi   *Courtesy of the Art Institute of Chicago, S. P. Avery Fund Collection*

PIETÁ

Christ willingly submitted His body to the dominion of death, that He might redeem us from the death of the soul.

Our Lady, also, consented to drink of the bitterest pains to which her children are subjected, suffering not only at the death of her divine Son, but passing through the door of death herself. The knowledge that Christ and His Mother have known and conquered death gives us the hope and courage needed to face it calmly and confidently.

3. DEATH AND THE SOUL

The soul is not a material thing composed of material elements or parts. The soul is an immaterial being—simple, uncomposed, spiritual, and therefore naturally indestructible. The human soul is *by nature immortal,* that is, immortality is one of the natural qualities which God has bestowed on it. It possesses a natural spiritual life which can never end except by a direct act of annihilation on the part of God.

When, therefore, at the moment of death, body and soul separate and the body begins to decompose, the soul continues to live, apart from the body. Death, therefore, puts an end only to the physical life of the body, not to the natural, spiritual life of the soul.

To make clear a point that sometimes causes confusion it may be well here to repeat that, by a supernatural gift of God, the human soul may attain to a supernatural, spiritual life in addition to its natural, spiritual life. This supernatural life of the soul, acquired when God bestows sanctifying grace, is lost only by committing mortal sin. It is to the loss of this special supernatural life of the soul, then, to which we refer when we speak of the death of the soul. A soul in mortal sin still possesses its natural, spiritual, immortal life but not its supernatural, spiritual life.

4. DEATH—A CONSEQUENCE OF ORIGINAL SIN

Death is a consequence of original sin. God had warned Adam and Eve, "Of the tree of knowledge of good and evil, thou shalt not eat. For in what day soever thou shalt eat of it, thou shalt die the death." Gen. 2, 17.

- p.122

→

G. A. Douglas from Gendreau, N. Y.

THE HOUR GLASS

Life's sands run swiftly. They never stop. How much remains in the upper glass for us we seldom know. But this we do know: the state of our soul when our glass runs out, seals for all eternity the destiny of our immortal soul. That is why good Christians frequently repeat: "From a sudden and unprovided death, deliver us, O Lord."

This warning referred both to the loss of the supernatural life of the soul and of the natural, physical life of the body; it included not only Adam and Eve but all their offspring, that is, the entire human race. St. Paul assures us of this fact when he says that "through one man sin entered into the world and through sin death, and thus death passed into all men because all have sinned." Rom. 5, 12. That this entailed no injustice on God's part we learned in our freshman year—the children of a father who squanders his fortune must share in his consequent poverty and suffering.

5. THE CERTAINTY AND UNCERTAINTY OF DEATH

Death is one of the most certain things in human life. All men die; no one is exempt, be he ever so rich and powerful. Even our Saviour and His Blessed Mother submitted to death, although both were free from sin, original and actual, and, consequently, free from the penalty for sin which all men must pay.

Christ died to fulfill the prophecies, to complete our Redemption and to give us confidence, because He overcame death by rising again. Our Blessed Lady passed through the gates of death because she followed the example of her Divine Son, the perfect exemplar of the Christian life.

Although death is one of the most certain events of life as to its occurrence, it is one of the most uncertain as to its time and circumstances. Death comes as a thief in the night. We can all cite incidents to substantiate this sobering fact. The daily newspapers prove it over and over each succeeding day.

6. PREPARATION FOR A HAPPY DEATH

The practical conclusion to draw from this knowledge is to resolve to live so as always to be ready. Our preparation for a happy death must be both remote and immediate.

a. Remote Preparation

1) Virtuous Life

The best remote preparation for insuring that the angel of death will not surprise us and find us unprepared is to live constantly in the state of grace. An habitually *virtuous life* is the surest safeguard.

2) Prayer to the Blessed Virgin

Prayer is a part of this remote preparation; prayer in general, but particularly prayer for the grace of perseverance and for protection against a sudden and unprovided death. The *Hail Mary* and the *Memorare* are especially effective. In the former we ask the Blessed Virgin to pray for us "now and at the hour of our death." If we say this prayer in such wise that Mary *does* pray for us at the moment of our death our salvation is certain, for everything Mary asks of God is granted. Let us, therefore, always say it with attention and devotion.

3) Devotion to St. Joseph

Devotion to St. Joseph, the spouse of the Blessed Virgin, is also a part of this remote preparation, for St. Joseph is the patron of a happy death, having himself departed from this life in the arms of Jesus and Mary. It might be well for us then to take a brief look at the life of this great saint that we may revere him as he deserves and have confidence in his protection.

4) The Life of St. Joseph

The foster-father of Jesus was probably born in Bethlehem, the city of David to whose descendants he belonged. Why or when he left the city of his forefathers to become a humble carpenter in Nazareth is not known. Doubtless he sought this humble city in Galilee, guided by divine Providence, that the Scriptures might be fulfilled, for God had destined him to be the spouse of the Mother of God, and Mary dwelt in Nazareth.

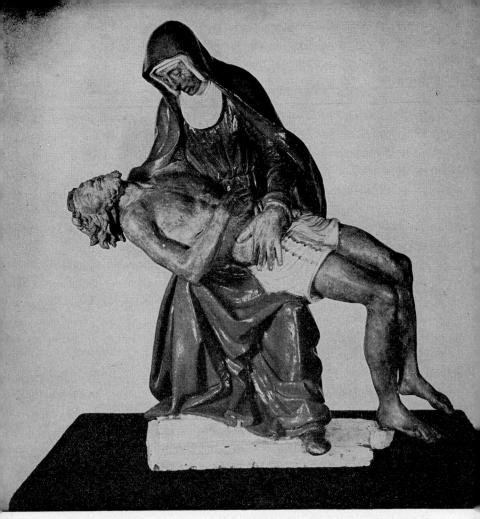

PIETÁ

In the preceding unit as we studied the life of Mary, we learned, in at least a small measure, to know and love St. Joseph, whose life was intertwined with hers. We read the beautiful story of the espousal and marriage of St. Joseph to her who was to become the Mother of God, and we loved St. Joseph for his tender care of Mary and Jesus. We sorrowed with him when he delicately refrained from putting away his stainless spouse but rejoiced with him when the archangel revealed to him the mystery of the Incarnation.

OBEDIENT, SELF-EFFACING

At the birth of Jesus we sympathized with St. Joseph, because the only shelter he could obtain for Mary was a stable. We marveled at the silent obedience of St. Joseph when in compliance with the Jewish custom, Mary's Son was circumcised, and we were happy when the name of Jesus, meaning Saviour, was bestowed upon Him as the angel said it should be.

Perhaps the prophecy of Simeon caused us anguish for Mary and her Son, but did we think how sorely Joseph was tried? The *Nunc dimittis* of Simeon could not crowd out the grief of St. Joseph for the two dearest persons in the world. The responsibility of the Flight into Egypt fell upon the shoulders of St. Joseph, but happiness came to him when he knew that Jesus and Mary were beyond the reach of Herod's soldiers. After dwelling for some time in Egypt, an angel bade St. Joseph return to Nazareth with Jesus and was not our heart glad when they again settled in the land of their fathers.

Once more St. Joseph suffered. Jesus, at the age of twelve, accompanied Mary and Joseph to Jerusalem to celebrate the feast of the Pasch. After the celebration, Joseph and Mary started for home but Jesus was not with them. After three days' search they found Him in the Temple, discoursing with the Doctors of the Law. Did not our heart expand with joy as we thought how happy St Joseph was? Or did we never think about him before? He was so self-effacing!

THE DEATH OF ST. JOSEPH

As we know, Jesus returned with His parents to Nazareth where St. Joseph led a simple but uneventful life, supporting himself and his family by his work and com-

plying with the religious practices of the Jews. The time of his death is unknown. He probably died before Jesus was thirty years of age, for there is no mention of St. Joseph being present at the marriage feast of Cana. Certainly he died before Jesus was condemned to death, for if he were alive at the time of the Crucifixion, Jesus would have commended His Mother to St. Joseph and not to St. John. St. Joseph probably died and was buried at Nazareth.

Although we have no information about the time and circumstances of St. Joseph's holy death, tradition tells us that Jesus and Mary were with him in his last hour. What more do we need to know! With Jesus standing at his bedside comforting him, encouraging him, cheering him with His grace; with Mary wiping the sweat from his moist brow, and holding his hand and pressing a sacred kiss of farewell upon his cheek, how could it have been other than a happy death. Do you begin to understand now why St. Joseph is the Patron of the Dying—the Patron of a Happy Death? Be his client then, and imitate him.

A JUST MAN

Holy Scripture calls St. Joseph a "just man." That single phrase says everything. He was obedient, humble, and chaste. He had faith in God and confidence in God's promises. He loved God and man. We would do well to resolve to imitate the resplendent virtues which shone forth in every act of this great man. The Church honors St. Joseph because he was chosen by God to be the foster father of Jesus and the spouse of the Virgin Mother. We celebrate the feast of St. Joseph on March 19th, and the

←

Courtesy of The Far East

ST. JOSEPH AND THE CHILD JESUS

This modern woodcarving of St. Joseph, in the church of St. Bartholemew, Long Beach, California, presents this loveable saint in a manner that helps one realize his quiet but heroic sanctity and devotion.

feast of the Patronage of St. Joseph on the Wednesday of the second week after the octave of Easter.

The Church also devotes the whole month of March to the honor of St. Joseph and requires special prayers to be recited. Let us invoke him as the Model of Workmen, the Head of the Holy Family, the Patron of a Happy Death, and Patron of the Universal Church.

We have digressed somewhat to speak of the life of St. Joseph and our devotion to him, all of which pertains to the remote preparation for death. Let us now consider the immediate preparation, which consists in the reception of the last sacraments: Penance, Holy Viaticum, Extreme Unction.

b. Immediate Preparation for Death

1) A Good Confession

Undoubtedly, the most important part of the immediate preparation for death is the confession of the dying penitent, and the reception of sacramental absolution. Penance is the ordinary means of reconciliation with God, so, if a person is conscious, he must make his confession to a priest in order to fit his soul for its departure from this life. When the person is incapable of sustained mental effort he may accuse himself of his sins to the best of his ability, sometimes merely answering the questions asked by the priest. If only the most general acknowledgment of the penitent's sinfulness is all that can be obtained by the priest, it may substitute for a detailed confession.

2) Reception of Holy Viaticum

After confession, the sacrament of Holy Eucharist is to be received by the dying person. The reception of Holy Communion, when in danger of death, is called Viaticum because it is the spiritual food by which we are supported on our last pilgrimage.

Because of the great value of the Holy Eucharist to a person who is dying the Church *obliges us* to receive Holy Communion when we are in danger of death. In her eagerness to console and to strengthen the soul the Church dispenses with her regular disciplinary measures and makes the reception of Holy Communion as easy as possible. The communicant is exempted from the traditional fast and may enjoy this privilege repeatedly during his illness.

Even if a person has already received Communion that same day, in danger of death he is allowed to, indeed he is urged to receive it again as Holy Viaticum.

3) Extreme Unction

In the immediate preparation for death, confession and the reception of Holy Communion are followed by the sacrament of Extreme Unction. It happens very often that the priest administers Extreme Unction after he has heard the confession of the penitent and before giving Holy Communion. The sacraments are given as time and circumstances allow, and every priest is most careful to see that the dying person is well fortified by all the helps the Church provides. As our most merciful Redeemer prepared the greatest aids, whereby, during life, Christians may preserve themselves from every grievous, spiritual evil, so did He guard the close of life with a most firm defense, the sacrament of Extreme Unction, which we shall now study in detail.

It would be well, by way of preface, to review the essentials of a sacrament and also the sacraments studied in previous years: Baptism, Confirmation, Holy Eucharist, and Penance. They all have some connection with the subject under discussion. Can you point out the connection?

REVIEW OF SECTION ONE

SECTION TWO: EXTREME UNCTION, THE SPECIAL SACRAMENT OF THE DYING

A. NATURE OF THE SACRAMENT
  1. DEFINITION
    a. The Outward Sign: Matter and Form
    b. Divine Institution
    c. Inward Grace: The Effects of Extreme Unction

B. ADMINISTRATION AND RECEPTION OF THE SACRAMENT
  1. Who Can Administer Extreme Unction?
  2. Who is Allowed To Receive Extreme Unction?

C. THE APOSTOLIC BLESSING AND OTHER INDULGENCES

A. NATURE OF THE SACRAMENT

1. DEFINITION

Extreme Unction is a sacrament which, through the anointing with blessed oil by the priest, and through his prayer, gives health and strength to the soul and sometimes to the body when we are in danger of death from sickness, accident, or old age. The word "unction" means anointing, and it is called "extreme" unction because it is usually the last anointing a Catholic receives.

a. The Outward Sign: Matter and Form

Extreme Unction, being a true sacrament, has an outward sign, was instituted by Christ, and gives grace.

The sensible or outward sign of each sacrament is made up of the "matter" of the sacrament and the "form" of the sacrament. See if you can recall the matter and form of each of the sacraments we have studied thus far.

$\longrightarrow$

Michelangelo　　　　　　　　　　　　*Alinari, Courtesy of The Far East*

VIRGIN MOST SORROWFUL

This head of the Blessed Virgin portrays a detail of the exquisite Pieta of Michelangelo in St. Peter's, Rome. The quiet fortitude of our Lady, etched so delicately into the marble, half conceals the craftsmanship of the master sculptor.

1) Matter

In Extreme Unction the "matter" of the sacrament is olive oil, or more accurately, the anointing with the *Oleum Infirmorum,* that is, the Oil of the Sick. This oil is blessed by the bishop at the ceremonies on Holy Thursday. The appropriateness and significance of oil as the matter of this sacrament is, without doubt, known to all seniors.

2) Form

The "form" of the sacrament of Extreme Unction is the recitation of the beautiful prayers by the priest as he anoints each of the senses.

The priest dips his thumb into the oil and makes the sign of the Cross on the eyes and at the same time he prays: "Through this holy unction and through His most tender mercy, may the Lord pardon thee whatever sins thou hast committed by seeing." Then the priest anoints the ears, nostrils, mouth, hands, and sometimes the feet, repeating this prayer each time, and substituting the words hearing, smelling, taste and speech, touch and walking, for the word "seeing." Should the person anointed be a priest, the holy oil is placed on the back of his hands because the palms have already been anointed in ordination.

In cases of extreme necessity only the forehead is anointed and the priest says, "Through this holy unction, may the Lord forgive thee whatever sin thou hast committed. Amen."

How beautiful and all-embracing is this prayer! Surely every Catholic should pray that he may have the consolations of religion in his last moments. The sign of the Cross, which the priest makes on each of the five senses, is like a seal which marks them for God. No longer need a Christian who bears the sign of his redemption on all his members fear to appear before his Judge.

b. Divine Institution

That Extreme Unction was instituted by Christ, is not as clearly evident from the Gospels as is the institution of some of the other sacraments, but it is insinuated in Mark 6, 13 when the Apostles anointed with oil many that were sick, and healed them. There is, however, a classic passage in the Epistle of St. James, "Is anyone sick among you? Let him bring in the presbyters of the Church and let them pray over him, anointing him with oil in the name of the Lord. And the prayers of faith will save the sick man, and the Lord will raise him up; and if he be in sins, they shall be forgiven him." Jas. 5, 14-15.

Even if the institution of this sacrament by Christ were not so clearly stated in Holy Scripture, the official teaching of the Church would remove all doubt in the matter, for the Council of Trent condemns those who say that Extreme Unction is not truly a sacrament instituted by Christ.

c. The Inward Grace

The third essential of a sacrament is the conferring of inward grace. Let us examine this and the other effects of Extreme Unction.

1) Increases Sanctifying Grace

Since Extreme Unction is a sacrament of the living, it *increases sanctifying grace* in the soul of the recipient, cleansing and strengthening it as it is about to leave the body.

2) Remits Sin and Punishment

From our catechism we have learned that there are only two sacraments of the dead, Baptism and Penance. The former remits original sin; the latter, actual sin. If, however, a sick person is unconscious or unable to confess his sins, and has imperfect contrition for them, the

THE GREAT PYRAMID AT GIZEH

The pyramids are monuments to an error in Egyptian theology—the false theory of the transmigration of souls. The Egyptians believed that the soul at death successively inhabited other bodies, even of animals, and would one day return to a human body created for it. Accordingly they carefully embalmed the bodies of their kings or pharaohs and built the pyramids as huge tombs to secrete and protect their remains. The teachings of our holy faith on the Last Things and the immortality of the soul keep us from such absurd errors.

The size of each stone and of the entire pyramid may be appreciated by a comparison with the automobiles in the foreground.

sacrament of Extreme Unction *can remit mortal sins* and restore the soul to the state of sanctifying grace.

The sacrament when received with attrition also *remits venial sins.* It effaces, moreover, sins which the sick person does not remember or know, and it remits, more or less, the *temporal punishment due to sin.* If all mortal sins have been forgiven in the sacrament of Penance, Extreme Unction can remove the *remains of sins* in greater or lesser measure depending on the disposition of the sick person. By the remains of sin we mean a spiritual weakness resulting from sin, and interfering with the full and vigorous actions of the life of grace.

3) Strengthens Soul

The strengthening of the soul for its final combat with Satan is another effect of Extreme Unction, and a very important one.

Though the devil seeks opportunities all during our life to ensnare us in sin, he is especially active and uses all his powers to ruin the soul when he perceives that the end of our life is near.

St. Thomas says that the spiritual healing of the soul granted to man in his last moments should be perfect, for none comes after it; and it should be soothing, so that hope, which is especially needed by the dying, may be encouraged in them.

4) Restores Health

Extreme Unction also restores the sick person to *health if God sees fit*. The fact that a person recovers after being anointed is, however, no guarantee that his salvation is assured; it merely means that new opportunities are being offered. Even when this sacrament does not restore health to the body it does take away the sting of death and its victory.

Poorly instructed Catholics and others who have not had much experience with sick people are at times afraid to receive Extreme Unction or to have it conferred on their sick relatives or friends. Priests and good Catholic doctors and nurses who have seen the wonderful effects which the sacrament frequently has, find it hard to understand such ignorance. Again and again they have witnessed sick people who are fretful, nervous, discouraged, and apathetic, change suddenly after having received the last sacraments and become calm, wonderfully happy, resigned to God's will whatever it may be, and not infrequently they have seen such persons recover, to enjoy many added years of life and happiness and service to God and man.

As a preparation for meeting and influencing such weaklings in the Faith you might try writing a paper on the effects of Extreme Unction listed here.

Put them into language that will reach the intellects and emotions of such people and thereby change their minds.

B. ADMINISTRATION AND RECEPTION OF THE SACRAMENT

1. WHO CAN ADMINISTER EXTREME UNCTION

Extreme Unction may be administered only by one who has been duly ordained to the priesthood. The reference to Extreme Unction in the Epistle of St. James says that if anyone is sick the priests of the Church should be called in to anoint him.

The right and duty of anointing a sick person devolves on the pastor of the parish in which the person lies sick. In case of necessity, however, any priest may administer the sacrament.

2. WHO IS ALLOWED TO RECEIVE EXTREME UNCTION?

Extreme Unction may be received by or administered to such baptized Catholics as have reached the use of reason and are in danger of death from sickness, accident, old age, or some other *internal cause,* that is, a cause internal to the organism.

A child or mentally defective person who has not yet reached the use of reason cannot be anointed; neither can a soldier about to enter battle or a criminal before he is executed. The same is true of a person who must undergo an operation, unless his condition is already serious, as

at the moment
once in the san
danger of deatl
person must de
contrition or lov
the name of "Je
be resigned to tl
ishment for sin.
that is, at the n
is not obtained v
moment of life.
it not prove the
children?

Besides the A]
be gained. If a dy
a crucifix, a mec
tolic Indulgences
gence if he is res
Penance and Ho
says an act of co
name of Jesus.

REVIEW OF SEC

Fra Angelico

DEATH AND A

The Blessed Virgin Mary
been subject to original si
punishment. Wishing, like
spare herself. Let her exan
God's children for her sak

---

for example, a person dangerously ill due to a burst appendix.

Note that the sacrament can be administered only to those who are in real *danger* of death. But observe also that it does not say that it can be received only by those who are actually dying. Here, as in other matters concerning a person's salvation, it is "better to be safe than to be sorry." When in doubt as to whether a person should be anointed or not, call a priest or a Catholic doctor and let him decide. Avoid needless self-recrimination.

If the person to be anointed is conscious he must be in the state of grace to receive the sacrament. Therefore, confession is advised, and, if the person is guilty of unforgiven mortal sin, confession is required. Consciousness is not an absolute requisite for the valid reception of the sacrament but it is greatly to be desired. If the danger of death is the result of sickness or old age one should not wait until the sick person has lost consciousness, but should call the priest as soon as he is aware of the seriousness of the patient's condition, that the priest may administer the sacrament while the sick person is able to receive it with attention and devotion.

Extreme Unction may not be repeated during the same danger. If the sick person recovers and falls ill again, later, it may again be administered. In certain cases of protracted illness or in certain diseases such as asthma where the danger of death recurs intermittently, the sacrament may be administered again.

C. THE APOSTOLIC BLESSING AND OTHER INDULGENCES

The Last Blessing is a special Apostolic Blessing of the dying. The power to bestow the Apostolic Blessing is vested in the pope, but since he cannot be present at the deathbed of every Catholic, he empowers his priests to give a blessing which carries with it a plenary indulgence

SECTION THREE: HELPING SOULS TO HEAVEN

A. THE SICK CALL
1. CALLING THE PRIEST
   a. In Cases of Sickness
   b. In Case of Accident
2. PREPARING THE SICK ROOM
3. RECEIVING AND ASSISTING THE PRIEST

B. ASSISTING THE DYING
1. ASSISTING DYING CATHOLICS
2. ASSISTING DYING NON-CATHOLICS

C. PERFORMING THE WORKS OF MERCY
1. THE CORPORAL WORKS OF MERCY
2. THE SPIRITUAL WORKS OF MERCY

This section has been given the very sedate subtitle "Helping Souls to Heaven," but we might also have given it the more exciting heading: Snatching Souls from the Devil! Saving souls for Christ is often just that; and it is a rare game, calling for great perseverance and at times for consummate cleverness. It can be a most enjoyable occupation and certainly it brings great satisfaction.

A. THE SICK CALL

1. CALLING THE PRIEST

How may we help the dying to attain heaven? If a person is near death from accident or illness, the proper one to call to administer the last rites of the Church, as we have already learned, is the *pastor of the parish* or one of his assistants. When the case is urgent any priest may be called.

a. In Cases of Sickness

The pastor should always be kept informed as to any cases of serious illness in his parish. He should also be notified about less grave illness if the general condition of the person is such as to anticipate sudden complications, as for example in those feeble with age, or having a serious heart condition or the like. (This rule also applies to unbaptized infants about whose health we are not certain.)

A good Catholic, when he suspects that he is in danger of death will request that a priest be called. If, as often happens, a person is more seriously ill than he realizes, he should be made aware of his condition. For instance he could be told: "John, you're a sick man. You are more sick than you realize. I'm going to ask (or I have asked) Father to drop in and give you a blessing."

Where the sick person is suffering from a lingering illness the priest should be called while the person is in complete possession of his faculties. This will insure that the sick person derives the fullest value from the last sacraments. In such cases the one who is sick has a right to know his own condition far enough in advance so that he may with a clear mind set his house in order and prepare for life's most important moment. He can be gently informed of the truth by saying, "John, it looks as if God will be coming for you one of these days. Is there anything you would like to set in order? I've asked the priest to call on you. I think you are entitled to receive Extreme Unction."

Notifying the priest early is a means of avoiding needless emergency calls in the middle of the night. It also relieves one of the responsibilities of answering for a person dying without the sacraments as a result of a sudden fatal turn for the worse.

b. In Case of Accident

When a Catholic or one who wishes to be a Catholic is seriously injured in an accident the first thing one should do is to call the priest, then the doctor or police. If the religion of a seriously injured person cannot be ascertained but it is possible he is a Catholic the priest may also be summoned.

1) Supplying the Priest with Needed Information

On all sick calls, but especially in accidents, one should be prepared to give the priest the information he needs: the name of the person, if possible, and the address of the house or place of the accident, whether the person is or was a Catholic, and how practical a Catholic, whether he asked for or refused the sacraments, whether or not he is conscious, in immediate danger, able to receive Communion and so forth.

It is also helpful for the priest to know other facts which may enable him to handle the case more successfully. There may be, for instance, the question of a mixed marriage or of an invalid "marriage," relatives or others who are anti-Catholic, or who do not wish the priest to "alarm the patient," and so forth. A person with Christian prudence and cleverness can be of great assistance to the priest on such occasions.

While waiting for the priest and attending the sick person's physical welfare we should not forget his spiritual needs. If the person is in grave danger we should endeavor to arouse him to make an act of perfect contrition.

2) Carrying Evidences of Catholicity

Accidents occur so frequently that we know not the day nor the hour that we ourselves may be involved in one. All Catholics therefore ought to carry with them something that identifies them as Catholics. A medal or rosary or pin will speak for us even if we are unable. This thought of the frequency of sudden death should also induce us to be always ready to meet God. If we live so

$\longrightarrow$

Fra Angelico   *National Gallery of Art, Kress Collection*

THE ENTOMBMENT OF CHRIST

The dead body of Jesus Christ knew the dark and quiet of the tomb. Therefore we, his followers, will never fear its solitude. Rather we will say
"In peace in the selfsame I will sleep, and I will rest:
For thou, O Lord, singularly hast settled me in hope."
Psalm 4, 9

that we are always prepared to leave this world, a sudden death is no misfortune. "As we live, so shall we die."

3) Anointing After Apparent Death

It often happens that persons who die suddenly, die alone, and are found later by some relative or friend. On all such occasions be sure to call a priest, because the sacrament of Extreme Unction may be given, at least conditionally, even two or more hours after death. *(3)*

Pray that your death will not be unprovided. Continue through life the practices of your youth—of frequent confession and Holy Communion. Because of our modern speed, industrial conditions, and the hazards in the home, sudden deaths by accident are more frequent than in former times. By performing the works of mercy you may gain for yourself the grace of being spared a sudden, unprepared death.

— p.152

2. PREPARING THE SICK ROOM

When a priest is called to administer the last rites of the Church, the face, hands, and feet of the sick person should be bathed, if time permits, and everything about the house, the room, and the sick person should be neat and clean.

It is customary to have in readiness a small table covered with a white linen cloth, on which there has been placed a glass of water and a spoon, a crucifix, and at least one blessed candle. These are the minimum essentials. The ritual of the Church asks that the following articles also be placed on the table: a bottle containing holy water, six small balls of cotton, and a plate containing several small pieces of bread for cleansing the oil from the fingers of the priest. The cotton and bread are used for Extreme Unction and should be placed on the table only if that sacrament is to be given. Most priests carry with them cotton and holy water, in case there is none in the home to which they have been called.

3. RECEIVING AND ASSISTING THE PRIEST

When the priest arrives he should be met at the door by a person carrying a lighted candle. This person should precede the priest and lead him to the sick room. All present should kneel as soon as the Blessed Sacrament is brought into the room. As the priest enters, he says in Latin, "Peace be unto this house and unto all who dwell therein." He places the Blessed Sacrament on the table, genuflects and then sprinkles the sick person with holy water while he says the prayer, *Asperges me.* When the priest has concluded this prayer he will give a sign to all present in the sick room to withdraw for a few moments if the person who is ill wishes to go to confession. When the priest is finished hearing the confession and is ready to give Holy Communion to the patient, all should return, kneel, and *pray* for the sick person.

a. Administration of Last Sacraments

The priest takes the Blessed Sacrament from the pyx, elevates the Host and says in Latin, "Behold the Lamb of God, behold Him who taketh away the sins of the world." Then he adds, "Lord, I am not worthy that Thou shouldst enter under my roof; say but the word and my soul shall be healed." As he gives Holy Viaticum to the person who is ill he says, "Receive, brother (or sister), the Viaticum of the body of our Lord Jesus Christ; may He protect thee from the malicious foe and bring thee unto everlasting life. Amen."

The priest then administers the sacrament of Extreme Unction with its accompanying beautiful and significant prayers. He ends the ceremonies with the Last Blessing.

A dramatization of the entire procedure of summoning the priest and assisting the dying person might help imprint some of this useful knowledge in our minds.

IN A CATHOLIC CEMETERY

The grace of the crucifixion and death of Christ enables us to face death calmly. It helps us say with St. Paul: "He who has not spared even his own Son but has delivered Him for us all, how can He fail to grant us all things with Him." Rom. 8, 32.

B. ASSISTING THE DYING

1. ASSISTING DYING CATHOLICS

It is a great act of charity to attend to the physical and spiritual needs of dying Catholics. We should pray for them and with them. If they are too feeble, we can pray aloud, making acts of faith, hope, love, and contrition, saying the Rosary, the litanies and other prayers, uttering the name of Jesus in frequent aspirations, and giving the dying person the crucifix to hold and to kiss.

Dying persons appreciate these things very much and we should not let human respect cause us to omit them.

a. Prayers

We should especially recite the prayers for the dying which are found in many prayerbooks. Read these prayers often while you are in good health that you may be able to recite them when an occasion arises, and may understand them when your own last hour will have come. Usually a priest says these prayers, but he may not be present during the last moments. Even if the priest has said them earlier, it would be well for someone to read them anew as the person is dying. They are very beautiful. In them we call upon the whole celestial court to come to the aid of the dying person, and to accompany the soul to the throne of God.

These and other prayers to assist us in helping the dying in their last moments have been made available in pamphlets and leaflets in recent years. It might be wise to procure some of them.

b. Sacramentals

When assisting the dying it is well frequently to bless the patient with holy water and to help him hold a lighted blessed candle in his hand. Holy water is a sacramental having special powers to keep away the evil spirits who are desirous of getting the soul as it breathes forth its last sigh. The blessed candle is a symbol of the faith which was infused into the soul at Baptism. Thus at the beginning and at the end of a Christian's life the candle is a symbol of his faith, of the grace which he has received, and of the eternal glory to which God has destined him.

See to it also that the sick person has a scapular around his neck, or is wearing a blessed scapular medal. In the previous unit you may have learned about the numerous blessings and indulgences granted for wearing the scapular. Provide for your own death by always wearing one. Be faithful to the Mother of God and resolve never to set aside the badge of her protection. He who at the hour of his death is clothed in the scapular, may hope to be saved from eternal flames and look forward to a speedy release from purgatory. This promise was given to St. Simon Stock by Our Lady of Mt. Carmel.

A crucifix should also be available in order that the dying person may look at it, hold it, and press it to his lips.

2. ASSISTING DYING NON-CATHOLICS

We have discussed the proper way to help the dying Catholic, but what should one do for a dying non-Catholic, Protestant, Jew, non-believer or pagan? One should urge him to make acts of faith, hope, and charity, tell him about the Passion and death of Christ, point out to him his sins and shortcomings, tell him to be sorry for them, and then recite with him an act of perfect contrition.

In endeavoring to dispose the non-Catholic to make an act of perfect contrition show him how his own sins helped to crucify Christ. Remind him that God is worthy to be loved because of His infinite goodness, and beg him to be sorry because he has offended so good a God. If the person is not baptized, tell him about the importance and necessity of Baptism and try to make him desire to receive it. If he consents, baptize him; if you cannot persuade him, encourage him by reminding him of the mercy and goodness of God or if necessary of His power and justice.

C. PERFORMING THE WORKS OF MERCY

In helping souls to reach heaven we are performing both the spiritual and corporal works of mercy. Do you know the seven spiritual and the seven corporal works of mercy?

1. THE CORPORAL WORKS OF MERCY

Our Lord mentioned six of the corporal works of mercy when He gave a description of the last judgment. They are:

> To feed the hungry
> To give drink to the thirsty
> To clothe the naked
> To harbor the harborless
> To ransom the captive
> To visit the sick.

The seventh,

> To bury the dead,

is added from the praise bestowed by Raphael upon the elder Tobias, who buried the Israelites that were slain in the streets. "When thou . . . didst bury the dead, and didst leave thy dinner, and hide the dead by day in thy house, and bury them by night, I offered thy prayer to the Lord." Tob. 12, 12.

To those who practice these works of mercy, Christ on the last day will say: "Come, blessed of My Father, take possession of the kingdom prepared for you from the foundation of the world; for I was hungry and you gave Me to eat; I was thirsty and you gave Me to drink; I was a stranger and you took Me in; naked and you covered Me; sick and you visited Me; I was in prison and you came to Me." Matt. 25,34-36.

You can probably recall the beautiful scene drawn by our Lord, as the elect in surprise ask Him, "Lord, when did we see Thee hungry, and feed Thee; or thirsty, and give Thee drink? And when did we see Thee a stranger, and take Thee in; or naked, and clothe Thee? Or when did we see Thee sick, or in prison, and come to Thee?" And you remember what Christ the King will answer: "Amen I say to you, as long as you did it for one of these, the least of My brethren, you did it for Me." Matt. 25,

37-40. The fact that Christ considers these acts of charity done to any fellow human being as done to Himself should be a sufficient reason to impel us to practice them.

a. Visit the Sick; Bury the Dead

The last two of the corporal works of mercy apply especially to the matters we are now studying. By making a practice of the former we may save many souls; by performing the latter we can bring Christian consolation, hope, and resignation to bereaved relatives. Therefore, attending Christian wakes and funerals and assisting in other ways at the time of a death are much to be recommended.

A *wake* or watch means passing the night with the remains and with the bereaved relatives of the deceased person. It is a mark of Christian faith in the doctrine of the resurrection of the body and an act of charity and a consolation to the sorrowing survivors. The practice of having the wake in the home seems more in keeping with the warmth of Christian love, although some, because of circumstances, find it necessary to have the remains waked in a funeral parlor.

All Catholics who come to view the body, after a word of sympathy to the bereaved relatives, should kneel and say a prayer for the speedy repose of the soul of the deceased. Friends and relatives, as a further expression of Christian sympathy, often give the family of the dead person a card indicating that the Holy Sacrifice of the Mass will be offered for the person's soul.

Albrecht Durer   _Cleveland Museum of Art, Print Club Gift_

THE FOUR HORSEMEN OF THE APOCALYPSE
(Woodcut)

In the Apocalypse, that is the Book of Revelations, St. John the Apostle, draws back the veil of the future and shows us the events of the last days of the world.
In the sixth chapter of the Apocalypse he mentions four horses. The first is a white horse, symbolic of victory in war. Tradition identifies the rider as Christ. The second is red; it recalls blood, and strife and war. The third is black, representative of famine. The fourth is pale green, denoting pestilence and death and hell.

It may be appropriate here to call attention to the fact that all theatrical display is out of place in connection with a Christian wake or funeral, whether it be in the preparation and laying out of the body or in any other matters. Is it necessary to add that the dignity of Christian decorum at a wake is a sign of faith?

2. THE SPIRITUAL WORKS OF MERCY

Besides the corporal works of mercy there are also seven works of mercy for relieving the spiritual ills of the soul.

(1) To admonish the sinner,
(2) To instruct the ignorant,
(3) To counsel the doubtful,
(4) To comfort the sorrowful,
(5) To bear wrongs patiently,
(6) To forgive all injuries,
(7) To pray for the living and the dead.

The fourth and the seventh have special interest for us in this unit, since we are considering death and the proper preparation for the soul in danger of death. As the fourth spiritual work of mercy indicates, words or acts of sympathy to bereaved relatives are acts of mercy; so is praying for the soul after it has left the body—the seventh spiritual work of mercy. As Holy Scripture says: "It is . . . a holy and wholesome thought to pray for the dead, that they may be loosed from sins." 2 Mach. 12, 46.

While remembering the dead we should not neglect the living in our prayers, especially the dying, and in particular dying sinners and non-Catholics. We should join with the priest at Mass in the Memento for the Living and the Memento for the Dead. Love of neighbor expresses itself in prayers and good deeds. In the story of the apparitions of our Lady at Fatima it is related that she said: "Pray, pray much for sinners. Many souls go to hell because there are none to make sacrifices and pray for them."

REVIEW OF SECTION THREE

SECTION FOUR: THE LAST RITES OF THE CHURCH

A. THE FUNERAL MASS
1. A SOURCE OF CONSOLATION
2. WHEN AND WHERE IT MAY BE OFFERED
3. THE DIES IRAE
4. THE PREFACE OF THE DEAD
5. THE MEMENTO OF THE DEAD
6. THE ABSOLUTION

B. CHRISTIAN BURIAL
1. THE CHURCH'S REVERENCE FOR THE BODIES OF THE DEAD
2. BURIAL IN CONSECRATED GROUND
3. NON-CHRISTIAN BURIAL
4. DENIAL OF CHRISTIAN BURIAL
5. CREMATION

A. THE FUNERAL MASS

1. A SOURCE OF CONSOLATION

How consoling to Catholics is the Funeral Mass! The Holy Sacrifice, the supreme act of adoration and petition and satisfaction, is offered for the deceased person. Repeatedly the priest begs God to give eternal rest to the soul and to let perpetual light shine upon it. What solace it is to feel that the soul, lately departed, becomes the object of the Church's greatest solicitude. In the words of her priest she pleads for that soul after it has passed beyond the pale of gaining reward for itself. If you have not already done so, read through the words of the Funeral Mass or one of the other Requiem Masses, not omitting the Preface and the Absolution. See what consoling thoughts are there presented.

2. WHEN AND WHERE IT MAY BE OFFERED

The Funeral Mass should usually be said in the church of the parish to which the person belonged during life. It may be offered any day of the year except on a few privileged feasts of the highest class, which include Christmas, Epiphany, Easter, the Ascension, Whitsunday, Corpus Christi, the Annunciation, the Assumption, the Immaculate Conception, the Nativity of John the Baptist,

Official U. S. Marine Corps Photo.

NUN ON TARAWA

This picture symbolizes, in a striking way, the fact that the Catholic Church cares for the living and the dead.

A nun from Australia, having dedicated her life to the noble work of making the unknown God known to the natives of the South Seas, pauses in her labors for the living to breathe a prayer at the grave of an unknown U. S. marine who died on the beach of her mission in Tarawa.

St. Joseph, Sts. Peter and Paul, All Saints, the last three
days of Holy Week, and during the Forty Hours' Devotion. A Funeral Mass may even be said on a Sunday, but
there is a custom to the contrary in the United States. On
account of this, the Holy See has recently granted permission to say a Funeral Mass on some of the feasts just
mentioned.

3. THE DIES IRAE

The Mass for the Dead has a well known Sequence—
the *"Dies Irae"* or "Day of Wrath." In this powerful
and moving mediaeval hymn, our holy Mother the Church
speaking in the name of the departed one, first takes
solemn occasion to remind us of the terrible signs of the
Last Judgment and of how souls will tremble when God
shall come to judge them. It tells how the faithful soul
begs God to overlook his transgressions because Christ suffered and died for him. The theme then changes by re-
calling God's mercy toward Mary Magdalen and towards
the Good Thief. Next, in mournful tones, the fettered
soul prays for light and rest. Finally, a last word of hope
breaks on the ear and sinks into the heart.

The *"Dies Irae"* is meant to arouse Christians to prepare for life hereafter by contemplating judgment while
yet living here below. It is as much for the instruction of
the living as for the relief of the departed. The exquisite
Latinity of this sequence has baffled many students of the
classics and has lured some to attempt a translation, but
there is no translation comparable to the flowing beauty
of the original hymn. The authorship of this masterpiece
is generally ascribed to Thomas Celano, O.F.M., who
lived in the thirteenth century.

The *"Dies Irae"* is said in the Masses on All Souls' Day, on the
day of the death, and on the day of the burial of a deceased Catholic; it is prescribed also for the Mass on the third, the seventh, and
the thirtieth day after death, the month's mind Mass, and on the
anniversary. Its recitation in other low Masses of Requiem is op-
tional with the celebrant.

4. THE PREFACE OF THE DEAD

The Sequence of the Mass of the Dead is strong, powerful, frightening, but the Preface of the Dead is full of the most wonderfully consoling thoughts. Let us set it down here in its entirety.

The prayers and ceremonies surrounding the Offertory, the first part of the Mass of the Faithful, have just been concluded. The priest announces the conclusion by chanting: "Per omnia saecula saeculorum." And the people say: "Amen" (So be it). Then the priest begins the second part of the Mass of the Faithful, the most solemn part of the Mass, the Canon, which contains the sacrificial action of the Consecration. He says, "Dominus vobiscum," "The Lord be with you." The choir and ministers reply what the people say in their hearts, "And with thy spirit."

The responses continue "Let us lift up our hearts." "We have, to the Lord." "Let us give thanks to the Lord, our God." "It is right and just." And then taking up the echo from heaven the priest launches into the Preface to the Canon, the beautiful Preface of the Dead:

Truly it is worthy and just, right and availing to salvation that we should at all times and in all places give thanks unto Thee: O Holy Lord, Father Almighty, Eternal God, through Christ, our Lord. In whom the hope of a blessed resurrection has shone upon us; that those whom the certainty of dying has saddened, those same the promise of a future immortality may console. For, to Thy faithful, Lord, life is changed, not taken away; and when the abode of this earthly sojourn is dissolved, an eternal dwelling is gained in heaven. And so, with the angels and archangels, with the Thrones, and Dominations, with the whole host of the heavenly army we sing the hymn of Thy glory saying without end:

Holy! Holy! Holy! Lord God of Hosts. Heaven and earth are full of Thy glory. Hosanna in the highest. Blessed is He that cometh in the name of the Lord. Hosanna in the highest!

Such is the Preface of the Mass of the Dead! How appropriate it is! We give praise to God through our Lord who has made us resplendent by the rays of hope in a happy resurrection and has consoled us by the promise of future immortality; for the life of the faithful is changed, not lost, and our earthly home is exchanged for a heavenly dwelling. How fitting to join with all the choirs of angels in their canticle of praise, "Holy, holy, holy, Lord God of hosts."

5. THE MEMENTO OF THE DEAD

After the Consecration the priest makes a Memento or Remembrance of the Dead. He asks our Lord to be mindful of those who have gone before us signed with the mark of faith, the poor souls who are still detained in purgatory. The priest names those for whom he especially desires to pray, and concludes by begging "a place of refreshment, light and peace," not only for those for whom he has just prayed, but for "all who rest in Christ." It is a comforting thought that the Church, not only in the Masses for the Dead but *in every Mass,* remembers all the souls in purgatory.

We ought to unite with the priest in praying for the ones whom he has remembered, and recommend to God those for whom we feel obliged to pray, and for whom we have promised to pray.

6. THE ABSOLUTION

Following the Funeral Mass and before burial there is pronounced the Absolution over the remains. Again the priest prays God to deliver the soul from every bond of sin, that, in the glory of the resurrection, it may rise to a new life. The cross carried by the subdeacon, or the server, is a fitting pledge of the resurrection; the candles, an appropriate symbol of the faith of the departed one. The sprinkling of the body with holy water helps us recall the resurrection of the body; it is a symbolic watering of the seed that must be placed in the ground before it can flower in eternity; the burning incense reminds us of the prayers of the Church for her deceased child, and of the virtues which this Christian practiced.

B. CHRISTIAN BURIAL

1. THE CHURCH'S REVERENCE FOR THE BODIES OF THE DEAD

The Church treats with greatest reverence and honor the mortal remains of every body which has been given the dignity of becoming a temple of the Holy Ghost in the sacrament of Baptism, and a tabernacle of the Holy Eucharist by the reception of Holy Communion.

Before the Funeral Mass, when the cortege reaches the portal of the church, the mortal remains are met by the priest with cross and holy water. They are blessed and brought into the church with the singing of the *Miserere,* a prayer for mercy. During the Holy Sacrifice the body is permitted to lie at the altar rail. During the Absolution, after the Mass, it is sprinkled with holy water and incensed. Finally, the priest sings the Benedictus, preceded and concluded by the beautiful antiphon, "I am the Resurrection and the Life, he that believeth in Me, although he be dead, shall live: and every one who liveth and believeth in Me, shall never die."

The Absolution over, the body is taken out for burial. Nor is the Church yet finished showing it reverence.

2. BURIAL IN CONSECRATED GROUND

In her respect for the former and future dwelling place of a soul sanctified by being made a temple of the Holy Ghost, the Church has ever been solicitous about the burial of the remains of her departed children. During the Great Persecutions her deacons and priests brought the bodies of the martyrs to their hiding places for burial. These sanctuaries of rest were called the Catacombs.

Today Catholics are required to be buried in cemeteries which have been consecrated, for the Church is unwilling that the bodies of the faithful when they crumble to dust should mix with anything but consecrated soil. She selects and prepares a fitting resting place for the bodies of her children who have partaken so frequently of the Bread of Life.

THE GATES OF GOD'S ACRE

Can you identify the symbols on the gates? Those on the left concern resurrection and eternal reward. Those on the right concern the Holy Spirit and His gifts and fruits.

To a good Catholic it makes a difference where his body shall rest until the angel summons it on Judgment Day. He desires to be buried in ground consecrated by the Church, because he knows that in the prayers said at the consecration of a cemetery there is a petition that the souls of those who sleep there will possess the heavenly Jerusalem. Moreover, prayers are said very frequently in our cemeteries by the faithful who visit the graves of their departed. Cemeteries are hallowed spots.

153

Should urgent and serious circumstances seem to make it necessary that a Catholic be buried in a non-Catholic cemetery, the pastor first must present the case for the approval of his bishop and secure permission to conduct such a funeral and to bless the grave in the non-Catholic cemetery.

3. NON-CHRISTIAN BURIAL

When we condole with the relatives of non-Catholics or of Catholics who have died outside the Church, of what small value are our expressions of sympathy! How full of comfort are the doctrines and the practices of our religion; how empty is the funeral ceremony without the consolations of the Church. For us there is the Mass, of infinite value; for them, only a few words of solace from a minister. Thank God each day for the gift of faith and do all in your power to bring others to the true fold.

4. DENIAL OF CHRISTIAN BURIAL

The right to a Christian burial is denied to all who have cut themselves off from the communion of the Church, and die without being reconciled. The Church also denies Christian burial to those who refuse to receive the sacraments and to those who deliberately take their own lives. In case of the latter, the Church gives Christian burial if she has reason to believe that the person was not mentally responsible for the act. Persons who affiliate themselves with forbidden secret societies, such as the Free Masons and Odd Fellows, are among those whom the Church excludes from Christian burial.

5. CREMATION

From the very beginning, the language and liturgy of the Church have been in accord with the thought that the bodies of the dead should be entrusted to the earth from which they were taken. Man, like the seed planted in the ground "is sown in corruption, but shall rise in incorruption." 1 Cor. 15, 42.

The burning of the body of a dead person, called cremation, outrages a Christian's finer sensibilities. It is condemned by the Church, among other reasons because it is usually associated with a public profession of irreligion and materialism, and is sometimes meant as a denial of or a taunt against the doctrine of a future life. Moreover, it is more fitting to bury the dead than to subject the body to burning, against which both love and friendship revolt. If one expects a seed to grow, it is more appropriate to plant it in the ground than to burn it in the furnace. In cases of epidemics or in other emergencies cremation may be permitted by the Church.

C. REQUIEM MASSES

The Church's care for her departed children does not end even with a Christian burial. After death she offers Requiem Masses enriched with the copious suffrage of the Church. To the Funeral Mass is attached a plenary indulgence for the departed soul. To Masses sung on or as near as possible to the third, the seventh, and the thirtieth day after the death of a person, and to the anniversary Mass there is also attached a plenary indulgence. The third day Mass is commemorative of the three days which Christ passed in the sepulchre. The seventh day Mass is symbolic of the eternal Sabbath of rest. The thirtieth day or month's mind Mass commemorates the thirty days of mourning for Moses. It is praiseworthy to remember our dear departed on each recurring anniversary. If we remember others we can hope also to be remembered after our death.

REVIEW OF SECTION FOUR

SECTION FIVE: MEETING MY MASTER FACE TO FACE

Although death does cause an interruption of the physical life of the body, it causes no interruption of the natural, spiritual life of the soul. The spirit of man is immortal. As the words of the Preface of the Dead phrase it: "... life is changed, not taken away."

Accordingly, when death comes, the body dies but the soul lives on and passes to another life, an eternal life, the first instant of which determines what all the rest of that eternity will be.

The Particular Judgment

At the very moment that the soul leaves the body it appears before its Judge, who is God Himself. "It is appointed unto men to die once but after this comes the judgment." Heb. 9, 27. The soul, suddenly enlightened, beholds all its works, whether good or evil, and the punishment or reward it deserves. Some theologians hold that the judgment takes place where the person dies, for the Judge is everywhere. God is the Judge, the soul is the accused, the guardian angel is the witness, and the devil is the accuser.

We are judged on our entire life, on all thoughts, words, or actions, on all evil deeds and every omission of good deeds. The verdict is determined by the condition of our soul at the moment death came. The sentence is executed immediately and the Judge being God, the sentence cannot be commuted nor can the culprit be acquitted. Hell, purgatory, or heaven becomes the dwelling place of the soul.

Christ, in His glorified human nature is the Judge. Not until the soul has received a favorable sentence, does it

Courtesy of the Art Institute of Chicago, A. A. Munger Collection

ST. JOHN AT PATMOS

The Apocalypse was written by St. John while he was in banishment on the Island of Patmos. What does the last book of the Bible treat of?

behold the Beatific Vision, for to see God for only a minute would be to enjoy Heaven, which reward is given only after Judgment.

The Particular Judgment is necessary, for without Judgment how could a just God render justice to all? Both the good and the wicked must give an account of their lives so that God may reward the good and punish the wicked. A judgment must take place immediately after death, for time, our term of probation, no longer exists and eternity has begun. Eternity is the reward or punishment one earns for the good or evil one has done during life.

SECTION SIX: MY LIFE IN THE OTHER WORLD

A. HELL—ETERNAL MISERY
1. EXISTENCE OF HELL
2. THE PAINS OF HELL ARE ETERNAL
3. THE TWOFOLD PAIN: PAIN OF LOSS, PAIN OF SENSE
   a. Limbo

B. PURGATORY
1. NATURE AND DURATION
2. PROOF OF EXISTENCE OF PURGATORY
3. NATURE OF PUNISHMENT
4. DEVOTION TO THE POOR SOULS
   a. All Souls' Day
   b. The Month of the Poor Souls
   c. The Heroic Act

C. HEAVEN—THE GOAL OF OUR QUEST
1. EXISTENCE AND DURATION
2. GETTING AN IDEA OF HEAVEN
3. THE JOYS OF HEAVEN
   a. Vision of God—The Essential Joy
   b. Glorified Bodies
   c. Companionship in Heaven
   d. Other Joys of Heaven

A. HELL—ETERNAL MISERY

Following the Particular Judgment one becomes for all eternity either a member of the elect, destined for eternal happiness or a member of the damned, suffering eternal woe.

The eternity of woe referred to is the everlasting fire to which the wicked will be condemned. Every soul stained with mortal sin must endure eternal misery in a state and place of torment "prepared for the devil and his angels." It is called hell.

Scripture sometimes uses the word hell to mean merely the grave or the unseen world. The words of the Creed that say that Christ "descended into hell" mean that He went to that unseen place, called Limbo, where the souls of the just were awaiting Him. Scripture, however, also uses the word hell for that awful place of eternal punishment, "where the worm dieth not and the fire is not extinguished." Mark 9, 43.

Many passages in the Old and New Testament seem to indicate that hell is somewhere under the earth. The location of hell is unimportant; its nature and duration are all important.

1. EXISTENCE OF HELL

That hell exists is proven from Scripture, from reason, and from the tradition and teachings of the Church. There are no less than fifteen references to hell in *Holy Scripture*. It is called "everlasting fire," "the furnace of fire," and "the bottomless pit."

Reason argues there must be a place of punishment for those who have refused to obey the laws of God. Just as there is a reward for the good, so there must be punishment for the wicked. The doctrine of hell may seem opposed to the mercy of God, but certainly it is in accord with the justice of God. If God treated the good and the bad alike, He would not be a just God, and so there must be a hell where souls who have turned away from God can be punished.

The *Fathers* from the earliest times have taught the existence of hell and they have proved their doctrine from Holy Scripture.

The *teaching of the Church* includes solemn pronouncements on this doctrine. The Council of Lyons (1274), the Council of Florence (1439), and the Council of Trent in the sixteenth century have maintained that the wicked shall receive everlasting punishment for their sins.

2. THE PAINS OF HELL ARE ETERNAL

That the pains of hell are eternal is evident from the kind of fire mentioned in the *Scriptures*. This is clear not only from the word "everlasting," but also from other expressions as, "Their worm dieth not, and their fire is not extinguished," and again, "It is better for thee to enter into life everlasting lame than, having two feet, to be cast into the hell of unquenchable fire." Mark 9, 44-45. If "life everlasting" has no end, neither has "everlasting fire" an end.

Our *reason* tells us that hell is eternal. Grave sin is finite and infinite; it is a transgression by a finite creature against an Infinite Being. Since the punishment cannot be infinite because it must be suffered by a finite creature, the duration of the punishment must be infinite or eternal. Moreover, by mortal sin, a person becomes an enemy of God by his own deliberate choice. If the end of his time of probation should find him in that state he will remain God's enemy for all eternity.

The *Church* has always taught that hell is eternal. Our Lord's words, "Depart from Me, ye cursed, into everlasting *fire*," plainly mean that the punishment is everlasting and the Council of Trent speaks of "everlasting punishment," "eternal punishment" and "eternal damnation." A synod held in Constantinople in 553, and confirmed by

$\longrightarrow$

Courtesy Rev. J. Cacella

OUR LADY OF THE ROSARY OF FATIMA

Our Lady, at Fatima, said: "Pray, pray much, and make sacrifices for sinners; Many souls go to hell because there are none to make sacrifices and to pray for them."

the pope, declared: "If anyone says or thinks that the punishment of the demons and of evil men is temporary, and that it will come to an end some time, or that there will be a restitution or a renewal of the demons and of impious men, let him be anathema."

It is of course not necessary to insist on or to prove a doctrine such as this to a good Catholic. However, it is well for all informed Catholics to know the full teaching of the Church and to be able to give the reasons for it, because there are many non-Catholics who challenge it.

3. THE TWOFOLD PAIN—PAIN OF LOSS, PAIN OF SENSE

The damned will suffer torments of two kinds: the pain of loss, which is the intense suffering caused by the loss of God and eternal happiness; and the pain of sense, which is pain caused by fire which is inextinguishable. The reference in Holy Scripture to the worm that never dies, indicates the pain of loss; the reference to the fire that is never extinguished indicates the pain of sense. To appreciate the intense agony of the latter read the story of Lazarus and Dives, in Luke 16, 19-31.

In hell all the senses will be horribly tormented. The ears will hear the most awful sounds, screaming, grinding, cursing. The eyes will behold the most terrifying and repulsive sights. The nostrils will be assailed; the sense of touch punished. The more spiritual punishment of man's higher faculties, however, will be far worse.

The sudden realization that one has lost everything the human heart yearns for, the knowledge that one will be hemmed in and held down by evil for all eternity will so beset the damned that they will be as men stark mad. They will hate everyone, even themselves; they will be hated and cursed by all the ghastly inmates of that terrible place, and of their suffering there will never, never be an end.

Their wills, by nature attracted to good, will be eternally bound to all that man shrinks from, and the knowledge that this was their own free choice, that it might have been different, will but add gall to the vinegar.

4. LIMBO

Besides the hell of the damned there are other abodes of the departed which are also called by the same name. The just who died before Christ ascended into heaven, were detained in *limbo,* so called because it was thought to be on the fringe of hell. This limbo which ceased to exist after the Resurrection of Christ, must not be confused with the Limbo of Infants, the abode of unbaptized infants.

The *Limbo of Infants* is a state of damnation in the sense that the souls there are deprived of the supernatural joy of heaven. The common opinion of theologians is that these souls suffer no pain of sense and enjoy natural happiness, although they do not see God.

B. PURGATORY

1. NATURE AND DURATION

Christians who depart this life in the state of grace may be in the friendship of God but may not be completely fit to enjoy the Beatific Vision. They may not be good enough for heaven nor bad enough for hell. There may be venial sins on their souls, or, though the soul may be entirely free from sin, there may be *temporal punishment* still due on forgiven sin. The soul must be cleansed from sins and must be freed from temporal punishment.

The place or condition where the soul is cleansed is an intermediate state leading toward eternal happiness. It is called purgatory, that is, a place of purgation or cleansing.

The souls in purgatory are really saved and will go to heaven as soon as they are fit to enjoy the Vision of God. The individual soul remains in purgatory only until it has paid the debt due to sin. "Thou wilt not come out from it until thou hast paid the last penny." Matt. 5, 26.

Purgatory as a state will last as long as the world lasts. After the General Judgment, there will be only two states, heaven and hell.

2. PROOF OF THE EXISTENCE OF PURGATORY

Reason dictates that there must be a state of purgation. "Nothing defiled can enter heaven," so there must be a state or place where the souls of those free from mortal sin but not free from venial sin or temporal punishment may make some sort of satisfaction.

Holy Scripture, in the last book of the Old Testament, records the story of Judas Machabeus who sent twelve thousand drachmas of silver to the Temple at Jerusalem for sacrifice to be offered for the slain, saying, "It is therefore, a holy and wholesome thought to pray for the dead, that they may be loosed from sins." 2 Mach. 12, 43-46. These words imply that there is a middle state where souls are detained, and where they may benefit from prayers said for them by the living. The *Council of Trent* defines these two points: "That there is a purgatory: and that the souls there detained are helped by the suffrages of the faithful, and chiefly by the acceptable Sacrifice of the Altar." Sess. 25, Chap. 6, Can. 30.

3. NATURE OF THE PUNISHMENT OF PURGATORY

What is the nature of the punishment in purgatory? Theologians have taught that the souls in purgatory satisfy the justice of God by undergoing the pain of loss and the pain of sense, but the pain of loss in purgatory differs from the pain of loss suffered in hell because it is not eternal and is assuaged by hope, whereas in hell there is only despair. The soul will certainly go to heaven, sooner or later, but while restrained in purgatory it suffers an intense yearning to see God. The pain of sense is said to be caused by fire, and the text "He himself shall be saved, yet so as by fire" has been interpreted by some to mean a material fire of purgatory.

Michelangelo   *Underwood and Underwood*

THE LAST JUDGMENT

Christ with upraised arm, and with great power and majesty judges all men.
This tremendous mural, by the incomparable Michelangelo, is on the wall of
the Sistine Chapel, in the Vatican Palace. With the passage of time it has badly
deteriorated.

When speaking of fire in purgatory we must remember that there will be no human bodies in purgatory but only human souls. How a material element like fire can make a spiritual soul suffer may not be easy to see. Yet even here in life we know our material bodies by their limitations, imperfections, and pains inflict suffering of mind and will on our spiritual souls.

4. DEVOTION TO THE POOR SOULS

Since the faithful on earth can help the souls in purgatory by their prayers, charity and prudence urge that we assist our brethren of the Church Suffering. Holy Mother Church, therefore, because she loves her suffering members, asks the faithful on earth to be especially mindful of those good souls who have preceded them into eternity. She sets aside a day and a month to be devoted especially to the Poor Souls suffering in purgatory.

a. All Souls' Day

On November 2, All Souls' Day, the Church offers many suffrages in behalf of the souls in purgatory. Each priest may say three Masses for the dead on that day; and the Church grants, under the usual conditions, a special plenary indulgence applicable to the souls in purgatory. This is called a *toties quoties* indulgence, an expression which signifies that a plenary indulgence, in this case applicable to the souls in purgatory, may be gained each time a person visits a church and says the prayers prescribed for the Pope's intentions (in this instance six *Paters, Aves,* and *Glorias* at each visit), provided that the person has been to confession and has received Holy Communion. Usually a plenary indulgence can be gained only once a day for the same prayer or act.

It was Pope Benedict XV who granted to priests the permission to offer three Masses on All Souls' Day. Of these Masses the celebrant may say one according to his own intention; one must be offered for the faithful de-to heaven in the Sacred Scriptures may open our minds to its glory. It has been called the City of Light, the Heavenly Jerusalem, the Eternal City, City of the Living God. It has been referred to as My Father's House, the Promised Land, a Secure Abode, Everlasting Life, Everlasting Rest, Everlasting Joy, the Place of God's Glory.

The best way to come to a realization of what heaven is, is to meditate on your knees. Study and wide reading will also help. Begin perhaps with the Bible, especially the mysterious chapters 4, 7, 14, 20, and 21 of the Apocalypse. After that, read pamphlets, magazine articles, books, anything you can find, about heaven; and when you have finished reading, think it over again, on your knees. Meditate!

Discussing the joys of heaven in class or with others may also be helpful. In addition, it would be interesting to find out what other, non-Christian people think or have thought about heaven—the Indians and their Happy Hunting Ground; the Greeks and Romans with their human deities, their Parnassus and Elysium, and so forth. The very imperfection of their conception of heaven will help us realize the treasure that is ours in the knowledge we possess in the riches of our Christian faith.

3. THE JOYS OF HEAVEN

a. The Vision of God

The joys of heaven are infinite and inexhaustible, supernatural and eternal. The *essential joy* of heaven consists in a living union with God in the Beatific Vision. We shall possess God with our intellects and our wills; we shall be overwhelmed by His beauty; we shall, as it were, be submerged in and transformed by the brightness of His glory. 1 John 3, 2. As a reward for faith we shall see God face to face; as a reward for hope, we shall possess God; as a reward for charity, we shall delightfully enjoy God, the beginning and end of all love.

The Beatific Vision, which is the direct intuition of God by the intellect and the possession of God by the will in beatifying love, comprises everything the blessed may desire to know, or be, or have, or do. It includes the answers to all the mysteries of our religion which the soul believed while on earth, all the riddles of science and knowledge.

b. Glorified Bodies

After the General Judgment, the glorified bodies of the just will also be in heaven, united once again to their souls. They will possess the qualities of impassibility, brightness, agility, and spirituality, as we shall see presently. They too will share the happiness of heaven, even as the bodies of the damned will suffer the terrors of hell.

c. Companionship in Heaven

In heaven, everyone shall be associated as friends with the Blessed Trinity, Father, Son, and Holy Ghost. Mary, the Mother of God, and her chaste spouse, St. Joseph, will occupy the highest places, next to their divine Son, and they will be our friends. Those bright spirits, who joined with St. Michael the Archangel to overthrow the rebellious spirits, will be our companions. The Apostles, with their special mark to distinguish them as founders of the Church and associates with Christ, will be there. Martyrs, confessors, and virgins will join with us in hymns of praise. In heaven, also, we shall know "our own"— a dear mother or father, a sister or brother, a son or daughter, a husband or wife. All will be happy in their reunion in Christ.

------   →

Veronese   *National Gallery of Art, Kress Collection*

THE ASSUMPTION

The body of the Blessed Virgin has already risen from the grave. The bodies of all other members of the human race will be revivified on the last day. All shall be perfect—free from every defect: the good, that they may enjoy heaven's bliss to the utmost; the bad, that they may suffer the full punishment they have so justly deserved.

Does the communion of saints add to the joy of the blessed in heaven? Can we increase that joy by giving the saints the honor they merit?

d. Other Joys of Heaven

In heaven there is the complete absence of all that is evil or unpleasant: death, suffering, sin, sadness. There is the presence and possession of all possible good.

In heaven all of man's faculties, especially the noblest, the intellect and will, will be brought to their highest perfection. They will be given supernatural capacities for knowing and loving far beyond that supplied by the supernatural virtues and the gifts of the Holy Spirit on earth. This will vary according to the capacity of each individual and will depend on the grace and glory which he has gained for himself while on earth.

The intellect on earth was aided in knowing God by the natural power of reason and by the supernatural power of the infused theological virtue of faith, of the infused moral virtue of prudence and of the gifts of wisdom, understanding, counsel, and knowledge.

The intellect having gained possession of Truth Itself will be given yet far greater supernatural knowledge and understanding. It will be aided to see and know God as He is by a special supernatural gift called the *light of glory*. It will see the unity of everything in the ineffable unity of the Triune God.

So too, the will, having possession of Uncreated, Eternal, Infinite Goodness will rest quietly in supernatural joy and peace realizing that it has attained the eternal possession of everything that is or could be desirable.

REVIEW OF SECTIONS FIVE AND SIX

SECTION SEVEN: THE GENERAL JUDGMENT

A. THE END OF THE WORLD
 1. THE SIGNS
 2. THE SECOND COMING OF CHRIST
 3. THE RESURRECTION OF THE BODY
    a. Qualities of the Risen Body
 4. THE LAST JUDGMENT
    a. Its Circumstances
    b. The Sentence

A. THE END OF THE WORLD

1. THE SIGNS

Although each person will be judged for all eternity at the Particular Judgment, there will be a second and public judgment at the end of the world. St. Matthew in his Gospel describes the signs which will precede the General Judgment:

(1) The Gospel shall be preached in the whole world.

(2) There shall be wars and rumors of war.

(3) Anti-Christs will appear; and false prophets shall arise.

(4) "The sun will be darkened, and the moon will not give her light, and the stars will fall from heaven, and the powers of heaven will be shaken." Matt. 24, 23-29.

When will the end of the world come? Again St. Matthew tells us, "But of that day and hour no one knows, not even the angels of heaven, but the Father only." Matt. 24, 36.

2. THE SECOND COMING OF CHRIST

When that day comes, Christ, who ascended into heaven, will come again, as the seventh article of the Creed tells us; "to judge the living and the dead."

St. Matthew portrays this second coming of Christ, thus: "And then will appear the sign of the Son of Man in heaven; and then will all the tribes of earth mourn, and they will see the Son of Man coming upon the clouds of heaven with great power and majesty. And He will send forth His Angels with a trumpet and a great sound, and they will gather His elect from the four winds, from end to end of the heavens." Matt. 24, 30-31.

3. THE RESURRECTION OF THE BODY

This brings us to another doctrine of our Faith, which proves the love of God for us and brings us great consolation. It is the doctrine of the Resurrection of the Body. Death indeed is hard on human nature. Death is bitter, for it is a punishment for sin; but Christ has overcome death. He conquered sin, the death of the soul, and also the physical death, which terminates the natural life of the body.

Not only the elect but all men who ever lived will rise again on that last day. At the sound of the trumpet, in the twinkling of an eye, "the dead shall rise incorruptible." 1 Cor. 15, 52. Our bodies will rise from the grave, the same bodies that we had on earth. The bodies of the just will be beautiful: the bodies of the wicked will be hideous.

Having risen, our bodies will live forever. In hell it will be rather a living death, but in heaven it will be the full life which has been promised those who worthily eat the Body and Blood of Christ. For the frequent, worthy reception of the Holy Eucharist is a pledge of our resurrection: "He who eats My flesh and drinks My blood has life everlasting and I will raise him up on the last day." John 6, 55.

a. Qualities of the Risen Body

The body in heaven will be perfected and freed from all defects. It will be endowed with many wonderful qualities. You can read some of them in the fifteenth chapter of St. Paul's first Epistle to the Corinthians. The four principal qualities are:

Giovanni di Paolo
(1403-1482)

PARADISE

THE RESURRECTION AT MONGUYON

The artist portrays the churchyard cemetery at Monguyon, France, as she conceives its appearance on the occasion of the resurrection of the dead.

In the foreground are a knight of the crusades and his family, an eighteenth century poet, and the priests' housekeeper. Above them appear a peasant and his family, a hermit (against the church), and others. Through the roof of the Church a priest, and the lord and lady of the fief rise from their tombs.

1) *Impassibility,* including incorruptibility and immortality. "For this corruptible must put on incorruption; and this mortal must put on immortality." This quality means our bodies will be free from suffering, from disease, from sickness and all infirmities.

2) *Brightness,* by which the risen body shall shine like the sun, as the face of Christ shone at His Transfiguration. "Then the just will shine forth as the sun in the kingdom of their Father." Matt. 13, 43. The great St. Teresa of Avila was enthralled at the mere sight of the glorified hands of Christ. Our bodies will be bright with happiness and grace, beautiful indeed!

3) *Agility,* which is the power of moving from place to place. We shall have but to wish to be in a place, and immediately we shall be in the desired spot, with the speed of thought.

4) *Spirituality,* by which the body becomes so spiritual and so completely subject to the soul, that it becomes like to a spirit. "What is sown a natural body rises a spiritual body." 1 Cor. 15, 44. This quality is generally explained as subtlety or penetrability; a power by which the body can pass through material objects as did our Lord's glorified body.

4. THE LAST JUDGMENT

God wills that all men be saved; nevertheless, some will be saved and others will be lost. We shall all answer the call of the angels on the last day, for Christ will judge those who will be alive as well as those who will have died. "We will all stand at the judgment-seat of God." Rom. 14, 10.

⟶

Raphael   *Ewing Galloway, N. Y.*

THE TRANSFIGURATION

The three Apostles, Peter and James and John, were given a foretaste of one of the joys of heaven when they were allowed to see the body of Christ gloriously bright and changed in the Transfiguration. We too, with the eyes of faith, can catch a glimpse of this future glory of the elect by meditating on the qualities of a glorified body.

a. Its Circumstances

Those who will be alive on the last day, will experience such a change that in a moment they will die and awake to a new life. "And the dead in Christ will rise up first. Then we who live, who survive, shall be caught up together with them in the clouds to meet the Lord." 1 Thess. 4, 15-16.

The judge will be the Second Person of the Blessed Trinity, our Lord Jesus Christ in His human form. At His first coming Jesus "humbled Himself"; He came to suffer and to die. At His second advent He will come with great power and majesty, His divinity manifesting itself.

At the General Judgment Christ will publicly judge all the good and all the evil every man has done; even his most secret thoughts. The just will have no fear for sins that have been forgiven but only gratitude to God for His mercy; but the sins of the damned will cause them the utmost confusion, and consternation, and fear. The Apostles and the saints will assist Christ, but we do not know in what way. St. Thomas thinks that the Apostles and saints will notify souls of their sentence. The sentence passed at the Particular Judgment will be confirmed here at the General Judgment.

There is need of a general judgment so that the Providence of God, which at times allows the good on earth to suffer, and the wicked to prosper, may in the day of judgment, appear in all its justice to all men. "What I do thou knowest not now, but thou shalt know hereafter." John 13, 7.

b. The Sentence

When all the nations of the earth shall be assembled before Christ,

He will separate them one from another, as the shepherd separates the sheep from the goats; and He will set the sheep on His right hand, but the goats on His left.

To those on His right hand He will say,

" 'Come, blessed of My Father, take possession of the Kingdom
prepared for you from the foundation of the world;
for I was hungry and you gave Me to eat;
I was thirsty and you gave Me to drink;
I was a stranger and you took Me in;
naked and you covered Me;
sick and you visited Me;
I was in prison and you came to Me.'
Then the just will answer Him, saying 'Lord, when did we see
Thee hungry, and feed Thee; or thirsty, and give Thee drink? And
when did we see Thee a stranger, and take Thee in; or naked, and
clothe Thee? Or when did we see Thee sick, or in prison, and
come to thee?'
And answering the king will say to them, 'Amen I say to you, as
long as you did it for one of these, the least of My brethren, you
did it for Me.'
Then He will say to those on His left hand,
'Depart from Me, accursed ones, into the everlasting fire which
was prepared for the devil and his angels.
For I was hungry, and you did not give Me to eat;
I was thirsty and you gave Me no drink;
I was a stranger and you did not take Me in;
naked and you did not clothe Me;
sick, and in prison, and you did not visit Me.'
Then they also will answer and say, 'Lord, when did we see Thee
hungry, or thirsty, or a stranger, or naked, or sick, or in prison, and
did not minister to Thee?'
Then He will answer them, saying, 'Amen I say to you, as long
as you did not do it for one of these least ones, you did not do it for
Me.' And these will go into everlasting punishment, but the just
into everlasting life." Matt. 25, 32-46.

Having read the passage answer this question: Why
does Christ reward the good and punish the wicked?
The souls of the just shall follow Christ into heaven,
there to enjoy the Beatific Vision forever. The souls of
the damned shall be cast into hell, where "there will be
the weeping and the gnashing of teeth." Matt. 8, 12.

REVIEW OF SECTION SEVEN

CONCLUSION: THE SENIORS MAP A PLAN OF LIFE
NEED OF A PLAN

Such, in the main, are the tremendous truths which our faith lets us know about that Last Commencement—the commencement which graduates us into eternity. The wise person, who wishes to get that all-important diploma of success—that "Come, ye blessed of My Father," knows that he must plan his life in its essential practices and that he must follow the plan until these practices have acquired the stability of habit. There is no time like the present for concentrating on that task of habit formation, if it has not already been undertaken.

MAKING THE PLAN

Endeavor to be very sincere with yourself. There is danger of leading a slipshod life, and unless you make a resolution to be faithful to the practices of your youth, it will be easy to adopt the careless ways of living which you see all about you. Well-formed habits are advantageous in temporal affairs; they are indispensably necessary in spiritual matters. With the following points as a guide, let us first discuss and then draw up a plan of life, and resolve to adhere to it.

1. Daily Prayers: Morning, Evening, Meal, Angelus, Rosary.
2. Reception of the sacraments: Confession, Communion.
3. Habits and virtues to be fostered; acts and practices necessary thereto.
4. Vices and habits to be avoided or suppressed.
5. My predominant passion and methods for counteracting it.
6. Plan for the day, week, month, season, or year and for special days, weeks, months, and seasons.

REVIEW OF UNIT TWO

1. What is death?
2. Explain and illustrate the certainty and uncertainty of death.
3. How should one prepare for death remotely? proximately?
4. Why is St. Joseph the Patron of a Happy Death? What do you know of his life?

5. Mention and recite some prayers for a happy death.
6. What are the Last Sacraments?
7. What is Holy Viaticum?
8. What is Extreme Unction?
9. What is the outward sign of this sacrament? the matter? the form?
10. Can we prove the divine institution of Extreme Unction better from the Gospels or from the teaching of the Church?
11. What does Extreme Unction do? Explain each effect in such a way as to create a desire to receive the sacrament.
12. Who can confer Extreme Unction? Who can receive it?
13. How often can Extreme Unction be received? How long after apparent death?
14. What is the Last Blessing? What is necessary to gain it?
15. When should the priest be called?
16. What should one do if someone is suddenly hurt or becomes seriously ill?
17. What information does the priest need for a sick call? What can one do while awaiting his arrival?
18. Is there any advantage in having evidence of our religion visible on our person?
19. What is needed in a sick room?
20. How should one receive and assist the priest?
21. How should one attend and assist a dying Catholic? Protestant? Jew? Pagan? Non-believer?
22. What spiritual and corporal works of mercy apply particularly to the matters treated in this unit? How can we practice them?
23. Where should the funeral Mass be said?
24. What is the *Dies Irae?* Describe its contents.
25. What is the theme of the Preface of the Dead?
26. When does the Memento of the Dead occur?
27. What is the Absolution? Explain its prayers and symbolism.
28. Why does the Church treat the bodies of her dead children with such reverence?
29. Where should a Catholic be buried? Why?
30. Can a non-Catholic be buried in a Catholic cemetery? In a blessed grave? In consecrated ground?
31. Who must be refused a Funeral Mass and Christian burial?
32. Why does the Church oppose cremation?
33. Enumerate the various kinds of Requiem Masses.
34. What is the Particular Judgment? What verdicts may be given?
35. Define hell. Describe hell.

36. Prove from Scripture, from reason, and from the teaching of the Church that hell exists; that it is eternal.
37. Define and describe the pain of loss; the pain of sense, in hell and in purgatory.
38. Prove there is a purgatory.
39. Can the Poor Souls help us? Can we help them? How?
40. What is the Heroic Act?
41. What is heaven?
42. Prove from reason that there is and must be a heaven.
43. Describe the essential joy of heaven; the other accidental joys. Quote Scripture passages to support your answer.
44. What are the signs of the end of the world?
45. Describe Christ's second coming.
46. Prove from Scripture that the body shall rise from the grave.
47. Enumerate and explain the qualities of our glorified bodies.
48. Describe the Last Judgment (Matt. 25, 31-46). For the omission or practice of what acts are the wicked condemned and the good rewarded?
49. What is the importance and value of making a plan of life?
50. Describe what you consider a good, practical plan of life for a man or a woman living in the world; for a father, a mother, a single person.

PS. 109.4

UNIT THREE

The Great Choice

STATE IN LIFE, HOLY ORDERS, MATRIMONY

"We are all created to His glory—we are created to do His will. I am created to do something or to be something for which no one else is created; I have a place in God's counsels, in God's world, which no one else has . . . I have my mission—I may never know it in this life, but I shall be told it in the next."

CARDINAL NEWMAN.

PART ONE: PLANNING THE UNIT

INTRODUCTION

God made me so that I might give glory to His greatness by adoring Him and by enjoying and participating in His infinite perfections for all eternity. He has placed me on earth so that I may merit that reward by fulfilling

His will in my regard. I am created, as Cardinal Newman has said, "to do something or be something for which no one else is created." If God has not already led me to a knowledge of His all-wise designs for me, it is time that I begin to think of the path He wishes me to take.

Let us start then with a prayer that God may give each of us the grace to enter that state which will give Him the greatest glory, and which will be for us the safest on our journey toward the happiness of the Eternal Commencement.

DIAGNOSTIC DISCUSSION, OR PRE-TEST

1. On what basis should one make the choice of a state in life?
2. What choices are open to a man? a woman?
3. What are the duties and obligations of the religious life? the married state?
4. What are some of the qualifications for the religious life? the married state?
5. Are mixed marriages forbidden? Is divorce forbidden?
6. Is the marriage ceremony of a Catholic by a justice of the peace really a marriage? the marriage of a non-Catholic?
7. What is necessary for a valid marriage?

SOME OBJECTIVES IN STUDYING THIS UNIT

1. To help us make a wise choice of our state in life.
2. To encourage religious vocations among those who appear qualified.
3. To impart that information and to form those attitudes and habits which will be conducive to happy Catholic marriages among those called to that state.

Before turning to Part Two on page 194 to begin the study of this unit, examine the following Suggested Assignments and Activities to see whether they can supply or lead you to ideas for activities which will make the study of this unit more profitable and interesting.

————

→

Holman Hunt   *Ewing Galloway, N. Y.*

THE LIGHT OF THE WORLD

SOME SUGGESTED ASSIGNMENTS AND ACTIVITIES

*1. Write a paper or make a report on a topic such as:
  Three Roads to Heaven: Which is Mine?
  My Vocation in Life in the Light of My Capabilities—A Self-Analysis.
  How Saint Matthew, St. Augustine, St. John Baptist de la Salle, St. Ignatius (or any person or persons) Found the Right State in Life.

'2. Read and report on a biography of some saint, outstanding Catholic, or other person, e.g., St. John Vianney, Father Price of Maryknoll, Thomas Edison, Elizabeth Seton, Francis Xavier, Napoleon, etc., etc.

*3. Make a list of the various religious orders of priests, brothers, sisters in your diocese or in the country. Briefly indicate the work of each.

4. Make a bar graph showing the main occupations of people in your city, state, country; indicate the percent of the population in each occupation.

*5. Report or write on:
  a) The Life and Obligations of:
     A Parish Priest.
     A Religious Order Priest (or Brother) Engaged in Teaching, or Giving Missions or In Mission Fields, etc.
     A Sister, Cloistered, or Non-Cloistered, Teaching, Nursing, Caring for Orphans, Aged, on the Missions, etc.
     A Doctor, or Lawyer, Dentist, Engineer, Architect, etc.
     A Business Man, Labor Leader, Industrial or Commercial Worker, Farmer.
  b) Benefits of the Religious Life in Church and State.
  c) Procedure to Be Followed by One Who Thinks He Has a Vocation to the Priesthood (or Brotherhood or Sisterhood).
  d) The Right to Decide One's Own State in Life.
  e) Termites in the Social Structure:
     Divorce, Birth Control, Mixed Marriage, "Career" Girls, Unlawful Steady Company.
  f. The Most Frequent Causes of Unhappy Marriages.

6. Analyze a movie, book, or story in which false ideas on marriage are presented and show the subtle ways in which the true view of marriage is attacked or ridiculed.

7. Make a list of saints, classified according to state in life and occupation.

8. Read the life of some famous married saints, e.g., St. Thomas More, St. Jane Frances de Chantal, St. Elizabeth, Sts. Marius and Martha, etc.

9. Debates:

Resolved: that the modern girl is less well prepared for making a happy home than her grandmother was.

Resolved: that newlyweds should own a modest home debt-free before buying an automobile.

Resolved: that girls who work before marriage should bring into marriage a dowry formed from their savings.

10. Report on an interview on causes of broken homes with a pastor, your parents, a divorce court judge, etc.

•11. Make a book report or book review on some book or pamphlet dealing with the priestly or religious vocation, or with married life. (See *Related Readings.*)

Priestly Life:

Via Dolorosa by a North Country Curate (Herder).

Magnificat by Rene Bazin (Macmillan).

My New Curate by Canon Sheehan (Longmans).

Uncharted Spaces by Monica Selwin-Tait (Longmans).

Come Rack, Come Rope by Benson (Herder).

Divine Adventure by Theodore Maynard (Stokes).

Convent Life:

Within the Enclosure by Hester Delgairn (Herder).

Gates of Olivet by Lucille Borden (Macmillan).

Back to the World by Champol (Benziger).

The Nun by Rene Bazin (Scribner's).

As the Morning Rising by Sigrid Van Sweringen (Benziger).

Sorrow Built a Bridge by Katherine Burton (Longmans, Green).

Mother Marianne of Molokai by L. V. Jacks (Macmillan).

Elizabeth Seton, An American Woman by Father Feeney, (America).

Mother Mary Chrysostom by Sister M. Aloysius and Sister M. Patricia (Kenedy).

Saint Therese of Lisieux by Lucie Delarue- Mardrus (Longmans).

Life and Letters of Janet Erskine Stuart by Maud Monahan (Longmans).

13. A Problem in Math! If 2,000,000 children were born in 1900, about 52% being boys and 48% being girls, and if, as usually happens, approximately 75% of the girls lived to grow up and get married, and about 85% of these were able to

have children, and if all of them decided to have only one child in the family, how many generations (20 years per generation) would it take before the original 2,000,000 persons would fall below 1,000,000? below 500,000? below 100,000?

If one-third of these families decided to have no children, and another third to have only one, how many children would the remaining third have to have to keep the population from declining?

14. Appoint a committee to plan, write, and produce a playlet entitled, "And So They Were Married." The following points are suggested:

    a. Boys meet girls (one good pair; one bad).
    b. Soliloquy of young men or women pondering the good and bad points of the proposed partners in marriage.
    c. Dialogue of each of the young men and each of the young women with different friends discussing the good and bad points of the proposed partner.
    d. Proposed partners in marriage have talks with parents.
    e. Proposed partners visit the pastor and make arrangements for nuptial Mass.
    f. Marriage ceremony in part or in whole.
    g. Five years later.

15. Learn the hymn: *Mother, Tell Me What Am I To Do?*

16. Dramatize the entire procedure of making arrangements for a marriage and the ceremony, formal and informal.

17. Prepare a discussion on:
    Mixed Marriages Weaken the Faith.
    How to Create Social Pressure Against Propaganda Favoring Birth Control (or Divorce, Mixed Marriages, etc.).
    The Art of Homemaking.
    Small Families—A Menace to Our Nation's Future.
    Money Quarrels and How to Avoid Them.
    Financial Preparation for a Happy Marriage.
    The Evil Results of Divorce.

18. Make arrangements for a question box and discussion and quiz periods on Fridays.

RELATED READINGS IN BOOKS AND PAMPHLETS

Books: ———, *A Catholic Appraisal of the Family Today*, N.C.W.C.
———, *Into Their Company*, Kenedy (Love and Marriage, for Girls).
Blunt, *Great Wives and Mothers*, Devin-Adair.

Code, *Great American Foundresses,* Macmillan.
Cronin, *The Christian Priesthood,* (T.F.S.) Macmillan.
Ernest, *Our Brothers,* Scott-Foresman.
Kelly, *The Romance of a Nun,* Kenedy.
Lord, *Our Nuns,* Q.W.
Meyer, *Youth's Pathfinder,* St. Francis Book Shop, Cincinnati.
Schmiedler, *Marriage and the Family,* McGraw-Hill.
Scott, *Convent Life,* Kenedy.
Williamson, *Great Catholics,* Macmillan.

Pamphlets:

————, *Companykeeping: When Is It a Sin?* O.S.V.
————, *The Service of the Queen,* Missionary Catechists.
————, *The Hidden Treasure,* Bengalese.
————, *Where do You Fit?* Bengalese.
————, *The Call Celestial,* Bengalese.
————, *The Working Sisterhood,* Bengalese.
————, *The Nuptial Mass,* I.C.T.S.
————, *Birth Control and National Decay.* O.S.V.
————, *How to Get Married,* O.S.V.
Bampfield, *Mixed Marriages* (Why the Church does not like them), I.C.T.S.
Bowdern, *Courtship and Marriage,* Q.W.
Cassilly, *What Shall I Be?* America.
Cassilly, *Who Can Be a Nun?* Q.W.
Connell, *The Catholic Doctrine of Matrimony,* America.
Conway, *Church and Eugenics,* Paulist.
Why Priests Do Not Marry, Paulist.
Cox, *The Divine Romance of Marriage,* Paulist.
Birth Control, Paulist.
Cunningham, *Have I a Vocation?* (For Boys), Paulist.
Dooley, *Our Priceless Heritage,* Mission Press.
Fenn, *Vocations to the Priesthood,* Paulist.
Fenton, *The Calling of a Diocesan Priest,* Newman Book Shop.
Fischer, *The Call of Christ,* Mission Press.
Forrest, *The Pearl of Great Price,* Paulist.
Garesche, *Teaching for God,* Loyola.
Gibbons, Card., *Christian Home,* Paulist.
Handly, *Dorothy's Divorce,* Paulist.
Harvey, *A Search for Happiness,* O.S.Vis.
Hogan, *The Priesthood, How Holy!* I.C.T.S.

Husslein, *The Wedding Ring,* America.

Hynes, *Farm-Family-Prosperity,* National Catholic Rural Life.

Kirsch, *Training in Chastity,* O.S.Vis.

Lambing, *Mixed Marriages,* Ave Maria.

Lord, *Marry Your Own,* Queen's Work.

What to Do on a Date, Queen's Work.

Shall I Be a Nun? Queen's Work.

The Wallflower, Queen's Work.

They're Married, Queen's Work.

Your Partner in Marriage, Queen's Work.

Mauer, *Training Your Child,* O.S.Vis.

McCormick, *The Terrors of Being Engaged,* Paulist.

McGill, *Company Keeping,* O.S.Vis.

Does That Man Love Me? O.S.Vis.

Meyer, *Why and How to Become a Lay-Brother,* St. Francis Book Shop.

Meyer, *I'm Keeping Company Now,* Paulist.

Mueller, *Family Life in Christ,* Liturgical.

Norris, *Unreasonable Mothers,* Paulist.

O'Brien, J., *Brides of Christ,* St. Anthony Guild.

Soldiers of Christ, St. Anthony Guild.

O'Brien, J. A., *Catholic Marriage—How to Achieve It,* O.S.Vis.

Courtship and Marriage, O.S.Vis.

Is the Church Woman's Enemy, O.S.Vis.

Marriage: Catholic or Mixed, O.S.Vis.

The Christian Home, O.S.Vis.

Why Not Get a Divorce? Paulist.

Marriage: Why Indissoluble? O.S.Vis.

The Priesthood, O.S.Vis.

Youth's Struggle for Decency, O.S.Vis.

Passionists, *Follow Me (On Vocations for Boys),* Thomas More Book Shop, Chicago.

Follow Him (On Vocations for Girls), Thomas More Book Shop, Chicago.

Pope Pius XI *Encyclical on Christian Marriage,* America. (See Treacy).

Redt, *Aids to Purity,* O.S.Vis.

Reger, *Our Catholic Sisterhoods,* Mission Press.

Ross, *What Is Love?* Paulist.

What God Hath Joined, Paulist.

Scott, *Marriage Problems,* Paulist.
Schmiedeler, *For Better—For Worse,* O.S.Vis.
   Vanishing Homesteads, Paulist.
Treacy, *Love Undying,* Paulist (Pius XI's Encyclical on
   Marriage, Simplified).
Ullathorne, *The Conventual Life,* Paulist.
Welfle, *Our Precious Bodies,* Q.W.

Periodicals:
   Land and Home, National Catholic Rural Life Conference.
   Family Digest, Huntington, Ind.

PARALLEL READINGS IN OTHER HIGH SCHOOL RELIGION TEXTS*

	Campion	Cassilly	Falque	Graham	Laux	Manual of Chr. Doctr.
Religious Vocations	I, 232	24		234	III, 30	342
Holy Orders	I, 228	292	II, 148 282	230	II, 121	480
Vows	II, 269	25; 90	I, 185	289	III, 76	254
Evangelical Counsels	I, 134	24; 471			III, 32	339
Marriage	I, 237 II, 286	303	I, 196		III, 107	489
Sacrament of Matrimony	I, 239 III, 70	304	II, 308	238	II, 129	488
6th Precept	II, 396	152		242	II, 133	333

*Given in volumes and pages, except Gaume which shows volume and chapter.

PART TWO: THE GREAT CHOICE

SECTION ONE: MY STATE IN LIFE, WHAT SHALL IT BE?

A. IMPORTANCE OF PROPER CHOICE
   1. THE THREE GREAT ROADS

B. CRITERIA FOR CHOOSING OR KNOWING ONE'S VOCATION
   1. PHYSICAL
   2. MENTAL
   3. MORAL
   4. THE SUPREME CRITERION—GOD'S GLORY
   5. MY OWN SALVATION

C. AIDS IN MAKING THE RIGHT SELECTION
   1. PRAYER AND RECEPTION OF THE SACRAMENTS
   2. SEEKING COMPETENT GUIDANCE

A. IMPORTANCE OF PROPER CHOICE

My choice of a state in life is intimately connected with my eternal happiness as well as with my happiness on earth. If I deliberately make a poor choice, through cowardice, love of pleasure, desire for ease and honor or because of any other ignoble motive I not only jeopardize my eternity and that of others, but, in addition, I almost certainly insure for myself an uneasy, miserable life of constant self-reproach.

1. THE THREE GREAT ROADS

There are three roads leading to the gate which admits us to the Eternal Commencement: first, the broad and crowded road of *marriage,* next, the more solitary avenue of *single blessedness,* as it is often rather dubiously called; and thirdly, the white road of the *religious life.* On one of these three ways you will walk towards eternity. *You* must make the choice. The question then is, which shall it be? What state of life shall I choose?

I may have made my decision already. I may still be debating the problem. I may have not as yet begun to consider it.

Of course not every one gets a clear decisive call to a definite state. In fact, in many cases, as with St. John

THE CAPUCHIN MONASTERY
Amalfi, Italy

Baptist de la Salle, it is a slow, almost imperceptible process which finally produces the situation which gives the answer; but in all cases if I am but docile in responding to the influence of grace I shall find the state in which I can do that "something" or be that "something" which divine Providence wishes me to do or be.

B. CRITERIA FOR CHOOSING OR KNOWING ONE'S VOCATION

God does not call everyone as he called St. Paul, that is, by giving him an invitation direct from heaven. Usually we must decide our vocation by considering certain criteria: physical, mental, and moral.

1. PHYSICAL CRITERIA

If I do not possess the *physical fitness* required for a certain state of life I can be certain God is not calling me to that state. If I am blind I can hardly be an aviator. If I do possess the physical requirements, then I must check the mental demands.

2. MENTAL CRITERIA

If I cannot learn algebra, I am in all probability not destined to be an engineer. If I can not learn Latin I hardly have a vocation to be a priest. Lack of *mental qualifications* is a positive sign that I am not called to a state, whatever may be my inclination to it. I should possess at least that minimum mental ability sufficient to enable me to carry out the essential duties and fulfill the minimum obligations of the state in life which I choose.

In this connection, however, one will do well to read the early life of St. John Baptist Vianney, the Curé of Ars. He was almost dismissed from the seminary because in spite of his best efforts he found it very difficult to learn, yet he applied himself so assiduously and used the grace of God so faithfully that he became the most successful parish priest in France and a great saint.

3. MORAL REQUISITES

Possession of both the physical and mental requirements is still not enough in deciding my vocation. There are also *moral criteria* that must be taken into consideration in making my choice.

A certain moral uprightness and stability of character is certainly demanded of one who aspires to the religious life. Lack of such would indicate that a person did not have a calling to that state.

4. THE SUPREME CRITERION—GOD'S GLORY

A fourth and very important criterion to guide one in the choice of a state of life is found in the answer to this question: Will the *glory of God* and the salvation of souls, mine as well as those of others, be best promoted by my choice of this particular state or would God wish me to choose another?

I was created to give glory to God. I should choose that state which, all things considered, will best increase His glory.

5. MY OWN SALVATION

As I give glory to God by sanctifying my own soul and those of my fellow men, the influence of a given state in life on my eternal welfare is also a criterion I must use in choosing my state in life.

C. AIDS IN MAKING THE RIGHT SELECTION

With the foregoing and any other useful criteria as guides, a person should *examine* the three basic states and the variety of possibilities within each state for which he considers himself called or to which he feels himself adapted or inclined.

1. PRAYER AND RECEPTION OF THE SACRAMENTS

In this examination of the different states and in the estimating of a person's fitness for a particular state and calling, prayer is indispensable as an aid to a proper choice. To decide on one's state in life without having invoked the assistance of God, His Holy Mother, and the angels and saints, to rely solely on our feeble human intellect and prudence, would be foolhardy and unchristian. If the main aim of life is to adore and worship and glorify God and if the choice of a state in life affects this duty so vitally then prayer should be relied upon to help us choose correctly. It should be unnecessary to remind a

Catholic that frequent Confession and Holy Communion are essential to this part of the preparation.

2. SEEKING COMPETENT GUIDANCE

Another very helpful aid for those who are somewhat hesitant in deciding, is to consult with persons competent to advise. Among these one's *confessor* ranks first, then one's parents, other priests or religious, and other informed and qualified persons, especially those marked with the virtue of prudence. If one is considering some specific vocation within a certain state it is also wise to have a talk with someone in that vocation or well acquainted with its requirements and duties. Good books also can sometimes supply the needed information to help reach a decision.

SECTION TWO: THE HIGHEST CALLING—SERVING GOD AND MAN IN RELIGION

A. THE RELIGIOUS VOCATION IN GENERAL
  1. ITS GRANDEUR
  2. SIGNS OF A RELIGIOUS VOCATION
      a. Physical
      b. Mental
      c. Moral
      d. Favorable Inclination
      e. Good Motive
  3. IMPEDIMENTS TO A RELIGIOUS VOCATION
  4. NEGLECTING A RELIGIOUS VOCATION
      a. Love of Pleasure—A Frequent Cause
  5. TESTING ONE'S VOCATION

B. THE PRIESTHOOD
  1. TWO CLASSES
      a. The Diocesan Clergy
      b. Priests of Religious Orders and Congregations
  2. DUTIES OF THE PRIESTHOOD
  3. DIGNITY AND RESPONSIBILITY OF THE PRIESTHOOD

C. THE SACRAMENT OF HOLY ORDERS
  1. DEFINITION
  2. THE STEPS TO THE PRIESTHOOD
      a. Tonsure
      b. The Four Minor Orders
      c. The Major Orders

3. THE OUTWARD SIGN OF HOLY ORDERS
4. THE MINISTER AND SUBJECT OF HOLY ORDERS
5. EFFECTS OF HOLY ORDERS
   a. Spiritual Power
   b. Sanctifying Grace
   c. Sacramental Grace
   d. Character

D. THE BROTHERHOODS
   1. KINDS OF BROTHERS
   2. NEED OF BROTHERS
   3. SIGNS OF A VOCATION
   4. THE PREPARATION OF A BROTHER

E. THE RELIGIOUS LIFE FOR WOMEN
   1. THE ACTIVE AND THE CONTEMPLATIVE LIFE
   2. THE VOWS OF RELIGION
      a. The Vows and the Evangelical Counsels
      b. Solemn and Simple Vows
   3. TYPES OF WORK PERFORMED BY ACTIVE ORDERS OF WOMEN
   4. AIDS IN DECIDING
   5. CORRECT UNDERSTANDING OF THE RELIGIOUS LIFE
   6. GREAT NEED OF MORE VOCATIONS
   7. TESTING THE VOCATION
   8. THE 'PRO'S' AND 'CON'S' OF RELIGIOUS LIFE
      a. Sacrifices Demanded
      b. Happiness of a Life of Service

A. RELIGIOUS VOCATION IN GENERAL

1. ITS GRANDEUR

The grandest privilege and the greatest honor that Christ can confer upon a young man or woman is to give him or her the call to serve Him in religion. To work for Christ and with Him, to labor for His Mystical Body, to make one's chief work in life the fashioning, in oneself and in one's fellowmen, of the virtues of the Incarnate Son of God, to forget self and to think of others, to serve God first, then others, and only lastly to serve self—what calling could exceed this in grandeur?

2. SIGNS OF A RELIGIOUS VOCATION

A vocation to the religious life is not offered to all, nor even to the majority, but those to whom it does come must accept it readily. Sometimes the call is clear and

THE MADONNA OF THE CARNATION

unmistakable, but more frequently it is indicated by a quiet inclination, a timid liking. Some boys and girls know from childhood that they want to be a priest or a brother or a nun. Others have gone on, never quite sure until they have been invited to take the final step. Yet both have had a vocation, for, in the final analysis, a vocation is determined not by the inclination or the liking of the person concerned but by the call issued by the proper authorities in the Church.

A religious vocation is *a call issued by Christ through His Church,* and we can never be certain we really have such a vocation, no matter how strong the urge within us may be, until the Church actually calls us. If we do feel, however, the inclination to enter the life of religion, we should present ourselves to the Church for testing and for a final decision.

a. Physical

In discussing the criteria which should serve as a basis for helping a person decide which state of life to choose we also gave the general criteria for estimating whether you may be called by God to the religious life. If you are lacking the health and physical fitness required in the religious life God evidently does not intend to call you to it; if you do possess that fitness you have at least one positive sign.

b. Mental

But more than physical fitness is required. Sufficient mental ability is also essential, although the amount needed may vary greatly in the different states and levels within the religious life. Average to high mental ability may be required for the priest, the teaching sister or brother, the sister-nurse. On the other hand, less than average ability might be amply sufficient in a contemplative order, or for a lay brother or for a non-teaching sister in a woman's community.

c. Moral

Moral fitness is also a sign of a possible vocation, just as lack of it is an argument against the existence of one. However, in this regard we must remember that all men are sinners, and that great sinners have at times become great saints. The conclusion from this is that, although great moral purity is desirable, sins in one's past life are not a bar to a religious vocation if there has been a genuine and wholehearted conversion. Recall the early life of St. Paul and of St. Augustine.

None the less, a person who persists in habits of sin, as well as a person who lacks the moral characteristics necessary for the religious life gives evidence of not possessing a vocation. Some of these requisite characteristics and potential habits would be: obedience, a habit of prayer and of frequent reception of the sacraments, ability to get along with others, forgetfulness of self, and so forth.

d. Favorable Inclination

A constant inclination toward the religious life is a good sign of a vocation, although it is by no means necessary or absolute. To many, a realization of their vocation has come like a flash of lightning at the end of high school, in college, even at the end of college or later in life. Usually, however, the final decision is reached somewhere between the ages of sixteen and eighteen; sometimes after a retreat, in confession, during a visit to the Blessed Sacrament, or in other ways.

e. A Good Motive

In trying to decide whether you might have a religious vocation so that you might present yourself to the proper authorities in the Church for testing, it is always very necessary to examine the motive which inspires you. If the motive is good, fine. If it is not good, you may be in danger of pushing yourself into a state of life where you can do great harm to yourself and others.

The *right intention* is a necessary sign of a religious vocation. If a boy or girl inclines to this life because of love of God or because of love of souls, a desire to help others, a love of virginity, a desire for perfection or a wish to atone for sins, a longing for his own salvation and that of others, his intention is right. But if a girl were to choose the religious life primarily because she thought it offered security, or freedom from the trials and worries of married life, or if a boy chose the priesthood because in it he thought he could live a soft, easy life, or because of some other selfish reason, he or she would be acting from a bad motive.

3. IMPEDIMENTS TO A RELIGIOUS VOCATION

In addition to these general signs of a vocation there is another: freedom from any impediments or irregularities.

Because the vocation to the priesthood is of such importance the Church sets up certain impediments in order to protect the good name and reputation of her clergy. Thus those born out of lawful wedlock may not be ordained unless the matter has been rectified or dispensed; neither may one who has taken another's life or cooperated in such a deed, whether by murder or by causing the death of an unborn child. Heretics, epileptics, and those who have been insane are also debarred from the priesthood.

There are also certain impediments forbidding entry into the novitiate of a religious community; for instance, age, marriage bond, dependent parents, etc.

4. NEGLECTING A RELIGIOUS VOCATION

If we have been insisting on matters which seem to deter persons from entering the religious life because

they are not fit, then we must insist with equal emphasis
on the great spiritual dangers which arise from neglecting
a vocation. St. Vincent de Paul said that it was very
difficult, if not impossible, to save one's soul in a state of
life in which God does not wish one to be. We must also
refer to the often heart-rending unhappiness of those who
have deliberately refused to respond to the clear signs of
a vocation.

a. Love of Pleasure—A Frequent Cause of Neglecting a Vocation

One of the most frequent causes of loss of a vocation
is a disordered love of pleasure and especially the failure
to develop the habit of *self-sacrifice*. As a result of the
lack of this habit people follow their natural inclinations
to indulge in worldly pleasures, and not having the assistance of a good habit of self-sacrifice they find themselves
unduly attracted by and attached to worldly pleasure and
goods. The consequence is that they smother the call of
the vocation.

The conclusion to draw from this is the following: If
you think you may have a vocation, foster it and protect
it, and especially train yourself to deliberate acts of sacrifice, regularly denying yourself perfectly lawful pleasures,
and avoiding all or at least any excessive indulgence in
those things which would make it difficult for you to follow the religious vocation. Persons who feel they may
have a vocation are to be encouraged to renounce completely or to indulge very infrequently in such activities
as parties, dancing and the like.

5. TESTING ONE'S VOCATION

A person who is free from any negative signs which
would prevent a religious vocation and who seems to possess the necessary positive signs, should first consult his
pastor, confessor, or other priest and, if encouraged,

should test his or her vocation by *applying for admission* to the seminary or novitiate. That is one of the purposes for which these institutions were established. They exist not only to train priests and religious but to allow them to test the wings of their aspirations.

Some foolish persons consider it a disgrace for a boy or girl to leave the seminary or the novitiate; they think that when one enters either of these institutions his vocation is complete and assured. That is not the truth. It is no more a disgrace to withdraw after having tested one's supposed vocation to the religious life and having found out that one does not really have the call, than it is to take a pre-medical course in college and drop out because one finds he has no liking or aptitude for that work. One might compare it to trying out for the football team, or the debating society, or the like. Those who feel capable are urged to try but the coach or moderator finally decides.

a. The Seminary and Novitiate

We have just mentioned the *seminary* and the novitiate. Let us say a word about them. The seminary is the school for the training and education of priests. A *novitiate* is a place for the training of members of religious communities, whether of men or of women.

There are in some dioceses, minor or preparatory seminaries which take boys as early as the beginning of high school or college. There are major seminaries with a six-year course, the first two of which correspond with the third and fourth year of college and are devoted chiefly to the study of philosophy, while the last four years are devoted to the study of theology, which is concluded by ordination to the priesthood.

If you are positive you have a vocation to the religious life and are free to follow the call, let nothing interfere with it. If you are sure you do not have a vocation, be just as decisive in resisting the pressure of fond parents or others who may wish to gratify their own desires by forcing you into a state of life to which God has not called you and in which you may lack the special graces you need.

B. THE PRIESTHOOD

Let us now examine the variety of ways in which a person can serve God in the religious life. First and highest of all is the priesthood. The word "priest" comes from the Greek word *presbyteros* meaning "elder." It is generally conferred on those engaged in the service of God, especially such as offer sacrifice. At present it is reserved almost exclusively to the Catholic priest who alone offers a sacrifice pleasing to God.

1. TWO CLASSES

There are two great general classes of Catholic priests. First, there are those who work in and are permanently bound to a certain diocese and are therefore called *diocesan priests,* or less aptly secular priests, that is, priests who work out in the world. Secondly, there are priests of the various *religious orders;* they are subject to the head of their order, and generally remain in monasteries, houses of study, and similar institutions. The priests of the religious orders which follow the religious life strictly so-called, add the three vows of poverty, chastity, and obedience to the other obligations of the priesthood. They vow to lead a life of Christian perfection.

a. The Diocesan Clergy

The diocesan clergy are the more numerous. They are mostly engaged in parish work, in direct contact with souls, although some of them may be in special fields such as hospital or youth work, directing or teaching high school, college or seminary and so forth. The priests of the many religious congregations, although originally engaged in special work now often have some of their mem-

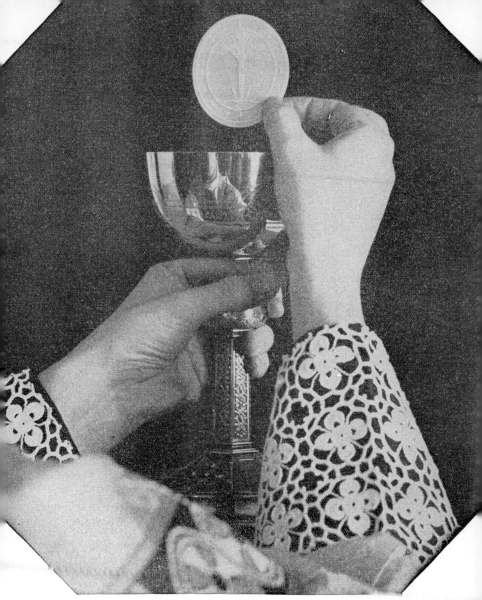

"OMNIS HONOR ET GLORIA"

The priest offers to God for men, that adorable, and solely acceptable Sacrifice which reenacts Calvary and communicates to men the graces of the Redemption. By performing this great Action the priest not only adores his Maker but he also serves his brothers and sisters in Christ in a manner more august and more beneficial than any other that is possible to man.

bers in parish work also. In 1940 there were about 22,000 diocesan priests and about 11,000 priests of religious orders in the United States.

All priests take upon themselves the obligations of the solemn vow of chastity by which they bind themselves to remain unmarried and to live a life of highest purity. For the diocesan priest this is included implicitly in his acceptance of the obligations of subdiaconate. In addition to this he makes a solemn promise of reverence and obedience to his bishop at his ordination.

· b. Priests of Religious Orders

The priests of religious orders and communities are engaged largely in the special work for which the order was founded.

To this end they take the three vows of religion mentioned above. We shall study these vows later in the unit. If these three vows are what the Church calls *solemn vows* then the religious community is known as a religious *order*. If these vows are *simple vows* they are known as a religious *congregation*. The main difference between solemn and simple vows is that the former are much more difficult to be released or dispensed from.

In addition to these two subdivisions of religious communities there are religious societies of priests like the Oratorians, the Maryknoll Fathers, the Sulpicians, who usually do not take the three vows but, while remaining technically diocesan priests, bind themselves to the work of that community by a special promise. It might be well to locate and report on articles about such orders as the Benedictines, Franciscans, Dominicans, Carthusians, Carmelites, Jesuits, Marianists, Redemptorists or the Servites.

2. DUTIES OF THE PRIESTHOOD

The first, the most august, and most important duty of a priest is to offer to God the *Holy Sacrifice of the Mass* as the supreme act of adoration, thanksgiving, satisfaction, and petition.

Filippino Lippi
(1457-1504)

TOBIAS AND THE ANGEL

Young Tobias, faithfully fulfilling the instructions of his angel guide, was led
to a happy marriage. Beginning his married life, as Raphael had suggested, by
spending three nights in prayer with Sara his wife, he avoided the death which
the devils of lust had brought to the seven former suitors for Sara's hand.

His second duty is to bring supernatural life to souls and to guard and foster that divine life by *administering the sacraments.* The third duty is to *preach and to teach* the glad tidings of God's love for man contained in the Gospel of Jesus Christ.

A fourth duty is to recite daily the *Divine Office;* a fifth, to observe celibacy; a sixth, to lead a holy life. Over and above these are the special duties of the particular work in which the individual priest is engaged.

The obligation of celibacy arises from a Church law which is binding on the clergy of the Latin rite but not on some of the clergy of the oriental rites. Among these latter the general practice is to permit married men to be ordained but not to allow marriage after ordination. The oriental bishops are unmarried men. Can you see any advantages in having an unmarried clergy?

3. DIGNITY AND RESPONSIBILITY OF THE PRIESTHOOD

The duties just enumerated, especially the first two, reveal the sublime dignity of the Catholic priesthood. For a human being to be allowed to consecrate the sacred Body and Blood of Christ in the renewal of the great sacrifice of Calvary, for a man to be allowed to say for Christ: "This is My Body," "This is My Blood"; to say, "I absolve thee," this is indeed a great dignity, but at the same time it is a tremendous responsibility. Only the grace of God can enable a man to shoulder it safely. God bestows this grace in the sacrament of Holy Orders.

C. THE SACRAMENT OF HOLY ORDERS

A man is made a priest by ordination to that office in the sacrament of Holy Orders.

1. DEFINITION

This sacrament can be defined as follows: Holy Orders is a sacrament of the New Law, by which spiritual power is bestowed and grace conferred to enable a man to offer the Holy Sacrifice and perform the other ecclesiastical

duties and functions. This sacrament confers not only grace but spiritual power also—power over the real and Mystical Body of Jesus Christ.

2. THE STEPS TO THE PRIESTHOOD

There are ascending steps in the conferring of the powers and graces of Holy Orders, each approaching closer to the Holy Eucharist. These are usually referred to as the four minor and the three major orders, seven in all.

a. Tonsure

Preceding the reception of the first minor order, tonsure is conferred. Tonsure, from the Latin *tondere*, to shear, or cut, is a sacred rite which changes a person from the lay to the clerical status. The ceremony consists in cutting the hair in five places in the form of a cross, to indicate the renunciation of the world; and in the reception of the surplice, indicative of the "new man created according to God."

b. The Four Minor Orders

The first of the minor orders is that of *porter* or doorkeeper, then comes the lector or *reader* of certain lessons or scriptural passages; next the *exorcist* who receives and once used the power to exorcise or cast devils out of possessed persons—a function now usually reserved to priests. Fourth and last of the minor orders comes the order of *acolyte* which confers the power to serve at the altar, to carry the candles, light the lamps, and to present the wine and water which is to be changed into the Holy Eucharist.

Kenneth Rogers, Atlanta, Ga.

THE CONTEMPLATIVE LIFE

By cutting himself off completely from the world and from all secular pursuits, and by dedicating himself in poverty and silence to the glory of God by the supernatural perfecting of his own soul, the contemplative chooses a life, than which no other is of greater service to man—than which no other is closer to that life of eternal praise and peace which is the lot of the blessed in heaven.

c. The Major Orders

Following tonsure and the four minor orders the candidate, if he is deemed worthy, is promoted to the first of the major orders, the *subdiaconate* in which among other things, he receives the sacred vestments of that office, is given the power to handle and prepare the sacred vessels, and obliges himself to a life of celibacy by a solemn vow of chastity.

The minor orders and the subdiaconate are of ecclesiastical institution; that is, they were established by the Church. However, the second major order, the *diaconate,* is of divine institution and it confers definite spiritual powers, for it enables the deacon to preach the word of God, to baptize solemnly, and to give Holy Communion. A deacon may not exercise these powers without permission granted for a sufficient cause.

All the orders which we have thus far considered are a preparation for the final step, the *priesthood* of Jesus Christ, which confers the power to offer sacrifice and to communicate to the faithful the real Body of Jesus Christ, to baptize, to forgive sins, to preach and to perform all the sacred functions the priestly office entails. By being ordained a priest a man becomes, as it were, another Christ, distributing the grace of God.

The priest during the ordination ceremony receives the stole, the sign of priestly power, and the chasuble, the Mass vestment symbolic of Christ's all-inclusive charity. His hands are anointed with the oil of catechumens, and a chalice containing water and wine, and a paten holding an unconsecrated host are placed in his hands. The ceremony is impressive with symbolism and venerable with antiquity.

←——

Courtesy of the Far East

SEMINARIANS

Prayer, study, recreation, sleep—such is the life of a seminarian as he prepares himself for the priesthood.

The *episcopacy* is not considered by all as a separate major order, but is looked upon rather as the conferring of the fulness of the power of Christ's priesthood, including the power to consecrate other priests and bishops, to administer Confirmation and to rule in Christ's Church as a successor of the Apostles.

3. THE OUTWARD SIGN OF HOLY ORDERS

Each sacrament, as you remember, has an *outward sign* by which its grace is signified and conferred. This outward sign is composed of two parts called matter and form. In the *minor orders* the *matter* is the handing over to the person on whom the order is to be conferred, of the respective instruments such as the keys, the book of lessons, the book of exorcisms, and the candle and cruets. The *form* for the minor orders, as indeed for all the orders, is found in the words which accompany the action by which the instruments are presented.

In the *subdiaconate* the matter is the handing over of the chalice and paten and the book of Epistles. In the *diaconate, priesthood,* and *episcopacy* it is the imposition of hands which constitutes the matter of the sacrament as all theologians agree, although some claim that the handing over of the book of the Gospels or a Missal in the diaconate and the handling of the chalice and paten in the priesthood also are part of the matter. In practice there is no difficulty, for both are always done.

4. WHO MAY ADMINISTER AND RECEIVE HOLY ORDERS?

The bishop is the *ordinary minister* of Holy Orders. Cardinals and abbots who are not bishops, together with others who have a special indult from the Apostolic

←

Far East Photo.

SEAT OF WISDOM

This statue of Our Lady, Seat of Wisdom, stands in St. Mary's Seminary, Baltimore—the oldest seminary in the United States.

See, may confer certain orders, usually tonsure and the minor orders. They are thus the *extraordinary ministers* of Holy Orders.

As for the *subject* of Holy Orders, that is, the person who can be ordained, the general principle is this: Any validly baptized male can be validly ordained. Thus a baby boy who has been baptized could receive Holy Orders. It would, however, be gravely sinful to confer the sacrament on an infant, and he would be allowed to make his own free choice of state when he had attained sufficient use of reason. For an adult to be validly ordained he must have the desire and intention to receive the sacrament.

5. THE EFFECTS OF HOLY ORDERS

Some of the effects of Holy Orders have already been mentioned; to summarize them here they are these four:

a) The sacrament of Holy Orders confers the *power* to exercise certain sacred functions, as for example, offering the Holy Sacrifice of the Mass. This, as you may recall from last year, is known as the power of orders.

b) Moreover, like all the other sacraments of the living, Holy Orders increases *sanctifying grace* in the soul.

c) Thirdly, like the other sacraments, it also confers special *sacramental graces* peculiar to this sacrament, giving the right to the actual graces needed for the proper discharge of the order received.

d) Lastly, Holy Orders, like Baptism and Confirmation, imprints a special, indelible spiritual mark or *character* on the soul, in this case the mark of a sacred minister of Christ's Church. This mark will remain for all eternity —a priest will be recognizable as such forever.

The religious life, strictly so called—that is the life devoted to Christian perfection, lived in a community, and made stable by the three vows to observe the evangelical counsels of poverty, chastity, and obedience—is lived not only by priests of religious orders but also by brothers, nuns and sisters. Let us now turn to the first of these.

D. THE BROTHERHOODS

Besides the call to the priesthood in either the diocesan clergy or that of a religious order or congregation, there is a third possibility for a Catholic young man—the religious state in the various Brotherhoods.

In most religious communities of men there are both clerical and lay members—priests and brothers. In some, all or most of the members are brothers. Many of these brothers have deliberately renounced any aspirations to the priesthood although they may possess the mental, moral, and physical qualifications. They do this in order to be free to devote themselves without interference of other duties to such noble tasks as teaching in schools, high schools, and colleges.

1. KINDS OF BROTHERS

Brothers do any and all kinds of work for God and for souls. There are three prominent divisions: working brothers, nursing brothers, and teaching brothers. Their name indicates their chief occupations.

As far as the working brothers are concerned some of them are mechanics, carpenters, gardeners. Others do farming, printing, janitorial work. Some do the cooking, others administer the temporal affairs and property of the community, and so on, but all of them in addition to these pursuits have their regular daily religious exercises and sanctify themselves and others by observance of their vows.

Nursing brothers, like the Alexian Brothers, are able to do tremendous service to souls in the spiritual as well as the physical care of the sick. The contribution of the teaching brothers to the progress of religion and the welfare of mankind is difficult to estimate; it is so far-reaching.

There are some communities of brothers like the Christian Brothers or Brothers of the Christian Schools and the Xaverian Brothers who have no priests; while others, like the Brothers of the Society of Mary and the Congregation of the Holy Cross have both priests and brothers. In addition to these, remember, as we said above, nearly every one of the hundred or more religious orders of men in the United States accepts brothers in various capacities.

If you wish to learn about the various communities of brothers look up the article "Lay Brothers," or the names of the various communities in the *Catholic Encyclopedia*. You can find a list of all of them in the *Official Catholic Directory*. You could also read some books such as the following:

The Training of a Brother—Congregation of the Holy Cross, Notre Dame.

Brother Ernest's *Our Brothers*—Scott-Foresman.

Rev. E. F. Garesché's *Teaching for God*—Loyola Press.

National Catholic Almanac, 1941—*Franciscan Clerics*.

2. NEED OF BROTHERS

There is today great need for brothers of all kinds; a fact which may mean that many young men to whom God has given the call are neglecting it. The thing for anyone to do if he is in doubt whether or not he has a vocation to the religious life of a brother is to *test it out* by becoming a candidate for a period, usually of six months, at the end of which time both he and the community are usually able to tell if the candidate should be accepted into the novitiate.

Persons who are interested in the spread of Christ's kingdom on earth will pray for vocations to the brotherhoods. They will learn of the work of the brothers and make it known, that others hearing of it may be attracted and join them. Finally they will encourage worthy aspirants to dedicate their lives in this noble state which in many ways calls for much greater sacrifices of one's own will and desires than does the priesthood, diocesan or religious. Can you think of any other good ways to encourage vocations to this state of life?

3. SIGNS OF A VOCATION

The signs of a vocation to be a brother are in general

the same as those for choosing the religious state, attention being called to the fact that the qualifications, especially the mental qualifications, may vary greatly depending on the type of work to be done.

4. PREPARATION AND TRAINING OF A BROTHER

The preparation for the life of a religious brother usually begins with a period known as the *postulancy* which in some communities commences as early as the first year of high school. After this, the young man is given the religious habit and is admitted to the *novitiate* if he has completed his fifteenth year and is judged fit. The novitiate lasts one or usually two years, one of which is to be spent in spiritual preparation and formation in the religious life. It includes a retreat, instructions, prayers in common, meditation, and study.

The brother also receives the special training for his work. If he is to teach he finishes high school—should he have entered before graduation—and he completes his teacher preparation in a normal school or college. Teaching brothers are highly educated men, many possessing masters' and some even doctors' degrees.

Having completed at least the minimum preparation necessary for their work, the brothers begin their life career, joining to their daily work further study and training to become ever more proficient in their selected tasks. They also devote themselves every day to the religious exercises prescribed by their rule, for the main purpose for which brothers and all other religious choose that state of life is their own sanctification and salvation and the greater glory of God.

E. THE RELIGIOUS LIFE FOR WOMEN

Although Christ our Lord in His divine wisdom did not see fit to admit women to the sacrament of Holy Orders, he has called them, even as he has called men, to

the state of highest perfection. In fact, the most perfect purely human being is a woman, our Mother, the Blessed Virgin Mary.

1. THE ACTIVE AND THE CONTEMPLATIVE LIFE

As with the men, the religious orders and congregations of women are divided into contemplative, active, and mixed. Just as the men have the strictly cloistered Carthusians and Trappists or Cistercians, so do the women glory in the life of the greatest self-abnegation in orders such as the Carmelites, the Franciscan Poor Clares, and others. Cut off completely from the world and its distractions, they pray and work for God and the souls He has created. By their great function of public worship of God, and by the severity of the penances they impose upon themselves for the good of others, they contribute more to the welfare of the world than most men realize.

Other communities do not withdraw from the world so completely. They also devote themselves to the duty of worship by direct acts of the virtue of religion, but to prayer and meditation they join external works of charity. They can be said to lead the active or mixed life in religion.

A PRAYER FOR CHOOSING A STATE OF LIFE

O my God, Thou who art the God of wisdom and good counsel, Thou who readest in my heart a sincere desire to please Thee alone and to direct myself in regard to my choice of a state in life, in conformity with Thy holy will in all things; by the intercession of the most holy Virgin, my Mother, and of my Patron Saints, grant me the grace to know that state of life which I ought to choose, and to embrace it when known, in order that thus I may seek Thy glory and increase it, work out my own salvation and deserve the heavenly reward which Thou hast promised to those who do Thy holy will. Amen.

300 days, once a day. *Raccolta* (official edition), p. 544.

TRAPPISTS AT PRAYER

The Trappist monks at Conyers, Georgia, recite the Divine Office in their austere choir stalls.

2. THE VOWS OF RELIGION

Like brothers and priests belonging to religious orders, all professed members of the religious institutes of women bind themselves to strive for Christian perfection and toward that end take the three vows of religion: poverty, chastity, and obedience. By these vows they renounce for God, first, worldly possessions, and secondly, bodily pleasures; thirdly, they submit their wills to a religious superior whom they obey as the instrument of the will of God.

a. The Vows and the Evangelical Counsels

By observing these three vows a religious fulfills the evangelical counsels, that is, the Gospel advice given by our Lord. In regard to *poverty,* the first and lowest step in this self-denial, Christ in His talk with the young rich man said: "If thou wilt be perfect, go, sell what thou hast, and give to the poor." Matt. 19, 21. He completed this statement by saying, "and come, follow Me." Thereby Christ recommended the third and most difficult of the evangelical counsels—that which asks us to give up our own will and desires and to practice perfect *obedience* to the will of God by cheerfully complying with the commands of a superior. The second counsel, *chastity,* was recommended by Christ in that same chapter of St. Matthew when, reestablishing the law of the unity of marriage, which had been relaxed under the Mosaic dispensation, He ended His teaching by praising those who deny themselves the pleasures of the flesh for the sake of the kingdom of heaven. While admitting that not all are called to accept this, He concluded by saying: "Let him accept it who can." Matt. 19, 12.

b. Solemn and Simple Vows

In some religious orders of women these vows are *solemn,* which means among other things that they are more firm and binding, that they prevent a valid marriage, and that they are much more difficult to dispense. All vows which are not declared solemn by the Church are *simple vows.* In all religious communities the first vows are simple, and in most communities the final vows are also *simple* although perpetual. Both solemn and simple vows bind under pain of mortal sin.

It might be well at this point to review what you learned in your freshman year or in the elementary school in regard to vows, their nature, kinds, and obligation.

3. TYPES OF WORK PERFORMED BY ACTIVE ORDERS OF WOMEN

"The greatest religious fact in the United States," said Bishop Spaulding some years ago, "is the Catholic school system." It is a tribute to the sisters engaged in the active life in the profession of educating and teaching our Catholic children. This is the phase of the active life in which the majority of our nuns and sisters are engaged. Large numbers also are to be found in hospitals, in orphanages, and in institutions for the care of the aged, the crippled, the deaf, the blind, the insane, the wayward and the delinquent. Many also are in missionary fields at home and abroad, acting as catechists or performing any of the countless other corporal or spiritual acts of mercy that go to make up a sister's life.

Do you know of any other types of work in which sisters are engaged, or can you describe the details involved in any of those enumerated above? Would the scarcity of nuns lead you to believe that many girls are receiving a call from God but are neglecting it?

4. AIDS IN DECIDING

The young woman in making up her mind as to whether she is called to the religious life or not, and if so to what particular type, has the same aids as the boy in deciding whether to be a priest or brother. Though the final decision in all cases must be made by the person concerned, the advice of one's confessor, parents, teachers, and other persons capable of giving prudent guidance should be sought and carefully weighed. Prayer to the Holy Spirit and our Blessed Lady for light and courage are prerequisites, and an examination of one's self for

Correggio   *By Ewing Galloway, N. Y.*

THE MYSTIC MARRIAGE OF ST. CATHERINE

St. Catherine, by cooperating with God's grace, achieved that highest union with God by love, which spiritual writers call "Mystical Marriage." She became indeed a spouse of Jesus Christ.

Women who enter the religious life and bind themselves by vow to the practice of Christian perfection by the fulfillment of the three evangelical counsels also unite themselves to Christ in love. For this reason they are often referred to as Spouses of Christ or Brides of Christ. For this reason also some religious orders prescribe that on the day of entry into the religious life the new candidates attire themselves as brides.

the absence of any impediments and the possession of the required qualifications are also necessary.

5. CORRECT UNDERSTANDING OF THE RELIGIOUS LIFE

All Catholics and young people in particular should know at least the essential facts about the religious life, both for their own information and guidance, and to enable them to guide others, perhaps their own children, some day. In this way they can prepare themselves to correct the numerous erroneous ideas which many uninstructed Catholics as well as most non-Catholics entertain concerning convents and monasteries and the religious life in general. If you want to find out some of these queer ideas look into such books as the *Question Box, Radio Replies* or the like.

For the girl who is considering entering the religious state such information is necessary and it should be secured by consultation, visitation, or by reading books on the subject that are sensible and not ultra-romantic. Life in a convent is not a lark; neither is it unwilling slavery. It is a life of abnegation, freely chosen, and it can be made very happy by a deep personal love of God and His Divine Son and an abiding charity towards the souls created and redeemed by Him. Accordingly, it is wise to look ahead not only to the immediate demands of the novitiate but also to the subsequent obligations of the religious life. It is beyond the possibilities of a textbook to supply this information on the many communities, but the *Related Readings* will supply much information on this matter.

6. THE GREAT NEED FOR MORE VOCATIONS

The Church in our country, and in many other countries, is prevented from growing and developing as much and as quickly as it should by a great dearth of religious vocations, especially among the girls. God is undoubtedly issuing the call and giving the necessary grace, but it is

LORD, WHAT SHALL I BE?

being neglected. Can you think of things in modern life which would smother a vocation or cause a boy or girl to neglect God's call? What remedies are called for?

Would one reason for the falling off in the number of vocations be that many have never learned that sacrifice of self is the key to happiness and that they have accepted the anti-Christian doctrine that pleasure is man's final goal? Would other reasons be that they have given themselves over to an almost completely externalized life, deliberately plunging into unceasing activity lest the small voice of conscience be heard; that they have been misled by much reading of over-romantic literature; that the girls have allowed creatures like finery and jewelry and parties and perfume to ensnare their hearts and to befuddle their usual common sense?

A vocation is a fragile flower. Like an orchid it needs sacrificing care and protection. It must not be exposed to searing heat or killing frost. It should not be put out unguarded to compete with weeds and hardy plants in the fields of the world; it should be shielded, and put in the nursery of the novitiate or seminary until it is properly developed and full blown.

7. TESTING THE VOCATION

At the same time a vocation must be tested. The Church has carefully arranged for this, testing a young woman's adaptation to convent life.

First, there is the *postulancy* which lasts at least six months in communities taking perpetual vows. Then the candidate enters the *novitiate,* is clothed in the habit, and usually receives the white veil. Here the testing and preparation become more intensive.

Under the direction of a novice-mistress and separated from the rest of the community, the novices receive their training and spiritual preparation for a period of one or usually two years. At the end of the novitiate the candidate, if willing and judged worthy and adapted to the life, is called by the Church to make her profession and to take *temporary simple vows* for a specified number of years. These temporary vows may be repeated for another period and then, usually after six years, comes the infallible sign of a vocation, the *official call* issued by and for the Church to take the *final or perpetual vows,* simple or solemn, according to the community concerned. There is no danger, then, of entering into the convent and taking perpetual vows when one does not have a vocation. A young woman has years to think it over; to test herself and be tested. And even after this, if the case justifies it, there is still the possibility of a dispensation.

8. THE PROS AND CONS OF RELIGIOUS LIFE

a. Sacrifices Demanded by the Religious Life

The sacrifices demanded by the religious life are many and not easy. The observance of the evangelical counsels demands control of the three strongest wayward tendencies in human nature: pride, covetousness, lust. The renunciation of the pleasant association of home and friends and of the possibility of a home and family of one's own are by no means small sacrifices to many. The leading of a common life, subject to rule and thrown together with many persons, all of whose personalities will not be equally attractive—these and other things demand abnegation, self-control, and sacrifice.

b. Happiness of a Life of Service

Yet these very sacrifices lead a person to a life of closer union with God; they allow her to follow in the footsteps of Jesus Christ, practicing the virtues of a divinely perfect life. They permit her to satisfy an urge which is deep in the heart of all human beings, the urge to make a worthwhile contribution to the world in which we live.

The religious life enables one to serve our Lord and Saviour, Jesus Christ, in the person of people He has

created, but especially those who have been made sanctified members of His Mystical Body. To those who really
love God, this is happiness enough for all the sacrifices
they may be called upon to make. But added to it there
are the joys of living together with people of the same
high ideals, the happiness of being occupied in congenial
work, and many other satisfactions, difficult to describe
and hard to enumerate. But best of all is that peace, and
contentment, and satisfaction that results from a life of
unstinting sacrifice and service.

God made me to do something or to be something for
which no one else was made. When I find it and do it I
can be supremely happy.

REVIEW OF SECTION TWO.

SECTION THREE: THE UNMARRIED STATE IN THE WORLD

We now come to the second road—the unmarried state,
or the state of virginity in the world. This road is traveled
perhaps by fewer people than any of the three, and with
reason, for it is not easy to save one's soul when unsup-
ported by the special graces of the religious life on one
hand, or the special helps and safeguards of the state of
matrimony on the other.

A. ADVISABILITY OF THE UNMARRIED STATE

Virginity is a higher state than the married life, but
the unmarried state in the world is usually not to be advised. It is a matter, however, which depends on circumstances, and if God wishes a person to choose this state of
life He will supply the necessary graces to meet its greater
temptations and problems. Fundamentally, the choice of
this state is a matter of motives.

1. A MATTER OF MOTIVES

Some persons who are in the unmarried state are there
because of *unworthy motives,* such as selfishness, a desire

to enjoy greater freedom, an unwillingness to follow an inclination towards the married state and its obligations, or the religious life and its abnegations. A person who chooses the unmarried life because ot these or other unworthy motives may find it extremely difficult to save his soul. It is dangerous to make personal pleasure and comfort the basis for selecting a state in life, when the glory of God and the salvation of one's soul is the only safe basis.

There are, however, *worthy motives* which make the choice of the unmarried state a noble decision, and in some cases perhaps an even greater act of self-sacrifice than the religious life. Such would be a desire to serve and support others as, for instance, aged parents or relatives, a desire to allow younger brothers and sisters to enjoy the advantages of a Catholic education, or the conviction that one can best serve God and save his soul by remaining in the unmarried state in the world.

Some, particularly girls, remain unmarried because the opportunity of a suitable marriage did not present itself; others, however, pass up reasonable opportunities. Suffering from "movie-mirage" they determine to wait for some fabulous partner who is a combination of movie star, multimillionaire, and saint. They forget that they may be lacking a few perfections themselves.

B. DIFFICULTIES OF THIS STATE

Before a person chooses the unmarried state he should have a talk with his confessor or other qualified persons and consider the special difficulties which this vocation presents.

First, there is the necessity of leading a life of *virginal purity* and absolute continence without the special assistance of the graces of the religious life and against the numerous and constant temptations of a pagan-minded world. Over a short period of time this might not be serious, but over the span of a lifetime there is great danger

THE CATHEDRAL OF NOTRE DAME
Rheims, France
As it looked before World War I.

of being gradually anaesthetized into moral blindness and lack of spiritual sensitivity by the influence of the non-Christian culture and standards and attitudes of the world in which one must daily live.

Another thing to be considered before choosing the life of virginity in the world is the problem of *loneliness* especially in old age. In the religious life one has the necessary companionship; so too in marriage, especially when blessed by a large family. But the single person in the world can be very lonely. If the person is really called by God to this state His grace will be sufficient to enable him or her to meet the situation, but if the choice were unwisely made it may be a grievous burden to be left alone in the evening of life.

SECTION FOUR: CAREERS

A. CAREERS FOR MEN
1. KINDS OF JOBS
2. FINDING THE RIGHT JOB
3. CATHOLIC EDUCATION AND CATHOLIC LEADERSHIP

B. CAREERS FOR WOMEN
1. THE NOBLEST CAREER—THE CHRISTIAN MOTHER-EDUCATOR
2. OTHER FIELDS
3. A CAREER AND MARRIAGE?
   a. The Alleged Excuse
   b. The Catholic Remedy

It is not only necessary to choose the right state of life, but within that state Christian prudence requires that we place ourselves there where our talents will be of most use to God, to ourselves, and to our fellowmen. At times this choice is easily made. Yet God leads some people by His secret, and often devious, but ever wise ways; as for instance the priest who was kept teaching Greek, much against his will, for more than ten years, but who felt it was all repaid when he was able to hear and understand enough of the confession of a modern Greek to give him absolution on his deathbed.

There are many more different kinds of careers and many more varied types of occupations than most young people are aware of. A recent United States census showed that there were over 20,000 different types of work in which people were occupied. A prudent Christian does not just drift along life's way. God has given him an intellect and He expects him to use it to plan his life. Certainly the choice of a fitting career is an essential in this plan and has a definite influence on the work of saving our soul. It is to be highly recommended, therefore, that boys especially make a detailed study of the main classification of careers or jobs in relation to their abilities.

In choosing a career Catholic boys and girls should remember that the Church and the world need men and women who are ready to forego serving their own little selfish purposes and are prepared to devote themselves to serving God and their fellow men. In business and industry, in journalism and radio, in government and in science there is a crying dearth of men who are willing to serve the cause of Christ and of humanity even at the cost of great personal sacrifice. Key men must dedicate their lives to the task of preparing themselves for and getting themselves into key positions where they can present and explain and defend the true principles and practices which can alone save a sick world.

A. CAREERS FOR MEN

The great majority of men in our country are now employed, and in the future will be employed, in occupations to which there is attached no glamour or public acclaim. Work is and always will remain work—a medicinal punishment for sin. "In the sweat of thy brow shalt thou eat bread," said God to Adam and his offspring.

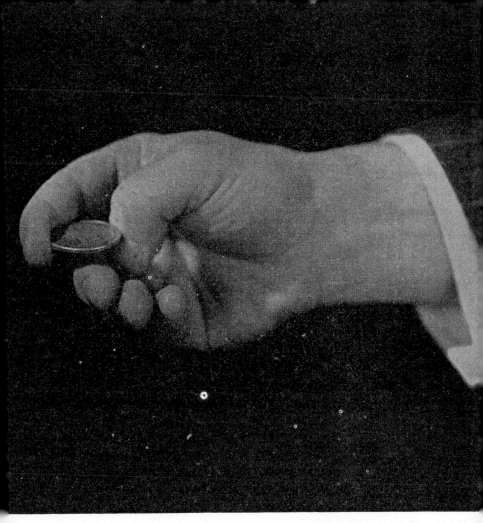

Philip Gendreau, N. Y.

NO WAY TO CHOOSE A VOCATION!

A toss of the coin may be a proper way to choose one's goal in a football game; but in selecting one's state in life, it would be a poor method indeed. God gives us our intellect and His grace to help us choose aright.

1. KINDS OF JOBS

By far the largest percentage of jobs to be found require little initial skill or training. On the average only one person in seven is needed in the professions and in the management positions; and about one in five in the skilled occupations. Many are needed in industry, agriculture, distribution.

The young man planning his future should face this fact and determine whether he has or can develop in himself the necessary qualifications for the more honored positions. If not, he should recognize that normally there are thousands of more or less simple tasks to be done— some interesting and challenging, others quite colorless.

2. FINDING THE RIGHT JOB

God has created men of many degrees of ability and temperament and if they find the work for which He has given them the capacity they can be most happy themselves and at the same time useful to their fellowmen. Moreover, their work may be as necessary and beneficial to mankind as many of the so-called better jobs.

Did you ever consider that the man who collects the garbage and cleans the street contributes to a community's health and well-being as much or more than the doctor? Without the aid of these men in checking the growth and spread of deadly germs, the doctor might strive in vain to maintain a community in health. The importance of the farmer, the factory worker, the truck driver, the store clerk needs but be considered to be appreciated.

The Christian realizes that his reward and place in heaven does not depend on his social or financial status on earth but on how well or how poorly he employed the graces and talents which God bestowed on him for the honor of his heavenly Father and for the service of mankind.

It is hardly necessary to remark that men should not be satisfied with lesser jobs if God has given them the talents with which to serve their fellowmen better and if they can as safely save their souls in the better calling.

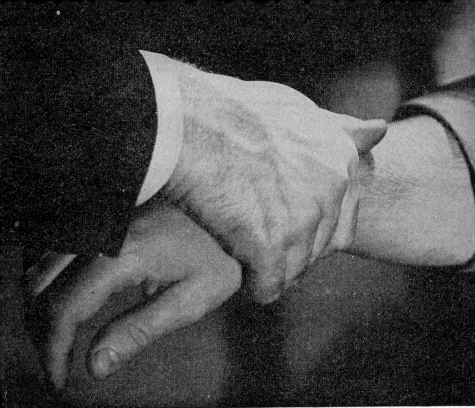

Philip Gendreau, N. Y.

SERVING GOD'S CHILDREN IN THE MEDICAL PROFESSION

Medicine is a noble calling when pursued nobly.
A good Catholic doctor serves God by caring for the physical life and health of men's bodies. He also finds countless opportunities for helping them to the grace that gives supernatural life and health to their immortal souls. A full measure of devout service in this state, free from the taint of avarice, and full of the cheerfulness of giving, is a benediction on earth and a joy in heaven.

At the same time persons of lesser ability should recognize that all cannot be "white-collar" workers. Such self-delusion creates social unrest which favors communistic agitation.

3. CATHOLIC EDUCATION AND CATHOLIC LEADERSHIP

As only a minor percent of our Catholic youth, however, are able to enjoy the benefits of a Catholic high school education, the percentage of those in our schools who dedicate themselves to the task of preparing for leadership in all fields should be greater than in public high schools. Catholic high school students should appreciate the fact that they must carry the burden for those not thus privileged. And they must realize their responsibilities to prepare themselves by earnest study and persevering work for the task of serving God's Church and of leading our nation and our world to happiness, to peace, and to God.

All men seek the truth. All human minds are attracted by truth, as all human wills are drawn by goodness. America needs leaders! Catholic high school boys and girls should prepare and be prepared for leadership, for they alone have, in their fulness, the sound principles on which a happy future can be built. But they must *learn* these principles. They must *preach* these principles. They must *live* these principles. Senior! The Catholic Church invites you and challenges you to *be a Christian Leader!*

B. CAREERS FOR WOMEN

1. THE NOBLEST CAREER—THE CHRISTIAN MOTHER-EDUCATOR

What shall it be, a career or marriage? This is the silly question many women whom God has not called to the convent ask themselves. As if the grandest career in all this world, next only to the religious life, were not the art of being a perfect *Christian mother!* Indeed, Pope Pius XII has said: "Every woman is made to be a mother- -a mother in the physical meaning of the word, or in the more spiritual and exalted, but no less real, sense."

What are social work, and teaching, and nursing, and journalism, and all other positions compared with the task of taking living human personalities, one's own flesh and blood, and molding them, with the help of God's grace, into images of Jesus Christ! Indeed all these activities are part of the work of a mother. Truly then, the greatest career for a Christian woman, outside the religious life, is that of a Christian wife and mother. Here a woman can do the most good. Here is the career for which a woman is by nature best adapted. And, as most women ultimately choose this career and spend the greater part of their adult years in it, they have an *obligation in conscience to prepare* themselves for the proper fulfillment of its duties: the care of a house, the rearing of children, the selection and preparation of food, and all the rest.

Many women today, under the influence of the non-Christian standards and attitudes of our times, and motivated by pride and selfishness, choose a "career" in preference to marriage. Some, indeed, have a just reason. Many, it seems, do not.

2. OTHER FIELDS

There are many opportunities for those who have a good cause for choosing the unmarried state in the world, as well as for those who wish some career which they will follow for a time without detriment to the proper preparation for their main career—marriage. In each of the basic fields for women: professional, social, commercial, industrial, and domestic, there are a great variety of opportunities. We cannot list them here, but you could look them up and report on them.

3. A CAREER AND MARRIAGE?

Lastly, there is the problem of a career *and* marriage. Are they compatible? Can one have a career without detriment to the family obligations? The answer is "No," except in the most rare cases. The founding of a happy home and the bearing and training of children is in itself such a big career that it requires the undivided effort and attention of any woman.

a. The Alleged Excuse

It is not unusual today for married women to be gainfully employed outside the home. It is often said that modern conditions make it necessary for the wife to work. Occasionally that may be so, but for the most part is it not true that frequently the reason will be found in a covetous desire for earthly possessions and luxuries?

Do not many young people expect to begin married life at the same level as that reached by their parents after years of sacrifice, hard labor, and careful saving? Have not many young women learned to spend all their earnings on themselves, instead of regularly saving a portion of their salary so as to bring a reasonable dowry into marriage, as in justice, they should? Is it not a fact that after marriage they are unwilling to abandon this unreasonably high standard of living and insist upon working because they say they cannot live on their husband's salary?

Would it not be better for many women to get married earlier, without having worked or started on a career, and without having built up habits that, times without number in the past, have made husbands discontented, homes unhappy, divorces frequent, and society restless? Would not men's wages be higher if women did not compete with men for jobs?

b. The Catholic Remedy

If it is true that the family "encounters difficulties by reason of the fact that the man and wife are in straitened circumstances," as Pope Pius XI said in his encyclical on Christian Marriage, the general remedy lies not in "a job for every wife" nor in degrading, enervating govern-

←

Raffaellino del Garbo *Philip Gendreau, N. Y.*

VIRGIN AND CHILD

ment relief and subsidy, or local charity, but in a *"living family wage"* for every husband and prospective husband. This is the proper goal for society and all good citizens, Pope Pius maintained, citing the same principle from Pope Leo XIII.

REVIEW OF SECTIONS THREE AND FOUR.

SECTION FIVE: THE HOLY STATE OF MATRIMONY (PART ONE)

A. IMPORTANCE OF THE TOPIC
B. NATURE OF MARRIAGE
  1. MARRIAGE IS A CONTRACT
  2. THE NATURE OF A CONTRACT
  3. CONDITIONS OF A VALID CONTRACT
  4. THE MATRIMONIAL CONTRACT
    a. Essential Nature, Purposes, Conditions Fixed by God
    b. Requisites for a Valid Marriage Contract
      1) Persons Capable of Marrying
      2) Mutual Consent
      3) Matter Subject to Contractual Obligations
      4) Observance of Prescribed Formalities
    c. Effects of the Matrimonial Contract
  5. DIVISIONS OF MATRIMONY
  6. QUALITIES OF MARRIAGE:
    a. Unity
    b. Indissolubility
    c. Necessity of these Qualities in Marriage
  7. THE PURPOSE OF MARRIAGE
    a. The Essential Purposes of Marriage
      1) Procreation of Offspring—Primary
      2) Mutual Help and Allaying of Concupiscence—Secondary
    b. Other Purposes of Marriage
    c. False Modern Ideas on the Purpose of Marriage
      1) Happiness not the Prime Purpose of Marriage
      2) Sources of False Ideas on Marriage

A. IMPORTANCE OF THE TOPIC

We must now turn our attention to the third road leading to the gate marked "Eternity"! It is the crowded road called *matrimony*. It is crowded because God so constituted human nature that, for the great majority of men and women, it is the safest way to heaven. By reason, then, of the numbers who choose this state, it is important. But there are other reasons why it is important.

Much of the trouble in our modern world can be traced to a disregard of the laws of nature and the laws of God concerning marriage. You can most likely point to cases in your own immediate neighborhood or among your acquaintances, which illustrate the religious and social consequences of disobeying the laws of marriage. If you want a classic example from history you could discuss the results of Henry VIII's disregard of marriage laws. It has helped keep a whole nation in heresy for four centuries.

The third reason for the importance of this topic is the fact that the sacred union of husband and wife effected by the contract of marriage is vital for the continuation of the human race on earth and the salvation of immortal souls.

B. NATURE OF MARRIAGE

1. MARRIAGE IS A CONTRACT

Matrimony or marriage is a *contract* between a man and a woman—a sacred contract. It is both a natural contract and, for Christians, a sacrament. We shall first consider marriage in its essential nature, that is, in those things which are common to it both as a sacred natural contract and as a sacrament. First, what is a contract?

2. THE NATURE OF A CONTRACT

A contract is *an act of the human will* consisting in an agreement between two or more people, about a certain matter or right. Marriage is a mutual agreement between a man and a woman, with God as a silent third partner. By this agreement the man and woman consent to live together as man and wife, and they mutually accept those responsibilities and confer upon each other those rights and privileges which are necessary for the begetting and rearing of children for God, and for the sanctification of their own souls.

3. CONDITIONS FOR A VALID CONTRACT

Because *marriage is essentially a contract,* it is necessary to understand well the conditions for entering into a valid contract. What we will say here will be true of all contracts.

Perhaps you can already answer the question: What is necessary for a binding contract? The usual conditions for a valid contract are these:

1. Persons capable of making a contract.
2. Mutual consent.
3. A matter subject to contractual obligations.
4. Observance of the prescribed formalities.

As regards the first condition for a valid contract, namely, persons capable of making a binding contract, would you think an idiot or an insane person could make and be held to a contract? or an infant? or a drunken person? Of course not! To enter a contract a person must have *sufficient use of reason.* In addition to this, there may be other restrictions set up by law which render a person unable to make a valid contract. For instance, minors usually need the consent or approval of their parents in matters of some importance. According to the civil law in most states marriage is such a matter.

The second requirement for a valid contract is *mutual consent,* freely given and with sufficient knowledge of the nature of the thing one contracts to do. A person who signs or agrees to a contract because someone holds a gun at his back is not free and consequently the contract is not valid.

Thirdly, the matter on which the contracting parties agree must be something which is possible, good, and under the control and possession of the persons who make the contract. A man could not agree to sell Lake Erie and move it to Texas. First, he does not own it, and secondly, the thing is physically impossible. Neither could a person make a valid contract to commit murder for a certain amount of money.

Girolamo da Santa Croce　　　　　　*National Gallery of Art, Kress Collection*

THE ANNUNCIATION

At this moment, Mary, the ever blessed and spotless Virgin, became Mother of God.

Lastly, the law may require that certain formalities be observed before it will recognize a contract as valid. For instance, it may require witnesses, signed and dated agreements, and the like.

4. THE MATRIMONIAL CONTRACT IN PARTICULAR

Marriage is a contract. But it is a contract which, in certain important respects, is different from any other contract. Marriage, even as a natural and civil contract, is *sacred;* and for Christians this contract is also a *sacrament.* The sacramental character of marriage will be explained later. Here we are speaking about marriage, whether sacramental or not, as a sacred contract.

a. Its Essential Nature, Purposes, Conditions Fixed by God

The nature, purposes, and conditions of other contracts are usually left to the will of the parties concerned. This is not the case with the marriage contract. In marriage *the essential nature, purposes, and conditions of the contract* have been *fixed by God* Himself, the author of matrimony. Gen. 1, 27-28 and 2, 18-24. The marriage contract, therefore, must be accepted unchanged in all its essentials as God has instituted it. The contracting parties are free to marry or not to marry as they see fit. They are free to add any lawful condition to the contract as, for instance, regarding division of property; but *they are not free to reject any of the essentials of marriage* either as regards its nature, or its purpose, or its conditions; neither may they change any of these essentials. *In all basic essentials the marriage contract must be accepted as God instituted it.*

If the contracting parties make a marriage contract in which one of the essential qualities or purposes is rejected or has been changed or omitted, the contract *is invalid;* in other words, it is no contract, no marriage. In this matter of marriage, then, the rule is: take it as God instituted it or leave it. Man cannot change it.

The encyclical of Pius XI on Christian Marriage clearly states this when it declares:

"The sacred partnership of marriage is constituted both by the will of God and the will of man. From God comes the very institution of marriage, the ends for which it was instituted, the laws that govern it, the blessings that flow from it; while man, through generous surrender of his own person made to another for the whole span of life, becomes, with the help and cooperation of God, the author of each particular marriage."*

*Five Great Encyclicals—Paulist Press, New York—1939, p. 79.

b. Requisites for a Valid Marriage Contract

We have studied the requisites for a valid contract in general; let us now apply these to the marriage contract.

1) Persons Capable of Marrying

First, we must have *persons capable* of validly and licitly making such a contract. This means that both the man and woman must have sufficient use of reason to know the nature of marriage and its obligations. It means that they cannot be already validly married to another person; that they are not held by any impediments; and that they are physically capable of consummating the union by the sacred physical relationship which marriage implies.

2) Mutual Consent

Secondly, there must be *mutual consent* on the part of the two persons concerned. If only one party consents, there is no marriage contract, no marriage. If a parent forces a girl into a marriage, and the girl even goes through the ceremony and says the words but absolutely does not consent to the marriage, there is no contract, no marriage. This fact, however, of lack of consent may be difficult or impossible to prove in an ecclesiastical court.

3) Matter Subject to Contractual Obligations

The third requisite for a valid contract is that the contract concern itself with a matter subject to contractual obligations. As regards marriage, this matter is the right which the contracting parties mutually give and accept to perform that holy act which has for its purpose the generation of human lives for God's glory.

4) Observing of Prescribed Formalities

Lastly, there are the prescribed formalities. Marriage of and by itself requires no definite formalities; but since

Church and State have prescribed certain formalities, they must be observed. Usually these consist in this, that the marriage contract be made in the presence of witnesses and also in the presence of an authorized person.

c. The Effects of the Matrimonial Contract

Marriage is a mutual agreement about a definite matter. It has certain effects. First, it produces a *matrimonial bond* between the two parties, binding them to the duties and entitling them to the rights which marriage implies.

A second effect of matrimony is the reception of the right and duty to rear, *educate and train children* for heaven. What this includes shall be seen later.

Third, by marriage the man is constituted *head of the family,* for as St. Paul says, "The husband is head of the wife, as Christ is head of the Church." Eph. 5, 23. The wife, as you learned in your sophomore year, is not a slave of the husband, but a helper and companion enjoying all the rights of a human being, although subject to the husband in the administration of the family.

Next it requires them to lead a *common life* according to the word of Genesis—that a man shall leave mother and father and cling to his wife.

As a result of the marriage contract, the two parties have an *obligation to be faithful* to one another to the exclusion of all others, to observe strict conjugal chastity, and to love one another with a deep, abiding, life-long love. These obligations when fulfilled make for happy marriages.

Among other effects, by marriage a wife takes the family name of the husband and his residence; he is obliged

$\longrightarrow$

Flemish Tapestry   *Courtesy of the Metropolitan Museum of Art*
Fifteenth Century

   The upper left panel portrays an artist's conception of the marriage of Adam and Eve in the Garden of Eden. Beneath it, a sixteenth-century wedding is depicted. On the upper right David begins his life's work by being anointed by Samuel. Below a dying man receives Extreme Unction.

to support her, and she is obliged to make her contribution of service to the mutual well-being. Concerning this matter of finances, however, it might be well to remind young married people and prospective spouses that they should look to the deliberate simplicity of the home in Nazareth for their cue to happiness.

5. DIVISIONS OF MATRIMONY

A marriage may be legitimate or ratified; and either a legitimate or a ratified marriage may be consummated or not.

A *legitimate* marriage is a valid but *non-sacramental* marriage between *non-baptized* persons. It results in a sacred natural bond.

A *ratified* marriage is a valid *sacramental* marriage between *two baptized persons,* which has not yet been confirmed or consummated by living together as husband and wife.

A *consummated* marriage is a valid marriage, whether legitimate or ratified, which has been confirmed and completed by living together in the relationship of husband and wife.

6. QUALITIES OF MARRIAGE: UNITY AND INDISSOLUBILITY

Matrimony has two chief qualities or characteristics: unity and indissolubility.

a. Unity

Unity means that marriage may take place only between one man and one woman. When God instituted matrimony He decreed that marriage should be monogamous (*mono,* one; *gamy,* marriage to). "They shall be two in one flesh." Later on, our Lord informs us that, because of the hardness of the hearts of the Jews, God, under the Mosaic dispensation, permitted polygamy (*poly,* many; *gamy,* marriage to).

The original law of monogamy, however, was *rein-stated by Christ* for the entire human race. When, in discussing this question, the Pharisees asked Him: "Is it lawful for a man to put away his wife?" Christ replied: "Whoever puts away his wife, except for immorality, and marries another, commits adultery; and he who marries a woman who has been put away commits adultery." Matt. 19, 9. You can read the whole discussion of this topic in Matthew 19, 3-12.

St. Paul clarified the whole question when he said: "Do you not know brethren . . . that the Law has dominion over a man as long as he lives? For the married woman is bound by the Law while her husband is alive; but if her husband die, she is set free from the law of her husband. Therefore, while her husband is alive, she will be called an adulteress if she be with another man; but if her husband dies, she is set free from the law of the husband, so that she is not an adulteress if she has been with another man." Rom. 7, 1-3. Cf. 1 Cor. 7, 39-40.

The Catholic Church, therefore, speaking for Jesus Christ and with His authority insists on the unity of marriage—one man and one woman, until death dissolves the bond. Remarriage after the death of one's lawful spouse is not forbidden.

b. Indissolubility

In the same passage in St. Matthew in which Christ teaches the world the unity of marriage He also teaches the second great quality of matrimony—indissolubility. As this will be treated more in detail later, in connection with divorce, we will restrict ourselves here to a brief presentation of the basic principles in this matter of indissolubility.

First, a man and woman once having entered a valid marriage contract have no power to dissolve that contract.

Secondly, no person or institution on earth, whether in the Church or in the State, has the power to dissolve a ratified, that is, a sacramental marriage, which has been consummated. *No power on earth can dissolve a ratified consummated marriage.*

Thirdly, if a *ratified* marriage has *not* yet been *consummated* the bond is not yet indissoluble and the pope, in special cases, has power to dissolve such a bond.

Moreover, as the fourth basic principle, the bond of a *legitimate,* that is, non-sacramental marriage, even if consummated, can be dissolved by the so-called *Pauline Privilege,* the scriptural authorization of which may be found in 1 Cor. 7, 12-16.

An example of a case in which a legitimate, non-sacramental marriage can be dissolved by this Pauline Privilege is as follows: two non-baptized persons enter a valid, legitimate, non-sacramental marriage with one another. After their marriage one of these parties is converted to the true Faith, and the other party refuses to live peaceably with the new Catholic. In this case Christ our Lord granted a privilege in favor of the Faith, namely, that the newly-converted party could marry *another Catholic,* the former matrimonial bond of the legitimate marriage being dissolved at the moment the new sacramental bond is formed. This Pauline Privilege may not be used if the non-Christian party is willing to live in peace with the Catholic. There are many more details to it than we have time to explain here.

From what we have just said it can be seen that the bond of a legitimate, that is, a non-sacramental marriage, and of a non-consummated marriage can be dissolved under certain circumstances; but the bond of a ratified (sacramental) and consummated marriage can be dissolved only by the death of one of the parties. No power on earth either in the Church or in the State can dissolve it. Remember this when you study divorce.

c. Necessity of Unity and Indissolubility of Marriage

Both unity and indissolubility are necessary qualities

of marriage if it is to attain the purposes for which God instituted it. Reasons affecting both the individuals and society demand these two qualities in the marriage bond. Perhaps you can think of many of these reasons. Let us mention just one or two. If a man were allowed to have more than one wife at a time there would be dissension, discontent, and jealousy between the wives and between their families. The opposite situation of a wife having a plurality of husbands at the same time is a violation of the laws of nature, as is proved by the fact that it prevents the primary purpose of marriage, the procreation of children.

We shall not delve any deeper into this question of the necessity of these characteristics of marriage, as the matter of indissolubility will be handled later when considering divorce. The necessity of unity both for the individual and for society will become clearer as we study the next topic. You would do well, nevertheless, to read what Pope Pius XI says in his encyclical on Christian Marriage about this and other topics upon which we have touched.

7. THE PURPOSE OF MATRIMONY

a. The Essential Purpose of Marriage

The essential purposes of matrimony have been determined by God himself. Of these essential purposes one is primary, another is secondary. The *essential primary purpose* of marriage is the *procreation and proper rearing of children.*

God created two sexes and instituted marriage in order thus to provide for the continuation of the human race on earth and to fill with human beings the places in heaven lost by the fallen angels. In the Garden of Eden God said to Adam and Eve, "Increase and multiply and fill the earth." Gen. 1, 28. The first and most important purpose of marriage, then, is children—children to glorify God and to be glorified by Him.

This means not only the bringing of children into the world, but, even more, the training, the forming, the instructing and educating of those children so that they will be able to lead good and useful lives on earth and, above all, attain to eternal salvation. This is the chief purpose of marriage. This is why a man and a woman must form a stable, indissoluble union.

Does the dignity of marriage now dawn upon you? Does its importance begin to become clear?

If the essential primary purpose of marriage is children and their eternal salvation, the *essential secondary purposes* of marriage also have a relation to the salvation of souls, this time *the salvation of the souls of the husband and wife*. These essential secondary purposes are the following:

1) *The mutual assistance* of husband and wife in all things, especially in their spiritual welfare, and in the saving of their own souls; in domestic affairs, in the rearing of the children.

2) The *quieting of concupiscence* by providing a holy and a lawful outlet for the satisfaction of those tendencies which God has placed in human nature to insure the continuation of the race on earth and the peopling of heaven with saints.

God has created in human beings a strong attraction between man and woman. By His grace He makes it possible for some, whether in the religious life or in the unmarried life in the world, to lead a life of virginity and to control this tendency of concupiscence without the slightest indulgence. In others, this tendency is stronger or God's grace is less freely given, and for these people God has supplied the grace of the holy state of matrimony to allow them, without sin, to satisfy this tendency and beget souls for Him. Thus matrimony is a remedy for concupiscence, and another proof of God's loving solicitude for our eternal salvation.

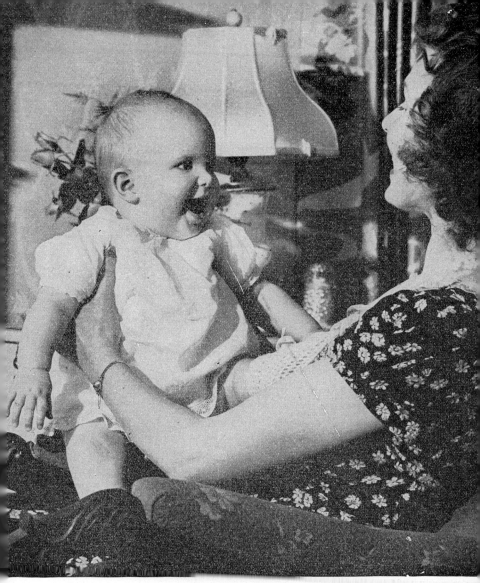

Philip Gendreau, N. Y.

CHILDREN: THE PURPOSE OF MARRIAGE

God instituted the holy state of matrimony that He might bring immortal souls into existence, and indeed, that He might bring them into this world under the protection of a stable family unit that would have the right and duty of forming the children unto the image of God.

255

b. Other Purposes of Marriage

Marriage, like all created institutions, is ultimately for the glory of God and the sanctification of souls. Marriage can and should be, to a man and woman, a means of "perfecting themselves in the interior life," and of advancing "ever more and more in virtue," as the encyclical on marriage says. In fact, if matrimony be viewed in a broad way the "earnest pursuit of helping one another to perfection, may in a very real sense be regarded . . . as the elemental cause and reason for matrimony."

Without doubt, people have many reasons for getting married, some good — love, companionship, security; others not so good—passion, pleasure, money. God and His Church have no objection to any of these additional purposes or reasons for marriage if they are good and if they do not oppose or prevent the attainment of the essential purposes—procreation and proper rearing of children; mutual help and the allaying of concupiscence of the parties. The higher the motives which inspire the parties to the marriage the nobler will the union be and the more likely to achieve the full measure of happiness and blessing which God intends it to confer.

c. False Modern Ideas on the Purpose of Marriage

Our hardly-Christian world is full of pagan ideas and irreligious theories as to the purpose of marriage. Perhaps you know some of them. Perhaps you yourself have already accepted some of these evil principles without realizing how shockingly opposed to the teaching of Christ and the welfare of the human race they really are. Many Catholics have been deceived into adopting some of these errors, and it is up to you to learn the truth about the purpose of marriage and help set these misguided people right.

—>

Donatello   *National Gallery of Art, Mellon Collection*

THE VIRGIN MOTHER WITH HER CHILD

1) Happiness Is Not the Primary Purpose of Marriage

The primary purpose of marriage is not the pleasure or happiness of the contracting parties. The primary purpose of marriage is souls for heaven—children. All else is secondary. God does indeed intend that a man and woman should enjoy deep happiness in marriage; He does allow them great pleasure in order to lead them to assume the none-too-light burdens of rearing a family. But this happiness, this *pleasure is not the first purpose of matrimony* and to make it such is to offend God.

2) Sources of False Ideas on Marriage

The *movies* have created many of these erroneous ideas. Produced largely by persons guided by non-Christian moral principles, the movies have built up—deliberately it almost seems—ideas about morals which have been condemned by Christ. They have made "love" the great aim of marriage. "I have a right to be happy" emotes the poor "mistreated" heroine, as she throws herself, married woman though she may be, into the arms of her big, good-looking "lover," married though he may be. Have you swallowed any of this sort of trash? Have you "fallen for" such anti-Christian propaganda? Or have you been wise enough to see that movie "love" is often only gilded lust? Analyze a number of current or recent movies to discover how some of them strive to influence our people to form false ideas as to the purposes of matrimony.

The same sort of poison is hidden in many *romantic novels and magazine stories*. One often suspects that those who write and publish them hope to wreck Christian civilization by ruining Christian morals and destroying the foundations of society so that the world revolution of the communists may make our country a welter of blood. Are we going to stand idly by and permit such a condition to develop? Do we not have an obligation to shout forth the truth that *true love* is identical with *sacrifice?* Christ proved that. But the modern world tries to tell us that love is a selfish thing, based on the pleasure it gives, that a man loves a woman when he gets pleasure from being with her. But Christ has shown us that he who loves forgets self and serves others. This is Christian love, even in marriage.

REVIEW OF SECTION FIVE.

SECTION SIX: THE HOLY STATE OF MATRIMONY (PART TWO)

C. MATRIMONY AS A SACRAMENT
   1. MATRIMONY AND THE ESSENTIALS OF A SACRAMENT
   2. PRESCRIBED FORMALITIES FOR A VALID MARRIAGE
     a. Justice of Peace Marriages Not Valid for Catholics
     b. Marriages of Non-Catholics
   3. EFFECTS OF THE SACRAMENT OF MATRIMONY
     a. Increase of Grace of Justification
     b. Sacramental Graces
   4. THE BLESSINGS OF MATRIMONY
     a. Offspring
     b. Conjugal Faithfulness
     c. Indissolubility and Sacramentality
   5. OBLIGATIONS OF THE MARRIED STATE
     a. Duties to One Another
     b. Duties to Children

D. MODERN ERRORS CONCERNING MATRIMONY
   1. BASIC ANSWER TO ERRORS
   2. BASIC FALSE PRINCIPLE CAUSING ERRORS AND EVILS
   3. VICES OPPOSED TO CHRISTIAN MARRIAGE
     a. Contrary to the Blessing of Offspring
       1) Frustrating Power of Marriage Act to Generate Life
         a) A Violation of Natural Law—Intrinsically Evil
         b) Causes of, or "Excuses" Offered for Birth Control
       2) Killing The Unborn
       3) Sterilization
     b. Contrary to the Blessing of Conjugal Fidelity
       1) Adultery
       2) Unchristian "Emancipation" of Woman
       3) Incompatibility
     c. Contrary to the Blessing of the Sacrament
       1) Marriage, A Completely Civil Function?
       2) Mixed Marriages
         a) Disparity of Cult and Mixed Religion
         b) Church Law Forbids Mixed Marriages
         c) Reasons for Forbidding
         d) Conditions For Dispensing with Law
         e) How to Avoid Mixed Marriages
       3) Divorce
         a) Church's Teaching on Divorce
         b) Scripture concerning Divorce
         c) The Church and Civil Divorce
         d) Ecclesiastical Separation
         e) Declaration of Nullity

E. REMEDIES FOR THE ABUSES AND ERRORS OPPOSED TO MATRIMONY
  1. BASIC PRINCIPLES FOR CORRECTING ERRORS AND ABUSES
     a. Return to the Divine Plan—Exemplar of All Right Order
     b. Means to This End

F. THE MATRIMONIAL IMPEDIMENTS
  1. DIRIMENT IMPEDIMENTS
  2. PROHIBITING OR IMPEDING IMPEDIMENTS
  3. DISPENSATIONS

C. MATRIMONY AS A SACRAMENT

Up to this point we have been discussing marriage mostly as a natural contract. Even as such every marriage is sacred, but for Christians marriage is more than that. *For Christians, the matrimonial contract is a sacrament.* For Christians the marriage contract is one of those seven sacred signs to which Christ has given the power to confer grace, *ex opere operato.*

The Council of Trent says: "If anyone says that Matrimony is not truly and properly one of the seven sacraments of the evangelical law instituted by our Lord Jesus Christ, but that it was invented by man and that it does not give grace, let him be anathema."

It might be useful at this point to review for the last time in our high-school career, the *essentials of a sacrament* and to apply them to this great sacrament of Matrimony.

1. MATRIMONY AND THE ESSENTIALS OF A SACRAMENT

A sacrament is an external sign, comprised of matter and form, instituted by Christ, to signify and confer grace. Some sacraments were instituted to give grace to a soul sunk in the death of sin. These are the two sacraments of the dead. The other five presuppose that the person receiving them is already in the state of friendship with God.

$\longrightarrow$

Raphael   *From Ewing Galloway, N. Y.*

THE ESPOUSAL OF THE BLESSED VIRGIN

They increase grace. Among these latter is Matrimony which must be received in the state of grace before it can confer the special graces it bears.

Christ did not institute marriage as a state. That existed from the beginning. But Christ did institute Matrimony as a sacrament. He took the holy contract of marriage, raised it to a higher plane and gave it special supernatural powers it did not possess before. By it He caused special graces to flow into the lives of Christians, graces most helpful and necessary for a happy, successful marriage.

Our Lord took the outward sign which had always constituted marriage—the outward sign of a mutual agreement between a man and a woman to take one another for husband and wife—and He gave this external sign the power to confer grace when the contract was made between Christians.

The matter and form are somewhat different in this sacrament of Matrimony than they are in the other sacraments. The *matter* of the sacrament of Matrimony is the matter of the contract—the right to those sacred relations which constitute marriage. These are the remote matter. The proximate matter is the mutual offering and giving of that right. The *form* is the mutual acceptance of that right by some external sign. The matrimonial contract therefore includes the matter and form of the sacrament.

2. PRESCRIBED FORMALITIES FOR A VALID MARRIAGE

A Catholic is either married right or he is not married at all, even though he goes through a marriage ceremony. The Church prescribes two formalities in making the contract and giving consent. These formalities must be observed, otherwise the marriage contract is not valid, that is, there is no real marriage. The first of these is this: A Catholic of the Latin rite cannot be validly married except by the *pastor of the parish* in which the marriage

takes place or by a priest delegated by him or by the
bishop. The second is that *two witnesses* must be present
for the validity of the marriage contract.

All Catholics of the Latin rite are bound by these for
malities, whether they marry another Catholic or a non-
Catholic. The priest of course is only a necessary witness,
not the minister of the sacrament of matrimony. The
contracting parties are themselves the ministers of this
sacrament.

Before the time of the Council of Trent, the presence of
the priest was not required for a valid marriage, as it
is not the blessing of the priest but the consent of the
parties which makes the contract, confers the sacrament,
and produces the marriage bond. Now, however, the
presence of an authorized priest is required by the law of
the Church, so that marriages not performed by him are
not valid, that is, are not marriages.

The only exception made to the compliance with these
formalities would be an emergency marriage when one of
the parties is in *danger of death* or when it is foreseen
that a duly authorized priest cannot be had within a
month. This latter situation might arise in sparsely settled
regions, especially in the winter. In these very exceptional
cases the matrimonial agreement entered into in the *presence of two witnesses* would be valid if everything else
were in order.

a. Justice of Peace Marriage Not Marriage for Catholics

If you have grasped the foregoing it will be clear to you
that *any* Catholic who goes through a marriage ceremony
before a *justice of peace* or any other civil magistrate is *not
married* at all, even if she or he be recognized and held as
married by the civil law. Moreover, a person who is guilty
of an act which shows such a lack of faith and gives
such scandal, commits a mortal sin which the Church

considers very grave. Some bishops reserve the power to absolve from it to themselves, as it is an offense which borders at least on a denial of faith.

Moreover, if a Catholic should attempt marriage by going through a marriage ceremony before a *non-Catholic clergyman,* he or she suffers *excommunication* and is suspected of heresy. Matrimony is a sacrament and to go to a non-Catholic minister to be married is just as sinful as going to one to be baptized. It shows either great ignorance or partial or complete loss of faith.

We now have learned the two requirements for a valid marriage when one or both of the parties is a Catholic—namely, marriage in the presence of an authorized priest and before two witnesses. In addition to these, there are many other details which the Church prescribes in order that the marriage may be licit or lawful—prescriptions, for example, as to time, place, banns, impediments, etc., etc. We shall discuss these in detail as we proceed.

To see if you have grasped what has been said on this point, discuss the following problems and answer the questions.

Problems: 1. John, a Catholic, got "married" by the court. He says he is married, all right, but just not married "in the eyes of the Church." Enlighten poor benighted John as to the true situation.

2. Edward, an Episcopalian, asks Joseph, a Catholic, to be "best man" at his wedding to Joseph's sister, Louise, also a Catholic, at the Episcopal church. May Joseph accept? Why? May Joseph be a baptismal sponsor for any of Edward's children? Why? What about Louise and her marriage?

b. Marriages of Non-Catholics

Although all validly baptized persons are bound by the laws of the Church, when both baptized parties are non-Catholic they are excused from these formalities. Thus, a

THE CATHEDRAL
Rouen, France

marriage between two validly baptized Protestants before a justice of peace is both valid and sacramental. A marriage between non-baptized persons is not subject to the laws of the Church. However, it is subject to the laws of nature and to the just prescriptions of civil authority. If it complies with the requirements of natural law and civil law it is a valid though non-sacramental marriage. The bond such a marriage produces is not as firm as the sacramental bond.

3. EFFECTS OF THE SACRAMENT OF MATRIMONY

The effects produced by the *natural contract* of matrimony we have discussed above. They include the matrimonial bond, the obligation of leading a common life, the installation of the husband as head in the family circle, the right and duty to rear and educate the children, the duty of fidelity and chastity and love, and the other effects regarding name, residence, support, property, and so forth. In addition to all these effects produced by every valid matrimonial contract there are some very *special effects* which only Christians receive, because for them the matrimonial contract is a sacrament.

a. An Increase of the Grace of Justification

The first of these sacramental effects is an *increase of sanctifying* grace, that is, the producing in the soul of a greater likeness to God, a fuller participation in the divine nature by grace.

In connection with the increase of grace by the reception of Matrimony we should recall that in order to receive a sacrament of the living with fruit, it is necessary to be in the state of grace. For a Catholic, then, to be married while in the state of mortal sin is to commit another mortal sin and to be guilty of a great sacrilege. Sac-

raments are holy things. And Matrimony is a sacrament.
Such a marriage would of course be valid, if everything
else were in order, but it would confer no grace until such
a time as the guilty party made an act of perfect contrition
or love or made a good confession.

b. Sacramental Graces

The second effect of the sacrament of matrimony is the
conferring of special *sacramental graces* which are available to the Christian husband and wife during their entire
married life. Among these can be mentioned: 1) the elevation and *sanctification of the love* of husband and wife,
lifting it from the base thing it often is to a beautiful, holy,
sacred love that resembles the love of Christ for His Spouse
the Church, which love and union is the model for the love
of Christian spouses; 2) special sacramental graces which
enable the parties more easily to *bear each other's weak-
nesses* and to withstand the trials and temptations of married life—you certainly ought to be able to mention quite
a few of these when you think of the duties of fathers and
mothers—3) the grace to help parents to *rear and form
their children* properly and carefully as children of God,
loaned to them from on high and committed to them for
training.

The use of and cooperation with these graces is, of
course, essential.

Much of the foregoing as well as the following material of this treatment on marriage deals with matters
which have been emphasized in the *Encyclical on Christian Marriage* by Pope Pius XI and follows in general the
sequence of that encyclical. It may be well, therefore, to
include on pages 268-269 a brief outline of that encyclical,
and to recommend that you read and discuss at least some
sections of the encyclical in class.

OUTLINE OF THE ENCYCLICAL *CASTI CONNUBII* ON CHRISTIAN MARRIAGE, OF POPE PIUS XI

INTRODUCTION

Dignity of marriage—Made a Sacrament.
Need of 1) Knowledge as to nature of Matrimony.
       2) Grace to think and act with Christ.
Growing errors and evils against marriage.
Matters to be treated in the Encyclical.
    1) Nature and dignity of Christian marriage.
    2) Advantages and benefits to family and society.
    3) Errors concerning matrimony.
    4) Vices opposed to conjugal union.
    5) Principal Remedies to be applied.

1. NATURE OF MATRIMONY and ITS BLESSINGS.

A. Fundamental principles regarding nature of marriage.
Marriage instituted and restored by God.
Free contract between parties necessary.
Base unions must be opposed.
Freedom to marry must be safeguarded.
Institution, ends, laws, and blessings of marriage from God.

B. Blessings of Matrimony.
    1. Blessing of OFFSPRING.
    Value of human being.
    Members of God's household.
    Education and training of children—right and duty of parents.
    2. Blessing of CONJUGAL FIDELITY.
    Its nature.
    Is based on *unity* of marriage.
    Also on conjugal *chastity* in act and desire.
    Blooms when rooted in mutual *love*.
        Husband is head.
        Dignity and liberty of wife.
        Obedience of wife.
    3. Blessing of the SACRAMENT.
    (Indissolubility and sacramentality.)
    Indissolubility and firmness of bond.
        True in all marriages.
        Rare exceptions—not dependent on human will.
    Benefits of indissolubility.
        Guarantees stability to spouses.
        Defends chastity.
        Mutual aid.
        Necessary for rearing children and social well being.
    Sacramental benefits.
        Sanctifying and actual graces.
        Need of cooperating with these graces.

2. ERRORS AND EVILS OPPOSED TO MATRIMONY.

Errors are spread openly.
Writings, theatre, novels, movies, etc.
Basic Principle of these errors and evils:
    Matrimony claimed not divinely instituted nor a sacrament
        —but invented by man.
    Proof of error of this principle.
    Temporary, experimental, companionate unions.

A. Evils opposed to the Blessing of OFFSPRING.
   1. Sinful avoidance of having children.
      This is intrinsically against nature.
      Church condemns it; confessors must oppose it.
      Observance of God's law is possible.
   2. Taking life of unborn infants.
      No one has power to destroy life of child.
      Public authority should protect unborn.
   3. Sterilization.
      State has no direct power over body except for crime.
      Individual may not mutilate own body.
B. Evils opposed to the blessing of CONJUGAL FAITH.
   1. Adultery.
   2. "Emancipation" of woman: social, economic, physiological. Debases woman.
   3. Compatibility of temperament as basis of bond.
C. Evils opposed to the blessing of the SACRAMENT.
   1. False claim that marriage is a purely profane and civil affair.
      Even natural contract is sacred.
   2. Mixed marriages.
      Cause loss of faith and growing indifference.
      Lack of unity of mind and heart.
   3. Divorce.
      Four arguments advanced for it.
      Refutation of these arguments.
         Law of God, confirmed by Christ.
         Infallible decree of Council of Trent.
      Separation may be allowed.
      Benefits of indissolubility.
      Evils arising from divorce.

3. REMEDIES FOR THESE ABUSES.
   1. Basic Principle—return to the divine plan for right order of nature.
      Lust, the great cause of sins against Matrimony.
      Remedy for it—subjection to God, sense of duty and reverence for Him.
   2. Supernatural means.
      Prayer and the *sacraments,* devotion to God.
   3. Submit reason in humble obedience to the Church.
   4. No undue trust in our own reason.
      Be guided by Church and Supreme Pontiff.
   5. Thorough instruction of faithful concerning Matrimony (intellect).
   6. Bishops, priests, laity welded together by Catholic Action oppose error by truth; vice, by chastity; etc.
   7. Instructions should avoid exaggerated physiological emphasis.
      This teaches art of sinning not chastity
   8. Strong determination of husband and wife to observe divine and natural laws on marriage (will).
   9. Faithful fulfillment of duties by married parties.
  10. Proper preparation for marriage.
      Remote: Proper training of self control in child and youth.
      Proximate: Care in choosing a partner.
  11. State to enable man to support family.
      Family wage.
      Rich helping poor.
      State to relieve poor by laws and funds.
  12. Religious authority of Church must be supported by civil ordinances.

4. THE BLESSINGS OF MATRIMONY

a. Offspring—The First Blessing

"Among the blessings of marriage," says the encyclical of Pius XI, on Christian Marriage, *"the child* holds the first place." You know how true this is, for as freshman you learned the grandeur and dignity of the image of God found in a human body and a human soul, especially one which has been given not only a natural but also a supernatural likeness to God by the reception of sanctifying grace. There is no treasure on earth comparable to the riches which is a child, especially a child of God, in whose soul God lives. *Offspring, therefore, are the first blessings of Matrimony.*

b. Conjugal Faithfulness—The Second Blessing

The second blessing is conjugal fidelity. The encyclical says that this "consists in the mutual fidelity of the spouses in fulfilling the marriage contract, so that what belongs to one of the parties by reason of this contract sanctioned by divine law, may not be denied to him or permitted to any third person; nor there be conceded to one of the parties anything which, being contrary to the rights and laws of God and entirely opposed to matrimonial faith, can never be conceded." The elements which compose this blessing of conjugal fidelity are, according to the encyclical: "unity, chastity, charity, and honorable, noble, obedience."

c. Sacramentality and Indissolubility—The Third Blessing

The two previous blessings of marriage are completed and crowned by the blessing of the *Sacrament,* "by which is denoted both the indissolubility of the bond and the raising and hallowing of the contract by Christ Himself whereby He made it an efficacious sign of grace." Firmness, inviolable stability, indissolubility, and sacramentality are all elements in this blessing of the Sacrament.

Raphael

Phillip D. Gendreau, N. Y.

THE MADONNA OF THE CHAIR

5. OBLIGATIONS OF THE MARRIED STATE

In our sophomore year, while studying the fourth commandment we learned the duties of parents to one another and to their children. As the obligation to undertake these duties as well as the grace to fulfill them both spring from the sacrament of Matrimony, it is in place here to review them.

a. Duties to One Another

First, there are the duties to one another. The husband and wife owe one another mutual love, and mutual help in all things, that is, in their physical needs and in their spiritual needs. The husband who really loves his wife will anticipate her needs and wishes, even before they are spoken. So too the wife. Neither will ever let that loving thoughtfulness which characterized the days of their courtship and early married life grow less observant.

b. Duties of Parents to the Children

Secondly, come the obligations of parents *to the children* with whom God blesses them. To each and every child they owe a deep and life-long Christian love. To each and every one they owe care of body, mind, and soul.

On the *spiritual side* parents must cooperate with the Church in her task of bringing supernatural life to men. They must have their children baptized; see that they receive the other sacraments, and train them in the ways of religion.

On the *physical side* parents must provide food, shelter, and clothing. The father should supply the means, while it is the mother's duty to know how to feed and clothe her children properly, so that they may have healthy bodies which will assist them in saving their souls, rather than bodies which will cause discouragement and bitterness because they are weak and sickly due to being improperly fed and cared for.

Parents are also obliged to prepare and *train their*

HOLY FAMILY

The highest ideal of truly Christian family life has been given to the world in
the example of the virtues of the three members of the Holy Family.

children for a state in life in keeping with their condition, and to equip them with that *knowledge* and mould them in those habits which will secure for them the possession of eternal happiness with God in heaven and what earthly happiness and success is compatible with this supreme goal of life.

Parents should train their children in permanent and consistent *good moral habits* from *earliest infancy,* helping them to control the basic tendencies of human nature by the development of the seven basic virtues which underlie a really Christian life. To do this they must first *instruct* their children, that is, illuminate and guide their intellects with correct knowledge. Then they must *train* their children, habituating their wills and bodies to correct ways of acting. Part of their obligation consists in sending them to a Catholic school unless that should be absolutely impossible. But in this matter they should remember that the school relieves parents of only a very small, restricted part of their obligation, even when the children are in school. The home educates; the school instructs.

The world today is in great need of good Christian fathers and valiant Christian mothers who will consecrate their lives to the arduous but richly satisfying task of molding children unto the image of Jesus Christ.

1) Parents' Right to Educate Based on Natural Law

The right and duty to rear and *educate and train children* for heaven is founded in the natural law, that is, it springs from the very nature of the relationship between child and parent, and it may not be taken away from parents who are fulfilling their obligations in this regard. Today there is prevalent in many nations a dangerous and erroneous theory which claims that the State alone has any rights in education and that all rights of parents and Church in education are derived by grant from the State.

Lauren Ford *Courtesy of the Liturgical Arts*

BAPTISM OF ARNAULD

The first obligation of parents as regards the religious care of their children is to have each child baptized as soon as possible after birth. These scenes depict a Catholic baptism in twentieth century France.

In this connection it would be well to summarize the contents of the encyclical on the "Christian Education of Youth" by the same Pope Pius XI. It shows that education belongs to the Church by supernatural right, to the family by natural right, and to the State, only indirectly, in as far as the common welfare requires. It shows that the *whole child* must be educated in body and soul—will as well as mind, for eternity as well as for time, by supernatural means as well as by natural means.

Seeing that parents have these grave duties, those who intend one day to become married and raise a family must prepare themselves for that sacred task. They must learn how to instruct and train their offspring in the habits needed for a successful and happy life on earth and for attaining an eternity of bliss in heaven.

D. MODERN ERRORS CONCERNING MATRIMONY

One of the most important causes of the widespread social unrest of the present day is to be found in the many wrong notions, and in the errors and the vices which are opposed to the true nature of marriage. When family life is not healthy and normal, society is necessarily disturbed. The encyclical on marriage, as you perhaps have noticed, devoted great attention to these matters, listing ten errors or evils opposed to marriage.

1. BASIC ANSWER TO THESE ERRORS

Let us give a *general answer to all these errors* and vices before we go into detail. It is this: The Catholic Church, the infallible voice of Jesus Christ on earth in matters of morality as well as those of doctrine, condemns these theories or proposals as wrong and evil. Good Catholics need know no more, but that they may show how reasonable our position is on these questions it is well for them to know the answers from reason as well as those from faith.

NOTRE DAME

The famous golden dome of the main building at the University of Notre Dame rises in the center of the campus and dominates the entire scene. A great statue of our Lady, her hands in a gesture of invitation, stands atop the dome.

2. BASIC FALSE PRINCIPLE CAUSING THESE ERRORS AND EVILS: MARRIAGE REGARDED AS A HUMAN INSTITUTION

First, let us consider the most dangerous error—the opinion that marriage was not instituted by God or made a sacrament, but was *invented by man*. This fallacy the Pope calls the *basic principle* which is the *source of the evils opposed to matrimony*. We have already proved that God instituted marriage from the words of Genesis; we have proved that it is a sacrament by quoting the decree of the Council of Trent. We can also show the falsity of this principle, that marriage is a human institution, by enumerating the terrible consequences which are the sequels of adopting this theory. Marriage is made a thing of human caprice, social disorder results, there is no stable family union for the proper rearing of children, the smashing of homes follows, with the placing of a premium on impurity, on wilfulness, on infidelity.

Because many wayward or poorly instructed Catholics are acting on or are being influenced by this false principle that marriage is of human origin, the Catholic Church, speaking with an infallible voice, proclaims incessantly that marriage is sacred, having been instituted by God and made a sacrament by Jesus Christ.

3. VICES OPPOSED TO CHRISTIAN MARRIAGE

We have already learned that there are three main blessings of matrimony. There are evils opposed to each of these blessings.

a. Contrary to the Blessing of Offspring

Against the first blessing, offspring, there are three such abuses: the unnatural frustration of conception, abortion, and sterilization.

1) Frustrating the Power of the Marriage Act to Generate Life

The first of these vices is preached as a virtue by the modern apostles of chaos. They call it "birth control," but it is only uncontrolled indulgence in lust. The encyclical says of it: "Since the conjugal act is destined primarily by nature for the begetting of children, those who in exercising it deliberately frustrate its natural power and purpose sin against nature and commit a deed which is shameful and intrinsically vicious."

a) A Violation of Nature's Law—Intrinsically Evil

The power of speech is given to us to convey the truth to others; the appetite for food and drink and the pleasure attached to its indulgence were placed in man by God to lead us to take what nourishment we need to preserve life and health. To enjoy the pleasure which God has placed in an act, while allowing that act to attain the purpose for which God instituted it, is not only no sin but can be a virtue; but to indulge in the act and deliberately frustrate its essential purposes is wrong.

Thus, to use the power of speech to tell a lie is to do a thing intrinsically evil. To indulge the liking for food and drink solely for the pleasure it gives and, like the pagan Romans, to introduce artificial vomiting so as to be able to begin eating and drinking all over again, is an abominable excess. It is the misuse of a gift of God, the enthronement of physical pleasure as the supreme purpose of life; it is an act which can never be permitted or excused for it is intrinsically evil.

$\longrightarrow$

Philip Gendreau, N. Y.

PRAYER—AN ACT OF THE VIRTUE OF RELIGION

The primary essential purpose of marriage is the begetting of new life—the procreation of children—and the formation and training of them unto the image of God in the model of Christ and of Mary His Mother.

The formation and development of children in all good habits is the duty of parents. The Church cares for the supernatural formation; the school helps parents and Church and State. All four should work in perfect unanimity. If even one works at cross-purposes to the others, the success of all is gravely imperiled and impeded.

So too is the indulgence by married people in sexual intercourse when they desecrate the act by the deliberate frustration of its natural effects. They too make physical pleasure the supreme purpose of life. Such an act is intrinsically evil and *no circumstances whatsoever can ever make it good or permissible*. It is a *violation of the natural law*. The Church recommends self-control and continence to married people, but she absolutely condemns and forbids sinful birth control.

In his encyclical on marriage, Pope Pius XI speaking for Christ's Church to the world in a matter of morals says: "Any use whatsoever of matrimony exercised in such a way that the act is deliberately frustrated in its natural power to generate life is an offense against the law of God and of nature and those who indulge in such are branded with the guilt of a grave sin."

The proponents of birth control advance many "arguments" for it. As sophomores you learned the basic principle which proves them wrong: *An act intrinsically bad can never become good no matter what the purposes or excuses, no matter what the circumstances.* The unnatural frustration of conception is an act intrinsically evil. This vice is founded on the false idea that the first purpose of marriage is pleasure. It is directly opposed to the true primary purpose of marriage—children.

After considering what you have just read would you think that a Catholic who refused to accept the teaching of the Church in this matter of birth control should be suspected of heresy?

———

$\longrightarrow$

Richard King   *Courtesy of the Catechetical Guild*

THE SCOURGING

Christ expiated sins of the flesh by enduring the merciless scourging at the pillar. Sins of lust within the holy state of Matrimony play their cruel part in these sufferings of our Divine Saviour.

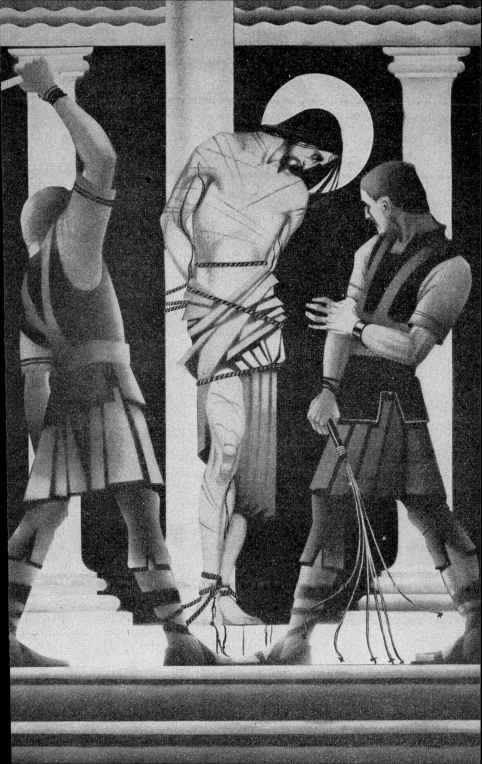

b) Causes or "Excuses" Offered for Birth Control

The causes of birth control and the resultant social calamity of small families may sometimes be partly traced to a wage scale which provides less than a family wage. But American wages and standards of living are the highest in the world. More often, therefore, it arises from a pagan desire for pleasure divorced from duty, or from vanity, or the desire for "freedom," or unwillingness to make sacrifices which accompany the task of bearing and rearing children, from expensive tastes, extravagant living, poor financial management, desire for luxuries, and so forth.

Do you know any of the false reasons people allege in order to excuse themselves for committing this sin? How do you think Christ will deal with them on Judgment Day?

Should Catholic young people advocate simple, inexpensive weddings, very simple engagement and wedding rings, and modestly furnished homes, so as to have money enough to avoid the temptation to limit the size of their family by sinful means?

Would you and your school be interested in gathering together those students who were willing to make a solemn pledge to promote Christian simplicity in these matters? Would you also wish to induce as many as possible to pledge to aid full observance of God's law in these matters by their own personal example and by openly speaking against the principles of the "apostles of doom" wherever they meet them?

2) Killing the Unborn

The second vice, abortion, is the deliberate taking of the life of an unborn infant. It is a form of *murder* and is considered such a heinous crime by the Church that she excommunicates those who are guilty of it or cooperate in it. It sends a human soul into eternity without Baptism.

3) Sterilization

Lastly, there is the vicious practice called sterilization which, by surgical means, interferes with the body's natural power of generation. Individuals may not permit sterilization except when the health of the entire body demands it, neither may the State prescribe sterilization in the vain hope of preventing the birth of defective children.

The Pope gives the following *basic principle* regarding this matter: "Public magistrates have no direct power over the bodies of their subjects; therefore, where no crime has taken place and there is no cause present for grave punishment, they can never directly harm, or tamper with, the integrity of the body, either for the reasons of eugenics or for any other reason."

b. Contrary to the Blessings of Conjugal Fidelity

Against the second blessing of marriage, conjugal fidelity, there is the sin of adultery, the error of false liberty or "emancipation of woman," and the breaking up of a marriage for "incompatibility."

1) Adultery

Marriage permits to husband and wife the enjoyment of the sacred relationship which is the means of begetting children and the object of the marriage contract. This act then is not only no sin for them, but it can and should be an act of virtue, if it is in keeping with the laws of God and of nature. To be unfaithful, however, to one's marriage vows and to permit this relationship to any third party is the grievous sin of adultery for both persons involved. It is a double sin if both are married, for in that case it violates two marriages. Moreover, it is not only a grave sin against chastity but it is also a grave sin against justice. It violates the marriage contract.

ST. NICHOLAS

An ancient story records that St. Nicholas saved three young women from a life of shame and made it possible for them to enter honorable marriages by secretly supplying their father with the dowry which, in former times, was required of a young lady desiring to be married.

Would it promote the leading of truly Christian lives in marriage today if girls who work before being married were expected to bring a proportion of their earnings into the marriage with them? Would it be real Christianity to set this money aside for the purpose of having a fine large Catholic family?

2) Unchristian "Emancipation" of Woman

The second error opposed to the conjugal faith that husband and wife have pledged to one another in solemn contract is the exaggerated emancipation of woman. Woman is not a slave but a helper and companion, possessing the essential liberty of any child of God, yet she is subject in all love to the just authority of the husband. "Let wives be subject to their husbands as to the Lord." Eph. 5,22.

A prevalent modern error, however, would "free" women from all the duties and burdens of the married state, would "emancipate" them from the duty of bearing children, and would allow them to follow careers and manage their own affairs rather than take care of their family and home. It is an attempt to drink all of life's pleasures and avoid all of its duties. Many women who live this way try to ease their consciences by plunging into so-called social-uplift work, but such works of charity and humanitarianism are no substitute for neglected obligations of justice.

3) "Incompatibility"

Concerning the dissolution of a marriage because of alleged incompatibility of temperaments, we shall say but few words. This abuse is so opposed to common sense and reason, so contrary to the finer instincts of any decent man or woman, so wholly inimical to the interests of society and the generation and rearing of souls for heaven that it is easily shown to be the suggestion of persons whose aim is to justify their own lust or to disrupt the home and family and with them Christian civilization.

c. Against the Blessing of the Sacrament

As we have learned above, the third and greatest blessing of matrimony, called that of the sacrament, includes especially the firmness and permanency and indissolubility of marriage and all the graces of the sacrament. Against this blessing there are several great errors or evils; first, the idea that marriage is a completely civil affair to be controlled by the State.

1) Marriage, a Completely Civil Function?

A dangerous error, sponsored by enemies of the Church and accepted by many non-Catholics and at least in part, even by some poorly instructed Catholics, is the false principle that marriage is and should be a completely civil act. It would take away from the Church the right to control and assist at marriages and give this power exclusively to the civil authorities.

Christian marriage is a sacrament, and even non-Christian marriage is a sacred act. This false theory, which favors making marriage a purely civil act, is therefore an attack on the sacredness and sacramentality of marriage and an affront to the religious character of the marital union which is a symbol of the union of Christ and His Church.

Good Christians will oppose this false doctrine by striving to encourage the celebration of all marriages as distinctly religious affairs.

2) Mixed Marriage

We now come to mixed marriage—the second great evil opposed to the third blessing of marriage, for mixed marriages do offend against that unity of mind and heart and soul which should characterize a Christian marriage.

a) Disparity of Cult and Mixed Religion

There are *two kinds* or, one might say, two degrees of mixed marriages. The first and most serious is one in which a baptized Catholic marries an unbaptized person; this is known as *disparity of cult*. The second class also seriously objected to by the Church is the mixed marriage between a Catholic and a heretic—that is, a validly baptized person belonging to some heretical Christian sect, or a schismatic—that is, one who refuses to listen to the proper established authority in the Church. This is known as *mixed religion*.

b) Church Law Forbids Mixed Marriages

The *Sixth Precept* of the Church, as well as the Church's Code of Canon Law forbids mixed marriages not only in cases of disparity of cult but also in cases of mixed religion. Here is the law of the Church concerning the latter case:

Everywhere and with the greatest strictness the Church forbids marriages between baptized persons, one of whom is a Catholic and the other a member of a schismatical or heretical sect; and if there is, added to this, the danger of the falling away of the Catholic party and the perversion of the children, such a marriage is forbidden also by divine law. Canon 1060.

If this is the Church's stand on the milder case, how do you think she regards marriage with a person who is not even validly baptized?

c) Reason for Forbidding Mixed Marriages

Mixed marriages very often lead to a gradual lessening of religious practices, thence to laxity, religious indifference, and loss of faith. These latter cases frequently pass unnoticed, because such persons usually are regarded by their Catholic neighbors as lifelong non-Catholics.

See how many cases of loss or weakening of faith due to mixed marriage you can discover in your own range of knowledge.

The promises which must be made before a mixed marriage is permitted are more often broken than kept. The usual modern attitude of the average non-Catholic on birth-control, divorce, need of Baptism, First Communion, and attendance at Catholic schools, causes great temptations or difficulties to the Catholic party and frequently gives rise to the most bitter arguments and family quarrels. Children of mixed marriages tend to be less strong in the Faith and more prone to indifferentism than children of Catholic marriages. Moreover, the essential unity of mind and heart being absent in all mixed marriages, they are *always less happy,* and frequently absolutely unhappy. The relatively few non-Catholics who come into the Church as a result of mixed marriage are almost unanimous in recommending that the Church should become much more strict in forbidding mixed marriages than she is at present.

d) Conditions under Which the Law May Be Dispensed

The Church has the right to put a complete ban on mixed marriages if she sees fit. At present, it is only with great reluctance that she relaxes the law forbidding the marriage of a Catholic with a baptized non-Catholic, and it is with far more reluctance that she permits a marriage with an unbaptized person. She gives permission for a mixed marriage only if, first, the natural and divine law does not forbid the marriage; if, secondly, there is a genuinely grave reason; and if, thirdly, both the Catholic and non-Catholic party make certain promises.

A grave reason would be, for instance, the case where marriage is necessary because, due to sinful intimacy, a child is to be born, or the case where it is necessary to avert or remove a great scandal or a grave spiritual danger.

Even in these cases, if there were direct and serious danger to the faith of the Catholic or of the children of the marriage, a dispensation could not be granted because the divine and the natural law forbid it. Even the pope cannot dispense from the obligation to observe either of these two laws which are founded in the law of nature established by God.

1) The Promises

The promises are usually in writing and preferably in legally binding form. They are:

1. That all children born of the marriage, boys and girls alike, will be baptized and reared in the Catholic religion.
2. That the Catholic party will be given complete freedom to exercise his or her own religion.

If these two promises are not seriously given with the honest intention of keeping them, the divine law still forbids such a marriage. In addition to these two promises, the local bishop may also require others, as for instance,

Gaddi   *National Gallery of Art, Mellon Collection*

THE MADONNA ENTHRONED

In the center of this triptych is seen our Blessed Lady with the Divine Child. Christ, blessing, appears above. St. Andrew the Apostle and St. Benedict are on the left panel, with Gabriel, the angel of the Annunciation above. On the right are St. Bernard, a great lover of the Blessed Mother, and St. Catherine of Alexandria. Above them is the Virgin Annunciate.

a promise that there will be only the one marriage ceremony, that namely which is performed in the presence of the authorized priest.

The fourth and final requirement before the Church can grant a dispensation for a mixed marriage, is that there be moral certainty that the promises will be faithfully fulfilled.

But even if all these requirements are fulfilled, the Church still is under no compulsion to grant a dispensation, for a *dispensation is a favor* on her part and she has no obligation to grant favors.

e) How to Avoid Mixed Marriages

The best way to avoid being burned is to *keep away from fire*. The best way to keep from the danger of getting embroiled in a mixed marriage is for Catholic young men and women to make it an unbreakable rule to restrict all socializing to Catholic circles and to *avoid all dating and company-keeping with non-Catholics*. The first question to ask in all social contacts is: Is he or she a Catholic? If the answer is "No," the proper reply is, "I'm sorry but I won't be able to make it"—and, *sotto voce,* "My Faith forbids it." In addition, a firm resolution never to marry anyone but a Catholic should be made by all. It is a great help. Catholic parents should forbid their children to date or keep company with non-Catholics. On the other hand, they have the duty of providing their young sons and daughters with opportunities of social contacts with good Catholics.

If a person has allowed herself or himself to become enamored of a non-Catholic who definitely refuses to join the Church, or says he will become a Catholic after marriage, the prescription is: Break it up! Such promises are usually worth about a dime a dozen. They are seldom serious, and hardly ever kept. Ask any priest.

A non-Catholic knows that the Church forbids mixed marriages. If you enter such a marriage, the non-Catholic already has the upper hand, for he knows that he is more important to you than the most serious commands of your Church.

Meditate, too, on the *coldness* of the ceremony for a mixed marriage, and contrast it with the beauty and splendor of a marriage at Mass, with the nuptial blessing, Communion, and all the grand liturgy of the Church. Think also of the fact that there can never be true happiness, with the mind at ease, where wife and husband disagree diametrically on the "one thing necessary," and on many other important if less essential matters.

Think also of this possibility. If a person marries one who is not baptized or whose baptism is invalid—as is often the case with non-Catholic baptisms—the union, although it is a marriage, is certainly *not a sacramental marriage* for the unbaptized person, for only a baptized person can receive a sacrament of the living. Moreover, according to the more common and truer opinion of theologians, even the baptized or Catholic party in such a marriage would not receive a sacrament, and therefore would not receive the sacramental graces needed for a happy, successful marriage. Remember this if you are ever tempted to consider marrying an unbaptized or a doubtfully baptized person.

At the present time there is very little social pressure in Catholic circles against mixed marriages. Can you think of any way by which to make mixed marriage something socially frowned on by your circle? by all Catholics?

3) Divorce

Every graduate of a Catholic high school is to be expected to know the Church's teaching on divorce and the reasons therefor, so that he may not only obey it but also explain it to those who misrepresent or misunderstand it.

Divorce is understood to mean the severing or dissolving of the marriage bond so completely as to permit remarriage.

a) The Church's Teaching Concerning Divorce

The Catholic Church, speaking for and with Jesus Christ, opposes and forbids divorce. She says that the bond of any valid marriage is firm and permanent. She says that the bond of a valid, legitimate marriage, that is, a valid non-sacramental bond is firm and permanent and may not be dissolved except in those rare and thoroughly investigated cases in favor of the Faith. The bond of a ratified but unconsummated marriage she also maintains as firm, and declares that only the profession of solemn perpetual vows or the supreme authority of the Vicar of Christ on earth can dissolve it. The true Church further says, as we have seen, that the bond of a valid, consummated, sacramental marriage is so unbreakably firm that *no power on earth,* in Church or State or anywhere else *is able to dissolve it.* Such is the teaching of the Church, the Infallible Spouse of Jesus Christ.

b) The Scripture Concerning Divorce

In the Garden of Eden God forbade divorce, saying, "A man shall leave father and mother, and cleave to his wife: and they shall be two in one flesh." Gen. 2, 24.

Later He permitted divorce, under the Mosaic Law. Deut. 24, 1-4. Christ our Lord, however, again enforced the law forbidding divorce when He said: "What therefore God has joined together, let no man put asunder." Matt. 19, 6.

When the Jews challenged Him on this point and asked why Moses permitted divorce Christ replied:

"Moses, by reason of the hardness of your heart, permitted you to put away your wives; but it was not so from the beginning. And *I say to you,* that whoever puts away his wife, except for immorality, and marries another, commits adultery; and he who marries a woman who has been put away commits adultery. Matt. 19, 8-9,

By the words "except for immorality" Christ shows that a separation may be granted because of infidelity; but His final words in the passage quoted show that neither divorce nor remarriage is permitted, even in case of infidelity. There may be sufficient cause for separation, but the marriage bond remains intact. This is and remains God's law for all human beings, Catholic or non-Catholic.

THE MIRACULOUS PICTURE AT GUADALUPE, MEXICO

Here, above the Blessed Sacrament exposed on the high altar of the great basilica of Guadalupe, is the miraculous picture of the Blessed Virgin which our Lady caused to appear in the cloak of the Indian, Juan Diego, on the occasion of her second apparition at Guadalupe on Tuesday, December 12th, 1531. Is our Blessed Lady known to have appeared at any other place in the Americas? Is this her first American shrine?

c) The Church and Civil Divorce

The Church has always opposed the granting of divorces by the State and has ever declared that a civil "divorce" has no effect whatsoever on the bond of a valid marriage.

There are circumstances, however, under which the Church permits Catholics to institute civil divorce proceedings because of certain civil or legal effects of a marriage ceremony which the civil law regards as constituting a valid marriage.

Consider this example: Chauncey, a Catholic, but not a very good one, went through a marriage ceremony with Alyce before a justice of the peace. The attempted "marriage" was of course no marriage at all. The contract was invalid because a Catholic, to enter a valid marriage, must make the contract in the presence of a Catholic priest authorized to perform this ceremony. But the civil law considers it a valid marriage. Chauncey finally wakes up, and, realizing that his "marriage" is invalid, breaks up with Alyce. Later he wants to marry another girl. Here a civil decree of divorce from Alyce would be necessary, otherwise Chauncey would be guilty of bigamy in the eyes of the civil law. Remember, however, that it is not a divorce, but only a civil formality, since no marriage bond ever existed between Chauncey and Alyce.

Can you think of other circumstances under which a person would be permitted to secure a similar civil "divorce" decree?

d) Ecclesiastical Separation

Although the Catholic Church forbids divorce, there are circumstances, one of which we have already indicated, in which she permits a separation of husband and wife, the marriage bond remaining intact and remarriage being impossible. This separation may be temporary or permanent, and for natural or supernatural causes; it may be for reasons of virtue, it may be because of the sins of one of the parties. For instance, if a Catholic husband or wife apostatized, or was causing the children to be brought up as non-Catholics, or was a confirmed drunkard, or was gravely endangering the health or eternal salvation of the other party, or was guilty of being unfaithful to the marriage vows, a temporary or even a permanent separation might be permitted or even be necessary. In all such cases, however, the matter is to be submitted to the bishop for his approval.

e) Declaration of Nullity

There are occasions when a man and woman have been living together as husband and wife for years, perhaps, and have raised a family, and still the ecclesiastical court issues a declaration of nullity and the parties concerned proceed to marry someone else. This declaration of nullity is *not a divorce,* it is merely a declaration by the Church, after long and very thorough investigation, that no marriage bond had ever existed between the two parties from the beginning, owing to some hidden defect or impediment in the ceremony or in the persons.

For instance, it has happened more than once that a Beau Brummel suddenly appears in town, sweeps Mary Ann off her feet and gets "married" in church, but contrives somehow to conceal the fact that he has a wife still living. Everyone thinks it a valid marriage, but ten years later when the two people have a family of three or four children, the "wife" discovers the previous marriage and submits it to the matrimonial court of the diocese. After due investigation, the validity of the first marriage is clearly established; the court, therefore, issues a declaration of nullity for the second "marriage" and the "wife" is allowed to marry again, or is "again" the proper word? No? Why not?

Who Can Issue a Declaration of Nullity?

In some cases the bishop or his diocesan tribunal is able to issue the declaration of nullity; in other cases the matter must be referred to the Roman Rota or to the appropriate Roman Congregation. All questions as to the validity of Christian marriages are decided by the Church and her various ecclesiastical courts. In all cases the Church presupposes that an apparent marriage is a valid marriage until the contrary is clearly proved. The ecclesiastical laws on matrimony, however, are extremely intricate and in many involved cases the ordinary person, even the ordinary parish priest, may not be able to give the correct answer. Therefore, *never make rash judgments!*

Famous Marriage Cases

There have been some world-famous declarations of nullity, such as the Marlborough-Vanderbilt case, and the Marconi-O'Brien case.

There have been many more *declarations of validity*, some even more famous; for example, in the marriages of Henry VIII and Catherine of Aragon, and of Count Boni de Castellane and the wealthy American, Anna Gould. If you would read the decisions in these cases you would find how meticulous the Church is before declaring nullity. She always holds a marriage as valid unless it can be proved clearly invalid.

Problems

1. Pretty Helene Anne Martin, a Catholic, marries good-looking, well-to-do J. Carson Smythe, a non-Catholic, after the necessary promises have been made and a dispensation secured. Four years later, after two children have been born, the husband starts "running around" with another woman. Shortly thereafter he abandons Helene

$\longrightarrow$

Press Association, Inc.

HENRY VIII
The Church Refused Him a Divorce

In his younger days Henry was a good and intelligent Catholic. He defended the doctrines of the Church against the heresies of Luther. Getting lax as regards chastity, he fell lower and lower, breaking with the Church, plunging England into schism, confiscating church properties, disrupting countless works of charity, scandalizing a nation—and indeed the whole world—with his adultery, and finally stooping to murder—even the murder of women who had lived with him as wives. Here indeed is striking proof of the necessity of chastity for true social peace and prosperity, as well as for national and domestic happiness and security.

and "marries" the other woman after securing a divorce from Helene Anne, who is given custody of the children. Helene, only twenty-six, has a heartbreaking time of it. After three years of unequal struggle alone, she meets a fine young man and they fall deeply in love—or can it be love? Feeling herself the innocent victim of her first husband's infidelity and saying she has a right to be happy, Helene marries the man before a justice of the peace, knowing she cannot marry him "in the eyes of the Church."

Ten years later her conscience prods her into going to the priest to see if he cannot "fix up" her second marriage and give it the blessing of the Church. What do you think about it? What will the priest advise her to do? Why?

2. James and Loretta, both Catholics, get properly married at a fine ceremony in her parish church. Five years later, after three children have been born, Loretta goes completely insane and is committed to a state institution for life, being declared incurable. After a very difficult struggle for six years James marries Jeannette before a justice of the peace. Was he justified? Is an individual's happiness or the common welfare more important in marriage?

E. REMEDIES FOR THE ABUSES AND ERRORS OPPOSED TO MATRIMONY

Because good marriages are so indispensable, both for the happiness of individuals and for the peace and order of society, Catholic youth must do everything in their power to inform their fellowmen as to the correct principles governing marriage; and then they must exert the full extent of their influence, by word, pen, example, ballot, and in every other way, to lead a pagan world back to *marriage in Christ*.

1. BASIC PRINCIPLE FOR CORRECTING ERRORS AND ABUSES

Pius XI, in his encyclical, gives an extended list of remedies which must be applied to bring about this result. But first he tells us the basic general principle to follow.

a. Return to the Divine Plan—the Exemplar of All Right Order

Pius XI lays down the basic principle that, to bring things which "have deviated from their right order . . . back to that original state which is in harmony with their nature," it is necessary that there be a *"return to the divine plan"* which is "the exemplar of all right order."

The key to this right order is that men subject the lower nature (the body and its passions) to the higher nature (the reason and will), and then that they subject themselves, body and soul, to their Creator and Redeemer and Sanctifier.

b. Means to This End

We will briefly indicate the remedies recommended to achieve this goal. They could be discussed in class.

First, supernatural means are suggested: prayer, reception of the sacraments, the exercise of the virtue of religion.

Second, the submission of the human intellect to the Church in humble obedience and the avoidance of undue reliance on our own reason is proposed.

Third, it is necessary that all men know the correct principles governing marriage. They must, therefore, be told what these principles are.

Fourth, since knowledge alone is not enough, it will be necessary for the laity to bind themselves together with their priests and their bishops, in true Catholic Action, to oppose error with truth, vice with chastity, slavery to created things with detachment, and divorce with unbroken fidelity.

Harmon

FAMILY ENTHRONMENT OF THE SACRED HEART

By gathering together the family and consecrating all its members to the Sacred Heart, enthroned in the home, parents not only invoke the special love and protection of our Blessed Lord on themselves and their children, but, at the same time, they teach their children the value of religion and train them in habits and attitudes which will protect them from sin and lead them to happiness.

Catholics should feel it their sacred duty to encourage what is right in marriage by bringing strong organized *social pressure* against the abuses and errors opposed to true and good marriages, and by giving social support to those who lead the married life as God wishes. Are they doing this today?

Fifth, sex instruction should avoid an exaggerated emphasis on the physiological aspects of sex and marriage, as this only causes sin and temptation.

Sixth, a strong determination on the part of the husband and wife to observe the divine and natural law on marriage will be of great assistance, as will also the faithful fulfillment by both parties of their marital obligations.

Seventh, there must be proper preparation for marriage—a matter which we will study more at length, later in this unit.

Eight, the husband should be assisted in his task of supporting his wife and family by the existence of sound economic conditions. His own savings and financial preparations should be carefully planned and if necessary supplemented by private charity of the rich, and also by the assistance which public authorities can lend by encouraging proper housing, a sufficiency of jobs, a proper balance of prices, wages that free the wife from the necessity of working and that enable the family to secure necessary medical attention, food, and the like.

Lastly, the civil authorities should assist the true Church in her important and necessary task of helping souls to reach heaven.

F. THE MATRIMONIAL IMPEDIMENTS

To safeguard marriage and promote the welfare of the offspring, of the parties, and of society in general, certain impediments to marriage have been created.

An impediment is an obstacle set up by God or by the Church, and prohibiting or preventing a marriage.

Of the impediments set up by God, some of them come from Him by direct positive revelation, as for example, when Christ made it clear that an existing valid marriage prevents the forming of another bond. Other impediments come from God through the natural law, as for example, the impediment of blood relationship in the first degree, and physical incapacity for marriage, that is, impotence.

There are two kinds of marriage impediments: first, diriment impediments, and, second, prohibiting or impedient impediments.

1. THE DIRIMENT IMPEDIMENTS

A diriment impediment is one, the presence of which prevents a marriage contract from being valid. It makes no difference whether the contracting parties are aware of the existence of the impediment or not. If a diriment impediment exists, then no matter how much everything else may appear to be in proper order, no marriage results.

There are thirteen diriment impediments:

1) *Age*. The Church advises young people to get married at an age in keeping with the reasonable laws of the place in which they live. Under no circumstances will she recognize as valid a marriage contract entered into by a Catholic boy before the beginning of his seventeenth year of life, or a Catholic girl before the beginning of her fifteenth year of life.

2) *Physical incapacity—impotence*. A matrimonial contract is invalid if it is made between persons one or both of whom are incapable of the sacred physical act which God has made necessary for the procreation of offspring.

3) *Existing marriage bond*. A marriage contract cannot be made by a person already held by an existing valid marriage.

4) *Disparity of worship*, that is, mixed marriage with an unbaptized person. A contract of marriage between a baptized Catholic and an unbaptized person is not valid, unless the proper dispensation has previously been obtained.

5) *Sacred Orders*. A man who has received the subdiaconate or a higher major order cannot validly enter a marriage contract.

6) *Profession of solemn vows in religion*. A man or woman who has taken the solemn vow of perfect chastity in a religious order cannot validly enter into a marriage contract.

7) *Abduction to force a marriage.* The impediment consists in this: that a man who has abducted a woman against her will in order to make her marry him cannot enter into a valid marriage with that woman as long as she is held in his power.

8) *Criminal attack* against an existing marriage by murder or by adultery. There is a diriment impediment preventing a valid marriage between a man and a woman who, though married, a) have promised to marry or have attempted to marry one another and have committed adultery together, or b) who take the life of one of their spouses with intent to marry.

9) *Blood relationship.* A diriment impediment of consanguinity or blood relationship exists between blood relatives up to and including the third degree, that is, second cousins.

10) *Relationship by marriage—affinity.* A diriment impediment exists between a man and his wife's relatives up to and including her first cousins, and between her and his relatives up to and including his first cousins. In other words, if a man's wife dies he may not validly marry her mother or sister or aunts or first cousins, and vice versa.

11) *Public propriety.* A man who has contracted an invalid marriage or who has lived publicly with a woman in a life of sin cannot validly marry certain of her near relatives, e.g., her mother or her daughter by another union. Neither could the woman in the case marry the man's father or son by another union.

12) *Spiritual relationship from Baptism.* One cannot validly marry the person who acted as sponsor for him in Baptism, nor the person who baptized him if it were a Baptism of necessity.

13) *Legal Adoption.* If a person has been legally adopted he contracts a legal relationship which prohibits marriage to the same extent and degree of relationship as that set by the civil law of the state or nation.

Some of the diriment impediments come from God, and these divinely established impediments the Church has no power to dispense or change. Such, for instance, is an existing marriage bond. Other diriment impediments, however, have been made by the Church and these can be changed or dispensed by the Church as she sees fit. From some of these impediments set up by herself the Church never or hardly ever grants a dispensation. From others, for example, disparity of worship, and the more remote degrees of affinity or consanguinity, if there is a grave and urgent reason, she may grant the favor of a dispensation.

2. THE PROHIBITING OR IMPEDING IMPEDIMENTS

In addition to these most serious or diriment impediments which we have just considered, there are others known as prohibiting or impeding impediments. They also forbid the contracting of a marriage but, unlike the diriment impediments they do not render a marriage invalid if through ignorance or some other reason a marriage contract is made without having secured a dispensation from the impediment.

The impeding or prohibiting impediments make it unlawful to contract a marriage but do not prevent the contract from being valid. It would indeed be a mortal sin to get married while held by one of these prohibiting impediments, but the marriage would still be valid.

The prohibiting impediments are these:

1) *A vow opposed to the state of matrimony* prohibits a marriage. Such would be a simple vow of chastity, a vow of virginity, simple vows in religion.

2) *Mixed religion.* Disparity of cult is the diriment impediment which prevents a valid marriage between a baptized Catholic and an unbaptized person. Mixed religion is the prohibiting impediment which forbids a mixed marriage between a baptized Catholic and a baptized non-Catholic.

3) *Legal adoption.* In places where the civil law makes adoption a prohibiting but not invalidating impediment Canon Law does the same.

These, then, are the impediments set up by God or by Holy Mother Church to promote marriages which will bring honor to God and salvation to spouses and children.

ST. JOACHIM AND ST. ANNE

The incident here portrayed, though imaginary, is in complete keeping with Christian feeling. The saintly parents who bore, and trained, and gave us the Blessed Virgin Mary, in true liberality and Christlike detachment, freely shared the temporal goods with which God blessed them with the poor and unfortunate.

The wise Catholic observes them religiously and by so doing, finds happiness. The unwise and disobedient Catholic, trying to secure his own will, sometimes forces the Church to relax her laws and grant a dispensation. Usually he ends up by bringing unhappiness and misery on himself and many others.

3. DISPENSATIONS

The Church may grant dispensations from some of the ecclesiastical impediments—that is, impediments established by the Church—but she always does it reluctantly. A dispensation, as has been insisted upon already, is a *favor* granted by the Church to deserving people for sufficient reasons. By it the Church relaxes her law in a special case.

The Church does not have to grant a dispensation at any time; she may do so if she wishes and if there are sufficient and proportionately grave reasons. But *she can dispense only with the impediments she herself has created.* Those set up by God in the divine positive and divine natural law she may not touch. Even as regards some impediments set by herself, the Church seldom or never dispenses; for example, from the diriment impediment of minimum age.

As there are expenses incurred in the recording, the preparing and the handling of a dispensation, the Church has a right to direct that he or she who asks the favor bear such expenses. In addition to this the Church often prescribes an alms for the poor in connection with the granting of a dispensation.

REVIEW OF SECTION SIX.

SECTION SEVEN
THE SACRAMENT OF MATRIMONY (CONCLUDED)

G. BUILDING A HAPPY AND SUCCESSFUL MARRIAGE
  1. REMOTE PREPARATION
     a. Good Life
     b. Christian Habits
     c. Knowledge and Skill in Duties of Married Life
     d. Financial Preparation
  2. THE PROXIMATE PREPARATION
     a. Company-keeping—Courtship
        1) Its Purpose
        2) Dangers
        3) Unjustified Dating or Company-keeping
        4) Controlling The Dangers of Courtship
        5) Length of Courtship and Engagement
        6) Aids in Choosing a Good Partner
  3. IMMEDIATE PREPARATIONS
     a. Seeing the Pastor
     b. The Engagement or Betrothal
     c. The Banns
     d. Confession
  4. THE MARRIAGE
     a. The Time
     b. The Place
  5. THE MARRIAGE CEREMONY
  6. HAVE CHRIST AT YOUR MARRIAGE
  7. THE NUPTIAL MASS AND THE NUPTIAL BLESSING
     a. The Mass
     b. The Blessing

H. AFTER MARRIAGE
  1. LOVE
  2. SELF-SACRIFICE
  3. SUPERNATURAL AIDS TO A HAPPY MARRIED LIFE
  4. CHASTITY
  5. INTELLIGENT MANAGEMENT OF HOME AND CHILSDREN
  6. AVOIDING MONEY QUARRELS
  7. THE SACRED HEART, THE IMMACULATE HEART

G. BUILDING A HAPPY AND SUCCESSFUL MARRIAGE

We now have studied the main facts about marriage which a high-school senior might be expected to know. Knowledge alone, however, will never build a happy marriage; so those who think that God is calling them to this holy state of matrimony as He does most human beings, should also know and put into action the things which will be conducive to a happy marriage. There is both a remote and a proximate preparation that should be made.

1. THE REMOTE PREPARATION

a. A Good Life

The first preparation for a successful and happy marriage is a *virtuous, chaste, innocent life.* If you have made the virtues allied to purity and temperance habitual in your life you will have that self-control which will make for a happy married life. If you are lacking in any of these virtues, set to work at once to develop them.

b. Christian Habits

One of the first habits that is needed is the habit of *frequent reception of the sacraments* of Penance and Holy Eucharist, as well as the habit of regular daily prayer. Many other virtues are essential to living with others peaceably. Pride must be overcome and controlled, selfishness must give way to thinking oftener of others and of their needs and likes. All sensuality and softness of living should be repressed; marriage requires stern control of one's body.

c. Knowledge of and Skill in Duties of Married Life

Next in the remote preparation for marriage, one must include a knowledge of, and a skill in performing, the *duties of married life.* For example, the man must acquire the ability to support and direct a family, the woman must learn how to select foods, prepare them, care for them. She must learn how to run a house economically and efficiently; how to care for children, not only physically and mentally, but, above all, morally, by training them in religious knowledge and habits.

d. Financial Preparation

You will be able to think, no doubt, of many other things which should enter into this remote preparation. Let us conclude with one that is very important, *financial preparation.* No one can live on "love" for many days. It takes money to establish and to run a home and to support a family. Therefore, it is the duty of those looking forward to marriage as their state in life to make the necessary financial preparations.

Young men and women who squander all their money on themselves and on pleasure, on automobiles and shows and parties and costly clothes when they should be saving an appreciable part of their earnings regularly week after week, are heading for a marriage made unhappy with poverty, spendthrift carelessness, and constant quarrels about money and such like.

The virtues of prudence and justice demand foresight and moderation. Girls, especially, should remember that they should bring something besides a pretty face and expensive habits with them into marriage. In former days when girls worked at home and contributed to the family welfare, they were given a dowry by their parents when they were married. In these days when girls work away from home they should see their obligation to save a part of their earnings as their substitute for a dowry when they get married. What would be a fair amount? How much would one have to save each week to accumulate that sum for a marriage four years after graduation from high school?

2. PROXIMATE PREPARATION

a. Company-keeping—Courtship

Company-keeping is part of the proximate preparations for marriage. Before we discuss this subject, try to answer these questions: Are boys and girls allowed to go out with one another? Is steady company permissible? To whom? When?

———————   ⟶

A CATHOLIC MARRIAGE

A marriage before God's altar, in the presence of one's family and friends, with the full pomp and splendor of the Catholic liturgy, with organ ringing and candles flickering, is a blessing indeed, and a memory to cherish.

1) Its Purpose

The purpose of company-keeping is to allow a man and woman to get acquainted with one another, and to enable them to learn how they are adapted to one another, mentally and temperamentally, in order to make it possible for them to decide whether they should marry one another or not.

Many today keep company merely for the pleasure it affords, without any prospects of marriage with one another and without intention of possible marriage. Such company-keeping is wrong.

2) Dangers of Company-keeping

Because human nature is what it is, because the attraction between two young persons who like each other is inescapably strong, dating and company-keeping are always accompanied by temptations and by occasions of sin which grow in strength and frequency as the parties become better acquainted. Company-keeping, therefore, is not permitted except to those who have the possibility of getting married within a reasonable time, say, a year or two.

From this last statement you can see that a girl is not allowed to keep company with a man who is not free and able to marry. If any doubt exists, especially as to a person's freedom to marry, say, perhaps because of a previous marriage of doubtful or even almost unquestionable invalidity, the matter should be referred to one's pastor or confessor. Freedom to be married should be ascertained *before* company-keeping begins.

3) Unjustified Dating and Company-keeping

Steady dating between persons who definitely do not intend to get married is wrong, no matter what the practice in pagan America may be. Steady dating between boys and girls, who cannot possibly get married for a long time to come, is also unjustifiable and, if it results in serious occasions of sin or even worse in actual mortal sin, it *must be discontinued.*

Let it be said here again that, what is right and wrong, what is sin and not sin in boy-girl relations is to be learned, not from the customs of non-Christian America but from the infallible moral teaching of the Catholic Church. Too many young Catholics are forming *lax and erroneous consciences* by telling themselves that this or that is "all right" because "why everybody does it." That is a poor criterion of morality, especially in a country eighty percent non-Catholic. What is the correct criterion of morality? Why are some things right and others wrong? Does the fact that birth control and divorce are the custom in America make them morally right? Why not?

4) Controlling the Dangers of Courtship

Knowing the dangers of company-keeping, wise Catholic boys and girls will not begin to keep steady company until they are ready to consider selecting a partner in marriage. They will lessen the temptations of courtship by greater care in praying, by more frequent reception of the sacraments, and by exercising Christian prudence in avoiding being alone together.

The good Christian boy will pride himself on being the protector of the virginity of the girl who is to be the mother of his children. The wise Christian girl will realize that the passions are far more strong and violent in the man and she will act as his guardian angel by judiciously seeing to it that occasions for temptations are avoided.

A period of company-keeping sanctified by prudent reserve, and spotless, reverent admiration is the best foundation for a lifetime of happiness and unshaken confidence in one another. No young couple can expect to found a happy marriage on mortal sins.

5) Length of Courtship and Engagement

How long a period should be devoted to company-keeping as well as to the engagement? The sensible answer is: *neither too short nor too long.*

Marriages rushed into with an unholy haste are *hardly ever happy.* A large proportion of quick marriages, entered on short acquaintance end in complete failure. Therefore, there should be sufficient time before the marriage to let the first infatuation cool off a bit and to permit reason and grace to ask a few questions.

But protracted company-keeping or engagements are just as inadvisable, often giving rise to serious temptations and sins, and not infrequently ending with the girl being left to start all over again by a man who perhaps never had any serious intentions from the beginning.

6) Aids in Choosing a Good Partner

In Catholic countries even today, as in former ages, marriages are frequently arranged by the parents of the bride. They choose the husband and if the girl accepts, the marriage takes place. There is only a very short or perhaps no period of company-keeping. Such marriages have, time without number, been eminently happy, especially when Christian parents who really love their daughter choose a good man well suited to her in temperament, education, and other points.

If such a method of selecting a partner in marriage is no longer considered "democratic," at least young moderns who know that their parents are sincerely interested in their happiness should go to them and *talk over the*

$\longrightarrow$

By Frank Maguire   *Courtesy of Fordham University*

CHRIST, THE TEACHER

This unusual statue of Christ at the age of eighteen was conceived by the president of Fordham University and executed under his directions. It stands in the foyer of one of the university's halls.

matter of choice of a partner and discuss with them the possibilities of a successful marriage with a given party. Every one is free, of course, in the choice of state of life and in the choice of partner in marriage, but the advice of good parents should have a large influence in the final decision, being given careful, thoughtful, prayerful consideration.

Consultation with one's *confessor or pastor* or another priest who knows both parties concerned is also a very wise procedure. Most priests can predict with a great degree of accuracy the future result of a certain union. They have had special training and much experience in these matters. Be wise. Ask for and listen to their advice. It may save you many heartaches.

Lastly, in the proximate preparation for a happy marriage the parties should not omit earnest prayer and frequent confession and Holy Communion. The grace of God is of greater value than all human means. To neglect it is to do a very foolish thing. As a good summary of this point look up in the catechism the answer to the question: "How should Christians prepare for a holy and happy marriage?"

3. IMMEDIATE PREPARATIONS

a. Seeing the Pastor

When a couple has finally made up their minds to marry, before announcing their engagement, they should *go to the bride's pastor* to see if they are free to marry. The pastor will make the necessary investigation, and request the baptismal certificate and other necessary documents to insure that a valid and lawful marriage can take place. Never announce an engagement, and, above all, never announce a date for a wedding, until this examination has been completed and the pastor has given his assurance that the marriage can take place. Foolish young people have sometimes placed themselves in very embarrassing situations because they have made their announcement and then have gone to see the pastor, only to find that the marriage is impossible, or must be long delayed.

This examination should take place at least a month, and preferably two or more months before the proposed date of marriage. It is also highly advisable for both the man and the woman to have a physical examination before marriage, to give themselves and each other the assurance of the absence of any disabilities, defects, or diseases which would prevent a happy marriage.

b. The Engagement or Betrothal

When a prospective husband and wife have promised to marry one another they are said to be engaged. An engagement or betrothal is a serious matter, and not to be made or broken lightly. It creates obligations binding under the virtue of justice. The formal engagement recognized and advised by the Church is one made in writing, with full date, and signed by both parties and the pastor, in his presence; or before two witnesses and signed by them and the contracting parties.

c. The Banns

If the pastor finds that there is nothing to prevent the marriage he then proceeds to publish three times the banns or marriage proclamations. The purpose of the banns is to supply another guarantee that an invalid marriage will be prevented. Occasionally there are hidden impediments which even the careful investigation of the pastor does not disclose, but which may be known to people in the parishes where the parties concerned reside or have resided. There is a grave obligation on persons who know of impediments to reveal them to the persons concerned or to the pastor if necessary.

d. Confession

Finally, just before the marriage both parties should go to confession, for Matrimony is a sacrament of the living, and to confer grace it must be received while in the state of sanctifying grace. The confession before marriage should be preferably a *General Confession* of a person's entire life. Thus one begins the new life by turning a clean page.

4. THE MARRIAGE

a. The Time

A marriage may take place at *any time* during the year, but the *solemn blessing* of marriages is forbidden during Lent and Advent. The Sixth Precept of the Church says that we are not allowed to solemnize marriage at forbidden times. The marriage itself is not forbidden, but the special Votive Mass and the *Nuptial Blessing* of the bride, are forbidden, as is also the usual external pomp and celebration. The reason for this prohibition is, of course, that such things do not well agree with the penitential spirit of Advent and Lent. The Nuptial Mass is also forbidden on certain of the greater feasts, but the Nuptial Blessing of the bride may be inserted in the Mass of the day.

b. Proper Place for the Marriage

The proper place for the wedding ceremony, according to Canon Law, is the *parish church,* the parish of the bride being designated by custom. The practice of getting married in churches or chapels other than one's own parish church is discouraged by the Church and may be allowed only with permission of the bishop or the pastor. Requests for such permission, unless based on really sufficient grounds, are generally an indication of a lack of that proper relation with one's own parish which is a mark of a good Catholic.

Mixed marriages take place in the parish of the Catholic party and are usually devoid of all ceremony.

5. THE MARRIAGE CEREMONY

A Catholic marriage, with full ceremonial, is a thing of beauty and a memory to cherish. Being a sacrament, it takes place in church, before the altar. Therefore none but practical Catholics should be in the bridal party, and all should receive Holy Communion. When the bride and groom have arrived at the altar, the priest addresses a few words of instruction to them and then asks the man:

"(John) wilt thou take (Mary) here present for thy lawful wife, according to the rite of our Holy Mother, the Church?" and (John) answers, "I will." The same question is then asked of the bride.

"(Mary) wilt thou take (John) here present for thy lawful husband according to the rite of our Holy Mother, the Church?" and she answers, "I will." Then the priest orders them to join right hands and asks the groom to repeat after him:

"I, (John——) take thee (Mary——), for my lawful wife, to have and to hold, from this day forward, for better, for worse, for richer, for poorer, in sickness and in health, until death do us part."

The bride repeats the same words, inserting her own name in the proper place. The priest then says in Latin, "I join you together in marriage, in the name of the Father, and of the Son and of the Holy Ghost. Amen." Following this he sprinkles them with holy water and proceeds to bless the wedding ring. You might read the beautiful prayer in a Ritual or in a prayerbook.

Having blessed the ring, he gives it to the groom and directs him to place it on the third finger of the bride's left hand, and to say: "With this ring I thee wed and I pledge unto thee my fidelity," or as the Old English had it, "I plight unto thee my troth," i.e., truth. The priest confirms the pledge by saying "In the name of the Father, and of the Son, and of the Holy Ghost, Amen." Finally, the priest reads several versicles, says the Our Father, and ends with a prayer to God to look down "upon these thy servants and graciously protect thy institutions, whereby Thou hast provided for the propagation of mankind, that those who are joined together by Thine authority may be preserved by Thy help, through Christ our Lord. Amen."

The marriage ceremony over, Mass follows.

6. *HAVE CHRIST AT YOUR MARRIAGE*

Do you want a beautiful marriage? Do you want a happy married life? Yes? Then *have Christ at your marriage!* Be married in church, in the state of grace, at Mass, with all the beautiful ceremonial of the Church, receiving the Nuptial Blessing and sanctifying your union by receiving Christ in Holy Communion. Then your marriage will be gay. Then it will be happy. Then it will have the intense but restrained Christian joy of the marriage of Joseph and Mary.

7. *THE NUPTIAL MASS AND THE NUPTIAL BLESSING*

a. The Mass

Following the marriage, the *Votive Mass for Groom and Bride,* usually called the Nuptial Mass, is said or sung, unless a greater feast or privileged octave forbids it. In this latter case the Mass of the day is said with a commemoration from the Nuptial Mass added to the collects or orations.

The Epistle is from the Letter of St. Paul to the Ephesians. Ponder over its many lessons, as for example: "Let wives be subject to their husbands as to the Lord," and "Husbands, love your wives, just as Christ also loved the Church, and delivered Himself up for her." Eph. 5, 21 and 25. The Gospel is from the nineteenth chapter of St. Matthew in which we have already seen Christ proclaiming the New Testament law on the unity and indissolubility of marriage.

b. The Nuptial Blessing

After having said the Pater Noster of the Mass, the priest turns to the bridegroom and bride kneeling before the altar and says over them the first two prayers of the Nuptial Blessing. The first is a short prayer which asks a blessing on the marriage; the second is longer and is a special prayer for the bride. A third prayer comes after the Postcommunion, just before the Last Blessing. It asks a blessing on the bride and groom that they may see their "children and their children's children, even to the third and fourth generation, and afterwards may . . . have life everlasting by the grace of our Lord Jesus Christ."

This Nuptial Blessing is especially a blessing of the bride and she may receive it *only once*. If for some reason it was omitted when the marriage was contracted, for example, because it could not be conferred due to the closed season, it should be received as soon after as possible. This blessing is not given to those who contract mixed marriages, or to widows who are contracting a second marriage. It may be given, ordinarily, only at Mass.

H. AFTER MARRIAGE

1. LOVE

The early days of wedded life are usually days of wonderful happiness because both husband and wife are so deeply in love with one another that they completely forget themselves and think only how to please each other. Even the severe sacrifices necessary to adjust to a completely new and different mode of life, as well as the necessity of abandoning the habits of years, and of accustoming one's self to new manners of acting—all these great sacrifices seem as nothing to true love. If they are cheerfully made until they become habitual, married life can be very happy.

2. SELF-SACRIFICE

Sad to say, in most marriages, selfishness soon creeps in. Each wants his own way. Arguments, quarrels, even fights and violence may follow. Love may turn to hate, and quickly, too, unless the wholehearted, self-sacrificing, mutual love of the early days of married life is practiced by both partners without ever a deviation or exception until sacrifice becomes a habit. This is the foundation stone of a happy marriage — *lifelong mutual self-sacrifice*

Von Uhde   *From Ewing Galloway, N. Y.*

GRACE BEFORE MEALS

The home in which Christ is a welcome guest, is a happy home, a bit of heaven on earth, though it be humble and possess but few of life's luxuries.

founded on true Christian love of God and of one another.

Christian self-sacrifice will guarantee that there will be *beautiful refinement and moderation* in all the relations of married life.

The necessity of self sacrifice in marriage becomes apparent when one considers that no man or woman is free from faults. All of us have failings and imperfections. Most of us have serious faults. But faults always annoy and cause friction and, unless each party constantly and permanently bears with the other's shortcomings, knowing that his or her own failings also cause irritation, trouble will not be avoided.

Trials and misfortune come to every marriage: loss of work, sickness, accident, death, for no human life can completely avoid them. A bad husband, an unfaithful wife, ungrateful children, jealous "friends"—these too, may bring misery. But the spirit of sacrifice, in honor and memory of the suffering Christ, will ease the burden and bring peace to the heart in spite of the tears in the eyes.

3. SUPERNATURAL AIDS TO A HAPPY MARRIED LIFE

Human means are never sufficient to effect a successful marriage. Grace also is necessary, and in copious quantities. Grace is secured from prayer, the sacraments, good works of mercy. *Lifelong fidelity to daily prayers,* said in common when possible, and great *frequency in confession,* and the reception of Christ in the *Holy Eucharist* are among the principle means of gaining the grace needed for the cheerful bearing of the sacrifices of married life. Meticulous care in the fulfillment of religious duties and prompt and *complete obedience to all laws of the Church* are an integral part of this pattern for happiness.

4. CHASTITY

Holy Scripture says: "They who in such manner receive matrimony as to shut God out from themselves, and from their mind, and to give themselves to their lust . . . over them the devil hath power." Tob. 6, 17.

Conjugal chastity is indispensable for married happiness. This virtue must characterize the relations within the marriage, by avoidance of all indulgence contrary to the laws of God and the laws of nature; it must also characterize the relation of husband and wife with others.

After marriage the husband is not allowed to look with sinful desire on another woman, nor the wife on another man. They now, by contract, belong to each other alone; they have no right to attempt to be or even to want to be attractive to any other than their lawful wedded partner. From this you may be able to draw some conclusions as to the dress, behavior, and demeanor of a married woman; also as to the behavior of a Catholic husband toward other women. Compare present practices with your conclusions. Does your comparison suggest any recommendations or resolutions?

5. INTELLIGENT MANAGEMENT OF HOME AND CHILDREN

In addition to religious duties there are countless other obligations comprised in the married state. They also must be fulfilled with prompt and exact care. A good Catholic wife and mother takes great pride in a tidy, clean house; in children well trained in all virtues; in skill in the kitchen; in clever and prudent management, and so forth. The father, too, has his duties in regard to training the children, caring for the home and its surroundings, planning the future, and guiding the financial affairs. This last point calls for a further word.

6. AVOIDING MONEY QUARRELS

Quarrels over money are a frequent source of trouble in family life. The husband should ordinarily manage these affairs. It may be, however, that the husband knows his wife to be a better manager than he and consents to her taking care of the finances. Whoever it be, he should be neither sinfully spendthrift on one hand, nor miserly on the other. Prudence, foresight, and saving for the "rainy day" are, of course, indispensable; but money and possessions and luxuries are not life, and *Christian detachment* from worldly goods *plus Christian prudence* should dictate the proper financial policy in the family.

In this connection let us repeat what was said above when speaking of careers. Marriage and a job are incompatible terms for any woman. Marriage is in itself *a full-time job*, a twenty-four-hour-a-day job. To attempt to hold down two jobs always means one will be neglected; and the duties which usually suffer are those of the married state.

7. THE SACRED HEART, THE IMMACULATE HEART

Real Catholics dedicate their married life through the Immaculate Heart of Mary to the Sacred Heart of Jesus for the honor and glory of God. The first decoration which they secure for their new home is a crucifix, the symbol of sacrifice; the second and third are pictures or statues of the Sacred Heart of Jesus and of the Immaculate Heart of Mary, symbols of love. *Sacrifice and Love.* In marriage, as in all life, these two words spell *happiness.*

REVIEW OF SECTION SEVEN.

CONCLUSION

We have now considered the three states of life, the three roads towards eternity. There is much that we still could say about each, but you must find that out for yourself. At least, if you have studied well, you know the essentials. Now, you must make your choice. Let it be for the glory of God and the sanctification of your own and other souls. Let it be for the building up of the Mystical Body of Christ and for the safety and progress and happiness of our own beloved country and that of the entire world.

REVIEW OF UNIT THREE

1. Why were we created?
2. What criteria should one use in choosing his state in life?
3. What aids does one have to assist him in choosing well?
4. What are the three main choices?
5. Explain the nobility of a religious vocation.
6. What are the signs of a religious vocation?
7. Why is it dangerous to neglect a religious vocation?
8. What is a frequent cause of neglect of a religious vocation?
9. How can one test whether he or she has a religious vocation?
10. What various choices of vocation in the religious life are offered to a young man? a young woman?
11. Define Holy Orders. Name the various steps toward the priesthood.
12. What are the effects of the sacrament of Holy Orders?

13. What are the duties of a priest?

14. What are the vows of religion?

15. Explain the work done by brothers; the preparation of a brother for his life and work.

16. What are the steps before a nun takes her final vows?

17. Describe the postulancy, novitiate, and the religious life. Tell its sacrifices and joys.

18. Name some worthy and unworthy motives for choosing to remain unmarried in the world.

19. Tell the difficulties of that state in life.

20. What are the main types of employment in our country? What percent of the population is in each?

21. What is the noblest career for a woman in the world?

22. Are a career and marriage compatible? Why?

23. What is marriage?

24. What is a contract? What are the conditions for a valid contract?

25. Who is the author of the marriage contract?

26. Can the contracting parties change the conditions or provisions of the marriage contract to suit their own wishes? Explain.

27. What are the requisites for a valid marriage contract?

28. What are the effects of the marriage contract?

29. What are the essential qualities of marriage? Define and explain each.

30. Define each of the following terms: monogamy, polygamy, indissolubility, unity, legitimate marriage, ratified marriage, ratified and consummated marriage.

31. What is the primary essential purpose of marriage? the secondary essential purpose? What are some of the other purposes?

32. What are some false modern ideas on the purpose of marriage? Whence do they arise?

33. Define marriage as a sacrament.

34. Show that matrimony has the three essentials of a sacrament.

35. Is it a sacrilege to get married while in the state of grievous sin? Would such a marriage be a real, valid marriage?

←

By Ewing Galloway, N. Y.

LOVE AND SACRIFICE

Christ loved men, sacrificing Himself for them on the altar of the Cross, and thus saving them from the effects of their sins against Him. In the example of this great love, must man and wife love one another. So too must they love the children God gives them. Love and sacrifice spell happiness.

36. What formalities are prescribed for a valid marriage of Catholics?

37. If two Catholics, two non-Catholics, and a Catholic and non-Catholic, go through a marriage ceremony with one another before a justice of the peace, are they married? Why?

38. What are the effects of marriage as a sacrament?

39. What are the obligations of married people to one another? to their children?

40. What are the three great blessings of matrimony? Explain each.

41. What is the basic false principle regarding marriage?

42. Name three vices opposed to the blessing of offspring.

43. Why is the sinful prevention of the conception and birth of children so serious?

44. Name two great errors relating to the blessing of conjugal fidelity.

45. Name three errors opposed to the blessing of the sacrament.

46. What are the two kinds of mixed marriages?

47. What precautions should be taken to avoid mixed marriage?

48. Why does the Church forbid mixed marriages?

49. Under what conditions might the Church grant a dispensation for a mixed marriage?

50. Is divorce forbidden? Prove it.

51. Does the Church sometimes permit persons to secure a civil decree of "divorce"? Why? Does this civil decree dissolve the marriage bond?

52. Are husband and wife ever allowed to separate? Why? May they remarry?

53. Who has the right to determine the validity or nullity of the marriage of Christians? to make laws concerning the sacrament of Matrimony? Why?

54. What is the basic principle needed to correct the modern errors and abuses opposed to Matrimony?

55. What supernatural means are available to oppose and correct these errors? What natural means?

56. What is meant by an impediment to marriage?

57. What two kinds of impediments are there? Explain the nature and effects of each.

58. Name the more important of the diriment impediments.

59. Which of the following are diriment impediments? Which are prohibiting impediments? Which are required formalities for validity? Which are not impediments?

Age 15	Abduction	Criminal Attack
Vow	Engagement	"Common law"
Physical Incapacity	Cousin	marriage
Blood relationship	Spiritual relationship	Affinity
Adoption	Two witnesses	Habitual drunkenness
Priesthood	An existing marriage	Marriage by pastor
Novitiate	Unbaptized	
Solemn profession	Tuberculosis	

60. May blood relatives marry?
61. What is a dispensation?
62. Is the Church obliged to grant dispensations? Explain.
63. What preparations should one make for a happy marriage? remote preparations? proximate? immediate?
64. What advice does Pius XI give in his encyclical on marriage concerning choosing a partner?
65. What financial preparation should be made for marriage?
66. When and to whom is company-keeping permitted?
67. Are high-school boys and girls permitted to keep steady company?
68. Mention some aids in choosing a proper partner in marriage.
69. How long before marriage should one call on the pastor to make arrangements? Why?
70. What are the banns? When are they published?
71. When can Catholics get married? When can marriage be solemnized with the Nuptial Mass and Nuptial Blessing?
72. What is the Nuptial Blessing?
73. Where should the marriage take place?
74. What must be done after marriage to insure a happy married life?
75. Find five more practical questions on this unit.
76. Present to the class five practical situations related to choice of state in life, religious life, and marriage. Ask the class to give the Catholic solution to each.

LEX · LUX

REX

Human Rights come from God and not from the State.

All men are members of the same human family redeemed by Christ.

Dignity of the individual as a human being.

Right evaluation of the riches of the world.

Co-operation among nations for peace.

UNIT IV

Building a Better World

Justice, the Seventh, Eighth, and Tenth Commandments

PART ONE: PLANNING THE UNIT

Your school and its teachers, particularly the religion teachers, have spent four years trying to show you how much *God loves you.* Let us rest in the confidence that they have succeeded in opening your mind to that wondrous fact; and let us trust that you have been inspired to go forth from your Alma Mater determined to prove to the entire world that *you love God;* and that you love Him more than anything on earth.

Let us hope also that you have made the firm resolution not only to glorify God by leading a virtuous life yourself, but even more than that, that you will consider it as your solemn duty to be a leader in the movement

toward *Building a Better World* by preaching everywhere
and at all times, especially by your own life, the virtues
needed for a happier world. Thus you can make the future
your debtor; thus you can pay your debt to the past,
your debt to your school. Thus you can prove your love
for God and at the same time satisfy that yearning which
all of us have to make a worthwhile contribution to the
scene on which we live.

BASIC GOOD HABITS—KNOWLEDGE VERSUS PRACTICE

Your religion course, in these years, has presented for
your consideration the seven basic habits which are the
only valid proofs of a real love of God. You should know
them by heart now—faith, hope, and charity, the theological virtues; and prudence, justice, fortitude, and temperance, the cardinal moral virtues. Any other virtue is
but an allied part or a subdivision of one of these.

As you have studied these virtues and their parts you
have in all probability agreed mentally to their necessity
or have accepted them on faith. But there is something
far more important than merely accepting them, and you
know what it is. Yes, it is more important that you practice and *develop these habits* than that you know how to
define them. But that is something only you can do. No one
can do it for you.

SOCIAL IMPORTANCE OF VIRTUE

In addition to being the only good proof of a real love
of God the practice of these seven basic virtues is socially
important, for the modern world is in dire need of them.
But the world hardly knows them, so it must first be told
about them, and as it will hardly listen to the Church, you
must do the preaching by your lives. You must live these
virtues, that the world may see them, and be attracted to
them, and imitate them. Even as the Blessed Virgin Mary
did, you must prove to all you meet that charity, that is,

supernatural love of God and all God's creatures, is a habit which produces a happy society.

You must let men see, as Mary did, that charity springs from divine hope. You must let them see that charity, together with hope, is founded on faith. You must let them see that faith is a humble virtue by which the proud intellect of man takes its first long step toward God by bowing down in complete submission to His revealed word and to the authority of His Church.

As with the theological virtues, so with the moral; they, too, are a proof of your love of God and the world needs a demonstration of their worth also. Will you supply it? Will your Church and school be disappointed in the hope that you will?

You have studied all these virtues in the course of the past four years, but there is a phase of one which we have only lightly explored—it is the social side of the virtue of justice. It is of great importance today. We must examine it thoroughly before we conclude our course.

The study of social justice has been reserved for this last year because of a desire that it be fresh in your minds as you step out into society; but also because it requires the greater mental development and social maturity which you should now possess. It will call for your best efforts.

DIAGNOSTIC EXPLORATION

To discover what you already know about this topic, try to answer the following questions:

What is justice? What is the purpose of property and possessions? Who has the right to possess property? the individual? the State? What are the rights and duties of capital and labor? What is the social importance of the eighth commandment? What has the Church done for the social improvement of the world?

SOME OBJECTIVES FOR THIS UNIT

To learn the importance of justice, especially social justice and to encourage the development of the attitudes and acts necessary to make it a deep-rooted habit.

To show how our Church has a program of morality and social justice which needs only to be practiced to transform the world.

To fire us with a desire to become leaders in a movement for a better world, by practicing all the virtues, justice prominent among them.

We are now ready to turn to Part Two on page 335 to begin study of this unit. The following or similar activities, assignments or readings may be of assistance.

SUGGESTED ASSIGNMENTS AND ACTIVITIES

1. Discuss at least five dishonest business practices which would violate justice or the seventh and eighth commandments.
2. Write a character sketch of a thoroughly just, honest, upright, truthful man.
3. Examine the social encyclicals to discover the reasons why the Church says that the communist or socialist solution of social problems will bring misery and chaos.
4. Discuss some social problem affecting justice in your community, in this nation, in the world. How might it be solved?
5. Describe:
   a) the advantages that would accrue for individuals, families and society, if nearly all men could become property owners; or,
   b) cases where privately owned property must submit to limitations on its use for the common good; or,
   c) cases where, according to the principles of Pius XI, public ownership might be required or advisable.
6. Look up the recommendations of "The American Bishops' Reconstruction Program of 1919." List them and tell how many have been followed.
7. Estimate how much a "living wage" should be in your community for a family with six children. Draw up a budget if possible.
8. John borrows $200 to finance a car. If he pays back $20 a month for 12 months, what rate of interest per annum is he paying on his average unpaid balance? Is it usurious?
9. Write an address to be delivered to a group having communistic leanings; in it present the Catholic principles for the solution of the social and economic ills of the world; or, give your reasons why the Communist solution is bound to be a failure and cause great disorder and unhappiness.

10. Debate or discuss the statement that many families fail to attain the independence of debt-free ownership of their own homes:
    a) because of the expense of buying and maintaining an automobile, or,
    b) because of the interest burden of a mortgage on a too expensive home, or,
    c) because of uncontrolled liking for pleasure, finery, jewelry, personal adornment, or extravagant living.
11. Report on the youth movement activities for social justice and moral betterment in other countries.
12. Have a report or discussion on Cooperatives and Credit Unions. (cf. Related Readings.)
13. Report on how much it would cost to own, maintain, replace, insure, and operate a medium priced automobile for twenty years.
14. Explain the obligation of restitution in cases of stealing or cheating or in damaging property or unlawfully interfering with its use.
15. Summarize the chief duties of employers toward their employees; of employees toward their employers; of both to society.
16. Discuss the Catholic attitude toward labor unions; strikes.
17. Report on labor unions, their kinds, activities, power, benefits, dangers, etc.
18. Write a paper on some topic such as:
    a) Reputation: Its Value and Importance.
    b) Sacredness of the Reputation of My Neighbor.
    c) Justice and Charity: A Prescription for a Sick World.
    d) The St. Vincent de Paul Society.
    e) The Mediæval Guilds.
19. If their is any special social problem in which you or the class are interested, present it to the teacher for approval as an assignment.
20. Discuss the responsibility of newspapers, etc., as regards the protection of a person's character, e.g., in alleged crimes, during political campaigns, etc.
21. If you know of any movie, novel, short story, etc., which attempts to spread erroneous social and economic principles, report to the class on what it tries to do and how.
22. Arrange a Definition Bee on new or difficult words or phrases in this unit. Ask for the other meanings of the same word.
23. Make posters or placards presenting Catholic social principles in snappy slogans.

24. What social teachings of Christ are to be found in the follow-
ing scripture passages: Matt. 19, 19; Gen. 4, 9; Luke 10, 7;
Matt. 20, 6; 2 Thess. 3, 10; Jas. 5, 4; Matt. 6, 9; Matt. 22, 21;
Col. 4, 1; Luke 10, 30 ff.

25. Report on the life of a saint or other Catholic who was outstanding in his labors for the social betterment of his fellowmen,
e.g., St. Vincent de Paul, Pope Leo XIII, etc.

RELATED READINGS IN BOOKS AND PAMPHLETS

Books: Five Great Encyclicals, Paulist.

Coady, *Masters of Their Own Destiny,* Harpers.

Consilia, Sr., *Christian Social Principles,* Kenedy.

Ghéon, *Secret of St. John Bosco,* Sheed & Ward.

Kerr, *A Catechism of Catholic Social Principles,* Herder.

La Farge, *Interracial Justice,* America.

Ligutti-Rawe, *Rural Roads to Security,* Bruce.

Maurin, *Easy Essays* (On Social Topics), Sheed & Ward.

Michel, *Christian Social Reconstruction,* Bruce.

Walsh, *The Saints and Social Work,* Prop. Faith, Boston.

Richardson, S., *A.B.C. of Cooperatives,* Longmans.

Ross, *Sound Social Living,* Bruce.

Vaughn, *Divine Armory of Holy Scripture,* Herder (Pt. 5, p.
341 sqq.).

Weismantel, *Mantle of Mercy* (St. Vincent de Paul), Bruce.

Periodicals:

Catholic Action, N.C.W.C.

Catholic Family Monthly, O.S.V.

Catholic Rural Life Bulletin, Dubuque.

Land and Home, Natl. Cath. Rural Life, Des Moines.

Pamphlets:

Bishop's Program of Social Reconstruction, N.C.W.C.

Catholic Action Series, N.C.W.C.

Christian Democracy Series, N.C.W.C.

Cunningham, *The Gossipers,* Paulist.

Curran, *Facts about Communism,* I.C.T.S.

Flynn, *Catechism of Communism for Catholic High School
Students,* Paulist.

McDevitt, *Communism and American Youth,* America.

McGowan, *Towards Social Justice,* Paulist.

Michel, *Labor and Industry,* Wanderer, St. Paul.

N.C.W.C., *Organized Social Justice* (An economic program for the U.S.), N.C.W.C.

O'Brien, *Does the Church Serve Humanity?* O.S.V.

O'Hara, *Credit Unions,* N.C.W.C.

Rumble & Carty, *Jewish Problems,* Radio Replies Press.

Schmiedeler, *Catholic Rural Life,* N.C.W.C.

Schmiedeler, *Consumer Cooperatives,* N.C.W.C.

Sheen, *The Tactics of Communism,* Paulist.

Thorning, *A Primer of Social Justice,* Paulist.

Treacy, *Deal Honestly and Justly,* Paulist.

Treacy, *Curb Thy Tongue,* Paulist.

Treacy, *Labor's Charter of Liberty* (Encyclical of Leo XIII on labor, simplified), Paulist.

Treacy, *Rebuilding Society's Social Order* (Encyclical on Reconstructing the Social Order, simplified), Paulist.

Treacy, *God and Liberty against Satan and Slavery* (Encyclical on Communism, simplified), Paulist.

PARALLEL READINGS IN OTHER HIGH SCHOOL RELIGION TEXTS

	Campion	Cassilly	Falque	Gaume	Graham	Laux	Manual of Chr. Doctr.
Commandments...	I, 131	33	I, 104; 156, 165	II, 25	271	III, 9; 22	233
7th and 10th Commandments...	II, 350	124	I, 212	II, 31	313	III, 90; 108	290
8th Commandment	II, 378	133	I, 216	II, 32	316	III, 90; 105, 110	302

Given in volumes and pages, except Gaume which shows volume and chapter.

PART TWO: BUILDING A BETTER WORLD

"If thou followest justice thou shalt obtain her . . . and she shall protect thee forever." Ecclus. 27, 9-10.

SECTION ONE: THE VIRTUE OF JUSTICE

A. NATURE OF JUSTICE
    1. DEFINITION
    2. NATURAL AND SUPERNATURAL JUSTICE
    3. JUSTICE — A SOCIAL VIRTUE
    4. JUSTICE — A VIRTUE OF THE WILL
    5. DIVISIONS OF JUSTICE
        a. Legal Justice
        b. Distributive Justice
        c. Commutative Justice
        d. Social Justice
    6. JUSTICE AND ITS RELATED VIRTUES
        a. Religion
        b. Piety, Reverence, and Obedience
        c. Other Virtues Related to Justice
    7. CHARITY DISTINCT FROM JUSTICE
    8. JUSTICE AND THE TEN COMMANDMENTS
        a. Justice and the First Three Commandments
        b. Justice and the Fourth Commandment
        c. Justice and the Remaining Commandments
    9. SOCIAL IMPORTANCE OF JUSTICE

A. NATURE OF JUSTICE

Every human being has rights. A right is a moral power which entitles a human being to something which is distinctly his own. The basic human rights are personal, inalienable, inviolable, and moral. They come from God. Such among others are the rights to life, to true liberty, to work, the right to marry, the right to educate one's own children.

These natural and inviolable rights belong to every human being precisely because he is a human being, possessing a rational soul and an eternal, supernatural destiny. They may not be unjustly infringed upon. No human being can abolish these basic rights nor render their exercise impossible; neither can public authority suspend them without a just and serious cause. Of course there are certain other rights which may not be so fundamental

or so inalienable. The virtue which protects these and all of man's rights is the virtue of justice.

1. DEFINITION

The word justice has a wide meaning, as, for instance, in the command of our Lord: "Seek first the kingdom of God and his justice." In this sense, justice includes the practice of all virtues and is synonymous with sanctity. In this sense the virtue of religion, filial reverence, obedience and the like are said to be part of the virtue of justice.

The word justice, however, is most frequently used in a more restricted and proper sense. In this sense it is defined as follows: Justice is the cardinal moral virtue which inclines and supports the will towards giving to everyone what is his due.

Justice, then, is a good moral habit perfecting the human will and consisting in an inclination and a facility of the will in acting in such manner that it constantly, permanently, promptly, and easily tends to perform those actions by which we give to all men what is rightfully theirs.

2. NATURAL AND SUPERNATURAL JUSTICE

A virtue may be natural or supernatural. A virtue, you remember, is a good habit. A *natural* virtue is a habit or facility for acting *gained by practice*. Thus the natural

---

THE SHEPHERDS

Christ by word and act taught His followers the proper relation to wealth and earthly possessions. The first persons to whom He revealed His presence on earth were the shepherds, men devoid of all wealth and worldly influence. For Himself He deliberately chose a life in most modest circumstances. He repeatedly called for detachment from worldly goods on the part of His followers.

Our modern world and many modern Catholics need to learn again this part of Christ's program for reconstruction.

virtue of justice is a facility for rendering to everyone what belongs to him, which facility has become habitual with practice.

A *supernatural* virtue is a divinely infused capacity and ability to act on a supernatural level. You will recall that the supernatural virtue of justice, together with the other of the seven basic virtues, is *infused* into the soul with the reception of sanctifying grace.

But, as the definition just given states, this infused virtue is in the nature of a capacity or a power for acting justly rather than the fully developed good habit of always acting justly. It is only by repeated *acts* and by consistent cooperation with grace that the infused capacity is developed, until finally the human will easily and consistently tends to give to every human being what is rightfully his.

3. JUSTICE—A SOCIAL VIRTUE

The other cardinal virtues are not always and necessarily social, but justice never lacks a relation to others—it is a social virtue. We have already studied some of its social implications and applications. For example, in our sophomore year, we treated of justice particularly in relation to those obligations which concern the proper submission to and use of authority, whether in family, Church, or State.

4. JUSTICE—A VIRTUE OF THE WILL

All the moral virtues have reference to the human will in its choice of good and bad; but not all of them are directly intended to support and perfect the will.

Prudence is the moral virtue which guides and strengthens the *intellect* in its pursuit of the true. The intellect is also perfected by the theological virtue of faith which gives it supernatural light and assistance in knowing and believing what God has revealed to us.

Temperance, as we learned last year, is a virtue which guides and supports us in our control over the lowest part of our nature, the bodily urges and tendencies, or the *sense appetites* as they are usually called. Justice and fortitude are the moral virtues which perfect the *will* in seeking the good. They are assisted and elevated by the theological virtues of hope and charity which give supernatural support to the human will in its efforts to reach genuine happiness.

5. DIVISIONS OF JUSTICE

Justice has two divisions: general and particular. The first, that is, general justice, is more often called legal justice. The second has two subdivisions, distributive justice and commutative justice. There are, then, three kinds of justice: legal, distributive and commutative, but only these last two are parts of the cardinal moral virtue; legal justice is not.

a. Legal Justice

Legal justice inclines citizens to render to the community what belongs to it and to obey the *legal prescriptions* set down by the civil authority of the community or state for the common good. Thus tax laws and other similar laws necessary for the public welfare bind under legal justice.

b. Distributive Justice

If legal justice is the obligation binding citizens to civic duties, then distributive justice is in a way the very opposite. It is distributive justice which binds civil authorities to distribute public benefits, goods, and burdens with equity to all citizens.

c. Commutative Justice

The third kind of justice is justice in a more proper sense than the previous two. It is called commutative justice. Commutative justice is that moral virtue which inclines all men to observe the strict rights of others. It

regulates the mutual relations of individual to individual.
When commutative justice is violated, it demands restitution in conscience.

d. Social Justice

There is a new term in use today, namely, social justice.
It includes legal justice and certain elements of distributive and commutative justice.

6. JUSTICE AND ITS RELATED VIRTUES

Many virtues are related to justice and are considered
parts of that virtue, although in varying degrees. We say
that in justice we owe God all we have. In a natural sense
and to a certain degree we can say the same concerning
our parents and our country. We can never repay God, our
parents or our country, the debts we owe them, at least
not in full equality, as would be required in an obligation
of justice, taken in its strict sense. The virtues, therefore, which govern these acts are not identical with justice,
but related to and allied with it. Such are the virtues
of *religion,* by which men render to God the honor and
worship due to Him; the virtues of *piety* and *reverence*
and *obedience* by which children and subjects render to
parents and others in authority the love and service they
owe them; as well as the correlative virtues by which those
in authority fulfill their duties to those under their charge.

There is another group of virtues which are related to
justice but to which our neighbor can lay no such strict
claim as he can to his property. These virtues include
truthfulness, fidelity to promises, gratitude, the vindication or reasonable punishment of crime, friendliness, liberality, and a natural love of neighbor.

7. CHARITY DISTINCT FROM JUSTICE

Although both charity and justice support the human
will in its search for the true good, the divine virtue of

THE MAGI

After first revealing Himself to the poor shepherds our Blessed Lord disclosed His coming to the wealthy kings from the East. Men of means they were, indeed; yet they were truly poor in spirit. They were detached from their wealth, and attached to Christ and to the task of finding and serving Him. Having found Him they gave richly of their possessions.

charity is distinct from justice and not a part of it. The virtue of justice helps us to give to every one what is due to him—what is his by right. The virtue of charity carries the will even further, for it takes us where no obligation of justice binds us and causes us to add what is needful also, not merely what is due by right.

Justice can be commanded and guided by law. A judge may demand that one person pay his debt to another, no matter how wealthy the creditor already is. Where there is no obligation of justice, however, he may not command. Here charity reigns, here love of man for love of God leads one to do things which are not required by justice.

On the other hand, *charity is no substitute for justice* as many a so-called "philanthropist" will learn to his terror on Judgment Day. Giving money to the poor in charity will never serve as a substitute for paying them just wages. In this sense, *justice comes before charity.*

8. JUSTICE AND THE TEN COMMANDMENTS

All the precepts of the Decalogue pertain to and have relations with the virtue of justice. Some of them indeed pertain to other virtues also, as we saw last year when we learned that the fifth and sixth commandments fall under the virtue of temperance, but all of them pertain to justice, and in practicing the virtue of justice perfectly, one includes the observance of all the commandments. That is why when the Scripture says a person is "a just man," as it says of St. Joseph, it conveys the highest commendation of that person.

a. Justice and the First Three Commandments

The connection between the virtue of justice and the first three commandments is by way of the virtue of religion. The first three commandments, St. Thomas Aquinas tells us, deal with acts of the *virtue of religion* which is the most important part of the virtue of justice. No man can be just, no Christian can even think that he practices the virtue of justice and of its major subordinate virtue, religion, unless that man gives God what is due to Him as the source from which he has sprung and from which he derives all good.

As regards the *first commandment* the virtues of justice and religion require that we render to God what we owe Him, by internal acts of adoration and by sacrifice to the one true God. All idolatry and worship of false gods, all superstition and superstitious practices and observances, all worship of God by and in false religions are violations of the virtue of religion and therefore of justice. God has a right to our service. God has the right to demand that we serve only Him, the one true God, and that we serve Him in the manner He prescribes.

As regards the *second commandment,* the virtue of religion says that God has a right to demand and expect honor of His Holy Name and person, as well as due reverence to all holy persons and things, to mention but a few of these latter: the sacraments, the Church, relics, images of holy persons. The second commandment also requires that we keep our vows and promises to God, our oaths witnessed by the invocation of His Name and His omniscient truthfulness. On the negative side this commandment forbids all profanity, cursing, perjury, sacrilege, simony, and tempting of God. In a word, it forbids everything that would verge on contempt of God as a violation of the reverence which in justice we owe Him.

The virtue of justice in relation to the *third commandment* insures that man, a social being, will pay to God external, social worship, freeing himself from other duties for the performance of public acts of the virtue of religion. God's perfection is so great that this worship also is due to Him from all of His rational human creatures.

b. Justice and the Fourth Commandment

The first three commandments then, are related to the virtue of justice by means of the virtue of religion and the acts which this virtue prescribes for all just men. The fourth commandment falls under the virtue of justice by way of the *virtue of filial piety* which is the second part of the virtue of justice. The first three commandments regulate our debt of justice to the *Supreme Source or Principle* from which we have sprung, that is, God, the principle and fountain head of our being. Similarly, the fourth commandment defines and regulates the debt of justice children owe to parents as the *proximate principle* of their being under God, and the duties which parents

owe to children as their own offspring and images of God. *Obedience* to and the *proper use of authority* are the main virtues under justice and piety relating to this commandment. How much do you remember about the details of this double relation to authority from your sophomore year?

c. *Justice and the Remaining Commandments*

The remaining six commandments, that is, the fifth to the tenth, refer to justice in its more strict and proper sense, that is, as our duty to respect the rights of others. The *fifth commandment* details the sequels to our right to expect others to respect our health and integrity both in body and in soul. It is a violation of justice and at the same time a sin against the fifth commandment to kill a man, to cripple, maim, or injure him in his body. It is a violation of justice to cause or even to give the occasion of the spiritual ruin of another by scandal or bad example.

As regards the *sixth commandment,* among other things, it is a transgression of the strict right acquired by the contract of marriage to violate a marriage by adultery; and it is a violation of the right which the unborn child has to a proper chance of salvation, to terminate its life before birth or to cause it to be born outside of the love and protection of a stable marriage bond.

The *ninth commandment* fosters justice by controlling thoughts and desires which lead to violations of the sixth commandment in act, as does the *tenth commandment* in regard to sins transgressing the seventh.

It is when we come to the seventh and tenth and the eighth commandments that we are in the most proper

---

Thomas McGlynn, O. P.   *Courtesy of Liturgical Arts*

BLESSED MARTIN OF PORRES

This humble Negro, a Dominican lay brother, led a life of hidden holiness and devotion to his daily tasks.

domain of the virtue of justice. The *seventh command-ment* protects, by way of precept, the right which every human being has to own and use his property, according to reason and the laws of God. The virtue of justice regulates the use of this right by commanding liberality conjoined with prudence. It forbids avarice, that is, the unreasonable and inordinate attachment to earthly possessions; and it also forbids prodigality which means carelessness and wastefulness in regard to the property which God has committed to our care to help us lead a healthy, virtuous life.

The *eighth commandment* is related to justice because of the right that every human being has to expect others to use the power of speech to convey the truth, and because of every person's right to his reputation and good name. Justice, therefore, as well as the eighth commandment is violated by lying, hypocrisy, boasting, flattery, slander, and other like vices.

As we are to study these two commandments at length in this unit we shall not go into further detail here.

9. SOCIAL IMPORTANCE OF JUSTICE

From what has been said thus far about justice all can see that the virtue of justice guides us in the three main relations of life: first, in our relation to God, secondly, in relation to those subject to us or to whom we are subject; and thirdly, in relation to other men as to equals. All can also understand that he who practices the virtue of justice perfectly and completely is indeed a virtuous Christian, a "just" man.

GRINDING MEAL

→

The conveniences and comforts of living are not enjoyed by all people and nations in such abundant measure as they are in the great urban areas of some of the major nations of the world. This woman, living in Egypt in the second quarter of the twentieth century, must still grind her meal between two stones before she has the flour with which to make bread.

Is it possible that violations of justice on the part of powerful nations keep the people of smaller, weaker nations from enjoying that economic sufficiency that produces the security and confidence needed for living like children of God? Our Blessed Lady probably ground her meal like this.

The virtue of justice is a prerequisite for the happiness of the world; it is a foundation virtue in all social living. Without it society will ever be weak, discontented, disjointed, and unhappy. Without justice there is lacking one of the fundamental conditions necessary for social well-being on earth, as well as for ease of attaining to eternal salvation.

If, therefore, you find the world an unhappy place or not to your liking, change it. First, *practice* absolute and unflinching justice in all things. Become a just man. Secondly, *preach* justice by word and by example. Show the world its value by argument and reason as well as by the evidence of its visible results. Men have eyes to see and intellects with which to understand.

Let us now turn to a more detailed treatment, first, of the seventh and tenth commandments, in which the virtue of justice in its most strict and proper sense is prescribed; and then of the eighth commandment, which calls for veracity or truthfulness, a potential part of justice.

REVIEW OF SECTION ONE.

SECTION TWO: THE SEVENTH AND TENTH COMMANDMENTS

A. GENERAL PRINCIPLES
1. PURPOSE OF CREATED THINGS
2. MAN'S RIGHT TO PROPERTY
   a. Individual and Social Rights of Property
3. PURPOSE OF THE SEVENTH AND TENTH COMMANDMENTS
   a. To Protect and Control Ownership
4. OWNERSHIP
   a. Kinds of Ownership
   b. Ways in Which Ownership is Acquired
5. NECESSITY OF PRIVATE OWNERSHIP

B. VICES AND SINS VIOLATING JUSTICE AND THE RIGHTS OF OWNERSHIP
1. STEALING AND ROBBERY
   a. Influence of Attendant Circumstances
   b. Stealing by Cooperation
   c. An Exception — Extreme Necessity
2. KEEPING PROPERTY

3. UNJUST INTERFERENCE WITH LAWFUL USE OF PROPERTY—STRIKES, JUST AND UNJUST
   a. Conditions for a Just Strike
4. DAMAGING PROPERTY
5. NON-FULFILLMENT OF CONTRACTS
6. CONTRACTING DEBTS
7. BETTING AND GAMBLING
8. CHEATING
9. USURY
10. OTHER FORMS OF INJURING PROPERTY RIGHTS OF OTHERS

C. RESTITUTION
  1. WHEN IS RESTITUTION REQUIRED?
  2. GOOD AND BAD FAITH
  3. RESTITUTION FOR DAMAGES AND THE LIKE
  4. RESTITUTION IN CASES OF COOPERATION
  5. GRAVITY OF OBLIGATION TO MAKE RESTITUTION

D. COVETOUSNESS AND THE OPPOSITE VIRTUES
  1. COVETOUSNESS
    a. The Desire to Possess
    b. Purpose of This Tendency
    c. Danger of Covetousness
    d. Other Effects
  2. THE OPPOSITE VIRTUES
    a. Liberality and Christian Prudence
    b. Detachment — A Needed Virtue
    c. The Saints and These Virtues
    d. Supernatural Christian Charity

A. GENERAL PRINCIPLES

The seventh and tenth commandments, by explicitly forbidding the chief external and internal sins against justice, that is, stealing and covetousness, condemn and forbid all other violations of that virtue and command those acts by which that virtue is practiced. They protect men in the possession of property and the rights of ownership. They prescribe justice in all things.

1. PURPOSE OF CREATED THINGS

Before entering into a discussion of this commandment, let us take a look at the purpose of created things.

a. God's Glory and Man's Sanctification

As freshmen we saw how God created everything that exists, whether visible or invisible. He created it all for His glory and man's sanctification. The material objects in this world were created for man, that by having and holding and properly using them, he might be able to lead such a life on earth as to fulfill the purpose for which he was created, and thus attain the happiness which was to be his reward. God created man for Himself, and God created material objects to help man reach Him.

To put this in a metaphorical way, man is a diamond, the precious jewel of creation. He is to use all the less noble objects of creation, in so far as he needs them, to help him cut the facets which will reflect to all men the great glory of God that shines on and in him.

2. MAN'S RIGHT TO OWN PROPERTY

Accordingly, every man, by the laws of nature, has a *strict right* to acquire and possess such temporal goods as are necessary at least for the preservation and protection of his own *supernatural life* and the spiritual welfare of those placed in his charge. He also has a right to acquire and own such property as is necessary for the *physical well-being* of himself and his dependents. However, the spiritual welfare of others and the common temporal welfare of society may confer rights on others which are superior to the temporal welfare of any individual. Created things, therefore, and the possession of them are a means to an end, and the end is God's glory and man's temporal and eternal happiness.

Titian (Tiziano Vecellio) $\longrightarrow$

                                 From Ewing Galloway, N. Y.

THE TRIBUTE MONEY

Several virtues allied to the virtue of justice require that we give "to Caesar the things that are Caesar's"; and the virtue of religion, which is also a part of the virtue of justice, commands that we give "to God the things that are God's".

a. The Individual and Social Rights of Property

The word *property* designates not only such real property as real estate but it also designates any material object, or good, or any right, title, or interest which a person has the stable right to use, to own or to dispose of. Thus a diamond ring or a copyright is property in the broad sense.

The ownership of property and the possession of rights is a two-edged sword. It brings with it obligations as well as rights, for there is a social as well as an individual aspect to ownership.

Everyone can see that it is against the laws of nature for any one person to get exclusive possession of any necessity such as food and deny all access to it to others so that they do not have even the barest essentials for the maintenance of life, of health, of liberty.

God created visible things so that *all* would have at least the minimum essentials required for human life and eternal salvation. Undue concentration of ownership or wealth is dangerous in nations and in the world. It leads to insecurity and unrest.

Ownership, then, although it is a matter of strict right, is not a matter of rights without duties. A man can, by labor and the use of his intellect, gain possession of worldly goods and of rights, perhaps in greater abundance than many of his fellowmen. He can justly expect all men to respect his rights, whether as regards property or other affairs. But he must not forget that the *common welfare* of the entire community places just *limitations* and obligations on property and the right of private ownership. Nor should he forget that the common good also places limitations on the amount of this world's goods which he acquires and withdraws from the possibility of ownership by others.

When it is necessary for the common welfare, then, the State can, by taxes or other means, take from the rich to give to the poor. Would it not be better socially if the rich gave the same money to the poor in better wages?

What is true between individuals is true also in the *economic relations of states.* No government has a right to deny to other nations access to those temporal goods or raw materials which are strictly necessary for the physical life and, above all, for the spiritual life of people of other nations. To repeat our basic principle, God created the goods of this world for all, and all have a right by work or purchase to gain for themselves possession of at least the minimum essentials for their physical and spiritual welfare.

3. THE PURPOSE OF THE SEVENTH AND TENTH COMMANDMENTS

a. To Protect and Control Ownership

In keeping with this right of access to and possession of the minimum essentials, the purpose of the seventh and tenth commandments, is to protect all men in the possession and use of created goods. This concerns especially those goods which are necessary for the preservation of life, health, liberty, and good name and, above all, those needed by men for the salvation of their souls. These commandments, therefore, *confirm and support the natural law* which, on the positive side, prescribes the virtue of justice by commanding us to give to everyone what is rightfully his; and on the negative side forbids any one to injure a man in his property and possessions or to infringe on his rights of ownership unlawfully.

The seventh commandment, supporting the virtue of justice both protects and limits the rights of ownership. But what is ownership?

4. OWNERSHIP

Ownership is the right and power to have, to use, and to dispose of things belonging to one's self, provided no right of another or any just law prohibits it. Ownership of created things, then, in its highest and most complete sense, belongs to God. He has supreme dominion over all

His creatures for He drew them out of nothing. But man has been made to the image and likeness of God, and has been appointed by Him to be the king and ruler of the creatures lower than himself in the scale of creation. Man, therefore, also possesses true, although not supreme, dominion over the created objects of which he becomes owner.

a. Kinds of Ownership

This human ownership and right to use and dispose of earthly possessions is of two kinds: first, that ordinary right to own, use, sell, and otherwise dispose of one's property which every private individual has. Secondly, there is what is called the right of *eminent domain,* which signifies the right of the State, for a just cause related to the public or common welfare, to make decisions or regulations governing the property and goods of its citizens. Thus, the State may compel a private landowner to sell or lease his property so that a needed bridge or road may be built.

b. Ways in Which Ownership is Acquired

How does one acquire the rights of ownership? In various ways.

In the beginning of the world, and even in early days in our own country, man became an owner of land or other goods or property by *taking possession* of something to which no one else had as yet laid a just claim. Do you remember the story of the days of the gold rush and how

←

Philip Gendreau, N. Y.

THE CHRIST OF THE ANDES

Justice must prevail between groups as well as between individuals, if peace is to be more than a vain hope. Between nations especially there must exist a spirit of confidence and good-neighborliness which only justice and charity can engender and promote. When Christ and His program of Christian justice and charity are introduced in the field of international politics and economics, peace and true progress may return to a world torn with mistrust and greed. If all nations would solve their difficulties in the Christian manner in which Argentina and Chile solved their border dispute—and signalized it as evidenced here—war would be less frequent.

the Forty-Niners staked and registered a claim? Here, of course, the government already had a general title to the land.

One also becomes owner *by finding* an object which as yet belongs to no one, as, for instance, a pearl in an oyster. Here civil law sometimes lays down certain rules. One may also become owner of an object when he finds something which has been lost and is unable to locate the owner even after careful search. The thoroughness of the search required depends on the value of the object found. One can also come into possession of property *by inheritance.*

The principal way, however, in which men today acquire the rights of ownership is *by purchase.* A man may buy an object, for example, some land, a house, some clothing; a man may also purchase the *use* of an object, as for example, by renting a house, leasing a truck, paying the royalty for the use of a copyrighted play or song or book. In the former case, you can easily see his rights of ownership by purchase will be greater than those he secures by only renting or leasing something.

Another important way in which human beings come into possession of the goods of this world is *by work.* God gave the whole earth to the entire human race, but He intended that each individual should gain for himself, by his own work and industry, that share of this world's goods which would be most in keeping with the best interests of his immortal soul. If this work is done on one's own property, the entire product belongs to the owner. If one works with another's property, he may take part of the result, or he may take wages for his work.

For instance, if a laborer cuts down trees for another man and makes posts of them, he may claim the agreed number of posts as his own, or the specified wages in money or other objects of value if such were the agreement or contract.

5. THE NECESSITY OF PRIVATE OWNERSHIP

There are those, such as the socialistic communists, who foolishly say that private possession of property is not necessary, or even that it is socially harmful. They would prohibit the private ownership of property and turn it all over to the State. They would "socialize" it or have it all held by the State and not by private individuals or companies. They promise great advantages as a result of this system of state ownership, especially to the poor and down-trodden. But sound reason and the solemn voice of the Catholic Church not only show their promises are vain or even insincere, but also advance unanswerable arguments to prove that the private ownership of property, real or personal, is necessary both for the liberty of the individual and for the progress of the social organism.

As regards government ownership of property, would the following principle seem to be sound and to protect best the liberty of peoples: Government should not own or control any more property than is required to protect and provide for the essentials of the common temporal welfare of its citizens?

B. VICES AND SINS VIOLATING JUSTICE AND THE RIGHTS OF OWNERSHIP

The rights which an individual or the members of any group, such as a company or corporation, have over their property may be violated by taking that property, by damaging it, or by interfering with the lawful use of it to the loss and detriment of the owner.

1. STEALING AND ROBBERY

The first sin against property rights is theft or stealing. It implies the stealthy and unjust taking of the property of another. The second is robbery, which is the open and violent taking of another's property by force or threat. Both are wrong, for they are a violation of the strict rights of another.

a. Influence of Attendant Circumstances

If the amount of property is sufficiently great, the sin committed can be mortal. However, the theft of a small amount of money or property, such as ordinarily would not constitute a grave sin, could be grave under certain circumstances. For instance, it might not be a mortal sin to steal a dollar from a very rich person or a large corporation, but it could be a mortal sin knowingly to steal the same amount of money from a poor widow who needed it very badly in order to buy necessary food. Here you see again an example of the case where circumstances affect the morality of an action. Moreover, if a person planned to steal a large sum, but to do so by repeatedly taking small amounts, he would still commit a grave sin.

There are other circumstances which affect the gravity of sins of stealing. For instance, when children take food or other things around the home it is usually considered as much less serious than if they were to take the same things elsewhere. When objects are out in the open and unprotected, as for example, fruit, it is usually necessary to take more than the ordinary amount or value to constitute a grave sin. Objects which have been definitely discarded or abandoned may be taken by anyone.

b. Stealing by Cooperating

Not only is it a sin to steal or rob, but it is also a sin knowingly to cooperate with or help a thief or robber in any way, whether it be by assisting him in stealing or robbing, or in advising him as to the time, place and so forth, or by accepting or keeping the stolen goods or by buying or selling them, or by conniving in the violation of justice in any other way. Could a lawyer be guilty in this regard? a storekeeper? How?

Fra Filippo Lippi   From Ewing Galloway, N. Y

ADORATION OF THE CHILD

c. An Exception—Extreme Necessity

There is one situation in which it is not a sin to take another's property. It is the case in which one's own life or the lives of one's dependents are at stake.

Let us illustrate this by an example. A certain man, John Smith, through no fault of his own, is actually in danger of starving. He has no food, no money. He will die of starvation unless he takes either some food or the money to buy food. In such circumstances it would not be a sin for him to take what is necessary for the preservation of life, unless by doing so he would place the person from whom he took it in the same dire straits. This is also true of a person who is in danger of freezing to death and takes the clothing necessary to keep himself warm.

The general principle in such situations is this: In cases of extreme necessity, that is, when one's life is genuinely endangered a person is allowed to take from another what is needed to save himself unless thereby he would put the other person into the same extreme necessity from which he is trying to escape. The right to life is higher than the right to private property.

2. KEEPING PROPERTY

Stealing and robbing are not the only sins against the seventh commandment. There are many varied ways in which a person can infringe on the property rights of others. For example, one can do an injustice to his neighbor by *unlawfully keeping* property or possessions which he should return. This is true when a person borrows a sum of money and unjustly withholds a payment or carelessly neglects to pay it back. It can also be the case when a person contracts a debt and refuses or unjustly neglects to make the necessary settlement, as happens when a person fails to pay his rent or bills, or when employers without necessity impose inadequate wage rates or refuse to pay, in full, wages due by agreement or under law.

TRAPPISTS PLOWING

Those who follow Christ realize that it is not only necessary but also good for man to eat his bread in the sweat of honest toil. Work is not merely a punishment for sin; in God's great wisdom it is, at the same time, a physical and mental requirement. Even those who devote their entire lives to the most strict regime of the cloistered religious life need work of some kind to preserve health of body as well as of mind.

Employees also would do wrong in not fulfilling a wage contract freely made. By so acting one infringes on the right which the other person has to his property.

3. UNJUST INTERFERENCE WITH LAWFUL USE OF PROPERTY—STRIKES, JUST AND UNJUST

A like situation occurs where the rightful owner is *interfered with* in the lawful possession or use of his property, or is actually prevented from taking or using it. This can happen in many different ways.

Thus, such a situation might obtain in an *unjust* strike, if the strikers, by picketing or taking over a plant, would unjustly force it to suspend operations with subsequent loss to the owners. Some strikes, however, are justified.

a. Conditions for a Just Strike

In this connection it might be well to lay down the requirements for a just strike. Since strikes are a sort of small-scale war, these conditions are rather strict.

a) There must be a real and grave injustice involved, such as unfair wages, excessive hours, harmful conditions of work, refusal to bargain with the workers' organization, etc.

b) The prospective gains must exceed the losses, remembering that neither can be measured in terms of money alone.

c) All other means of obtaining justice, such as persuasion, mediation, arbitration, should first have been attempted, and failed. The strike is a last resort.

d) There must be some likelihood of success.

e) The strike must be conducted fairly, without violence, or destruction of property, lies or fraud.

If a strike would cause serious harm to the common good it could hardly ever be justified. Here compulsory arbitration has its place.

These are the rules, and a Catholic must keep them in mind and try to apply them as best he can, as he would in forming his conscience on any other complex moral problem. He should endeavor to make these principles known and observed by his fellow-unionists. Do you think it would be of value to memorize these conditions?

The outsider often influences the success or failure of a strike by his support or opposition. This is true of customers as well as those who wield public power or control or influence public opinion. One, therefore, should try to learn the true facts in the case and take the side of justice.

The ultimate goal is the elimination of strikes, not by suppression but by intelligent use of organization, voluntary agreements, mediation, and arbitration to settle such disputes as may still arise even where both sides are reasonable and well-intentioned. All Catholics, and especially unionists and employers can and should hasten progress toward this goal.

As regards the purpose of the strike—to take advantage of an employer in order to extort exorbitant wages from him; to use a strike to promote social unrest and perhaps revolution as the communists do, to use it as a means of maintaining certain persons in charge of the union, or to remove those in charge in order to replace them with others—such are hardly honest and upright motives for calling or sponsoring a strike. They would constitute the matter for a violation of the rights of the employer and sometimes of the members of the union and an infringement of the virtue of justice. Moreover, to call a strike for some minor difficulty, or when there are available other means of getting a just settlement of the points at issue, is to violate the conditions of a lawful strike.

A strike is a serious matter. It causes loss of money to the workers and the employer, and adversely affects the common good. Strikes often lead to violence and public tumults. They tend to cause frayed tempers and unjust demands, and the use of unchristian methods. Therefore, a strike should be *a court of last resort,* and be used only when all other methods of obtaining justice have been patiently and fruitlessly tried out.

Catholic workmen and leaders of workingmen's groups should be well grounded in these principles governing strikes. By the promotion of justice and charity, and by the suppression of pride and avarice they should help our nation and its people toward a peaceful social existence in which there is a just wage scale and a just day's work, a fair profit, and decent working conditions.

Philip Gendreau, N. Y

What do these clasped hands symbolize? Cooperation? Friendship? A contract
made and sealed on a word of honor? The obligation in justice to fulfill honest
agreements freely arrived at? Yes, all this and more. They symbolize an answer to
this world's troubles. They symbolize man getting along with his fellowman in
justice and charity.

4. DAMAGING PROPERTY

In addition to the three ways of injuring others in their
rights to property which we have thus far considered;
namely, stealing or robbing, unlawful keeping or with-
holding, and the interference with the lawful possession
or use of one's property, we can mention, fourthly, the
damaging of the property of another, or the causing of
others to damage property or the failure to prevent such
damage when there is an obligation to do so.

Thus a night watchman who stands idly by while hoodlums hurl bricks through the windows of the store he has been hired to guard and protect; a jealous business man who, by ways direct or devious, leads others to do harm and damage to his competitor, whether by damage to his property, or by harming his business by spreading false and harmful rumors; and, finally, a person who himself directly causes damage and loss to another either by injuring him in his goods of fortune or by doing anything which would unjustly cause him loss—all these three men and all who are guilty of these or similar acts of injustice would be violating the seventh commandment and causing social unrest.

You can perhaps think of countless other ways in which one can damage the property or cause loss to the possessions of another. Such would be the case of a banker playing loosely with the funds entrusted to him and causing the bank to fail; a business firm poorly run, paying exorbitant salaries to its officers and because of dishonesty and culpable mismanagement going into bankruptcy and causing the stock- or bond-holders to lose the money which they had invested.

5. NON-FULFILLMENT OF CONTRACTS

A fifth way of violating the seventh commandment is by failing to fulfill our contracts.

In studying Matrimony we learned that a contract is a mutual agreement between two or more persons or groups by which they bind each other to a certain transfer of rights. A contract entails rights and duties for the parties who make it. Individuals or groups that make a contract and do not fulfill their part of it are guilty of a violation against justice and, if there is any loss arising from the failure to fulfill the contract, they are also responsible for that loss. Thus a company or a union that unjustly violates a contract can be bound in conscience to repair the losses unjustly inflicted on another group or person.

6. CONTRACTING DEBTS

Another violation of justice can be found in the not infrequent practice of contracting debts beyond one's reasonable ability to pay. This is usually an indication of the vice of covetousness and a proof of the lack of Christian detachment from created goods. It is unjust because it deprives the person who sold the goods of the payment of his money or at least defers such payment far beyond all reasonable limits.

A prudent Christian who is free from undue attachment to created things pays as he goes, lives within his income, and does not let his or her liking for clothes, or finery, or automobiles, or jewelry, or furniture, or any other such objects entice him or her into extravagant living and the unjust contracting of debts far beyond any prudent ability to pay. He does not mortgage his future except with reserved prudence.

7. BETTING AND GAMBLING

Betting and the playing of games for money are sinful if they violate the virtue of justice and due moderation. In itself, it is not sinful to wager a small or reasonable sum of money on the outcome of some event or on the truth or falsity of some statement or alleged fact.

However, betting and the playing of games of chance, speculating in the stock market, and the like, often quickly develop into the vice of gambling. What originally started out as perhaps a bit of justifiable recreation, or as an honest investment often degenerates into an abuse, into an obsession, into a craze for making easy money, a sinful overindulgence in recreation, a wasting of time or other similar forms of vice. If one senses such an attractiveness in these matters that he can prudently judge them to be a future occasion of serious sin or an occasion for contracting a vice which has ruined many individuals and families he should with all Christian fortitude avoid the dangerous situation.

These sins can become serious and form themselves into deep-seated and socially harmful vices if they lead a person to neglect his health or his work, or to wager and perhaps lose large sums of money which are necessary for the feeding, the clothing, and the Catholic education of one's self or one's family. In these latter cases you can surely detect the clear violation of the virtue of justice arising from the sinful disregard and infringement of the rights of wife and children.

The anti-social power and influence which petty gambling often gives to "racketeers" and "policy-kings" is another reason for avoiding betting and gambling.

8. CHEATING

Most people have tender consciences when it comes to the direct stealing of money from others, but not a few have rather calloused souls in regard to other violations of justice and of the seventh commandment. Many who would blush to steal will cheat most unblushingly. But cheating in all its various forms is wrong and displeasing to God. Using dishonest scales or measures, giving short weight, short count, or short change, charging excessive prices, and making excessive profits, falsifying goods as to kind or quality, or *cheating in any other shape or form* is a sin of injustice. Scripture says: "Thou shalt not have divers weights in thy bag, a greater and a less. Neither shall there be in thy house a greater bushel and a less . . . For the Lord thy God abhorreth him that doth these things, and He hateth all injustice." Deut. 25, 13-16.

If a storekeeper or clerk were to make a regular practice of cheating his customers of small amounts which at the end of the day or week would grow into major amounts, he could easily be guilty of grievous sin if he foresaw and especially if he intended thus to obtain a considerable sum for himself.

Not infrequently such cheating by clerks and store managers arises from greed, pure and unadulterated. But there are occasions when this vice finds at least a partial cause in the niggardly wages paid for such work. Owners and directors of stores and companies which pay wages so low that a decent standard of living cannot be maintained, may share the blame and guilt for the sins of injustice which their unchristian tightfistedness has caused. They fail to see also that such miserly wages almost constitute a tacit approval of cheating by the employee and encourage the formation of vicious practices and habits which are ultimately harmful to the owners as well as to the general public. It might be well to discuss this entire matter in class and to come to some conclusions as to what we as Catholics can do about it. The following suggestions may give you a start.

a. Purchasing Power and Fair Business Practices

Low wages are partly caused by sharp buying. Needless to say, everyone is in all justice allowed to drive a good bargain. But when bargain-driving becomes so hard as to deprive the seller of a reasonable profit, or, as more frequently happens, to cause him to lower the wages of his employees to meet the pressure of sharp competition, then the question arises: Am I allowed to drive such a hard bargain as to cause unjustly low wages to be paid?

To put it a better way, am I allowed to pass up the store of a merchant who is paying a living wage and patronize another store which is able to undersell him because it pays its employees unjustly low wages, or forces them to work under cheap, unhealthy conditions? Am I allowed to pass up goods produced by a just manufacturer and take advantage of the lower prices of similar goods pro-

----

$\longrightarrow$

Philip Gendreau, N. Y.

WHEAT

Man is a social being. God made him such. He needs the companionship of others. He needs the labor, the cooperation and help of others and they need his. The bread the city man eats is made possible by the hot work of the farmer who takes his chances with the elements to grow the wheat which is the staff of life and a symbol of the Eucharist food of our souls. On the other hand, the pitchfork the farmer uses is produced by the steelworker who stands over a hot furnace to make good steel. Therefore, by the law of nature—which is the law of God—all men, of all nations must be mindful of one another, cooperative, just, kind. They are all members of one human race created by God to be united with Him in bliss and glory for all the aeons of eternity.

duced by unfair competition or slave labor? Or, on the other hand, by the pressure of my buying-power do I have an obligation to exert my influence for fair wages, honest competition, and just business practices? What do you think? Women do 85 per cent of the buying in our country: do they have any special obligations in this regard? How can they help? Is it socially sound to eliminate the small business man?

9. USURY

A very common form of cheating is the practice of charging excessively high rates of interest on loans. Simple people are deceived when told they will pay an interest of only 1 per cent per month on a loan. They do not realize that this means 12 per cent per year if based on the unpaid balance, and that it may actually be as high as 20 per cent and 30 per cent per annum and higher if the monthly payments are all based on the original sum and are not reduced as the unpaid balance diminishes.

Would it be wrong for a Catholic to be engaged in usury? What interest do credit unions charge?

10. OTHER FORMS OF INJURING PROPERTY RIGHTS OF OTHERS

We have not begun to enumerate all the various ways in which a person can steal and cheat, nor have we listed all the other manners in which he can injure his neighbor in his property rights. It may be that you yourself can mention many ways in which men can and do violate justice and the seventh commandment.

Let us conclude this section by giving you a start on making a list of still further ways of committing sins in this matter: buying stolen goods, adulterating foodstuffs, making counterfeit money or tickets, etc.; unjustly cornering or manipulating the market whether in stocks and bonds or in produce or products of any kind; monopolies, bribery, going into bankruptcy unjustly and unnecessarily, evading just taxes, making no effort to find the owner of a valuable article which one has found; taking unjust advantage and cheating in examinations for jobs, as for example, civil service examinations, and thereby depriving qualified persons of the better remuneration; nepotism, and all other forms of injustice whereby persons related to us by ties of blood, friendship, etc., are unjustly preferred to more deserving and more capable persons who have a greater right thereto. These and many other ways there are of breaking the seventh commandment.

Would laziness, voluntary poverty, and the subsequent acceptance of government relief or charity when able to earn one's own living be an offense against justice? Does discrimination because of creed, color, or nationality violate justice? Does a Negro have a right to work? to fair wages? Does the bringing of unjust lawsuits also come under this head? What other situations can you think of in which a person can be done an injustice against his rights to acquire, possess, or use property, real or personal?

Would cheating by players or officials in athletic contests violate justice? How about unsportsmanlike conduct? "dirty" playing? doing anything to win? Is the main object in sports to win or to learn to be a man?

C. RESTITUTION

Restitution is the reparation of a loss which we have unjustly caused another to suffer.

1. WHEN IS RESTITUTION REQUIRED?

Restitution must be made in all cases of the unjust taking or keeping an object which belongs to another, and in cases of damage or financial loss unjustly inflicted.

The obligation to restitution arises only when there has been a violation of *commutative justice,* which you remember is that subdivision of particular justice which commands that every person give to every other person what is strictly and properly his own.

If a public official passes out public funds in such a manner as to favor unjustly a particular group of citizens, he commits a sin and violates distributive justice, but he does not incur the obligation of restoring to the less favored group its equal share of the benefits or money distributed. Thus if a politician arranged it so that all the money for good roads and other improvements were allocated to his part of the state, neglecting the others, he would violate distributive justice. However, he would not be bound to build roads for the others or restore them their taxes out of his own pocket.

Violations against legal justice and against distributive justice do not oblige one to make restitution.

But if a man steals from another man or a company, or organization, or embezzles, or cheats, or injures, or in any other way unjustly damages the property of, or inflicts loss on another person or firm or group, he is bound to make restitution if he is able.

The accepting of political graft, the charging of money for political appointments, stealing city or other property, passing an unjust sentence for the sake of a bribe, using public funds to control elections, and many other sins may involve sins against commutative justice and may therefore bind a person to restitution or to the reparation of the damages unjustly inflicted.

2. GOOD AND BAD FAITH

A person who in good faith possesses an object of value and then discovers that it actually belongs to another, is obliged to give back to the rightful owner whatever still remains. However, a person who is not in good faith, that is, one who has known that a thing which he has taken, or which he still has in his possession, really is the

$\longrightarrow$

Philip Gendreau, N. Y.

AGRICULTURE

Agriculture and its allied fields of employment provide men with the food they need for life. Justice requires that the man who produces the food receive a living wage for himself and his family. It also requires that he and all others who handle or distribute it do not unjustly control prices against their fellowmen.

property of another, is obliged not only to restore the entire object or its value but also to pay for the losses and damage caused by his unjust taking and retention of his neighbor's property.

For example, let us say that John steals Samuel's truck and keeps it for a month. As a result Samuel is unable to deliver his groceries which spoil, and, in addition, he loses a whole month's sale of goods. John is in conscience bound not only to return the truck but also to repair these losses in as far as he is able.

3. RESTITUTION FOR DAMAGE AND THE LIKE

In those cases where a person's property has been sinfully and maliciously destroyed or not properly protected or its use unjustly interfered with, the obligation of restitution also arises. Thus if a person were to cause another to suffer a serious loss because of failure to keep a contract, or because he prevented the owner from using or taking possession of his property or in any other similar way were the culpable cause of his sustaining a loss, he would generally be bound to make proper restitution for the losses incurred.

For example, if a lawyer unjustly kept the lawful heirs to a will from coming into possession of their inheritance he would be obliged not only to see to it that they got their allotted share but also that they were compensated for the damage or losses incurred, as for instance, loss of rents, dividends, and such like.

4. RESTITUTION IN CASES OF COOPERATION

There is likewise an obligation to make restitution in those cases where a person has not actually stolen or damaged his neighbor's property himself, but has commanded or advised or in other ways helped and cooperated with another in inflicting an injury on a third party in goods and possessions. The amount and degree of responsibility in this last case depends on the degree of cooperation and its influence on the injustice.

Would a politician or economic despot have any obligation to restitution for effecting the passage of laws which forced unjustly low wages or caused unemployment in order to make government relief and subsidies necessary and by this means build up the political support and control needed to keep himself and his party in office?

5. GRAVITY OF OBLIGATION TO MAKE RESTITUTION

The obligation to make restitution is a grave one if, first, the amounts concerned are in themselves grave and if, secondly, the taking of another's property or the damaging of his rights and possessions has also been gravely sinful. Of course, there is no obligation to restitution in those cases of damage or loss inflicted on another where no sin on our part has been involved. For example, if I by accident, but not through carelessness, destroy another's property, I incur no obligation to restitution.

6. TO WHOM TO RESTORE

The stolen money or object and the payment to cover the damages or losses unjustly caused must be paid back to the person who was thus injured or to his rightful heirs. If the rightful owner cannot be found or determined, then, but only then, must the money or goods be turned over to the poor, or to some charitable or religious purpose; they may not be retained by the culprit. A merchant who has defrauded his customers by cheating in making change or by using short weights could make restitution to them by giving over-weight in equal amount.

D. COVETOUSNESS AND THE OPPOSITE VIRTUES

1. COVETOUSNESS

a. The Desire to Possess

It has been repeatedly stated in the course of these last four years that when the basic tendencies of human nature are properly controlled they result in the virtues of an

THE HOLY STAIRS

The statuary group at the right depicts Judas, victim of covetousness, betraying Christ His Lord and Master. The staircase in the center covers the stairs which are said to have been in Pilate's palace in Jerusalem. They were brought from the Holy Land to Rome, where they are now revered as a most honored relic of Christ's Passion. Pilgrims ascend them on their knees. We could ascend them in spirit, saying an act of contrition on every step for our sins of covetousness and for all other sins committed by ourselves and by others, especially sins against justice.

upright life; and that when left uncontrolled, they degenerate into the vices of a sinful life.

One of these tendencies is the urge that is found in everyone to acquire and possess earthly goods. When properly guided by reason and faith this tendency leads to the formation of the cardinal virtue of justice and all its allied virtues. When uncontrolled, its acts gradually form the vices of covetousness, avarice, injustice, and all their accompanying sins and vices.

b. Purpose of Desire to Possess

From what has been learned already in this unit we know why God placed in man this natural inclination to acquire and possess things. His purpose was to lead men to acquire such a sufficiency of created goods as to permit them, with freedom and security, to care for the physical and spiritual life and health of themselves and those committed to their care. More especially, God intended that the freedom, the security, the health, and the other benefits arising from the possession of property—including the very uncertainty of its retention—might raise men's mind to Himself and to the hope of eternal salvation and security, and thus assist them in obtaining it.

c. Danger of Covetousness

Covetousness, which is the sinful perversion and vicious misuse of this inclination to possess, is a great and a dangerous vice, and the second of the capital sins. In our times Pope Pius XI tells us it has become *a prevailing passion* and the root of great social disorders. It binds men's wills to gaudy and attractive but worthless earthly baubles.

The covetous and avaricious man hoarding and guarding his property is like an unreasoning baby, chortling and gloating and beaming in the possession of a Christmas tree ornament. All tinsel and glitter it is—but hollow inside. Full of rosy promise, but empty of fulfillment. Attractive but fragile. And when it breaks, what pitiful nothingness!

So, too, it is with created riches. They are as empty as an ornament, yet they are as attractive; and the soft seductive whispers of the Great Deceiver keep coming: "Reach and take and taste. You shall be like gods." Nature already inclines. Earthly possessions are so pleasant—it seems. The temptation is great and unless the opposite habit has already been anchored by consistent practice we may reach to seize the bauble. And once it is seized we start reasoning and arguing with ourselves to justify our action in compromising our principles and violating our conscience.

Greed, avarice, and covetousness create within us an inclination to gloss over any excess or fault in our attitude toward or our possession of created goods. In more advanced stages greed creates *blindness to right and wrong in ourselves,* although we may clearly see and hate injustice in others.

d. Other Effects of Covetousness

Covetousness, avarice, greed, and unholy attachment to wealth and possessions are vices which never occur alone. They breed *harshness* in one's dealings with and in one's treatment of others. They foster *cruelty* and disregard of the feelings and even the extreme necessity of others. They approve *injustice,* and foster *dishonesty* of all kinds. They disrupt family life, cause arguments and fights and lawsuits, disturb community peace, help to split society and nations and have caused more wars than perhaps any other vices.

In truth, the inclination to have and possess can create havoc and unhappiness both for the individual and for the social organism. Like a rose it grows wild if neglected. Yet the root is good and God intended that it should bloom and glorify Him and serve man. It will do this, however, only if it is properly pruned, and faithfully trained, and eternally watched out of the corner of our eye.

2. THE OPPOSITE VIRTUES

We have already studied at length the key virtue which opposes covetousness and which controls the tendency to secure possessions—the cardinal virtue of justice. We have seen that it gives us that right to secure that share of this world's goods which is necessary to life and health,

$\longrightarrow$

Philip Gendreau, N. Y.

INDUSTRY

Ours is an industrialized civilization, with men working with tools and on materials supplied by others. In this relationship of employer and employee, of owner or manager on one side and worker on the other, laws of justice must be observed as Christ commands they should be; otherwise social unrest and disturbance will follow.

physical and spiritual. At the same time it obliges us to give to all other human beings that which is properly their own.

a. Liberality and Christian Prudence

Allied with justice is the daughter-virtue, liberality. If God has given freely to us He certainly expects us to share His gifts with others, with a free and open hand. This is especially true of those gifts which will assist our neighbor in his physical and his spiritual necessities.

In order to be truly liberal, prudence in the administration of our earthly affairs will be required.

We must avoid stinginess and penuriousness and over-carefulness in providing for the future on the one hand, and on the other, we must be equally careful not to indulge in a selfish spendthriftiness and the useless waste of money on idle objects of vanity, pride, and pleasure. The good Christian avoids both stinginess and prodigality in order that he may practice Christian liberality. And when he gives, it is always in the name of Christ who has already warned us that at the Last Judgment He will use the practice of this virtue of liberality as one of the criteria for separating the sheep from the goats. Read the account as it is recorded in St. Matthew 25, 31-46. You can also locate many scriptural passages on justice in the *Divine Armory* by Vaughn.

b. Detachment—A Needed Virtue

Before we can be liberal a certain mental attitude toward temporal possessions must be acquired. We call it the *spirit of detachment*. It means that we look on wealth and possessions merely as instruments intended to help us glorify God and save our souls, and that we use them only in as far as it is necessary to attain that objective. Instead of becoming unduly attached to them as our very own, we look on them as objects loaned to us by God for a certain period of time.

We can and must possess them and use them, but we should never become overly attached to them. Like the car, or bus, or public conveyance which takes us to school, we use them, we appreciate them, but we maintain towards them a sort of impersonal detachment. They are common human property to which God has given us the title and use for a brief period that they may help us reach Him.

St. Paul has described detachment: "And godliness with contentment is indeed great gain. For we brought nothing into the world, and certainly we can take nothing out; but having food and sufficient clothing, with these let us be content." 1 Tim. 6, 6-8. There is more to the entire quotation.

Detachment does not mean improvident carelessness about the future. The good Christian saves money, makes investments, plans for the rainy day, and protects his loved ones from abject poverty, which gnaws at virtue. But he also lives within his income and does not forget his soul and its eternal welfare in his cares about his body and its temporal needs and comforts.

c. The Saints and These Virtues

The lives of the saints afford examples of all the Christian virtues in operation, those concerning the virtues connected with justice no less than those allied to other virtues. It would be time profitably spent if you would read the lives of some of those who were outstanding for liberality and detachment, as for example, St. Alexis, St. Felix of Valois, St. Elizabeth, St. Martin of Tours, St. Francis of Assisi, St. John Baptist de la Salle, St. Vincent de Paul, and Don Bosco. You would see how they gave of their means and wealth in liberal alms to the poor, and how they founded, encouraged, and endowed charitable social enterprises for the relief of the poor and the spiritual welfare of their neighbor.

d. Supernatural Christian Charity

Justice, with its allied virtues, is a virtue of the will, and, when vivified with habitual or sanctifying grace, it is a supernatural moral virtue, giving us the capacity and, with practice, the facility for performing supernatural acts of justice. But there is, as has already been noted above, another, higher virtue which governs and supports the human will in its relations with material things as well as in its relations with everything that exists. It is the supernatural, or theological or divine virtue of Christian charity, the supreme virtue of a Christian life. It perfects justice and elevates it, as it perfects and elevates all other virtues.

From love of God is born fraternal charity, for if we have that perfect love of God which apprehends and serves Him as the highest good then we will also have love of His created images, rational or non-rational, angelic, human, or subhuman. We will love our fellow men and deal with them not only in complete justice but, far beyond that, we will treat them in all Christian charity. In our relations with them we will render to each not only what is due to him by right but we will add that, also, which is needful for body, and mind, and soul.

Would the virtue of charity favor the replacement of the profit motive with the motive of service of our fellowmen?

REVIEW OF SECTION TWO.

SECTION THREE: THE EIGHTH COMMANDMENT— THE VIRTUE OF TRUTHFULNESS

A. TRUTHFULNESS AND FIDELITY
  1. THE PURPOSE OF LANGUAGE
  2. MAN'S RIGHT TO EXPECT US TO TELL THE TRUTH
  3. PROVING THE NECESSITY OF TRUTHFULNESS
     a. From Reason
     b. From Revelation — Eighth Commandment
  4. FIDELITY TO PROMISES

B. VICES AND SINS OPPOSED TO TRUTH
  1. LYING
  2. EVASIVE REPLIES
  3. "WHITE" LIES
  4. HYPOCRISY
  5. FLATTERY
  6. BOASTFULNESS
  7. GRAVITY OF UNTRUTHFULNESS

C. SINS AGAINST OUR NEIGHBOR'S GOOD NAME
  1. CALUMNY OR SLANDER
  2. DETRACTION
  3. REPARATION OF SLANDER AND DETRACTION
  4. GOSSIPING, BACKBITING, CONTUMELY
  5. PERJURY
  6. HALF-TRUTHS — COLORING THE NEWS
  7. RASH JUDGMENT
  8. SHOULD I TELL?
  9. CARING FOR OUR OWN REPUTATION
  10. KEEPING A SECRET

A. TRUTHFULNESS AND FIDELITY

1. THE PURPOSE OF LANGUAGE

Man conveys his thoughts to other men by means of signs. Some of these signs are external motions—gestures, for instance; others are sounds, and still others are written symbols. God gave men this marvelous power of communicating ideas, whether by physical, audible, or written signs. He gave it to them in order that they might convey knowledge of the truth to one another. He wanted them to know the truth that the truth might make them free; that it might lead them to Him and make them like Him in wisdom and knowledge and truth and freedom.

He gave men the instrument of language to lead them to the Divine Word and to put them in possession of uncreated Truth Itself. If language is to succeed in doing this, man must use the power of conveying ideas only to impart the truth.

2. MAN'S RIGHT TO EXPECT US TO TELL THE TRUTH

Every human being has the right to expect that we speak the truth by whatever signs we may use: the spoken word, the written word, or by any other signs or symbols employed to convey ideas to others.

The virtue of justice then, demands not only that we do not rob others of their material possessions, but also that we do not rob or mislead them in their search for the truth. Justice requires that we speak the truth. Justice requires that no matter what signs we use in communications with others, we tell the truth, at least as we know it.

It does not require that we tell everything we know, nor that we always tell the full and complete truth about everything; in fact, there are times when, in justice, one may not tell what he knows, as for example, a priest or a doctor, but it does require that what we do say be in conformity with the truth, or at least with our knowledge.

3. PROVING THE NECESSITY OF TRUTHFULNESS

a. From Reason

The natural law reveals quite clearly to all men who have the use of reason that truthfulness or veracity in speaking or in any other use of signs to communicate ideas is a prerequisite for social living and social well-being. The work of the world would be disrupted and have to stop if man could not trust his fellowmen to tell and act the truth. If it were impossible to have confidence in the word of one's neighbor, how could society go on?

If the doctor were free to tell you to take a certain medicine to cure your cold when he knew it would kill you; if the banker could advise you to make an investment when he was certain that you would lose and he perhaps

SANTA MARIA DEL FIORE
The Cathedral—Florence, Italy

Religion, besides being a duty of a dependent creature towards his Creator, is a social necessity of man's nature, for, without it, man's spirit withers and the animal in him takes over. Being social, religion needs external expression, it needs churches, and ceremonies, and liturgical splendor.

gain; if the clergyman telling you how to get to heaven could be deliberately deceiving you and leading you to hell; if no one could trust the word of anyone else, how could any social living continue to be possible?

Truthfulness, then, by the very law of nature, by the very demands of social living is a necessary virtue. Without truthfulness life would be a jungle, a chaos.

b. From Revelation—The Eighth Commandment

What reason thus lucidly proves, God has placed beyond all possibility of doubt and *confirmed by direct revelation.*

It is just one more proof of the extent and the depth of His love for us. How many we have already seen! He has set His law to protect our bodies and physical being, our life and our health; He has set it to protect our spiritual welfare, our temporal possessions, and now we see Him making a divine revelation to protect our minds, and our good name against the invasion of deliberate error and falsehood.

On Mount Sinai, God revealed to man the moral code which was to guide the human race in its effort to participate in the freedom and happiness of God by liberating itself from the shackles of sin and vice and by practicing those virtues which mirror forth the perfections of God. In this code God included the eighth commandment which says: "Thou shalt not bear false witness against thy neighbor."

This is not the only text in the Bible concerning this matter. On the contrary the Holy Scriptures are full of references which show God's attitude toward lying and other violations of the eighth commandment. It might be illuminating to gather as many as you can and discuss them in class.

4. FIDELITY TO PROMISES

In addition to veracity or truthfulness, justice is also related to the virtue of fidelity.

Fidelity means faithfulness to promises. The good Christian is not only an honest man, honest in regard to property and possessions, honest in regard to telling the truth, but he is also *a man of his word.* A good Catholic never breaks his word.

The only exception in the matter of keeping one's word, and really it is not an exception, is when it is a physical or moral impossibility for a person to keep his word, or when he discovers that he has unwittingly promised to do something which would be *wrong*.

The world needs honest men, men whose reputations for untarnished honesty causes them to be trusted by all who know them. The world needs men whose word is their bond. How close are you to being such a man or woman? When you give your word of honor or your promise, do your friends accept it without doubt or hesitation? Are they ever disillusioned?

B. SINS AND VICES OPPOSED TO TRUTH

Let us now turn to the various ways in which the virtues of veracity, fidelity, and the eighth commandment in general can be violated. First, there is lying.

1. LYING

A lie is a word or other sign contrary to what we know or think to be the truth and used in order to deceive another. Usually the sin of lying is committed by word of mouth, but a nod, a pointing of the finger or any other sign used to deceive has the same effect as a spoken word and is therefore morally equivalent.

That lying can be a serious sin can be gathered from the passage in Sacred Scripture, which says of all liars that "their portion shall be in the pool that burns with fire and brimstone, which is the second death." Apoc. 21, 8.

Lying, like every other sin, is a matter of the will. For to lie it is not necessary that we actually deceive a person; it is enough that we *intend to deceive* him. The sin of lying rests in the will or intention to tell something that is false.

A man could actually tell something true to another and yet be guilty of lying if he thought, when telling it, that

Piero di Cosimo   *National Gallery of Art, Kress Collection*

THE VISITATION

St. Elizabeth, being free from envy and from any spirit of flattery, gives to her young cousin the honor which is her due. What a wonderful example to all members of her sex when they are tempted to jealousy, to backbiting, to gossip, and to damning their friends with slight praise!

it was false. On the other hand, a man who told a thing which was not true, but which he thought was true would indeed be in *error* but would not be guilty of the sin of lying, for he did not have the intention of saying something which was not true.

2. EVASIVE REPLIES

Although we are never allowed to tell a lie we are at times allowed and sometimes required to use evasive replies or to refuse to answer.

There may be occasions when a person is asked about something which has been revealed to him in confidence, as, for example, if he were a priest, a doctor, a lawyer, a close friend. There are also occasions when one is asked about some intimate matter in his own life or in the life of another which he would not wish to be known publicly or known by a certain person or group. There are occasions on which inquisitive busybodies ask questions concerning affairs about which they have no right to know. In all such and similar instances one may refuse to answer or may deftly parry the question, for example by asking, "Well, what would you think?" He may give an evasive answer which both avoids telling a lie and also avoids disclosing the information which one is in conscience, or in honor, or in prudence obliged or allowed to keep secret.

In this connection, however, it may be well to remark that there is such a thing as being too secretive. Perhaps the best general rule to follow is: In matters in which one is not obliged to keep a secret or in which Christian prudence would not seem to recommend it, Christian *candor* should be the general practice. If there were less "diplomacy" both private and governmental, and more Christian candor there would be less necessity for using a microscope on every word in peace treaties, contracts, and even everyday affairs. Pagans use words to conceal their real thoughts; Christians use words to tell and lead others quickly and easily to the truth which alone can solve personal as well as international problems. Candor is a virtue except when it becomes imprudent.

3. "WHITE" LIES

While discussing untruthfulness we should mention the matter of "white lies." Sometimes these are genuine lies intended to deceive and to avoid trouble of one sort or another. If such they constitute a venial sin. There are, however, certain formulae which should not be classed as lies but rather as evasive replies. For instance, if the manager of an office were to direct his secretary to inform all callers that he was "not in," that expression is generally accepted to mean that either he is actually not in or that he is busy with other work or that he does not wish to be bothered or interrupted.

4. HYPOCRISY

Three despicable sins and vices against the virtue of truthfulness are hypocrisy, flattery, and boastfulness. The first, hypocrisy, is a sin of false pretense.

A hypocrite is a liar in word or in action; he is a person who feigns to be or tries to make others believe him to be better than he actually is, especially in the moral order. A hypocrite is a sinner posing as a saint, a pretender to virtue. He is one who tries to gain credit for virtues which he himself knows he does not possess. Jesus Christ our Lord abominates hypocrisy, and on more than one occasion, as you will recall from your reading of the Gospels in the sophomore year, He excoriated those "whited sepulchres, which outwardly appear to men beautiful, but within are full of dead men's bones and of all uncleanness." Matt. 23, 27. An honest man is never a hypocrite and he hates hypocrisy in others.

5. FLATTERY

Similar to hypocrisy and equally as detestable, is flattery, that is, the dishonest, untruthful, and insincere praising of a person.

Honest praise is a good thing. Man needs it. It is a

tonic, a spur in doing good if it be but wisely given. Its use is all too infrequent. But flattery and adulation are not good. To give praise where no praise is due, where praise is dishonest or excessive, where praise is a lie and a contradiction of the truth is wrong. Flattery is no virtue, and it can be a very harmful thing if it confirms a sinner in vice.

The flatterer heaps lying or unmerited praise on a proud superior, or a person in power, in order to gain some favor for himself. He helps to blind that person and deceive him, and instead of aiding him to see and overcome his faults, as is his Christian duty, the flatterer only entangles him yet more hopelessly by encouraging him to consider faults as virtues, or little virtues or accomplishments as great ones. He who uses flattery, as well as he who encourages a flatterer, is no asset to this world.

6. BOASTFULNESS

Boastfulness is a mixture of self-flattery, excessive pride, noisy self-advertising, and usually some hypocrisy. Boastfulness is an attempt to raise one's self in the opinion of others. Whether this is in keeping with the truth, or as more often happens, in contradiction to the truth, it is sinful. Whether one tries to raise others' opinions of one's self to a true opinion of his merits or to a falsely inflated opinion of his merits, boastfulness is a sin. The latter kind would of course, be worse, being opposed both to humility and to truth, whereas the former is opposed only to humility.

At this point it may be well to observe that there is a theory which is held by some persons that, not infrequently, cases of *alcoholism* are a result of pride conjoined with a refusal of a person to be honest and truthful with himself. This at least is true, that a proud person striving vainly to become something or do something for which he lacks the ability, and at the same time encouraging an unwillingness to admit this lack of ability, often tends to use

ECCE AGNUS DEI ECCE Q

alcohol first to give him a false courage and later, as the excessive use grows, to give him the excuse or protection of an alcoholic stupor. Alcoholics are known to be the most brazen and inveterate liars. They are neither honest with themselves or with others until they master their habit. In this flight from reality they try to make themselves and others believe what pride and not what truth dictates.

Some types of mental aberration or *nervous breakdown* also seem to be the result of a similar excessive pride and an unwillingness to face the facts. This leads to the mental creation of a dream-world in which one's proud desires are satisfied. If this be true, and there is some evidence to support it, then the conclusion is in order that to avoid these two serious conditions of alcoholism and nervous breakdown one thing that must be done is in all humility to be *honest with one's self*. One must not flatter one's self, one must not be over ambitious, nor cowardly, one must not be boastful, one must not be a hypocrite, one must not lie to anyone, even to himself.

7. GRAVITY OF UNTRUTHFULNESS

Before passing from this general topic of lying we must say a few words concerning the gravity of this sin. If a lie offends only against the virtue of truthfulness it is generally a venial sin, but if in addition it also violates charity or the strict rights of justice then it can be a mortal sin.

For example, if I tell a lie which is the cause of a man losing a notable sum of money, I have violated both truth and justice and my sin can be grave if sufficient deliberation and consent are added to the grave matter.

See if you can find some scriptural quotations concerning lying, flattery, and similar sins and vices. Notice how strongly worded they often are.

←

Simone Martini   *National Gallery of Art, Kress Collection*

ST. JOHN THE BAPTIST

St. John was an honest man, with courage enough to speak for God and His Divine Son. He used the gift of language in a simple, direct, straightforward manner; avoiding the honeyed words of flattery and the deceptive phrases of "diplomacy." He gave testimony to the Lamb of God in all humility; he gave testimony against those in high places when they offended God.

C. SINS AGAINST OUR NEIGHBOR'S GOOD NAME

Every human being has a certain reputation, good or less good, merited, or more or less than merited. Even if a person's reputation is better than he merits he is entitled to that good name in all ordinary cases. In strict matter of fact nearly all men have a better reputation than they would enjoy were all the secret sins of their lives made public.

If the reputation which a person enjoys is founded on fact he has a strict right to it. If it is not founded on fact he still has a right to it unless the common good or the rights of others are thereby jeopardized. Therefore, all unjust and unnecessary attacks on a person's reputation are violations of the eighth commandment. There are two special sins which injure a person's reputation: slander and detraction.

1. CALUMNY OR SLANDER

Calumny, or, as it is more usually called, slander, consists in a violation of the reputation of our neighbor by telling *a deliberate lie* which harms his good name. This is usually done by accusing him of a crime or sin of which he is not guilty.

As you can easily see, slander is serious, whether it is considered in itself or in its social consequences. Do you remember the words of the poet to the effect that "He who steals my purse steals trash, but he who pilfers my good name . . ." Mud sticks more easily than whitewash. People by nature are more interested in startling details, salacious revelations, and crime than they are in efforts to restore a person's reputation. Hundreds who would listen to evil reports or read and be impressed by an accusation will not even hear or show any interest in the retraction of the falsehood. Lies stick like glue, and calumnious remarks often attach themselves to an unoffending victim and ruin his or her whole life.

2. DETRACTION

The sin of detraction is the violation of our neighbor's good name by unjustly revealing a secret sin or crime of which he has been guilty. It is also serious, and in some ways more harmful than calumny, for when one slanders another's character he can retract it by admitting and publicizing the fact that the accusation was a lie. But in the case of detraction one cannot do this. What the detracter has revealed is the truth, but he should not have revealed it. "The detracter is the abomination of men." Prov. 24, 9.

3. REPARATION OF SLANDER AND DETRACTION

Slander and detraction must be repaired, as far as one is able, otherwise they cannot be forgiven. A man who steals another's money must give it back. A man who steals or unjustly ruins another's reputation must also give it back in as far as possible. But it is difficult to make reparation when one has injured another's character. Stolen property or damaged possessions can be replaced, but a ruined character can hardly ever be fully restored.

All that the detracter can do is to attempt to restore the person's reputation by *speaking well* of him and by repairing any financial damage he may have caused by his unjust revelations. The slanderer must, however, *retract his falsehood* and do all he can to restore the damaged reputation. He, too, is bound to repair any financial damage his calumny may have occasioned.

If you want to engage in an interesting discussion, consider the position and responsibility of the newspaper or news magazine in relation to revealing real or alleged crimes or sins.

4. GOSSIPING, BACKBITING, AND CONTUMELY

When these sins of slander and detraction are committed in the absence of the accused they would be classified as backbiting and gossiping. Of such sins Scripture says, "The whisperer and the double tongued is accursed: for he hath troubled many that were at peace." Ecclus. 28, 15.

Gossiping is a sin of levity but its consequences are frequently anything but light. Backbiting is a meaner and more vicious sin. It adds a note of hypocrisy—a friend to one's face, a ruiner of one's character behind one's back. Backbiting often arises from pride and envy, for the proud and jealous strive to exalt themselves by belittling others. Did you ever catch yourself doing this?

When the sins of calumny or slander are committed in the presence of the accused person there is added to the violation of one's reputation a violation of the honor to which every human being has a right: this is the sin of *contumely*. It is not necessarily connected with slander and detraction for this injury to honor may be committed by any injurious calling of names, or by any word or sign or omission by which one shows and expresses contempt for another.

5. PERJURY

Perjury must also be mentioned here, although it is usually considered in connection with the second commandment because of the injury which it does to the name and honor of God. But perjury is not only a sin against the virtue of religion but also against justice; and a serious sin indeed. By it a man maliciously misleads his neighbor by guaranteeing a lie to be the truth and by calling God as a witness to support and confirm his lying statement. Certainly this is a grave sin if a person realizes what he is doing. Nor is it an uncommon sin today, as one can surmise from the number of flatly contradictory statements which people under solemn oath swear to in court.

6. HALF TRUTHS—COLORING THE NEWS

Falsification or coloring of the news, or the printing of only those facts which, though true, will cause a wrong impression or conclusion, are common today; so, too, is false and misleading advertising. It may be that you can add to this list other ways of violating the virtue of veracity. Vice has so many forms, such varied disguises and subterfuges. Would propaganda be a proper subject for discussion in relation to this topic?

7. CRITICIZING

A study of the eighth commandment calls for a word about a matter which is often merely an evidence of a very subtle form of pride, namely, the habit of criticizing others. Frequently it is an attempt to enhance one's self at the expense of the reputation of others. It usually involves one or more of the sins we have just studied. It is often a sin against charity in addition to being a sin against the eighth commandment. Do you habitually criticize or condemn others? How can one develop the opposite virtue?

8. RASH JUDGMENT

Rash judment is a sin consisting of a mental act by which we hold a person or a group guilty of sin without sufficient reason or evidence. It is not a mere suspicion or a doubt that the person may have committed a sin but a judgment that the person is guilty. Even if the person so judged were actually guilty of the sin and we found it out later, it would not relieve us of the responsibility for having rashly judged the person to be guilty before we had sufficient grounds on which to base such a judgment.

The Christian principle on which to act in matters of this nature should be similar to the principle on which civil courts act. The accused is always presumed innocent until proved guilty. It is always best to place the most

VENITE
FILII
AVDITE
ME
TIMORĒ
DÑI
DOCEB
OVOS

Fillippino Lippi *National Gallery of Art, Kress Collection*

ST. FRANCIS OF ASSISI IN GLORY

St. Francis, often called Il Poverello, renounced his right to riches and position to supply the world a most attractive example of the following of Christ in the humility and simplicity of the life of a mendicant friar. Today, in glory, he rejoices that he thus faithfully followed Christ.

favorable interpretation on the actions of others or to suspend forming a judgment until all the facts are available, or until it is necessary to come to a decision.

Experience proves that in most cases a charitable judgment is closer to the truth than an adverse judgment. Moreover, the golden rule can apply here. We would expect our friends and others to give us the favor of any doubt and even to suspend judgment of us if a decision were not mandatory. Should we grant others less, even in our mental judgments? You see, their honor is at stake, as ours would be; and everyone has a right to his just degree of honor until he has clearly forfeited his claim thereto.

Accordingly, not only actual rash judgments but even *unfounded suspicion* is contrary to our neighbor's right to honor and due estimation in our minds and thoughts.

9. SHOULD I TELL?

No one likes a tattle-tale, that garrulous busybody who tries to ingratiate himself with those in authority by telling on others. Indeed, tattling is a very ignoble trait in a person's character and the inclination towards it should be firmly suppressed. Yet, in spite of the fact that tattling and tale-bearing are seriously to be condemned and discouraged, no one should go to the other extreme and make it an unbreakable rule never to reveal the faults of others to the proper superior. There are circumstances under which it is not only advisable but even necessary and *binding in conscience* to report an offense or reveal the secret sin of another.

It can happen that a person of low morals can be an actual, grave danger to the spiritual welfare of a community or a group without the superior in charge being aware of the threat, or without the sins of this person becoming publicly known. If the spiritual welfare of the group cannot be safeguarded in any other way than by informing the person in charge about that grave danger, then there is an obligation on those who know its existence to reveal it to him.

A person can also reveal the secret crimes or sins of others to defend his own reputation or property. In all these cases, however, charity directs that none but necessary facts be disclosed and that they be made known to prudent persons who can do something about the matter, and not to talkative gossipers or persons without authority to act.

10. CARING FOR OUR OWN REPUTATION

It is a violation of justice to be a spendthrift with money, to be excessively prodigal or wasteful with our possessions, to neglect acquiring for ourselves and our dependents, at least what is necessary for a decent human existence. It can likewise be a violation of justice or of the charity we owe ourselves and those related to us to be sinfully careless about our own good name.

A good reputation is a protection to the person who possesses it and can be very necessary either to the individual or to his family and relatives. Think, for example, of the case of a person who disregards his or her own reputation and as a result makes it difficult not only for himself but for all his relatives to find suitable employment or to be accepted in their social group because of the public stigma on the family name.

11. KEEPING A SECRET

We have already mentioned the obligation resting on certain persons to hold in confidence knowledge which has come to them as a result of their official or professional capacity or services. The most notable example of this, of course, is the obligation of the priest to preserve in inviolate secrecy sins he has learned in confession. He may not reveal them even to preserve his own life. Doc-

ST. ILDEFONSUS

Pausing in the course of his study, St. Ildefonsus, with a glance and an unspoken word of love, with a prayer of praise and petition, turns his mind and his heart to the Blessed Lady.

tors, lawyers, and others who come to know facts of a confidential nature are also held by the obligation of secrecy, although it is not as binding as that on the priest.

In general, all are bound to keep secret any information which would cause harm or distress to the person or persons concerned unless one would thereby suffer a proportionately grave harm or inconvenience himself. The obligation to preserve the secret becomes more serious if one has made a promise to that effect.

Everyone has a right to keep certain facts secret if he so wishes and others have the obligation of respecting that right. They may not curiously pry into another's private affairs or use the knowledge thus obtained or reveal the matter to others. They may not read the letters or private papers of others without their express or reasonably presumed permission.

12. APPLICATION

God is truth. The Holy Ghost is the Spirit of Truth. The Son of God is the Way, the Truth, and the Life. Those who would follow the Son, those who would be temples of the Holy Spirit and children and possessors of the God who is Truth, must make themselves like to God by the practice of the virtue of truthfulness. To the God whose love they have seen proved by deeds at every step in the study of man's quest for happiness they, also, must prove their love, by deeds.

They must prove it by letting those virtues which are contained actually and eminently in the Divine God of Love shine in their lives and actions. They must avoid those acts and habits which contradict the nature of God. They must, together with all the other virtues, give proper place to a virtue allied to justice—the virtue of truthfulness or veracity, and they must avoid the sins and vices opposed to that virtue and to the eighth commandment.

REVIEW OF SECTION THREE.

SECTION FOUR: THE SOCIAL ENCYCLICALS

A. THE SOCIAL TEACHING OF THE CHURCH—A PROOF OF GOD'S LOVE
1. THE CHURCH'S CONCERN FOR MAN'S TEMPORAL WELFARE
2. THE ENCYCLICALS AND SOCIAL PROBLEMS
3. KINDS OF JUSTICE—A REVIEW

B. SYNOPSIS OF PIUS XI'S ENCYCLICAL ON THE RECONSTRUCTION OF THE SOCIAL ORDER
   I. SOCIAL BENEFITS OF THE EARLIER ENCYCLICAL OF POPE LEO XIII
      A. Benefits Arising From What the Church Has Done
         1. In Her Teaching
         2. In Applying These Teachings
      B. Benefits Arising From What Civil Authorities Have Done
      C. Benefits Arising From What Employers and Workers Have Done

   II. EXPLANATION, DEFENSE, APPLICATION, AND AMPLIFICATION OF POPE LEO XIII'S TEACHING
      A. Vindication of Right of Church to Speak on Economic and Social Problems
      B. Explanation, Defense, and Application of Specific Points
         1. As Regards Individuals
            a. Ownership, or the Right of Property
               1) Property Has an Individual and a Social Side
               2) The State Can Control the Use of Property for the Common Welfare
               3) Superfluous Income Has Obligations
               4) How Ownership is Acquired
            b. Teachings Regarding Capital and Labor
            c. Necessity of the Redemption of Property-less Workers
            d. Just Wages and Salaries to Enable Ownership
         2. As Regards the Social Order
            a. A Reform of Institutions is Needed
               1) Economic Life Must be Subjected to a True Directing Principle
            b. A Reform of Morals is Required

   III. EVILS OF THE MODERN ECONOMIC SYSTEM AND OF SOCIALISM; THE ROOT OF THE EVIL AND ITS REMEDY
      A. Changes Since 1891 in the Economic System and in Socialism
         1. Changes in the Economic System
            a. Concentration of Wealth, Power, and Control
            b. The Results   c. The Remedies
         2. Changes in Socialism
            a. Communism—Extreme Socialism
            b. More Moderate Socialism
            c. Catholic Deserters to Socialism
      B. The Root and the Remedy of These Evils
         1. The Root—The Uncontrolled Desire for Earthly Goods
         2. The Remedy
            a. A Return to Gospel Living and Right Order
            b. The Place of Charity
            c. Social Reconstruction—A Difficult Task
            d. The Course to Follow

A. THE SOCIAL TEACHING OF THE CHURCH— A PROOF OF GOD'S LOVE

We have now, after four years, completed our treatment of the commandments, and we have seen that everyone of them is an indication of the loving guidance and providence of a God who wants nothing more than that we live as faith and reason dictate so that He, in justice to His own divine perfections, can communicate to us His glory and blessedness and happiness.

We have yet another proof of God's unfailing love for men. It is to be found in the modern social teaching of the Church, some salient points of which we shall now consider.

To suit our present needs and to show the world the way out of its social and economic disorders God, through His Church, has made known the moral laws which must serve as guides if we are to live together in peace and prosperity in the twentieth century. These rules are mostly a new unfolding of the virtue of justice and of the obligations arising from the fifth and seventh commandments. Hence we can well take them up here, but with separate treatment, both because of their importance and newness, and because they have had separate treatment in the instructions given us by the popes.

1. THE CHURCH'S CONCERN FOR MAN'S TEMPORAL WELFARE

The Catholic Church, contrary to the accusations of some ignorant critics, has always shown concern for the temporal welfare of her children. The Church's main interest is the spiritual welfare and eternal happiness of mankind, but she knows that, unless man's temporal and physical needs are properly supplied, he will be subject to severe trials and temptations which will impede his spiritual progress. Accordingly, the Church has ever been interested in all the needs of her children, and indeed in

those of all men. She has encouraged learning and art and science; she, in her children, has fostered exploration and commerce; she has founded every type of social and charitable institution for the relief of humanity. We saw the proof of all this last year in our study of Church history. Can you give specific instances in which the Church has helped to protect the poor and defenseless and lift up the downtrodden?

Within the last hundred years new problems in our social and economic life have arisen. The Church saw that her age-old helps to society were no longer enough. She therefore took the lead in pointing out to men and nations the modern applications of the unchanging principles and laws which must be followed if our present-day world is to escape from hopeless confusion, disorder, and violent strife. She spoke chiefly through a series of encyclicals issued by the Supreme Pontiffs. If we examine these encyclicals we shall have another evidence that God through His Church cares for us, body and soul, and that He does everything possible, short of taking away free will, to guarantee man's happiness and well-being both in time and in eternity.

2. THE ENCYCLICALS AND SOCIAL PROBLEMS

Throughout the four years of our course in religion we have at times referred to or quoted from the various papal encyclicals. Some of these encyclicals, especially

POPE PIUS XI

The popes of the Catholic Church, in all ages, but especially in modern times, have been a most potent factor in promoting the social welfare of mankind. They have been the defenders particularly of the poor, the oppressed, the infirm, and the laboring classes. Even as Christ, their Leader, they have urged men not to let their hearts become too attached to created goods. Yet they have ever proclaimed that the world and all that is in it has been created by God for man, that he, by using it wisely, might lead a noble life on earth and more surely and easily reach the goal God has prepared for him.

the ones on marriage, education, communism, Catholic Action, and social reconstruction, deserve to be studied in their entirety, for they are masterly summaries of what reason and faith teach on these important topics. We have time for only one.

The word "encyclical" means "world letter," i.e., a letter or document sent by the Holy Father around the entire world. Encyclicals deal not only with dogmatic questions but also with problems that are social and moral in their scope. They are based upon natural reason and divine revelation and are issued primarily for the purpose of guidance, admonition or exhortation. They are not necessarily ex-cathedra pronouncements, although the pope could, if he wished, issue definitions in this way. We are obliged, however, to obey their moral precepts.

Most of the recent encyclicals touch in one way or another upon social problems. Pope Leo XIII wrote many encyclicals, among them, "On the Christian Constitution of States," "On Civil Authority," "On the Evils of Modern Society," "On True Liberty," "On Christian Marriage and Family Life," "On Prohibition and Censorship of Books," "On Christian Democracy," "On the Chief Duties of Christians as Citizens." Among the encyclicals of Pope Pius XI we find: "On Christian Marriage," "On the Christian Education of Youth," "On Catholic Action," "On Clean Motion Pictures," etc.

However, there are three encyclicals that deal in a special way with social justice—a most important subject today. They are:

1. *Rerum Novarum* (On the Condition of the Working Classes)—Pope Leo XIII, May 15, 1891.
2. *Quadragesimo Anno* (On the Reconstruction of the Social Order)—Pope Pius XI, May 15, 1931.
3. *Divini Redemptoris* (On Atheistic Communism)—Pope Pius XI, March 19, 1937.

Because the encyclical "On the Reconstruction of the

Social Order" includes a summary of "The Condition of the Working Classes" and a prefiguring of "On Atheistic Communism," we shall use it as the basis of our study of social justice, and as a proof of the interest of the Church in the temporal welfare of her children. But before we synopsize it let us review several important terms.

3. KINDS OF JUSTICE—A REVIEW

Justice, as we have seen, is a virtue or habit by which a person renders to everyone his due.

Commutative justice regulates the mutual relations of individuals within the community. The basis of commutative justice is an equality of exchange of goods or services such as in buying, hiring, loaning, etc.

Distributive justice binds civil authorities to distribute public benefits, goods, and burdens with equity to all citizens. The basis of distributive justice is not strict arithmetical equality, but rather a relative or proportional equality.

Legal justice inclines citizens to render to the community what belongs to it and to obey the legal prescriptions laid down by the civil authority of the community or of the State for the common good.

Social justice is a more recent term and includes what was formerly called legal justice, but it is a wider and more extensive term. Legal justice is that part of social justice which is defined and regulated by set laws. Social justice includes any actions that have a bearing on the common good. Social justice may be defined as that virtue of justice by which members of a society perform whatever actions are necessary for attaining or maintaining the common good of that society, and regulate their conduct in right relation to that common good. The object of social justice, then, is the general welfare of men as distinct from the particular interests of individuals.

In his encyclical "On Atheistic Communism," Pope

PEACE OR WAR?

These American warplanes passing the statue of Christ the Redeemer on the Corcovado overlooking Rio de Janeiro may be taken as symbols of the title of this picture. Might may bring victory, but victory without Christ or against Christ can never bring peace, but only more war. Christ alone is the Prince of Peace. Christ is also Prince of Justice. There can be no peace without justice, and justice includes the full practice of the virtue of religion.

Pius XI gives the following definition of social justice: "Besides commutative justice, there is also social justice with its own set of obligations, from which neither employer nor workingmen can escape. Now it is of the very essence of social justice to demand from each individual all that is necessary for the common good."

But let us turn to the *Quadragesimo Anno* if we wish to have a clear idea of the meaning of social justice. A study of it will afford a review of some of the important principles we have already learned in this unit.

B. SYNOPSIS OF THE QUADRAGESIMO ANNO

ENCYCLICAL LETTER OF HIS HOLINESS PIUS XI "ON THE RECONSTRUCTION OF THE SOCIAL ORDER"

Introduction

Pope Pius XI gave to the world his famous encyclical, "On the Reconstruction of the Social Order," on May 15, 1931. It is called from its opening words, the *Quadragesimo Anno;* in English, *Forty Years After.* It was published just forty years after Pope Leo XIII had issued the *Rerum Novarum*—"On the Condition of the Working Classes." Pope Leo's successor wished to commemorate the earlier document, reassert its teachings, and add new ideas to cover the developments of nearly half a century.

Pope Pius began with a brief review of events before and after the publication of the *Rerum Novarum.* The development and spread of modern industry in the nineteenth century had divided society more and more into two classes. By 1891 a few persons were extremely rich, comfortable, and arrogantly self-satisfied; but the great masses of workers were desperately poor, oppressed, and helpless.

Clergy and laity alike sent to Pope Leo pleas for instruction, guidance, and light. Like the workers they felt that so enormous an inequality in the distribution of this world's goods was not just. The Pope answered their requests with a long and scholarly document that chiefly opposed the wrongs of which labor was the victim, stated the rights and duties of workers and employers, of rich and poor, and proposed the means by which religion, government, and the two classes could help to solve the grave problems involved.

Much good resulted from the encyclical, as its doctrine gradually spread abroad, and was explained and inter-

preted. Nevertheless, after forty years Pope Leo's words
had not received due attention or acceptance. His meaning in many passages was under dispute. Furthermore,
changed conditions required that his teachings be ampli-
fied. These are the main reasons for the encyclical of 1931.

OUTLINE OF THE ENCYCLICAL

Before launching out into the main matter of the
Encyclical, Pope Pius XI gives an outline of what he intends to present. He proposes:

    I. "to recall the great benefits this Encyclical [The
        Rerum Novarum] has brought to the Catholic
        Church and to all human society";

   II. "to defend the illustrious Master's [Leo's] doctrine
        on the social and economic question against certain
        doubts
        "and to develop it more fully as to some points;
        and lastly,

  III. A) "summoning to court the contemporary eco-
            nomic regime
        B) "and passing judgment on Socialism,
        C) "to lay bare the root of the existing social
            confusion
        D) "and at the same time point the only way to
            sound restoration: namely, the Christian re-
            form of morals."[1]

I. THE SOCIAL BENEFITS OF THE EARLIER ENCYCLICAL OF POPE LEO XIII

A. BENEFITS ARISING FROM WHAT THE CHURCH HAS DONE

The first section of the Encyclical, *Quadragesimo Anno,*
is devoted to a review of the benefits of the earlier Encyclical of Pope Leo XIII, *Rerum Novarum.* The following benefits are those listed by the Pope as having resulted
from what the Church has done.

---

[1]Quoted from *Two Basic Social Encyclicals,* p. 91, with permission of Benziger Bros.,
New York.

1. IN HER TEACHING

As a result of the doctrinal and moral teachings of the Church on social and economic matters, as proposed and developed by pope, bishops, priests, and the laity, there has been evolved a true Catholic social science. Moreover, non-Catholics have begun to adopt Catholic principles in social matters; many of the social reforms which followed World War I seem to have been taken directly from the encyclical.

2. IN APPLYING THESE TEACHINGS

These teachings have been applied in constant efforts to improve the condition of the working classes. Better livelihood has been obtained, works of social improvement have been inaugurated, and organizations of workers, craftsmen, and farmers have been founded.

B. BENEFITS ARISING FROM WHAT CIVIL AUTHORITIES HAVE DONE

Pope Leo had urged civil authorities to protect workers and to develop better social policies. Many of them responded, and often, since 1891, social legislation sponsored by ecclesiastics has been voted and put into action. Laws to protect life, health, the family, proper wages, women and child laborers, and the like, have been enacted. Do you know of any in our country?

C. BENEFITS ARISING FROM WHAT EMPLOYERS AND WORKERS HAVE DONE

Pope Leo XIII had recommended the formation of organizations of workers alone, or of workers and employers. He discussed their nature, purpose, timeliness, rights, duties, and regulations. As a result of this advice many organizations sprang up for the defense of the workers, for their mutual economic assistance and for their religious, moral, and physical development and protection.

"AND HE GREW IN STATURE"

Pope Pius XI recommended that where these unions are secular and not Catholic, as would be best, religious associations be formed to parallel the workers organizations. Has this been accomplished?

Not only the industrial workers but farmers and those of the middle classes have also formed organizations as a result of the influence of the encyclical. Employers, however, for the most part, have not—though this has not been entirely through their own fault.

The sum-total of these benefits is so great that Pope Pius XI justly says that the *Rerum Novarum* has proved itself "the Magna Charta upon which all Christian activity in the social field ought to be based."

II. EXPLANATION, DEFENSE, APPLICATION, AND AMPLIFICATION OF LEO XIII's TEACHING

A. VINDICATION OF THE RIGHT OF THE CHURCH TO SPEAK ON ECONOMIC AND SOCIAL PROBLEMS

After reviewing the benefits of the *Rerum Novarum* Pope Pius XI turns to the task of removing doubts and settling controversies which have arisen as to the meaning of Pope Leo XIII. Pope Pius also makes more precise applications of the Leonine teaching to the changed needs and conditions of his own day and even makes certain additions. But he prefaces all this with a vindication of the right of the Church to make pronouncements on social and economic problems.

The *principle* which he enunciates in this important matter is that the grave duty of making known and interpreting the whole moral law which is incumbent on the pope, makes the social order and economic activities subject to his supreme jurisdiction. It is one and the same moral law which guides our actions in relation to our last and highest goal and to our more proximate goals. If we follow that law, then our individual and social economic goals will find their proper place in the entire order of goals and lead us to God, the Supreme Good.

B. EXPLANATION, DEFENSE, AND APPLICATION OF SPECIFIC POINTS

1. AS REGARDS INDIVIDUALS

a. Ownership, or the Right of Property

Pope Pius XI then turns to specific points in the social teachings of Leo XIII. First he takes up matters affecting the individual, beginning with the rights of ownership.

1) Property Has an Individual and a Social Side

Leo XIII defended the right of individuals to possess private property; Pius XI does likewise. On one side he rejects *individualism,* which denies or minimizes the social character of the right of property; and, on the other, he also rejects *collectivism,* which attacks the private and individual character of property. The pope therefore defends the rights of ownership but teaches also that the rights of ownership are circumscribed by the necessities of social living and by certain inherent duties. Property has both an individual and a social aspect.

2) The State Can Control the Use of Property for the Common Welfare

The State must safeguard the right of private property but regulate its use for the common good.

It is the duty of the State to determine what owners of property can do and cannot do in the use of their property if the necessity for such legislation arises and if the natural law has not already done so. But the State cannot by excessive taxation or otherwise take away the natural right of man to own goods and to pass them on to his heirs.

3) Superfluous Income Has Obligations

Superfluous income is income one does not need in order to sustain life and live fittingly and with dignity. Such superfluous income, says the encyclical, is not wholly at the free use or disposal of its owner but is bound by a very serious precept commanding almsgiving, largess, and magnificent liberality in sponsoring or supporting works of charity or of social benefit. An example of this latter would be the providing of gainful work in producing useful goods.

4) How Ownership Is Acquired

The encyclical then briefly mentions the two main methods of acquiring ownership of property—by taking possession of an object which as yet belongs to no one and by working.

b. Teachings Regarding Capital and Labor

A person working on his own property and in his own name gains a right to the entire fruits of his labor; not so, a person working on another's property. But it is just this union which has produced the wealth of nations. Indeed, says the pope, capital and labor need one another; but neither should claim the entire product for itself.

Capital, however, following the false doctrines of Liberalism, has long appropriated too much to itself, giving the worker barely enough to subsist on. On the opposite side, others have erred by claiming that everything above what was needed for repairs and replacement of capital belonged to the workers. This is a more dangerous error than that of some socialists who recommend that whatever contributes to the production of goods should be "socialized," that is, transferred to the State.

1) Principle of Just Distribution of Profits

The *correct principle* in regard to the division of the fruit of the labor of workers applied to the property of others is quoted by Pius XI from Leo's encyclical thus: "However the earth may be apportioned among private owners, it does not cease to serve the interests of all." The law of nature demands that there be a division of goods, and this division among individuals and classes should be such that the *common advantage* of all is safeguarded. Today, says the encyclical, there are a few exceedingly rich, and countless numbers who are propertyless. *This must be remedied* and brought into keeping with the requirements of the common good.

c. Necessity of Redemption of the Property-less Workers

Although in some of the more civilized and wealthy countries the lot of the worker is improved, still there

MONSIGNOR JOHN A. RYAN

Monsignor Ryan, long Director of the Social Action Department of the National Catholic Welfare Conference, devoted a laborious life and high talents to teaching and applying the social doctrines of the Church. His influence has been deep and wide. America today needs others like him, who will dedicate themselves to God and Church, to country and fellowmen.

are regions and countries where the property-less industrial and rural workers are in dire straits. Riches are not rightly distributed or made equably available. The resulting insecurity must be removed, warns the Pope, or peace and order cannot be maintained. To achieve this end *proper wages* are necessary.

To what extent would the purchase of unnecessary luxuries and the improvident, spendthrift habits of many propertyless workers be responsible for their lack of property? Do many persons who are earning good wages neglect to acquire the tangible or productive property which could give them some measure of security and independence? Would the owning of one's own home free from debt be a partial remedy for this?

d. Just Wages and Salaries to Enable Ownership

A contract by which a worker hires out his labor for wages is not unjust, but the Pope recommends that, as far as possible, the wage contract be modified somewhat by a contract of *partnership*.

To determine what are the proper wages many factors must be considered—among them is the twofold aspect of work, individual and social—from which conclusions may be drawn which should govern wages. They relate to the three parties concerned: the worker, the employer, and the public.

The first of these principles advanced by the encyclical is that a worker should be paid a *family wage,* that is, a wage sufficient to allow him to support himself and his family and, by frugal living, to attain some modest ownership of property. All members of the family should contribute their share towards the support of the family but women and children should be properly protected. The father's wages should be such that the mother particularly will not be forced to work outside the home to the neglect of her children and her other duties. The father's wages should be proportioned to his needs.

The second principle is that the *condition of the business* or its owner must be taken into account. Excessive wages might ruin the business, yet poor management must not be used as an excuse for low wages.

Thirdly, wages should be so adjusted as to promote the *common welfare.* Wages which are too low or too high cause unemployment. Therefore, wages should be set so as to provide employment to the greatest possible number. Moreover, there should be a *right proportion between wages* of various workers and also *between wages and prices,* for instance, between farm and industry.

1) Balance of Wage Scales in Various Occupations

There is a hierarchy of social value in various occupations so, generally speaking, there should be a hierarchy of wages corresponding to the value of the respective jobs. If industrial workers, or farmers, or doctors, or building trades craftsmen, or any other group, by force of organization, by power politics, or by other means force a wage scale for themselves that disrupts this hierarchy, social harm results. If one group has a wage scale out of line with its proper value others cannot buy, nor can it sell its products and services in due measure. Unemployment follows, economic insecurity also, and social unrest. Wages for all classes of work, then, should be kept in proper balance. No group should forget the common welfare for its own advantage.

2. AS REGARDS THE SOCIAL ORDER

Having concluded those points of social teaching which concern the individual, the Pope then turns to those which concern the social order. Here, he says, two things are needed: a reform of institutions, and a reform of morals.

a. A Reform of Institutions Is Needed

In earlier days, declares the encyclical, in addition to the individual and the State there were many small associations or guilds which promoted social well-being. Today, perhaps, larger associations are needed, but a large association should not be formed when a smaller asso-

Philip Gendreau, N. Y.

COOPERATION

Like the athletes in these racing shells the human race is striving towards the goal. To win, all must pull together. To win, they must have a wise and intelligent leader—a good leader who will not betray them. To win they must be in good condition. If one is out of condition, if one shirks, and especially if one rests or pushes on the oars, instead of pulling, how can he and his partners win? To achieve the peace of harmony in civil society all must pull together with, and **for,** and under Christ.

ciation can do the job. The State should let these smaller associations handle matters of less importance. It should abolish strife and promote the establishment and the harmonious cooperation of various branches or groupings of members of an industry or profession. The common good of the country should be the most important interest of each group.

1) Economic Life Must Be Subjected to a True Directing Principle

Free competition, says the Pope, may be justified and useful, if kept within limits, but it cannot be the directing principle in economic life. Neither can despotic economic dictatorship which has replaced free competition since 1891. Rather it must be *social justice* and *social charity* which are the directing principles. Indeed the nations should join to promote agreements and institutions which will result in international cooperation in economic life.

After reviewing the good and bad points of a newly-devised system of syndicates and unions of persons in various callings, the Pope declares that, to achieve a better social order *God's blessing* and the *cooperation* of all men of good will towards that end will be necessary.

b. A Reform of Morality Is Required

Pope Pius XI concludes the second part of the encyclical by reminding his readers that the reconstruction and the perfecting of the social order cannot be brought about without a reform of morals. He then turns, in the third and final section, to the task of passing judgment on the modern economic system and on its bitterest accuser, socialism. He also takes care to point out the chief cause of modern economic evils and the main remedy for them—a reform of morals.

III. EVILS OF THE MODERN ECONOMIC SYSTEM AND OF ITS BITTEREST ACCUSER—SOCIALISM; THE ROOT OF THE EVIL AND ITS REMEDY

A. CHANGES SINCE 1891 IN THE ECONOMIC SYSTEM AND IN SOCIALISM

1. CHANGES IN THE ECONOMIC SYSTEM

The Pope begins this part of the encyclical by conceding that the capitalistic system of economics is not by nature wrong, but that it becomes wrong when it so directs business to its own advantage that it neglects the worker and forgets its social obligations. Following this Pope Pius notes the extent of the spread of the capitalistic system with its good and bad features.

a. Concentration of Wealth, Power, and Control

The first evil he singles out is the dangerous *concentration of wealth* and of *despotic economic power and control* in the hands of a few persons, who are often not even the owners but only the managers of money invested by others. He particularly mentions the control of credit and loans which supply the very lifeblood of the economic system.
Would cooperative credit unions help counteract this evil?

This amassing of power is the result of *individualism* and of *uncontrolled "free competition."* It produces three kinds of conflict: first, for economic supremacy, then for control of the State, and finally, for mastery between states.

b. The Results

The result of free competition, therefore, has been economic domination or dictatorship, and the degradation of the State to the level of a tool in the hands of those having this economic power. In the international sphere the result has been economic internationalism or imperialism and financial internationalism or international imperialism.

c. The Remedies

The Pope has already suggested the remedies for these evils in the second part of the Encyclical. Do you recall them? He reviews them briefly: first, both the individual and the social character of ownership and of work must be given due consideration; then, free competition and despotic economic control must be brought under the control of public authority; and, finally, public institutions must conform to the common good and to social justice.

What specific suggestions can you make as to ways in which to secure better distribution of wealth in a just manner. Would thrift be included? taxation of excess profits? What else?

2. CHANGES IN SOCIALISM

a. Communism—Extreme Socialism

Socialism has split into two camps, both hostile to Christianity but also to each other. The first is Communism which strives to attain two objectives: bitter class warfare, and the complete abolition of private ownership. The Pope warns of the great dangers and evils of Communism and the folly of those who allow conditions which pave the way for it.

b. More Moderate Socialism

Some socialists in their economic doctrines are tending more towards true social principles, the encyclical tells us, yet there can be no compromise. Even if their economic doctrines do finally become sound, the socialist concept of society is completely *contrary to Christian truth,* ignoring, as it does, man's eternal goal and sacrificing man's dignity to the demands of production.

One cannot be a good Catholic and a genuine socialist at the same time, says the Pope; and he warns Catholics against the socialist program of education, particularly the program for the education of children to form them into socialists.

c. Catholic Deserters to Socialism

The Pope laments the Catholics who have left the Church and have become socialists, but he points out as a reason for their defections the fact that many Catholics neglect their obligations of justice and charity, exploit the worker, and even try to justify their conduct in the name of religion. He then invites these wronged and deceived former Catholics to return to the Church.

B. THE ROOT AND THE REMEDY OF THESE EVILS

1. THE ROOT—THE UNCONTROLLED DESIRE FOR EARTHLY GOODS

As if sounding a battle cry, Pius, quoting Leo says that *only a return to Christian life and Christian institutions will heal society.* Then, continuing, he calls attention to the worst result of the economic injustices—loss of immortal souls. After this he puts his finger on the root and source of the trouble—those inordinate tendencies and desires which lead man to prefer earthly riches to those of heaven.

The Holy Father enumerates some of the reasons why men fall victims to these passions: the insecurity of economic life; the easy profits of free competition; the opportunities afforded corporations to escape accountability or to defraud investors; and, lastly, those inhuman wretches who arouse man's baser desires for the sake of gain.

The leaders of economic life first deserted the right road, and the workers soon followed them, though not without grievance or occasion. Moral dangers in factories, shameful housing conditions, obstacles to the performance of religious duties, and a universal weakening of the true Christian spirit played a part.

2. THE REMEDY

a. A Return of Gospel Living and Right Order

All efforts to regenerate society will be useless, warns the Pope, and no real remedy for the loss of souls will be afforded unless men openly and sincerely *return to the Gospel teaching* and to that right order which makes God man's supreme goal, and regards all created goods as instruments to be used only in so far as they lead toward that goal.

Employment in gainful occupations, however, is not

wrong; increasing one's fortune is not forbidden, if done justly, and if the wealth is used rightly.

b. The Place of Charity

Charity must take *a leading role* in the task of social reconstruction. Justice alone cannot unite minds and hearts; justice alone is not enough. True cooperation in the one common good will be possible only when the various parts of society realize that they are members of one great family and sons of the same Heavenly Father— nay, more, one body in Christ, and members one of another.

How many means can you enumerate to promote sound social reconstruction? Would the Catholic Rural Life Movement provide a partial answer?

c. Social Reconstruction a Difficult Task

Pius XI admits the task of reconstruction is not easy, but he asks all to spare no labors and to let no difficulties deter them. He then reviews certain promising signs of a social reconstruction among the workers and among heads of organizations of workingmen, after which he concludes by sketching the way to proceed.

d. The Course to Follow

From among the workers, the tradesmen, and the leaders of industry must be recruited "auxiliary soldiers of the Church," who know the minds of these people and their problems and will strive to bring them back to Christ.

Albrecht Durer   *Philip Gendreau, N. Y.*

PRAYING HANDS

Prayer and the exercise of the other acts of the virtue of religion are indispensable in the solution of the social problems facing the human race. What are some of these other acts of the virtue of religion? What are the offenses which violate the virtue of religion?

The Pope directs the clergy to locate, select, and train these persons. They should choose those who have a most keen sense of justice, who are not afraid to oppose injustice, who have prudence, and above all deep Christian charity. They should use all means at their disposal, and avail themselves, in particular, of retreats or similar spiritual exercises, recommending them to all, especially workers' retreats for laboring men.

The Pope concludes by observing how shrewdly the enemies of the Church train their disciples and how they unite, in spite of internal quarrels, when attacked.

He asks Catholics *to unite,* to avoid dispersing their efforts in too many different directions, and to strive to contribute something to the Christian reconstruction of human society.

He ends by imparting his Apostolic Benediction to all his children, but especially to workers, and to employers and managers.

REVIEW OF SECTION FOUR.

SECTION FIVE: A LOGICAL ANALYSIS AND REARRANGEMENT OF THE *QUADRAGESIMO ANNO*—A REVIEW

A. WRONG AIMS AND METHODS IN ECONOMIC AFFAIRS
  1. INDIVIDUALISM AND FREE COMPETITION
  2. ELIMINATION OF MEDIAEVAL GUILDS; INTRODUCTION OF NEW BUSINESS METHODS
  3. DESPOTIC ECONOMIC CONTROL
  4. MORAL AND SPIRITUAL CONSEQUENCES
  5. COMMUNISM
  6. SOCIALISM

B. RIGHT AIMS IN ECONOMIC AFFAIRS
  1. GOALS REQUIRED BY STRICT (COMMUTATIVE) JUSTICE
  2. GOALS SET BY SOCIAL JUSTICE
  3. GOALS REQUIRED AT TIMES BY STRICT, AT TIMES BY SOCIAL JUSTICE

C. RIGHT METHODS OF RECONSTRUCTING SOCIAL AND ECONOMIC LIFE
  1. PARTIAL MEANS
  2. COMPLETE PLAN FOR RECONSTRUCTING THE SOCIAL EDIFICE
    a. Economic Measures
    b. Reform of Morals
  3. WHAT WE CATHOLICS CAN DO

A logical analysis and topical regrouping of the ideas suggested by the *Quadragesimo Anno* will serve as a review of this highly important Encyclical and help us grasp its lessons better. Let us summarize its principles under three headings: Wrong Aims and Methods in Economic Affairs; Right Aims in Economic Affairs; Right Methods. It will be good to know these principles and to recognize them when we meet them, but hardly necessary to learn them by heart.

A. WRONG AIMS AND METHODS IN ECONOMIC AFFAIRS

1. INDIVIDUALISM AND FREE COMPETITION

Individualism could not guide economic life toward the right goals. Some well-meaning theorists maintained that it could, that free competition was the best means of striking a balance and promoting general prosperity. But practical individualists consciously sought wrong goals, namely, all the profits and wealth they could ob-

Ugolino da Siena   *National Gallery of Art, Kress Collection*

CHRIST BLESSING

Without Christ's blessing nothing can prosper; with it, all is success, though a **world** may condemn or oppose.

tain. Human variations and freedom should have been part of the theoretical individualists' calculations. Some men are stronger, shrewder, harder or more unscrupulous than others. They rejected both the right goals (as we shall see under B) and the right means, that is, organic unity in society and government supervision.

The results are:

a. Enormous fortunes piled up by the few while millions live in perpetual want.
b. The terrible scourge of widespread and enduring unemployment.
c. Class welfare engendered and aggravated until it threatens society with ruin.
d. Governments burdened with endless tasks which private associations, destroyed by individualism, should be doing.
e. Elimination of powerful rivals and introduction of economic dictators.

2. ELIMINATION OF THE MEDIAEVAL GUILDS: INTRODUCTION OF NEW BUSINESS METHODS

Historically, individualism displaced a better and more workable system, that of the guilds. These mediaeval organizations may have needed adjustment, but instead of being adjusted they were wilfully destroyed. The ruling influence in the abolition of the guilds was not economic necessity but selfishness, exaggerated claims to liberty, and rebellion against all authority.

With the rise of industry:

a. Temptations to selfish individualism were greater.
b. Enormous profits became possible.
c. Sudden bankruptcy was permitted, making it a battle fit for keen, tireless, and conscienceless men.
d. Speculation opened up new wide avenues for greed.
e. The corporation, a new device, made possible the worst injustices and frauds without legal accountability. Huge sums were made available by countless small investors who placed their savings at the mercy of trustees.
f. Negatively, government contributed to the stampede of economic immorality by doing nothing to impede it. This was individualism in practice.

DOES CHRIST WANT THIS?

Voluntary poverty Christ does approve; but destitution? No! Can a father and mother care for the mental, moral, and physical formation and development of a Christian family under conditions as discouraging as these? Do leaders in business and industry, in finance and labor, in religion and education, in social welfare and government have an obligation in justice and charity to remove the causes for such conditions? Are the poor victims themselves perhaps partially responsible for their sad lot, because of their spendthrift habits and poor management? If so, would it be fair, to blame capital for their plight?

3. DESPOTIC ECONOMIC CONTROL

The successor of individualism, *economic dictatorship*, toward which individualism inevitably tended, is an even worse guide and controller of economic life. While competition was more or less free, some measure of balance and fairness would result periodically, although many would meanwhile perish. But as free competition decreased,

a. immense power and despotic domination, often exercised, for example, by those who control credit, but not necessarily identified with personal wealth, left the destinies of millions in the hands of a few men.

b. There were few checks upon these men; they were often stronger than government; swept along by pride and ambition, there was nothing in them nor in the relentless system with which they were identified to lead toward right moral goals.

c. They acknowledged no superior power to guide them aright— neither State nor Church.

d. Almost naturally they pursued, not full production and a good living for all, but more power—first in industry and commerce, then over their home governments, then over foreign business and other governments. This meant international economic war and eventually "shooting" wars.

e. Under the domination of business interests, governments used their power to promote the economic advantages of their citizens; conversely, they used economic power to settle political issues and extend their ascendancy over other peoples. In other words, economic overlords contributed a great deal to the growth of excessive nationalism and imperialism.

4. MORAL AND SPIRITUAL CONSEQUENCES

Both individualism and economic dictatorship are false guides for economic life. To bring home still further their harmfulness, and to illustrate why the Church is concerned, Pope Pius details many spiritual evils that have resulted under the system he condemns. Let us gather together some of those mentioned in the Encyclical.

Temporal disasters are bad enough; but, to the Christian, material loss is nothing in comparison with these results of individualism and of economic dictatorship:

a. The ruin of souls is widespread.

b. For multitudes salvation has been made very difficult.

c. Worldliness infects nearly all.

d. Economic life has become hard, cruel, relentless.

e. Civil authorities have betrayed their trust, yielding government to the service of passion and greed.

f. The primacy of profits and the instability of the system have led men to use any means, forgetting conscience, to increase or retain their wealth.

g. Trade, exchange, the speculative markets are open fields for sins of greed.

h. Corporation officers have been guilty of frauds, injustices, and betrayal of investors.

i. Appeals to the worst human passions, scandalous example to the weak, and extravagance are common.

j. Some employers even misuse religion, oppressing employees in its name, claiming to be good Catholics. They cause the Church to be accused of taking sides with the rich and neglecting the poor.

k. Many workers have found this scandal an excuse for leaving the Church. Multitudes of workmen have fallen to low spiritual levels, in yielding to the system and to the example of employers. They have forgotten their souls from long being treated as soulless.

l. Factory life has thrown men and boys, women and girls into frightful dangers.

m. Good family life has been made difficult, especially by poor housing conditions.

n. Most men do not find their work a path toward heaven; they have only one thing on their minds: how to obtain their daily bread in any way at all.

After a litany such as this it is evident that God's glory and man's eternal happiness are not the guiding star of modern economic life.

5. COMMUNISM

Communism presents a program for changing these evil conditions. It consists in the supplanting of private ownership by government ownership of all property. Its chief proposals are wrong because:

a. Communism violates a natural need for private ownership. It must not be our aim to abolish private property but to distribute it widely for a more secure and happier family life.

b. Government has no right to confiscate private property.

BYZANTINE MADONNA ENTHRONED

    c. Government has too many burdens now; owning and managing all property would multiply the evil.

    d. Communism proposes merciless class warfare as a necessary means to its end, with no limit on cruelty or inhumanity, and with open enmity against the Church and against God Himself.

Therefore, as a solution of the social problem communism is economically, morally, and socially unacceptable.

6. SOCIALISM

Another dangerous candidate for social-economic leadership in social reconstruction is socialism. There are many brands of socialism just as there are some schisms among the communists. Many socialists today propose

    a. not the abolition of private ownership, but some public ownership and rightful public controls over the use of private productive property, to be attained by peaceful means—discussion and legislation.

    This point in the economic program of some socialists may be unobjectionable in itself.

    b. However, as long as they insist on ignoring God and eternity and on making production and the sharing of temporal goods the supreme purpose of life, the socialists are in serious conflict with Catholic truth; no sincere Catholic can be at the same time a real socialist.

B. RIGHT AIMS IN ECONOMIC AFFAIRS

The supreme purpose of all material resources, of all economic activity and of all the human strength and brains and will that go into it, is the glory of God and man's eternal happiness.

How can economic life promote this purpose? By supplying all human beings with a good standard of living, by building universal prosperity wherein all men would have decent, honest work, and sufficient goods to supply their needs. But this would require full production and full employment, which is only possible if we use all our

resources and technical skill in a reasonably organized and balanced system.

1. GOALS REQUIRED BY STRICT (COMMUTATIVE) JUSTICE

Such an economic order would direct individuals, groups, and governments towards their ultimate end by showing them, and enabling them to pursue as their immediate goals, certain objectives which come under the demands of strict or commutative justice. These include:

a. The living family wage: enough, with good management, to support a family, put by some savings, and acquire a little property.
b. Freedom of mothers and children from the necessity of working for wages.
c. Avoidance of crushing taxes on individuals, confiscation of property.
d. The right of inheritance.

2. GOALS SET BY SOCIAL JUSTICE

Besides these, there are other goals which come under social justice or the pursuit of the common good. They include:

a. Full output—full use of a plant, a farm, a service valuable to the community—instead of restricted use, voluntary or involuntary, which in the past kept down living standards.
b. Rehabilitation of those companies or industries which have been unable to pay a living wage; where this is impossible equitable means of discontinuing such enterprises, making other provision for the workers.
c. Setting of wages at such levels as will best maintain full employment, which is impossible when wage scales become either too high or too low.

G. A. Douglas　　　　　　　　　　　　　　　　*From Gendreau, N. Y.*

BREAD LINE

When despotic economic and financial imperialism, aided by unchristian practices by management and labor cause the misery and dejection of a bread line like this, everyone suffers—everything suffers. Virtue and the leading of a Christian family life are most seriously impeded. Things of the mind and things of the spirit are forgotten. Resentment and desperation grow apace, and revolution, permanent world revolution—the goal of Communism, is just around the corner.

d. A reasonable relationship between prices; bringing about, for example, a fairer balance between the returns to the farmer and the returns to industry. Unbalanced prices injure not only this or that group but obstruct and break down the general prosperity.

e. Sharing in the profits by all engaged in a business, by labor as well as capital.

Where it is possible the way should be left open for some sharing by labor in ownership and management, too, although this does not mean that the wage contract must be eliminated.

f. A wider distribution of private ownership of all sorts.

g. Right use of private property, for the public as well as private good, enforced where necessary by law.

h. Public ownership of such property as cannot safely be left in the hands of individuals because it carries with it too great an opportunity for domination.

3. GOALS REQUIRED, AT TIMES BY STRICT, AT TIMES BY SOCIAL JUSTICE

There are certain other objectives which ought to be and can be attained, and which are required sometimes by strict justice, sometimes by social justice. For example, safety devices at work might be so necessary that the individual employee would have a strict right to them; or slightly unhealthful conditions might be harmful to the common good while not injuring any individual seriously. These goals are:

a. Working conditions good for both soul and body, spiritually and physically safe and healthful. The minimizing of danger at work, of industrial accidents, and of occupational diseases.

b. Good housing conditions, helpful to healthy, happy, and holy family life or individual welfare.

c. Special care and limitations where women workers and child workers are concerned.

d. Varying returns or shares in the fruits of production proportionate to the special contributions the individuals may make to the service of society and the development of its wealth.

C. *RIGHT METHODS OF RECONSTRUCTING SOCIAL AND ECONOMIC LIFE*

1. *PARTIAL MEANS*

We can begin at once to bend economic life towards its proper purposes. Complete conformity first to reason and then to the Christian ideal would represent a real revolution; but it can come only gradually, by forward steps here and there, by pursuing certain demands of justice and social justice with the organizations and institutions ready to hand, while we build the latter into an orderly and balanced system. These partial means which can attain in part the objectives already listed are:

a. Collective bargaining between *labor unions* and employers or associations of employers.

b. Unions striving to better the condition of their members. In Catholic countries they can effect spiritual as well as material improvements, strengthening religion and morality (including a spirit of collaboration with all classes).

c. Where Catholic unions are impossible, non-religious (but not anti-religious) workers' associations can defend the economic rights of their members.

Catholic unionists who belong to such non-religious unions should have also separate educational societies where they may learn the principles to be followed in their union activities.

d. *Employers' associations* should be formed or re-formed with a view to breaking down unfair business practices as well as class war.

e. Farmers' organizations, professional associations, associations of all special economic groups can look after the peculiar interests of their respective members (e.g., lawyers, fishermen, taxi-owners, etc.).

f. Government can help immediately by performing many tasks. Some of these would not normally belong to it and should not be left permanently on its hands. Just now there is no other agency ready in many fields. Among these needed activities are:

1. Laws governing wages and working conditions.

2. Care for the weak and needy.

3. Restrictions on the use of property.

MAN WAS MADE TO WORK

Happy workers build happy homes and happy nations. Happy nations can build a peaceful world.

4. Controls over free competition and still more over economic dictatorships.
5. Establishment of some public ownership.
6. In general, restoration of governmental control over economic forces that have gotten out of hand.

2. COMPLETE PLAN FOR RECONSTRUCTING THE SOCIAL EDIFICE

a. Economic Measures

We can fully attain the moral purposes of economic life only by rebuilding the whole structure according to a reasonable plan. Partial steps would still leave us with a certain amount of class war, with incomplete use of resources, unnecessary poverty, periodic breakdowns, and an overburdened government.

The Pope's plan is built on common sense, understanding of human nature, and belief in the ability of the common man as well as sympathy for his needs. The culmination of the plan is in the Gospel scheme of life. It includes these parts:

1. The economic system should govern itself, democratically, with a minimum of supervision by the political authority.
2. It can do this only if all individuals and all groups can be organized for the purpose of making their own part of the structure work well and of making the entire national economy, which is so interdependent, work well.
3. This requires a union of employers *and* employees in each industry, of all persons engaged in each trade, or profession, or avocation. Through their chosen representatives they would work together to turn out the best possible goods or services and to insure their own prosperity.
4. As each group depends on all the rest, it would be necessary for each to make plans, set goals, establish rules, in conference with all the other groups, through its chosen representatives.
5. As a consequence, we should need not only industry-wide associations, but a federation of these associations. This system might be compared to city, state, and federal governments, although it would be drawn up on different lines and would be quite separate from the political government and subordinate to it.

6. Nation-wide industries could also have local councils for handling local problems. When an agreement was reached by an established industry association, it would be given the force of law, unless in the judgment of the civil authority, it would impose on the rights of consumers or some other group. Separate unions of workers and employers could still meet and confer.

7. To set such a system in motion government will have to promote the initial steps; to keep it growing and going successfully government will have to watch and guide it.

8. Over and above this unified and balanced organism in the nation we shall need also international economic agreements and organization.

a. The dependence of men upon one another is now world-wide.

b. We need materials from other peoples; they need our help if they are to have prosperity and fulfill their divine destiny.

9. The "Pope's Plan" is an outline, not a fixed and detailed program. Details can be filled in and varied gradually, according to circumstances and experience and the advice of economic experts.

b. Reform of Morals

Neither the partial steps towards a right economic order can be made nor can the growth into the ideal of a social organism be possible without moral reform.

1. The hearts of men must be changed at the same time as their institutions.

2. Men will not want these institutions nor will they make them work unless the spirit of *justice* and *charity,* directed earnestly toward the pursuit of the common good, begins to prevail over selfishness, worldliness, and individualism.

3. Men must again place *God at the summit of society* as the object of their aspirations and strivings.

4. Men will work together for the common good only if they are convinced that all men are members of the same human family, children of the same Heavenly Father.

Some progress is possible with such motives and bonds of unity, which are available merely by the use of right reason. Progress will be hastened and complete, perfect order will be attained in the measure in which the supernatural teachings of the Gospel penetrate men's minds and operate in their lives. More than a rational acceptance of justice will be needed for a full realization of the "Pope's Plan." The message of Christ is the telling argument—above all, that grand truth that we are all "one body in Christ, but severally members one of another," so that "if one member suffers anything, all the members suffer with it."

3. WHAT WE CATHOLICS CAN DO—LEAD THE WAY!

A unique responsibility rests on Catholics to speed the pace of progress and carry the program forward beyond the range of mere reason to the ultimate heights which only faith can scale. Others can assist in "reconstructing the social order," but *we should lead the way;* for only true Christians can succeed in "perfecting it according to the principles of the Gospel." This is the distinction Pope Pius makes in his prefatory address.

He suggests special activities in which we Catholics should engage to prepare for and exert that leadership. They are:

1. Study circles.
2. Instructions to youth.
3. Catholic economic conferences.
4. Catholic schools in social sciences.
5. Courses in Catholic universities, seminaries, academies.
6. Lay retreats.
7. Training of leaders for "Catholic Action."
8. The action of priests as "social apostles."
9. The preparation of lay social apostles in every class, particularly among workers and employers.
10. The writing and publication of articles and works on Catholic social teaching.
11. The education of working men in their rights and duties.

Which of these activities are open to young people?

REVIEW OF UNIT FOUR

SEVENTH COMMANDMENT

1. What is justice?
2. What is the difference between the natural and the supernatural virtue of justice?
3. Why are some rights inalienable and inviolable?
4. What faculty of man does justice support and perfect?
5. How many kinds of justice are there? Define each.
6. Name four virtues related to justice. Which is the most important?
7. Is charity a substitute for justice? Explain.
8. Show the connection of justice with each commandment.
9. Why is justice an important virtue socially?
10. Why were created things brought into existence?
11. Does man have a right to acquire and possess property? Why?
12. What does the word "property" include?
13. Explain the individual and social rights and duties of property.
14. Is one nation allowed to throttle the economic life of another nation?
15. What is the purpose of the seventh and tenth commandments?
16. What is ownership? How is it limited? How acquired?
17. Is the private ownership of property good? Is it necessary?
18. Is stealing a mortal or a venial sin? Explain.
19. Mention as many ways as you can think of in which justice and the seventh commandment may be violated.
20. What are the requirements for a just strike? When may a strike be called?
21. Is it a sin to damage another's property? to break a contract? to go into debt beyond reasonable ability to pay? to gamble or make wagers?
22. How many forms of cheating can you mention?

M. E. Browning   *From Philip Gendreau, N. Y.*

ST. FRANCIS AND THE TURTLE DOVES

Christian detachment from worldly possessions is a necessary element in the Christian solution of the social problem.

In the story which this picture illustrates St. Francis of Assisi led the little boy to a spirit of liberality and detachment. The boy had trapped some turtledoves and was on his way to sell them so he could have the money to spend. St. Francis urged him to set free the doves, symbols of the human soul. The boy acceded to the urgings of the saint, and later, as St. Francis had predicted, he entered the religious life, to practice under vow the spirit of poverty which he had learned to love under the guidance of the saint.

23. What is usury? Is charging interest wrong?
24. What is restitution? When are we obliged to make restitution? Will absolution be denied when restitution is not made?
25. What vice arises from the failure to control properly the tendency to acquire and possess goods? Why is this vice dangerous? What are its effects?
26. Name the virtues allied to justice and opposed to injustice and covetousness?
27. What is detachment? What is its value? Give examples of detachment in the saints.

EIGHTH COMMANDMENT

28. What is the purpose of language?
29. Prove the necessity of truthfulness from reason and revelation.
30. What is fidelity? Is it a necessary virtue?
31. Define a lie.
32. What are evasive replies? Are they allowed?
33. Define: hypocrisy, flattery, boastfulness.
34. Does everyone have a right to protect his reputation?
35. Define: calumny, slander, detraction, backbiting, perjury, contumely, rash judgment. Explain the gravity of each.
36. Must we repair the damage to reputation caused by any sins mentioned in the previous question? Which? How?
37. Is tale-bearing a vice or a virtue? Are we ever obliged to reveal the sins or faults of another? Explain.
38. Must we protect our own reputation? Why?
39. Is it wrong to reveal secrets? to pry into them? to open letters? Why?

THE QUADRAGESIMO ANNO—SYNOPSIS

40. How is the modern social teaching of the Church a proof that God loves mankind?
41. Is the Church concerned about the temporal welfare of men or only their spiritual welfare? Give proof.
42. What is social justice?
43. What is an encyclical?
44. What are the main divisions of the encyclical "On the Reconstruction of the Social Order"?
45. What were some of the benefits of Pope Leo XIII's *Rerum Novarum*—"On the Condition of the Working Classes"?

46. Did Pope Leo favor unions?
47. Does the Church have any authority to make decisions in economic matters?
48. What are the two aspects of property?
49. Can the State control the use of property?
50. What are the social obligations of superfluous property?
51. Define: capital, labor.
52. What false theories have been advanced by capital? by labor? What is the true principle of just distribution of profits and wealth?
53. What is Pius XI's solution of the problem of the proletariat or property-less workers?
54. What is a just wage? a family wage?
55. What three principles help determine what is a just wage?
56. What is the proper function of the State in economic matters?
57. What are the effects of wages that are too high or too low?
58. What two reforms in the social order does the Pope ask for?
59. Does the Pope favor labor associations like the guilds? Does he favor large or small ones?
60. What should be the most important interest of such associations?
61. Is free competition good or bad? Economic dictatorship?
62. What are the true directing principles of economic life?
63. What is capitalism? Is it good or bad? Why?
64. What has replaced free competition since 1891? What are its results?
65. What are the remedies for the domination resulting from the concentration of wealth and power?
66. What are the two main branches of Socialism?
67. What does Communism teach?
68. Is mitigated or moderate Socialism permissible? Why?
69. What is the Christian concept of society? the socialistic concept?
70. What has caused some Catholics to become socialists?
71. What will bring about social reconstruction?
72. Do social and economic conditions influence the salvation of our souls? How?
73. What should be our battle cry in social and economic affairs?
74. What is the worst result of economic injustice?
75. What is the root and source of the trouble?
76. What are some reasons why men fall victims to these tendencies?
77. What is the remedy?
78. What role must charity play in economic reconstruction?
79. How does the doctrine of the Mystical Body apply to economic matters?

80. Whence are the leaders of the Christian Social Reconstruction to be chosen? Who is to train them?

THE QUADRAGESIMO ANNO—ANALYSIS

81. Name some economic objectives required by strict justice? by social justice?
82. Name some economic objectives which, depending on circumstances might be required either by strict or by social justice.
83. Name some economic results which prove that economic individualism and uncontrolled free competition are unsound.
84. What economic institutions were displaced by individualism? Was this good? necessary?
85. Show how economic individualism gradually led to despotic economic control and dictatorship. What were some of the results in economic and international relations? in moral and spiritual consequences?
86. Is there any connection between world wars and the struggle for economic dictatorship?
87. List some partial means of reconstruction of economic and social life.
88. Outline some of the economic elements in a complete plan for social reconstruction.
89. Outline the moral elements in the plan.
90. Do Catholics have a unique responsibility in this program of social reconstruction? Why?
91. What are some of the means we can employ toward that end?
92. Give an outline of this unit? What new things did you learn?

UNIT V

The Reasonableness of Our Faith

Apologetics: The Case for the Church

PART ONE: INTRODUCTION

FAITH HAS GUIDED OUR COURSE

Four years ago we began our high-school religion course with a unit entitled: *Our Guides to Our Goal*. In it we learned that our goal is God, and that human reason is one of the guides He has given us to lead us to union with Him—and a very good guide it is, too, when properly used. But we also learned that God in His infinite goodness supplied us with a better guide—a guide so superior to reason that the comparison of a flickering match to a million candle-power searchlight was an injustice to the power of faith, for it is faith that is this Master Guide.

God, in His love and mercy, saw fit to give us this gift

447

of faith. So, leaning more on faith than on reason, we have pursued our high-school course. With the aid of its powerful light we have studied about God's unity and Trinity, His works of love for men, men's obligations to Him. We have learned about the promise of a Redeemer made to our fallen first parents and the fulfillment of the promise in the Incarnation and Redemption. We learned that the guide which is faith is really faith in Jesus Christ. It is He who is our Leader. As juniors we took another step forward and came to the realization that it was the Mystical Body of Christ, the Catholic Church, which is our guide to our Lord in the world of today. She is the Infallible Teaching Voice of Jesus Christ for us.

WE MUST SHOW THE REASONABLENESS OF FAITH

All this we took on faith. It is better so; but now, both for our own sakes, as well as for the sake of any honest searchers for the truth whom God may send our way, we must pause before we come to the end of our course, both to show *how reasonable our faith is* and at the same time to let us see the steps to take in presenting to non-Catholics *The Case for the Church,* that is, the logical arguments which prove that the Catholic religion is the one, true religion.

To show the value of this, let us suppose that some one were to say: "What authority has the Catholic Church to tell you or me or anyone what to believe?" Of course we would answer: "Jesus Christ gave her that authority." Now if your friend should say, "I do not believe in Jesus Christ or in any Church He is supposed to have founded. In fact, I don't believe that religion is necessary at all. If I honor God in my heart and lead a good life, that is enough without belonging to any religion or Church."

How would you answer such a man? You should know, because there are many men in the world today who talk just that way. There are innumerable "learned" college professors in non-Catholic universities and colleges throughout the land who have shattered and are shattering the religious faith of thousands of American boys and girls, many Catholics included, sad to say. They are able to do it because they can bring up clever arguments and objections which at first sight appear unanswerable or very convincing, but which, with a little knowledge and training, can be shown false—most of them quite easily, although some of them only after profound study. It is the purpose of this unit to help you make a beginning in this science of justifying your faith, this art of presenting the proof which constitutes the case for the Church.

There are many steps in this proof and we shall not be able to expand all of them here. Rather we shall select the three most important steps and show how a noted modern apologist suggests that we handle them in order to prove them to an opponent. It may not be out of place, however, to give an outline of all the steps, first that you may know them and then that it may engender an interest in this intriguing field of Apologetics. It could easily become the delightful hobby of a lifetime.

OUTLINE OF STEPS IN THE ARGUMENT

Our purpose is to prove that the Catholic religion is a religion revealed by God, and indeed the religion which God recognizes as *the one and only true religion* in the world and therefore the religion which He wishes and commands all men to embrace.

Let us look at the series of things we must prove in order to show our claim is correct.

Our first step would be to prove the existence of God.

Our second step would be to prove the nature of God— that is, that He is a personal God, not an impersonal force, as atheistic evolution might wish to suggest.

Our third step would be to prove the nature of man—

particularly the spirituality and immortality of his
soul and his desire for perfect happiness.

Our fourth step would be to argue from the existence
and nature of God and from the existence and nature
of men to the necessity of some form of religion, that
is, of some form of worship of God by man.

Our fifth step would be to show the nature of natural
religion, that is, religion based on reason alone.

Our sixth step would be to show the possibility of revelation and the necessity of accepting any revealed, supernatural religion or religions, if we have clear proof
that God has revealed such to man.

Our seventh step would be to ascertain whether God
has actually revealed any religion or religions as the
one or ones by which He wishes to be served.

There are not a few claimants. So we would have to examine
their claims one by one.

One of the strongest claimants is the Catholic religion — the
Catholic Church.

The Catholic religion claims to be a supernaturally revealed
religion and also, and what is more important, it claims to be
the one and only true religion in the world—intended for all
men, alone acceptable to God.

If it can prove its claim to be the only true religion, as we
already know it can, our search is ended. For then one religion is not as good as another; all other religions are false,
and religious indifference is sinful.

If it could not prove its claim we would have to examine the
other religions claiming to be revealed. If none could prove
its claim we would then have to adore God according to the
precepts of reason and natural religion.

————
→

Follower of Giotto   *National Gallery of Art, Mellon Collection*

ST. PAUL

The great Apostle of the Gentiles preached "Christ and Him crucified."

The claim of the Catholic Church to be the one and only true Church of God is founded on the events recorded in the Bible, especially the New Testament. We cannot logically use the Bible as the *revealed* word of God unless we first prove it to be such. That will require several steps yet. In fact, we can only do it after we have completed our case for the Church. Can you see why?

Our eighth step, then, would be to prove first that the Bible, both Old and New Testament, as a *human* document, is authentic, reliable and trustworthy.

The ninth step would be to show how this trustworthy document, in the Old Testament, recorded the promise of a Redeemer and how, in the New Testament, it reveals that Jesus Christ claims Himself to be and actually *proves Himself to be that Redeemer* and also the very Son of God, a divine Person — God Himself.

The proof is based on the fulfilled prophecies of the Old and New Testament and the miracles of Christ, particularly the Resurrection, which He repeatedly predicted.

Our tenth step, after proving Jesus Christ actually to be God, would be to show that He revealed and founded a religion—that is, He established a Church.

In the eleventh step, then, we would have to show (a) that He founded just one Church, one religion, (b) to the complete exclusion of all others. Also that He promised (c) that this one true religion would be His mouthpiece on earth, and absolutely infallible as a guide to God; (d) that it would be a permanent, visible organization to which men are obliged to belong, and (e) that divine revelation was to come only by means of this Church and not directly by divine guidance in private reading and interpretation of the Scriptures as the Protestants hold.

As our twelfth and last step we would have to prove that Christ made St. Peter and his successors the infallible head of that Church and also show the Pope to be that lawful successor today.

Our proof would then be complete, and, by way of negative argument, all other churches or religions, whether natural or claiming to be revealed, would be proved to be deficient, false, and unacceptable to God.

Having proved the Catholic Church divine and infallible, we could now prove from her teaching that the Bible is not merely a trustworthy human document, but an inspired, revealed divine document. To all who will accept it as such, our proof both of the divinity of Christ and the truth of the Catholic Church then becomes much easier.

Such would have to be the trend of argument and the logical steps we would take to prove the case for the Church, that is, to prove that faith in the divinity and infallibility of the Catholic Church is justified and necessary.

It is easy to see that we could not begin to prove all of these steps in the time remaining this year. We will, therefore, choose the three most important steps and give a few good arguments to prove each. Then, if you are interested and grateful to God for the gift of faith, you may wish to prepare yourself to become a modern apostle, a modern apologist, carrying the warmth and happiness of the true faith to groping minds and to hearts yearning for the truth. For there are others who are also on a Quest for Happiness. Would you not like to be the instrument that God might use to place in their hands the searchlight of faith? Then study well this unit that you may take your first lessons in learning how.

DIAGNOSTIC EXPLORATION

Are you able to:
1) Prove the existence of God by arguments from human reason?
2) Prove the divinity of Jesus Christ to a rationalist, to a Jew; to a Protestant who believes in the New Testament?
3) Prove the Catholic Church to be the one true Church to the same three: rationalist, Jew, and believing Protestant?
4) Prove that the Bible is the word of God?

SOME OBJECTIVES FOR THIS UNIT

Our aims in this unit are:
1. To show how reasonable our Faith is.
2. To help us learn how to carry the happiness of Faith to others by leading them to the grace of faith from an appreciation of its reasonableness.

SUGGESTED ASSIGNMENTS AND ACTIVITIES

1. Appoint groups of two students each to prepare a dialogue between a Catholic and a non-Catholic in which the Catholic:
   a. proves the existence of God to an atheist or an agnostic;
   b. proves the divinity of Jesus Christ to 1) a Protestant, 2) a Jew and, 3) a rationalist;
   c. proves the divinity of the Catholic Church to a Protestant, a Jew, a rationalist.
2. Assemble facts or examples from any sciences you have studied which would help prove the existence of God.
3. Divide the class into three groups: one to prove the existence and nature of God to a modern rationalist; another to prove the divinity of Jesus Christ to him; and a third to prove the divine foundation of the Catholic Church. Let each member of each group write his paper as he sees fit and present it to the class. Choose the three best in each group and then analyze them to see why they were effective. Was it logic and argumentation? Was it good English? Was it examples and illustration? Was it delivery? Was it sympathy and understanding of the opponent? What was it? Then determine *the qualities of an effective presentation of the case for the Church.*
4. Write a paper on:
   Common Modern Objections to the Catholic Church.
   Methods of Approach to the Modern Mind.
   How to Present the Case for the Church without Arguing.
   Proving the Infallibility of the Church.

Prophecies about Christ in the Old Testament.
Prophecies Made by Christ.
Miracles Worked by Christ to Prove His Claim to Be God.
The Resurrection: Stumbling Block or Cornerstone?
Predictions of the Resurrection.
Historical Proof that the Resurrection Actually Took Place.
How the Life, Activity, Unity and Holiness of the Church Prove Her Divinity.
An Answer to a Man Who Denies the Possibility of Miracles.
Where to Start? or, Finding Out Where Your Opponent Stands and What He Believes.
The Need of Apologetics in the Modern World.

5. Prepare an Outline on The Teachings of the Catholic Church to serve as the basis for a talk to non-Catholics who know nothing about the Church. Make it simple, pleasant, convincing. Quote Scripture to prove your points.

6. How I Would Prove the Case for the Church:
To an evolutionist?
To a Jehovah Witness?
To a High-Church Anglican?

7. Have several students study the objections and line of reasoning presented by many people who are opposed to the Church. Then without previous preparation let each of them present these in a conversation to another student who is to answer the objections by presenting "The Case for the Church."

8. Report on the article, *What About the Hundred Million?* by James G. Keller, M.M., in the American Ecclesiastical Review, May, 1945, Vol. CXII, No. 5.

9. Report on the life and deeds of St. Francis Xavier, St. Francis de Sales, St. Irenaeus, St. Augustine of Hippo, Abbé Nicholas S. Bergier, Father Hecker, Cardinal Newman, Cardinal Gibbons or any other great apologist.

RELATED READINGS IN BOOKS AND PAMPHLETS

Books:
Conway, *The Question Box,* Paulist.
Falvey, *Apologetics,* Textbook Publ. Co., San Francisco, Calif.
Gibbons, *The Faith of Our Fathers,* Kenedy.
Hill, *The Catholic's Ready Answer,* Benziger.
Laux, *A Course in Religion for Catholic High Schools and Academies, Part IV, Apologetics for High School,* Benziger.

O'Brien, *The Faith of Millions,* O.S. Visitor.

Rumble and Carty, *Radio Replies,* Cathedral Press, **St. Paul.**

Schmidt, Perkins, *Faith and Reason,* Loyola U.

Scott, *Answer Wisely,* Loyola U.

Sheed, *Map of Life,* Sheed & Ward.

Sheehan, *Apologetics and Catholic Doctrine,* Gill, Dublin.

Smith, *An Outline of Catholic Teaching,* (T.E.S.) **Mac-**millan.

Walker, Fortman, *Sixteen Steps to the Church,* **Queen's** Work.

Read also books by or about prominent converts to see **the** reasons why they entered the Church, e.g.

Delaney, *Why Rome?* Dial, New York.

Lamping, *Through Hundred Gates,* Bruce.

Lunn, *Now I See,* Sheed & Ward.

Moody, *A Long Road Home,* Macmillan.

Stoddard, *Rebuilding a Lost Faith,* Kenedy.

Pamphlets:

Ginder, *This Is the Catholic Church,* Cath. Information **Soc.,** New York.

The Church of Christ, O.S.V.

Hurley, *Face the Facts Series,* Paulist.

Levy, *Is There a True Church?* I.C.T.S.

Moody, *The Outside Approach to the Church,* **Catholic Lay-**men's Assn. of Georgia, Atlanta.

Noll, *Why You Should Be a Catholic,* O.S.V.

O'Brien, *What Think You of Christ?* O.S.V.

O'Brien, *Which Is Christ's True Church?* O.S.V.

PART TWO: APOLOGETICS

THE SCIENCE OF PROVING THE CASE FOR THE CATHOLIC CHURCH

SECTION ONE: AN INTRODUCTION TO APOLOGETICS

A. NATURE, NECESSITY AND TECHNIQUE OF APOLOGETICS
  1. NATURE AND DEFINITION
  2. NECESSITY
  3. TECHNIQUE
     a. Not Merely Defensive
     b. The Approach Must Change With the Times
        1) The Easiest Case—The Non-Catholic Christian
        2) With Non-Christians
        3) With Atheists or Agnostics
     c. "You're right on the first point, John; but did you consider—?"
     d. The Handling of the Case for the Church
        1) Varies According to One's Own Ability to Present It
        2) Varies According to the Objector's Capacity to Understand
        3) Avoiding Slick Answers and Refusing Frivolous Discussion
  4. WHAT CAN APOLOGETICS DO?

A. NATURE, NECESSITY, AND TECHNIQUE OF APOLOGETICS

1. NATURE

A mere glance at the word apologetics would tell us that it must be the science of apology: but owing to the way the English language has changed, this piece of quite correct information may easily be misleading. Apology we tend to think of as what we are called upon to make if we have been late for an appointment or have spilt the soup. To our modern ears the word conveys the idea of regret expressed for wrongdoing. But there was an older meaning, by which apology was not the admission of wrongness, but the assertion of rightness. When Newman wrote an *Apologia pro Vita Sua,* it was not his apology for being alive: it was his explanation of the line his life had taken in religion, a line which had led him into the Church. Apologetics may be defined most simply as the science of proving the case for the Catholic Church.

2. NEED OF APOLOGETICS

Who needs to have the case for the Church stated? or proved? Not we. We already accept the Church because God has given us the gift of faith. Human arguments are a slight thing compared with the power of God's grace. The Faith that is in us does not need apologetics, for we already have a stronger support than the most overwhelming proofs could provide, the supporting hand of God Himself. But the majority of human beings do not belong to the Church. They either assail its claims and need to be answered, or ignore its claims and need to be stimulated toward acceptance. Either way, the call is for apologetics. The case of the Church can be so stated that even people with no faith at all will find it unanswerable. The object of your study of apologetics is that you may learn to state the case for the Church unanswerably.

3. TECHNIQUE

a. Not Merely Defensive

This must never be thought of as simply defensive. Our apologetic should be at once an explanation and a challenge: an explanation of our own position and a challenge to others to justify themselves for not holding it. In that sense we should welcome the man who assails the Church in our presence, because by that assault he gives us the right to state our case. If he had said nothing, we might have found it difficult to say anything. It is not easy to turn to the comparative stranger you find next to you at a dinner party and ask him if he would not like to hear some arguments for the Catholic Church. He *might* be delighted, but he might be furious, and most of us would not care to risk it. But if he attacks, nothing could be simpler. His attack is an invitation to us to state our case. All we have to do is to accept the invitation, state our reasons for belief and thus put it squarely up to him to justify his unbelief. Nothing, I say, could be simpler—

provided we know how. If we do not, we might do the
Church less harm if we let ourselves pass for Moham-
medans.

But it is our duty to know how. The sacrament of Confirmation made us soldiers, and this is part of our soldiering. If we cannot do it, then we may miss opportunities
of setting men's feet on the way of salvation: what is
worse, we may leave fellow-Catholics of weakened faith
to have their faith totally destroyed by seeing us lose an
argument we should have won.

b. The Approach Must Change with the Times

What makes apologetics particularly difficult is that it
must be always changing with the times. If it is out-of-
date, it is pathetic in its uselessness. The reason for this
may not immediately strike you. After all, you say, apologetics is a statement of the case for the Church, and the
case for the Church does not alter. This is perfectly true.
The whole case for the Church is that *it was founded by
Christ who is God.* This always has been its case and
always will be. What varies is not the case, but the statement of the case; and this must vary according to the
particular elements in the Church's claim that happen
to be attacked at any given moment, or by any given
person, and the reasons for the attack. One of the most
brilliant of all apologetical books is St. Augustine's *City
of God:* he wrote it because the pagans of his day were
violently asserting that the disasters falling so thick and
fast upon Rome were due to the anger of the old Roman
gods at the spread of Christianity. It was a powerful accusation at the time: St. Augustine brilliantly refuted it.
But who makes that accusation now? Most of the book is
still vital and effective; but those sections are not.

Let us look again at the argument for the Church—
namely, that she was founded by Christ who is God. This
involves three statements—

1. That there is a God.
2. That God became man.
3. That the God-Man founded the Catholic Church.

1) The Easiest Case—the Non-Catholic Christian

A man may deny the third of these truths, or the second and third, or all three. Or he may not even bother to deny them but may simply insist that they do not matter. Your statement of the case will vary according to what the assailant denies and why he denies it—and this involves finding out what he *does* believe. Thus, if a man believes that our Lord was God but does not believe that He founded the Catholic Church, you can concentrate on number three, and need waste no time in proving numbers one and two. But even in proving number three, it is important to discover whether your man believes that our Lord founded some particular church other than ours, or all Christian churches, or none of them.

2) With Non-Christians

Again, you may meet a man who believes in God, but does not believe that Christ our Lord is God. In that event, you need not prove number one, but you must certainly establish number two before proceeding to discuss number three. In other words, you will gain nothing by trying to prove that our Lord established the Catholic Church to a man who does not believe that our Lord is God. But here again, there are all sorts of people who deny our Lord's divinity: you must find out whether your man is a pagan, or a Jew, or a Mohammedan, or a Unitarian, or one of those Protestants whom we call Mod-

Underwood-Stratton

CHESTERTON

Gilbert Kieth Chesterton was one of the most brilliant proponents and defenders of Christian thought in modern times.

ernists. Indeed, he may deny that Christ our Lord ever existed at all: the view is mad, but it is held.

3) With Atheists or Agnostics

Let us consider the third group of opponents: those who do not believe that God exists. Here again your man may be an atheist, who asserts that there is no God; or an agnostic, who asserts that we cannot know whether there is a God or not; and again we must discover whether he is an old-fashioned materialist who bases his denial of 'God upon his view of science, or one of the newer Marxian sort, who bases his denial upon sociological grounds. The old-fashioned materialist thought that science could explain the universe without God; the Marxian's argument is that the belief in God is bad for the working classes. Clearly they require quite different answers.

c. "You're Partly Right on the First Point, John, But Did You Consider . . .?"

One thing, I hope, has become clear from all that has just been said: that if our study of apologetics is to be really useful, it is not sufficient to know it: *we must be able to say it*. We must so have mastered the case for the Church that we can make some reasonable statement of it when we are challenged. Being able to say it is the test, not simply knowing it, not even writing it: saying it. And again, not saying it as a set speech, but *leading into it from what the other man says*. Obviously you cannot study all the thousand ways of being wrong about religion: but if you try to master the Catholic case, then you will see for yourself just how to state it as against any particular line of objection. But always *begin by finding out what the other man believes* before answering the particular objection that he utters.

d. The Handling of the Case for the Church
1) Depends on Your Ability

There is one further word of warning. When trying to convince a man, your handling of the arguments in support of the Church's position must depend upon two things—your capacity, and his. It is not possible while you are still at school to master all that is concerned with the Church's case for herself. In this unit you are taking the first steps in a study of enormous usefulness for the saving of souls. But you cannot, at this stage, learn more than the first steps. Everything depends upon your willingness to train on for the rest of your life.

2) Depends on Objector's Capacity to Understand

But if your own capacity limits the arguments you may use, the capacity of the objector may limit them even more severely. He may of course be a man of powerful mind developed by hard study, and there is an exhilaration in coming to grips with such men, provided we are trained for the contest. But the ordinary assailant of the Faith has not had the years of study that you have had, and his mind may lack the "muscles" necessary to take hold of the truth even if you state it very well.

Consider a simple comparison. You may have studied geometry, and you may be able to prove fairly advanced theorems. But no matter how well you understand them yourself, you cannot prove them to a person who has had no mathematics at all. If such a person challenged you on the point, your reply would have to be that you could prove it to him in about five years, if he would devote those five years to the study of mathematics.

It is the same with the truths of theology. Theology treats of some of the most profound ideas that have ever been offered to the mind of man, and it is not to be thought that they can be conveyed, or defended, in a five-minute conversation with a man who has never studied any theology in his life and never means to.

3) *Avoiding Slick Answers and Refusing Frivolous Discussion*

Indeed you must beware of the temptation to think that you can give slick, quick answers to objections. If you fall into conversation with a man who raises difficulties about the Faith, you might begin by finding out if he is really asking his question seriously, or just having a game.

If he is serious, then he will give time to discussing the matter with you. If he is not prepared to give time to it, then he is not serious, and there is no point in thinking you can answer him, or that any good could be gained by discussing the matter at all. Men have been wrestling with these questions for centuries, and it is not to be thought that you can settle them between the soup and the coffee.

You will indeed have done your questioner a real service, if you merely teach him that he is handling profundities, not suitable for slick and easy settlement. Men have killed for religion, men have died for religion; men have given their lives for it, men have given their lives to it: it is not to be settled by some bright remarks from someone who has never given half an hour's thought to it in his life.

Against such a person, it will probably be more useful to attack his position, and his satisfaction with his position, by showing all the mysteries and seeming contradictions which arise where the truth is absent, rather than defending the mysteries and apparent contradictions which arise where the truth is present. In other words, we must be

---

<←—

A. Dürer   *From Ewing Galloway, N. Y.*

THE FOUR TEMPERAMENTS

The artist here, in the four personalities of St. Peter and St. John, of St. Paul and St. Mark, has attempted to portray the varying temperaments of human beings. In stating the Case for the Church the wise apologist, in addition to other matters, takes into consideration the type of personality and temperament of the one to whom he is presenting the proof of the Church's claim to be the one true Church of Christ.

clear in our own minds that religion does not bring mystery and the appearance of contradiction into a world which otherwise would be plain and straightforward: but that the world is in any event mysterious.

4. WHAT CAN APOLOGETICS DO?

What can you hope to accomplish with apologetics? You can state the case for the existence of God, or for the Godhead of our Lord, or for the divine foundation of the Church, and you can state it so that it is quite unanswerable. But apologetics can never force a man to believe. In the theological phrase the arguments for the Faith are conclusive but not compelling. They can bring a man to the point where he can see no argument against the Faith, but they cannot bring faith. It is important to see why not.

Faith remains a *gift of God*. If He does not give it, we cannot have it. God is not to be stormed by an argument. Arguments, after all, appeal to the understanding, the intellect. But salvation is not by the intellect only, or even principally. Most of all, salvation depends upon the will. It is not primarily understanding but loving which wins God to us. Yet apologetics may play an enormously important part in preparing the soul to receive God's gift, or, to put it another way, in bringing the soul to a state in which God will give his grace. God responds to humility, to love, to desire, to prayer. A man who has seen the unanswerable arguments for God and for our Lord and for the Church is helped towards humility and love and desire and prayer. Which is one reason why we must learn the key element in our own handling of apologetics: it is not sufficient for us to argue with a man on behalf of the great religious truths, we must pray for him actually while we are arguing with him. We must get him to pray.

REVIEW OF SECTION ONE.

SECTION TWO: PROVING THE THREE KEY TRUTHS

A. GOD EXISTS
   1. DIFFICULTIES OF THE ATHEIST—VOICE OF THE MINORITY
   2. UNIVERSAL AGREEMENT AS TO GOD'S EXISTENCE
      a. Its Nature and Value
      b. Tactics of the Atheist
         1) Throwing Stones
         2) Producing a Theory of His Own
   3. SOMETHING OR SOMEONE?
   4. THE ARGUMENT FROM THE ORDER IN THE UNIVERSE
      a. Blind Chance a Poor Explanation
      b. Order Presupposes an Intellect at Work
      c. Tremendous Complexity of Material Universe
      d. Minor "Disorders" Do not Disprove Major Orderliness
      e. The Conclusion
      f. Never Let an Atheist Bluff You Out of Position
   5. THE ARGUMENT FROM CONTINGENCY (MIGHT-NOT-HAVE-BEEN)
      a. What Causes Things to Exist?
      b. Receivers and Transmitters but not Originators
      c. There Must Be an Originator
         1) Simile of a Water System
      d. The Conclusion
   6. THE VALUE OF SUCH ARGUMENTS
      a. Enlargement of Our Own Ideas of God
      b. Value of Knowing *What* God Is and not Simply *That* God Is
      c. If There Were No God
         1) Then Men Would Not Be Brothers
         2) Then There Would Be No Hope
         3) Then Man's Life Would Be Purposeless
         4) Then Suffering and Pain Would Be Sheer Futility
   7. SUMMARY OF PROOFS OF GOD'S EXISTENCE

It has already been said that you cannot, while you are still at school, master the whole of apologetics; indeed an effort to master the whole of apologetics would probably mean that you mastered none of it. We have seen the three statements on which the case for the Church depends— 1) that there is a God, 2) that our Lord is God, and 3) that our Lord founded the Catholic Church. For each of these statements it would be possible, and even profitable, to produce half a dozen proofs, which might well be extended to hundreds and hundreds of pages. If you use the years of your maturity wisely, you will learn as much as that. But one cannot begin with so much. We shall consider one or two proofs of each point, and leave it to you to master them so thoroughly that you can state them against any objector—or rather not against him, but *for* him. Never get into an argument on religion to win the argument but to win a soul.

First, then, for the existence of God.

A. GOD EXISTS

1. THE DIFFICULTIES OF THE ATHEIST—VOICE OF THE MINORITY

In any argument with an atheist, it is well to remember that we are expressing the mind of humanity, and he is one of a minority so tiny as to be almost freakish. He is not always aware of this himself, or rather, even if he knows that he represents a minority view, he is rather proud of it. An atheist professor in a classroom may sound immensely impressive. And after all, so he should: it is his classroom. But outside he shrinks to life-size, and in this particular matter, life-size is not large enough. It is one thing to tell his students that they are wrong, quite another thing to tell the whole human race that it is wrong.

2. UNIVERSAL AGREEMENT AS TO GOD'S EXISTENCE

a. Its Nature and Value

As far back as we can trace human thought men have universally believed in the existence of a Supreme Being distinct from this world. The word "universally" is not too strong. The atheist individual has always been a rarity, and an atheist society scarcely known. If there is one thing upon which we may say that there is a universal agreement of mankind, it is this.

Now the value of this universal agreement may have to be weighed very carefully. The atheist may be disposed to say that the universal agreement of mankind might be wrong. But at any rate no man with a sense of proportion, or even a sense of humor, will say that the whole human

THE TEMPLE OF THESEUS—ATHENS

Men of all ages and times have acknowledged the existence of the divinity. They have built temples to show their reverence and to house their religious rites. This beautiful ruin of the Temple of Theseus in Athens, is a proof of the religious spirit of the ancient Greeks. The rugged power and simplicity of the Doric columns, without base, and with unadorned capitals, allow us to look into the candor and strength of the early Greek character.

race is wrong and he with a handful of others right, unless he feels sheerly and inescapably driven to it. He may feel himself forced to say it, but he will not say it lightly. He will want to have the strongest reasons for saying it.

As has been said, the value of the universal agreement of mankind upon a belief of this sort would require to be very carefully weighed before one dared to cast it aside. The fact that it has persisted through all the ages, in every variety of social system and geographical condition, at all stages of civilization, suggests that it is the decision of something very deep down in human nature. It cannot be explained by some special circumstance, operating at a particular time, for it is found in all circumstances and at all times.

b. Tactics of the Atheist

Yet the average atheist not only does not weigh it carefully, he does not weigh it at all. He simply tells the human race that it is wrong. But to tell the human race that it is wrong, one would need to be on a larger scale than the average atheist. Certainly if a man decides that he must make such an assertion, he might at least make a considerable effort to give his proof.

Now there is no such thing. No argument has ever been advanced that even claims to prove that there is no God. What the average assailant does is one or both of two things.

1) Throwing Stones

He throws stones at the belief in God. This stone-throwing has two main forms: attempts to make the idea of God sound unattractive, and attempts to explain why people hold it.

The *mockery of the idea of God* follows a very simple pattern: our atheist states it and then points out that it is silly: and as stated by him, it usually is silly, very silly indeed. It is the rarest thing in the world to find an atheist who could write down a true statement of the Catholic idea of God.

The *attempts to explain away* the plain fact that men do so persistently believe in God are usually inept beyond words. The favorite explanation at the moment is the one called Wishful Thinking. The theory is that we wish religion to be true and therefore believe that it is true. This is not likely to convince anyone who knows what the Catholic religion is. Wishful Thinking might possibly

NUESTRA SEÑORA DE LA SEDE
Seville Cathedral

This is one of the largest churches in the world. It's bell tower, called the Giral-
da, from the revolving weathervane on top, is a Moorish edifice with Christian
additions. It once served as the minaret of the mosque which formerly stood
where the cathedral now rises.

account for our belief in heaven, but could hardly account
for our belief in hell. Nor would wishful thinking account
for our acceptance of the commandments, which forbid
so many actions which we might easily find rather
agreeable.

2) Producing a Theory of His Own

None of this, of course, disproves that there is a God.
Nor does the second line that the assailant takes—namely,

to advance some theory of his own which might account for the universe without bringing in the idea of a creator. Even if you could imagine some way in which the universe might have come into existence without a creator, that would not prove that it did not in fact have a creator, but only that it *might* not have had one. Their theory would still be only a theory, and a minority theory at that.

But indeed all the theories brought forward to account for the existence of the universe without God suffer from the same defect; that they do not account, or even attempt to account, for the *existence of the universe,* but only for its present condition—the old fashioned evolutionist had one theory to explain how the universe developed to its present condition, the Marxian has another. But both of these, and practically all other theories, are an attempt to explain how the things *that were there to begin with* have reached the stage at which they are now. Not one of them attempts to explain why anything was there to begin with. They do not answer this question. They do not even ask this question.

But if you fail to ask this question, you will naturally fail to get the answer: and it is to this question: *"Where did the world come from?"* that the answer is God. The special distinction of the atheist lies not in getting a different answer, but only in not having seen the question!

But for any serious man, the question why anything exists at all is absolutely unavoidable. You cannot say that you will start with what you find and then proceed to do something with it. Because, whatever accounts for the thing being there at all may easily continue to have a very considerable bearing on what ought to be done with the thing. If you do not answer the question why anything exists, then you do not know what accounts for anything, you do not know the explanation of anything, you leave everything forever unexplainable. And this is not enlightened.

3. SOMETHING OR SOMEONE

Let us now consider what conclusion a little reflection upon the universe is likely to lead us to. Let us begin with that something that was there at the beginning, which the atheist refuses to look beyond. At any rate he and we agree that there must always have been something. Clearly, if there ever has been a condition in which nothing existed, then that condition would have had to be permanent. If ever there had been nothing, then there must always have been nothing, for nothing comes from nothing. So that we and the atheist are so far in agreement—there must always have been something.

What then is the point of our disagreement? Simply this, that he says that the original something was a mere *something,* whereas we say that it was a *Someone.* We say that the original Something had intelligence and will, that it knew what it wanted and knew how to get it. The atheist says that it had no intelligence and no will, that it knew nothing and could will nothing. This being the difference between us, why is the atheist so scornfully superior about it? After all, there is intelligence and will in the universe which has come from that original something; why should the atheist think it an odd superstition on our part to hold that intelligence and will were there always? If there were no further considerations, the atheist should at least concede that our guess is as good as his.

But there are many further considerations, and they all lead to the conclusion that the original something did have intellect and will, that it was not only a something but a Someone, that it was what we call God. Here we shall discuss two of these considerations, the basis of two of the great arguments for the existence of God.

4. THE ARGUMENT FROM THE ORDER IN THE UNIVERSE

a. Blind Chance a Poor Explanation

If the original being had no intelligence and no will, knew nothing, could aim at nothing, had no purpose, was simply blind, then you have a pretty difficult job to explain the universe as it now is. You would have to say that our universe is a matter of blind chance, that, merely by a process of stumbling on, the order of our inconceivably intricate world was produced. To make such an assertion requires a good deal of nerve.

b. Order Presupposes an Intellect at Work

If things are arranged in order, we know that intelligence has been at work. Chance working blindly can produce disorder to the point of chaos: it cannot produce order. If you found four sticks on the ground forming a perfect square, you would know that someone had arranged them. You would laugh at anyone who said that it merely happened so.

If a man sat down at a piano and played Beethoven's Fifth Symphony with no sheet of music in front of him, you would assume that he knew something about a piano and already had the Fifth Symphony in his mind. If you were told that the man knew no music, had never seen a piano before, and had in fact been stone deaf from birth, you would retort that it was impossible. If your informant demanded, "What is impossible about it? All the notes are on the piano. He merely happened to hit the right ones," you would not be moved from your certainty that only a mind which already knew the thing it wanted to play and knew how to play it could possibly have produced the music you heard.

c. Tremendous Complexity of Material Universe

The human mind revolts if it is asked to believe that

chance could account for the arrangement of notes in a piece of music, or even for so simple an order as that of four sticks meeting at right angles. Now the order of the universe is inconceivably more complex than the most complex music ever written. The whole vast system of suns and planets involves the inter-working, the organization, of things and energies on a towering scale, by comparison with which the Fifth Symphony is a billionfold simpler than a bar of Yankee Doodle. And almost any individual thing we like to contemplate presents a marvelously complex order. That the human eye may see, some 64,000 elements have to be rightly arranged.

d. Minor "Disorders" Do Not Disprove the Major Orderliness

There is, of course, a great deal of the universe of which we cannot see the explanation. We cannot see how it fits. It looks disorderly. But while these things may be a problem or a puzzle, the vast framework of the universe is a framework of order.

There is a famous analogy bearing on this. If in a dormitory you saw ten beds made and ten beds unmade, the presence of the made beds would prove that there had been a bedmaker in the room, and the unmade beds would not disprove this. Similarly, the vast amount of order we see in the universe proves that a mind produced it, even if there are things whose place in the order we cannot see.

e. The Conclusion

The obvious, indeed the only tolerable, answer to the problem of how any order exists is that some mind caused it; the obvious answer to the problem of an order in the universe that staggers the mind of man is that it has been caused by a mind immeasurably greater than the mind of man.

f. Never Let an Atheist Bluff You Out of Position

We should never let the atheist bluff us in this matter. He poses as the enlightened, commonsense person, who has liberated himself from the ridiculous superstition that the order of the universe is accounted for by a mind. His answer is that it merely happened so. If he dared to assert that chance accounted for some quite small example of orderly arrangement, we should know that he was talking nonsense—or at least that he was asserting something so extraordinary that it is very much up to him to prove it. Yet in this matter of the order of the universe he always acts as if he were propounding the obvious explanation, an explanation so obvious that no proof is needed, whereas we are producing a fantastic explanation which no serious person could for one moment accept.

In fact, it is the other way around. Our explanation, that here is a great framework of order and that it is produced by the operation of a great mind, is the simple and obvious one. His explanation, that blind forces produced it by operating blindly, is the fantastic one. And we should never get into an argument with an atheist without forcing him to accept the full burden of his fantasy.

5. THE ARGUMENT FROM CONTINGENCY (MIGHT-NOT-HAVE-BEEN)

Thus a consideration of the order in the universe leads us to the conviction that the original something must have had the mind to see the order that was to be produced and the will to bring it into being. And a something with

$\longrightarrow$

THE TEMPLE OF JUPITER AND THE ACROPOLIS, ATHENS

In the background we see the ruins of the Parthenon, atop the Acropolis. In the foreground is a Roman temple to Jupiter. Both give eloquent if mute testimony that man feels a natural need of religion. They, at the same time, show how fleeting are religions not based on God's revealed word.

Religions come and go. They build their temples and have their brief day. They disappear, though their ruined shrines remain. Only the true religion endures. Only the Church founded by Jesus Christ lasts through the ages. Its perpetuity is a sign of its divinity.

mind and will is a Someone. But there is another way of approach to the problem which brings us to still greater certainty. Let us consider not what comes from the original being, but why it or anything existed at all. In other words, *how are we to account for existence?* This, as we have already seen, is the question that no atheist attempts to answer. And it is *the* question. Certainly there is nothing enlightened in not asking it. Let us then reflect upon existence.

a. What Causes Things to Exist?

Everyday experience tells us that things do exist. We exist ourselves, and other things likewise. If we ask why this or that thing exists, we can usually find the answer quickly enough. Any given man exists because his parents met and mated. If they had not, he would not exist. His parents, likewise, exist because their parents met and mated. A particular valley exists, because a particular stream of water was seeking a lower level and gradually hollowed a bed for itself. If the spring had not been there or the melting ice, or if it had gone another way, then that valley would not have existed.

b. Receivers and Transmitters but Not Originators

There is no need to go on adding one example after another. We can already see certain truths about the existence of all the things of our experience. There is not one of them which might not have failed to come into existence at all if some other thing had not done what it did do. There is this mark upon all the beings of our experience. They did not have to exist: their existence is not necessary. They exist, but they might have failed to exist. This is what we call contingency: their existence is contingent upon some other thing having been what it was or having done what it did. In other words, the reason why they exist is not to be found in themselves, but

THE NATIVITY

in some other being. They have their existence, they can cause other things to exist, but they *do not originate their existence.* They receive their existence from something else.

c. There Must Be an Originator

At this point, I fear, you must think very closely. Try to think of a universe consisting only of the kind of being we have been describing—namely, beings which possess existence and can transmit existence, but only because they have already received existence from some other source. In such a universe, no one of the beings in question would be a source of existence, they would all be receivers. Very well, then: where would the existence itself come from, which all of them have, and none of them have originated?

In such a universe of contingent beings, there would be no place from which existence itself could flow, for *all* the begins in it would be *receivers* of existence. In other words, such a universe is impossible. By itself, it could not exist, for there would be no being in it from which existence could come. This means that, *behind the contingent beings* and ultimately responsible for them, *there must be a being* totally different from them, a being *which does not have to receive existence from any other,* a being which is the reason for its own existence.

We shall see in a moment how immeasurably different from all others such a being must be, but before proceeding to that, let us try to get a clearer view of the argument we have just been stating.

SIMILE OF A WATER SYSTEM

Imagine for a moment a very intricate system of water pipes, through which the water ultimately flows into our house. The water that reaches our house comes from a pipe, and it gets to that pipe from another pipe, and to that pipe from another, and so on in a complexity of water pipes as dizzying as you care to imagine. Every pipe contains water, and can pass on water to the next pipe; but no pipe originates the water: it has to receive it. The problem then is to account for the water.

If you ask where any particular pipe gets it water, you can always point to the pipe before it in the system. But how do you account for any water at all being in that system of pipes? Merely adding to the number of pipes will not explain the water, because, as no pipe produces water no number of pipes however great will produce water. Even if you multiplied the pipes, as the mathematicians say, to infinity, you still have not accounted for the presence of water in the pipes. Not even an infinite number of pipes, none of which produced water, can account for the existence of water.

What follows from all this is that somewhere or other the pipes must be in contact with a spring, that is, with something which is a source of water and not a receiver.

Transfer this notion from pipes which contain water but do not originate it, to beings which have existence but do not originate it. The water must flow to the pipes from something which is itself a source of water and not a receiver; similarly no being will have existence unless there is some being which is a source of existence and not a receiver.

d. The Conclusion

This source of existence we call God. Because He is the source of existence, He must contain in Himself the highest perfections of existence. Therefore He must contain the power to know, the power to will, since these things are a part of existence and their source is in Him. He is therefore *personal*.

Further if we think of the primary distinction between Him and all other beings, our whole mind must be enlarged by the new ideas that result. The primary distinction is that whereas other beings, including ourselves, exist but might not have existed, He *must* exist. For His existence we seek no reason outside His own nature. He alone of all beings totally accounts for Himself. It is His nature to exist.

A further study of philosophy would show that a Being whose very nature is to exist *must be infinite:* containing all perfection without limit, changeless because all perfection is already His, living in a timeless present—having no past because nothing goes from Him, having no future because nothing can be done to Him, Who has all in utter perfection and is the source of all perfection. There is no time to do it now, but if you continue your study to that point, and indeed beyond it, you will be well rewarded.

Meanwhile consider this one fact. This Being who alone exists of Himself is the reason for the existence of all other things. They exist because He confers existence upon them. He is the maker of all things other than Himself. Now it follows that if He makes all things whatsoever He must make them of nothing, for apart from all things there *is* nothing. Beings upon whom existence is to be conferred are not like pipes waiting for water; for until beings receive existence they are non-existent. This power of making from nothing, creating, is possible only to a Being who is Infinite.

6. THE VALUE OF SUCH ARGUMENTS

It is for us to think steadily about these arguments for God's existence until they become truly our own. Precisely because they call upon us to think at an unfamiliar level and to deal with ideas which are not our ideas of everyday, we do not find them easy to master, or, to start with, particularly luminous. We may be tempted to feel that they are doubtless good arguments, and not to be overthrown, but that our own faith in God's existence does not need them, and that we never shall be able so to master them that we can use them to bring conviction to others.

$\longrightarrow$

Vivarini   *National Gallery of Art, Kress Collection*
THE CORONATION OF THE BLESSED VIRGIN MARY

Apologetics may prove the truth of the Catholic religion but, of itself, it does not give faith. Faith is a free gift of God.

Prayer to Mary is one of the surest ways to obtain the grace of faith for oneself or another. He who will honor the Mother of Christ, and ask her to lead him to the truth, will, without fail, receive the needed grace.

a. Enlargement of Our Own Ideas of God

But the value of such arguments as we have used is not solely in that they demonstrate something we do not doubt—namely, the existence of God. If we keep our minds active upon them, we shall find that they give a new depth and richness to our idea of what God is. And gradually we shall find that they are becoming part of the very structure of our minds.

Anyone learning the piano finds a similar difficulty. The early exercises, which have as their object to make the fingers supple and competent, invariably have as their first effect to give us a new awareness of how clumsy and incompetent our fingers are. We never knew how useless were our fingers until we started on the exercises designed to make them more useful. But a time comes when those exercises do in a sense become part of the very structure of the fingers.

It is the same with the arguments for the existence of God.

b. Value of Knowing WHAT God Is and Not Simply THAT God Is

Unless these arguments do develop our own ideas of God, we shall find that they are not very useful in helping others to accept the fact of God's existence. The truth is that people will not be much moved by proofs that there is a God, unless first they have a real idea of what is meant by God. In practical fact, more people are won to God by a realization of *what God is* than by a proof *that* He is, and this is especially so of those people (who are, I believe, in the majority), who do not think very much about God but have never rejected Him and only need their belief re-awakened.

For us, then, along with the necessary task of learning the proofs, there is the necessary duty of deepening our understanding, that we may be able to convey it to others.

We must come to see some of the manifold magnificence that follows from the fact that the universe owes its existence to a Person who can know and love.

c. If There Were No God

One way to see this ourselves and to help others to see it is to consider some of the consequences that would follow if there were no God.

1) Then Men Would Not Be Brothers

Take the idea of Universal Brotherhood. Obviously, the word "brothers" means "sons of one father"; and if there is no one, who is the father of all men, what makes us brothers? If there is no God then men are not brothers. To call upon men to act like brothers while denying the one truth that makes them brothers is folly.

This is worth developing. Pose the atheist the question: "Why should I act like a brother to the man next door? Why shouldn't I do him a bad turn if I want to?" The answer usually is that it would be bad for yourself to rob the man next door, because it would be bad for the community as a whole, of which you are a member. In other words, don't rob your brother *because it won't pay:* this is simply an appeal to men's selfishness, when the evil of the world arises out of men's selfishness! Obviously it is no answer at all. Plenty of people have found ways of making their selfishness pay. And if there is no God, there isn't the faintest *reason* why we should treat our next-door neighbor as a brother.

2) Then There Would Be No Hope

Take the question of hope. What hope has the atheist to offer? A millennium upon earth. But you won't get it. Evolution will bring it to your great-great-grand-children, perhaps. But can you call that hope? For the individual himself there is nought but death. Strip the illusion away, and make them see that what they are choosing is despair when they bow out the God who alone can give them permanence of personal existence.

3) Then Man's Life Would Be Purposeless

Consider the question of purpose. You can't use anything until you know what it is for. You can guess what it is for, but if you act upon your guess the chances are you will make a mess of it. Now the only certain way of knowing what anything is for is to find out from its maker. Not only that: unless somebody made it, it isn't *for* anything. If a thing is a mere accident, it cannot have a purpose. Accidents do not have purposes. Only if somebody made man, has man a purpose; and only if you know what that purpose is, can you direct man's life—your own or another's. There is no test of right and wrong unless you know the purpose of a man's life. Here again is one of those gaps which men did not see when they dismissed God.

4) Then Suffering Would Be Sheer Futility

If we have the nerve to do it, we can take suffering as the key point in apologetics, as the thing the atheist has to explain away. Faced with this inescapable fact of suffering we have an answer which gives it significance. They have not. Here is the point where our superiority as believers in God is overwhelming. If the universe is directed by a mind, suffering is terrible, yet suffering *could* be directed by that mind for our good; but if the universe is merely blind, suffering is altogether intolerable because inescapably doomed to futility.

There are many more considerations of this sort and we should exercise our minds to find them. They do not, of course, prove the existence of God. But they show what the rejection of God would involve; and men who have

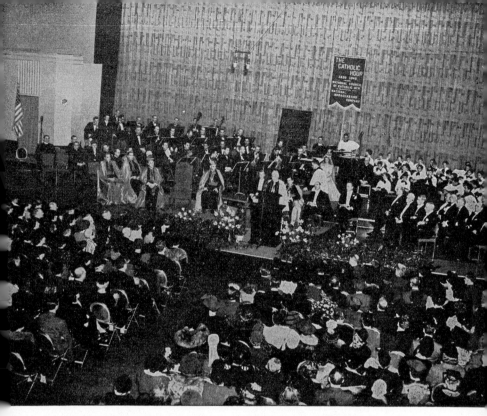

TENTH ANNIVERSARY OF THE CATHOLIC HOUR

For many years the "Catholic Hour", with other Catholic radio programs, has presented to the American public the teachings of the Catholic Church.

once grasped them are not going to reject God lightly, and almost certainly are not going to reject Him at all. And against those who have rejected God, they can be used very powerfully to show the utter darkness and helplessness of their Godless universe.

7. SUMMARY OF PROOFS OF GOD'S EXISTENCE

a. Where there is order—that is to say, where things fit together and work together—we know that a mind has (a) intended that order, (b) produced it. (When no mind intends a thing, that thing happens by chance: and chance cannot produce order but only chaos.) The stupendous order in our universe makes it certain that a stupendous Mind intended that universe and produced it.

b. All the things of our experience have this in common—that they might not have existed. They owe their existence to the fact that certain other things were what they were or did what they did. This means that no one of them is the source of its own existence. Where then does *existence* come from? There must be a Being who has existence without having to receive existence, who exists in His own right. He does not owe His existence to any other thing, but all other things owe their existence to Him. For all other things are receivers of existence, He is the Source. He brings the universe into existence by creating it from nothing, so that His power is infinite.

REVIEW OF SECTION TWO-A.

B. CHRIST IS GOD-MADE-MAN

B. CHRIST IS GOD-MADE-MAN
  1. SINCE GOD EXISTS RELIGION IS NECESSARY
  2. WE MUST FIND THE TRUE RELIGION
  3. THE CATHOLIC CHURCH CLAIMS TO BE THE TRUE RELIGION
  4. THE FOUNDER OF THE CATHOLIC RELIGION
      a. The Old Testament—A Redeemer Promised; Son of Abraham
      b. The New Testament—A Claimant Appears and Proves His Claim
          1) He Fulfills Old Testament Prophecies
          2) He Claims to be God and Proves It.
      c. Twofold Source of Knowledge of What Christ Did and Said
          1) The Word of His Church
          2) Reliable Documents
              a) The Gospels
              b) St. Paul's Epistles
              c) Authenticity of the Gospels
              d) Wealth and Value of Documentary Evidence
  5. WHO AND WHAT CHRIST IS
      a. Christ Claims to be God
          1) Claim is Guaranteed by Miracles
          2) Claim is Revealed Gradually
      b. Claim First Announced Implicitly in Christ's Words and Actions
          1) How a Claim Can Be Contained Implicitly in Actions
          2) Speaking and Acting as God
      c. The Explicit Claim To Be God
          1) "Before Abraham Came to be I Am"
          2) "I and The Father Are One."
          3) "My Lord and My God."
      d. Knowing *What* Christ Is
  6. SUMMARY OF PROOFS OF CHRIST'S GODHEAD

THE MASS COMES TO AMERICA

This scene reconstructs the first Mass celebrated at St. Augustine, Florida, on the feast of the Nativity of the Blessed Virgin Mary, Sept. 8, 1565, decades before the French Missions in Canada, and 55 years before the Pilgrims came to Plymouth Rock.

It is the first Mass of the first and oldest parish in the United States. It was celebrated by America's first parish priest, Father Lopez de Mendoza Grajales, a diocesan priest from Spain.

1. SINCE GOD EXISTS RELIGION IS NECESSARY

God exists and He is the supreme fact. To come to know of His existence and then ignore Him would be at least eccentric. It would be to act as though He were not there, or as though He did not matter.

2. WE MUST FIND THE TRUE RELIGION

A sensible man is always anxious to discover the right way to act in regard to any being he has to do with; the more important the being, the more anxious he is; but God is the Supreme Being, the only reason why any other being exists at all. Not to try to discover the right way to act in regard to God would be sheer madness. That is why we must try to find the True Religion.

Religion is the way men act in regard to God. True Religion is the right way to act in regard to God. Unless a man discovers that, he cannot be right about anything else: above all, he cannot handle his own life intelligently.

God is the only reason why men exist. What did He make men for? Unless He tells us, we do not know. How are men to carry out the purpose He made them for? Unless He tells us we do not know.

It is sometimes said that religion does not matter: a man, they foolishly say, can be a thoroughly good man without any particular views about God or even interest in God: it is not what a man believes that counts, but what he does. This is sentimental folly. A non-religious man may be a nice man, but he is a deaf and blind man. He does not hear the voice of his Maker, and he does not see where he is going.

3. THE CATHOLIC CHURCH CLAIMS TO BE THE TRUE RELIGION

Now the Catholic Church claims to have been founded by God for the very purpose of uttering His voice to mankind. It is interesting to trace the history of her founding and Founder.

4. THE FOUNDER OF THE CATHOLIC RELIGION

a. The Old Testament—A Redeemer Promised: Son of Abraham

Somewhere round the year 2000 B.C. there enters history the most remarkable of all races, the race we call the Jews. They steadily asserted that they were a people chosen by God, and that God had revealed and continued to reveal to them great truths about Himself and about humanity. All this was written down in books which, as they likewise asserted, were inspired by God. The chief of these revelations were that God was One (and not many, as the pagans taught); that the human race had been created in friendship with Him and had calamitously lost that friendship; that *it was to be restored by a Redeemer* who should come from this same Jewish people. With regard to this Redeemer their sacred books (which we now call the Old Testament) contained numerous prophecies.

That these things were claimed did not, of course, prove them true. All we can assert so far is that certain statements about God and His dealings with the human race, and certain prophecies about the Redeemer to come, were made and written down in the centuries before Christ.

b. The New Testament—A Claimant Appears and Proves His Claim

1) He Fulfills the Old Testament Prophecies Concerning the Redeemer

Then Jesus Christ came. The story of His birth and life and death and of the first years after His death are told in the books we call the New Testament. The *prophecies* certainly made about the Redeemer were verified in Him: He was of the line of David's father, as foretold by Isaias 11, 1-2; He was born of a Virgin (Isaias 7, 14) at Bethlehem (Micheas 5, 2); He suffered and died as Isaias described (Chapter 53), His hands and feet were pierced and His garments divided (Psalm 21).

He confirmed the teachings contained in the Old Testament and added new teachings of His own. We believe the Old Testament on His word; we accept His own teaching on His word. Why?

2) He Claims to Be God and Proves It

He claimed to be God and verified His claims by *making prophecies* and by *working miracles,* culminating in the great miracle whereby having died, as He foretold, after three days *He rose again as He foretold,* from the dead.

c. Twofold Source of Knowledge of What Christ Said and Did

So much being built upon what Christ did and said, how do we know what He did and said? There are two answers:

1) The Word of His Church

We have the living testimony of His Church: nineteen hundred years after, it is still living in the world, with unbroken history and unbroken memory. How powerful this testimony is we shall discuss later.

2) Reliable Documents

For the moment we shall concentrate upon the New Testament books written by men who wrote of what they knew and who proved their sincerity by the most searching of all tests—by dying for the truth of what they had written.

a) The Gospels

The most important of these books for the information they give us about Christ Jesus are the four Gospels and certain letters of St. Paul. Consider the Gospels:

The first Gospel was written by St. Matthew, one of the Apostles (that is, one of the twelve men who had been constantly in Christ's company). The second was written down by St. Mark: he was St. Peter's secretary and simply wrote down what Peter preached. This is Peter's Gospel. The third was written by St. Luke, secretary to St. Paul. He had gathered the materials for his Gospel—as he tells us in the opening verse—by a careful examination of what eye-witnesses had written and said.

These three Gospels were all written somewhere between the years 50 and 65 A.D., that is to say, within twenty or thirty years of our Lord's death. The fourth Gospel came somewhat later, towards the year 100 A.D.; but it was written by St. John, the beloved disciple.

b) St. Paul's Epistles

All these four books are lives of Christ, though written from different angles. The Epistles of St. Paul, written

STATUE OF FRA JUNIPERO SERRA
San Fernando Mission, California

Intrepid missioners, apologists for the true Faith, planted and tended the seed of God's truth in our land. Our modern age needs others to carry on their labors. Not only in the priesthood, but among the laity as well, apologists for Christ and God's Church must spread the word and answer the questions in men's minds.

roughly over the period 50-65 A.D., were not written with any such biographical purpose. But in the course of them St. Paul refers to most of the important facts about our Lord—not as informing his readers of them for the first time, but as mentioning things he assumes they already know. He is writing not only to Christians he had himself instructed, but also to Christians he had never even visited: he assumes that they will have heard the facts about our Lord exactly as he has heard them himself.

c) Authenticity of Gospels

Earlier in this century no book of Christian apologetics would have been complete without a detailed treatment of what was called the *authenticity* of the Gospels, that is, their genuineness as reliable authentic historical documents. This was because of an odd aberration of certain nineteenth century scholars, who asserted that the Gospels were written long after the time of Christ, consequently by men who did not know the events they claimed to be recording. This view has almost disappeared: there is scarcely any modern scholar of real competence in this very specialized field who holds it. But it is still occasionally heard from non-Catholic professors, for instance, whose reading has not been kept up-to-date.

They are usually professors of some other subject, and, if pressed, would not claim any special expertness in the field of Scriptural Origins. They are quoting things they read in their own student days, unaware that even non-Christian scholarship has abandoned those once modern positions. Should you meet such a man, there is no great point in arguing with him. The argument would require vast knowledge of Aramaic, first-century Greek, Syriac, third and fourth century manuscripts, recently discovered inscriptions and a score of other such things.

You have not such knowledge, neither, probably, has your opponent. Whether he has or has not, you might refer him to Adolf Harnack, a German historian and theologian of great reputation and perhaps the greatest of all non-Catholic scholars in this field. He is significant because having himself held the old-fashioned view that the Gospels were late documents he came to see that the view must be abandoned. By 1911 he had placed the writing of the first three Gospels between the years 60 and 70, and the fourth somewhere about the end of the first century.

These positions he still maintained at his death, in

1930, and they are close enough to what Catholic scholars have always held.

d) Wealth and Value of Documentary Evidence About Christ

Thus we are back at the position stated earlier. We have more and closer information about Christ our Lord than about any person before Him or for centuries after. It is information given by witnesses who have seen what they record, witnesses who have sealed their testimony with martyrdom. Had they only been eye-witnesses, they might be dismissed by enemies as untruthful; had they merely been martyrs, they might have been dismissed as sincere men but mistaken. But eye-witnesses who are willing to die for their statement of what they have seen —where can you get *guaranteed certainty* to equal that?

5. WHO AND WHAT IS CHRIST

a. Christ Claims to Be God

Everything that Christ our Lord did depends upon *what* He is. And any effort to decide what He is must begin with what He claimed to be. The Church He founded teaches that He is God. But no man could possibly know this if Christ our Lord had not said so. Miracles alone, even the mightiest of all miracles, the Resurrection, would not prove that the miracle-worker was God. He might be no more than a man *through* whom God was working.

1) Claim Guaranteed by Miracles

Yet miracles do mean, at the very least, that God is in action in the matter. If a teacher appears among men, and appeals to the miracles he works in support of his teaching, then it is clear that God is in fact guaranteeing his teaching. The Gospels with their continuous record of miracles thus make it clear that God Himself is guaranteeing to men the teachings of Christ. And Christ, thus guaranteed by God, claims that He is God.

2) The Claim Is Revealed Gradually

To understand just how our Lord made His claim, it is necessary to pause a moment and consider just how stupendous a claim it was, and what the effect would be likely to have been upon minds unprepared for it. The Jews of our Lord's day, whatever their faults, were men who believed most profoundly in God, and more particularly in the majesty of God. For our Lord to have begun His mission among men by claiming to be God would (at any rate, as far as the human mind can judge) have ruined that mission from the start. For either men would not have believed Him at all; or if they had believed Him, they would have been stricken with awe so profound as to be paralyzing. Our Lord had two problems to solve: He must bring them to the point where they can make the confession that He is God; and He must bring them to a richer, almost revolutionary, idea of what God is. As we have said, the Jew of that day thought of God primarily as a God of Justice and hardly at all as a God of Love. Had they believed at the start that Christ was God, they would have thought of Him as *that* God.

b. Claim First Announced Implicitly in Christ's Words and Actions

What our Lord did was so to act and so to speak that gradually those nearest to Him began to feel first that He was more than man; then, that He was immeasurably more than man; that He might be God; that He must be God; that He was God. It is a gradual process, but in the course of it something else, of enormous importance, has been achieved.

By the time His followers know that He is God, they are no longer simply paralyzed with awe by the knowledge. For in their three years of companionship with our Lord they have come to know all the love and compassion that is in Him. They will still be in awe of the Man who is God, but not only in awe. All their experience of Christ our Lord gave them a deeper and fuller, as we have said almost a revolutionary, idea of God.

This revolutionary idea one of them, St. John, expressed for them all in the phrase, "God is Love." They had come to this ultimate truth about God by realizing first that Christ was Love and then that Christ was God.

1) How a Claim Can Be Contained Implicitly in Actions

Let us look, then, at what our Lord did and what our Lord said in those years when He was leading the Apostles forward to the supreme truth about Himself, as bit by bit they grew towards certainty. We shall consider His way of action first. Quite apart from what He said about Himself, He continually did and said things which could make sense only if He were God. Put it this way. If God did become man, how would He act and speak? Christ our Lord acted and spoke just as only God would have any right to. A moment's reflection will show how very strong a claim this involves.

In ordinary life one can think of a score of examples of claims that are made by others, and accepted by ourselves, although the claims are not made in words at all. If a man invites you into a house, presses you to stay to dinner, orders the meal, sends the children to bed, invites you to stay the night, you do not need to hear him say that this is his home. Indeed, you would be a little surprised if at the end of all that he should find it necessary to say "This is my home." Why should he bother to say it, when his every action has said it? Now Christ our Lord for three years steadily was doing things and saying things that only God had a right to do and say. Let us take three instances out of a multitude.

2) Acting and Speaking as God

(a) Observe his attitude to the Law of Moses. Time and again in the Sermon on the Mount (Matt. 5-7) our Lord quotes commandments of that Law with the words: "It was said to them of old." He proceeds to amplify these with the phrase: "But I say to you" (Matt. 5). When we remember that the Law He is discussing was given to the Jews of old by God Himself, the phrase "But I say to you," would be astounding and even ridiculous on the lips of a man.

(b) Observe His attitude to other men in relation to Himself. With all His love and compassion, He never for an instant implies that other men are His equals. One of the commandments given by God through Moses was "Honor thy father and thy mother," Our Lord, of course, would not have us fail in any point of the honor due to our parents, but He says in the most natural way in the world: "He who loves father and mother more than Me is not worthy of Me." This would be the most monstrous egotism if Christ were only man, but the plainest commonsense if He is God. (It would be well to read the whole of the passage from which this phrase is taken. It is Matthew 10, 32-42.)

$\longrightarrow$

Boardman Robinson   *By Ewing Galloway*

JESUS CHRIST—THE GOD MAN?

This picture of Christ in the Department of Justice Building in Washington, D.C., represents our Lord as the founder of the Christian religion—the religion which stands as the basis of British and American jurisprudence. You will probably dislike this representation of Christ, and rightly so, for it omits all suggestion of the divine in Him. It is, however, a good illustration of the way in which many today regard Christ—a good man, a wise man, yes; but the Son of God? a God-man? No! It is to these modern minds that we must present the facts that will lead them to the grace of faith in Jesus Christ as the Promised Messias, God and Man, Redeemer of the World.

(c) Observe one other thing, His claim to pardon sins. You will remember, for instance, the man sick of the palsy who was lowered through the roof (Mark 2, 1-12). Our Lord said to Him: "Son, thy sins are forgiven thee." Very naturally the scribes thought He was guilty of blasphemy. They asked in their hearts: "Who can forgive sins but God only?" No question could be more natural. The Jews had a great expectation of the Messias to come; they had masses of literature about him both in the Old Testament and in other writings. But nowhere did they suggest that even the Messias could forgive sins. Yet here, and on many other occasions, our Lord simply does so, and always in His own name.

As was said earlier, we are giving only a few examples of the kind of action which would be natural as coming from God, and quite monstrous as coming from anyone not God.

Read any of the Gospels to yourself, and you will see that our Lord is acting thus all the time. If He was not claiming to be God by this kind of conduct, then some sort of explanation was certainly due from Him as to how He could possibly act thus if He were less than God.

In the face of such action, we should need the most explicit denials of His Godhead. But there are no such denials: on the contrary our Lord did quite clearly, as time went by, directly affirm that He was God. Here again, let us choose three instances.

——————

→

From Ewing Galloway

THE RESURRECTION

Christ proved the divinity of His mission by many miracles, the most astounding of which was His fulfillment of the prophecy that He had made, that He would rise from the dead on the third day.

c. The Explicit Claim to Be God

1) "Before Abraham Came to Be I Am"

Read the passage John 8, 37-59, culminating in our Lord's saying: "Before Abraham came to be I am." To the Jew of that day, this was the clearest possible claim to be God. Even reading it without any special knowledge, one is struck by the words "I am" where gramatically one would expect "I was." The use of the present tense would be natural only to the God for whom (as we have already seen) there is no past or future but only an eternal present.

So much anyone might see in the words. But the Jew would remember that "I am" was the name God had given Himself, when He appeared to Moses in The Burning Bush. Exodus 3, 14.

Moses had said to God: "Lo, I shall go to the children of Israel, and say to them: The God of your fathers hath sent me to you. If they should say to me: what is His name? What shall I say to them? God said to Moses: *I am who am.* He said: "Thus shalt thou say to the children of Israel: *He who is,* hath sent me to you."

Thus when our Lord says: "Before Abraham came to be I am," He was claiming for Himself the name of God. It is perhaps not surprising that hearing this the Jews took up stones to cast at Him: stoning was the penalty for blasphemy, and if our Lord was not God He was a blasphemer.

2) "I and the Father Are One"

Read again the passage John 10, 22-30. Here the culminating phrase is: "I and the Father are one." The Jews again took up stones to stone Him.

3) "My Lord and My God"

We go now to the week following our Lord's Resurrection. Read John 20, 24-29. Here at last the very word

THAT THE BEAUTY OF
HIS COUNTENANCE BE
NOT HIDDEN FROM
· · · HIS OWN · · ·
THAT HIS WOUNDS
AND WOE WHEREIN
HE WROTE
BE KNOWN
ALL THE
HE REDEEMED

INSCRIPTION BY
FATHER WALTER NOTT
1891 — 1932

A marine stops to read the inscription on the base of a beautiful roadside crucifix at Aquia, near Quantico, Va. What does the inscription mean when it asks that "His wounds and woe wherein He wrote His love be known by all the people He redeemed?"

"God" is used. Thomas had not been with the other Apostles at our Lord's first appearance after the Resurrection, and had refused to believe unless he should actually see and feel the wounds. Our Lord appeared and invited Thomas to make the test that Thomas had demanded. And all Thomas could say was: "My Lord, and my God." And our Lord accepted the phrase, declaring Thomas blessed for having believed.

d. Knowing WHAT Christ Is

We have seen that people are more likely to be won to belief in God by a consideration of what God is than by the mere proofs that God exists. Similarly, the arguments that Christ is God have immeasurably more power to a man who has come to *know* Christ: and immeasurably more again when he comes to realize what light is shed upon the nature of God Himself by the truth that Christ our Lord *is* God. We must develop this knowledge and this realization in ourselves, and then in those whom we wish to help. The way for us and for them is the same: to read and re-read the Gospels. We must be Gospel-soaked. Study each act and word of our Lord, having always in mind that He who acted thus and spoke thus was God. Thus we build up in our minds what that God must be, and there is no profounder way to that knowledge of God which is so much more powerful than any set of proofs.

6. SUMMARY OF PROOFS OF CHRIST'S GODHEAD

Christ's miracles, culminating in the Resurrection, prove that God is with Him guaranteeing His message, for God alone can work miracles and God would not guarantee an untruth. But Christ's message included certain claims about Himself. Whatever He claimed to be, that He was (and is). We know it on God's guarantee.

THE CHRIST ATOP THE CORCOVADO

This magnificent statue of Christ, one hundred feet in height and standing on the summit of the Corcovado peak, dominates the city and harbor of Rio de Janeiro, Brazil. It is eloquent public testimony that the citizens of that city and republic accept the divinity of Christ.

He claimed to be God:

By acting and speaking as only God would have a right to act
   or speak.
   His attitude to the law God gave through Moses.
   His attitude to other men in relation to Himself.
   His claim to pardon sins.
By direct statement.
   "Before Abraham came to be, I am." John 8, 58.
   "I and the Father are one." John 10, 30.
   Accepting St. Thomas's phrase, "My Lord and My God." John
   20, 28.

REVIEW OF SECTION TWO-B.

C. THE CHURCH CHRIST FOUNDED

C. THE CHURCH CHRIST FOUNDED
   1. THE NATURE OF THE CHURCH FOUNDED BY CHRIST
      a. The Catholic View
      b. The Protestant View
      c. Which View is Correct?
         1) Objectors to the Correct View
      d. Proving the Catholic Church the One True Church, Founded by
         Christ
         1) The Church of Christ was to Be Catholic
         2) The Church of Christ was to Be Visibly United
         3) The Church of Christ was to Be Papal
            a) Peter as Christ's Representative on Earth
            b) Christ Conferred His own Titles on Peter
            c) Power conferred on Peter by these Titles
         4) Summary on Nature of Church Established by Christ
   2. THE CHURCH CONTINUES CHRIST'S WORK ON EARTH
      a. Channel of Christ's Truth and Life
      b. We Go to the Church for God's Gifts
   3. ERRORS UPON NECESSITY OF CHURCH
      a. The Bible Only
      b. Indifferentism
   4. THE CHURCH HERSELF—WHAT SHE IS
   5. SUMMARY OF PROOFS THAT OUR LORD FOUNDED THE CATHOLIC
      CHURCH

1. THE NATURE OF THE CHURCH FOUNDED BY CHRIST

The question whether the Catholic Church is the one
true Church, or whether any Church is the one true
Church, or whether for a Christian it is a matter of vital

importance to belong to a Church—all these things are much discussed, and on the face of it a good deal of the discussion is off the point. All that matters is to find out what Christ our Lord intended. It is a curious kind of folly to approach the matter as though all we had to do was to settle it for ourselves, in the light of our own view as to whether it is more healthful to the soul to have One True Church, or a number of partly true churches, or a relation direct with God and no church at all. It is somewhat as though patients in a hospital chose their own treatment. For Christians, the one thing necessary is to discover what our Lord wanted.

Now it is not denied by any Christian that our Lord founded a Church, and wanted men to belong to it. That there is a Church in the world founded by Christ our Lord is, then, not in dispute. What is disputed is the kind of thing this Church was meant by our Lord to be.

a. The Catholic View

The Catholic view, which goes back to the very beginning of Christianity, is that the Church our Lord founded was a visible organization with officials, and with one of these officials in supreme control.

b. The Protestant View

What may fairly be called the Protestant view, which goes back to the sixteenth century, is that the Church our Lord meant to found is not a visible body at all, but an invisible society consisting of all who accept our Lord's redeeming act in their souls by faith. From this point of view everyone who makes the act of faith in our Lord as his Redeemer would by that very act be a member of the Church our Lord founded, and this invisible society of souls would be the only Church that matters. Members of the Church might, if they found it useful to their souls, form or join this or that religious body—Lutheran or

Calvinist or Methodist or what you will. These churches being only man-made, are considered valuable only if their members find them so. The only Church that matters would be the invisible society of all true believers.

c. Which View Is Correct?

As between these two views, we have already seen what is the only question that can be decisive. What did our Lord say on the matter? By this test it would seem to be as clear as crystal that our Lord intended to found the Catholic Church.

1) Objectors to the Correct View

If it is as clear as crystal, why does any believer in our Lord deny that our Church was founded by Him? It will be found that most objectors fall into one (or both) of two groups:

> those who dislike the Catholic Church.
> those who dislike the very idea of one organized Church.

Let us glance briefly at each.

a) Those who dislike the Catholic Church point to various episodes in her history, the ill deeds of certain of her leaders, the disedifying lives of many Catholics here and now: and argue that if our Lord did found a Church, it could not have been this one. But in the first place they are guilty of getting things out of proportion: for the Church does not have more or worse sinners than other institutions, whereas she has immeasurably more and more glorious saints. And in the second place they fail to grasp what the Church is for: Our Lord founded it *to give us His gifts* of truth and life: He gives these to us through men, and they are sometimes sinful men: but He guarantees the gifts: the men are but instruments in His hands:

NOMBRE DE DIOS, ST. AUGUSTINE, FLORIDA

Founded 1565

This is the venerable church of the oldest parish and mission in the United States. The parish was founded and served by diocesan priests from Spain in 1565. Many of them gave their lives that the true religion might strike root in the savage wilderness of the Western World. They were true apologists and missioners.

and it is for the gifts that we come to the Church, not for the men. Where the Church is not believed in, the very idea of our Lord's gifts of infallible truth and sacramental life has vanished away.

b) The second group consists of those who dislike the idea of one visible organized Church and value, as they say, their spiritual freedom. They claim that each soul has its own private relation to God, its own spiritual needs and problems; each mind has its own way of getting at truth and must not be enslaved by dogmas taught by men. Such people will deal with God and no one else, be taught by God and no one else. They mean well, but this refusal to form one body with their fellow-men, receiving God's gifts through them, united with them in the spread of God's kingdom upon earth, is a subtle sort of pride: and ends not in their doing what God wishes and believing what God teaches but in their doing and believing what seems good to themselves.

d. Proving the Catholic Church the One True Church Founded by Christ

But, as we have already insisted, the decisive fact in the case for the Catholic Church is that our Lord founded it. As upon all the other matters we have discussed, one could quote a great mass of proof. But here again it seems better to select two or three very clear, very unanswerable words of our Lord.

1) The Church of Christ Was to be Catholic

We might begin by considering the word *Catholic* itself. "Catholic," as everybody knows, means "universal." But this is not very enlightening. We have merely taken a Greek word and substituted a Latin word for it. What does "universal" mean? The word contains two ideas, the idea of *all* and the idea of *one,* in some way the Catholic Church must be the Church of all in one. But all what? And one what? Let us consider what our Lord had to say about the "all" and the "one."

Read Matthew 28, 16-20. At the very end of our Lord's time upon earth, just before His Ascension, He appeared to the Apostles and said this to them:

"All power in heaven and on earth has been given to Me. Go, therefore, and make disciples of *all* nations, baptizing them in the name of the Father, and of the Son, and of the Holy Spirit, teaching them to observe *all* that I have commanded you; and behold, I am with you *all days,* even unto the consummation of the world."

It will be noticed that the word "all" occurs four times in this passage. Once it refers to our Lord's own power, three times it refers to what He is ordering His Apostles to do. It is this threefold "all" which constitutes our Lord's comment on the meaning of the word Catholic. *All nations, all doctrines, all days.* The Church He is founding must be a Church which is one thing for all nations, and not simply a Church of this nation or that; it must be in the world from His day until the end of time; any Church which starts at some later date cannot be His; and it must teach all the doctrines He taught.

Our Lord is here speaking to the eleven Apostles, but from the mere fact that the orders He is giving are to be in effect until the end of the world, it is clear that He is speaking to them not simply as themselves, but as the first holders of an office in His Church, an office which is to go on until the end of time.

Thus it is not to them only, but to them and their successors, that our Lord gives His command, together with His guarantee that they will carry out the command without fail; for in their teaching and in their baptizing, our Lord Himself will be with them.

By itself *this excludes* the notion of a number of *sects,* all teaching different things as to our Lord's doctrines. He is to be with them in their teaching, therefore they

By Burton Holmes   From Ewing Galloway

ST. PETER'S, ROME

Unity is the first and most striking of the four marks which prove the Catholic Church to be the one true Church founded by Jesus Christ. The great basilica of St. Peter on the Vatican Hill in Rome gives visible evidence and testimony of this most remarkable and divinely effected unity, a unity of authority and belief of essential practice and worship.

must be united in their teaching; and men are to know that they have found the teaching and the sacraments guaranteed by Christ our Lord when they find the successors of the Apostles to whom our Lord gave the promise.

2) The Church of Christ Was to Be Visibly United

We have just seen that in giving His Apostles the commission to continue His teaching and His sacraments to the end of time, our Lord most clearly implied oneness as distinct from a multiplicity of religious bodies. But earlier, at the Last Supper, He had spoken explicitly of the kind of oneness He wanted. Every Catholic should be deeply familiar with the five chapters of St. John's Gospel, Chapters 13-17, which contain the discourse uttered by our Lord at the Last Supper. Towards the end of this discourse comes this: "Yet not for these [the Apostles] only do I pray, but for those also who through their word are to believe in Me, that all may be one, even as Thou, Father, in Me and I in Thee; that they also may be one in Us, that the world may believe that Thou has sent Me." John 17, 20-21.

Thus our Lord has in mind for His followers a *unity* comparable to the unity of the Three Persons within the Blessed Trinity, a unity which obviously excludes differences of doctrine. And this unity is not to be only in their souls, it is to be visible—for the world is to see it, and is to be so impressed by it that it will know that Christ who founded a unity so marvelous must be truly from God. In other words, Christ our Lord is staking the proof of His divinity upon the visible unity of the Church He is founding.

3) The Church of Christ Was to Be Papal

How is this unity to be secured? The answer to this question brings us to the one fact by which the Church is most instantly recognizable—namely, the position of Peter and the successors of Peter.

a) Peter as Christ's Representative on Earth

It is clear from what has gone before that our Lord did not mean that the Apostles should disband after He Himself had left this world. They were to continue as a band; they were now to do the work for which He had so long been training them.

But *men are not easily held together*. Differences of point of view, differences of temperament, are forever threatening to split men asunder. While our Lord was alive among them, He kept them united in obedience to Him. How were they to be kept united when He was no longer visibly with them?

Here again it is not for us to decide for ourselves what He ought to have done or might have done. Our only concern is to find what He did do. And what He did do was to choose one of the Apostles, who should represent Him when He was gone. How closely He made Peter to be His representative is not always realized. As the end of our Lord's life is approaching, we find Him conferring upon Peter the titles and functions which belong of right to Himself alone. Let us consider three such occasions.

b) Christ Conferring His Own Titles on Peter

Our Lord has been for all the Christian centuries, the Rock of Ages. St. Paul speaks of Him as the one Foundation. 1 Cor. 3, 11. In the last book of the New Testament we find our Lord described as "He who has the key of David." Apocalypse 3, 7. Remembering that our Lord is the *Rock,* the *Foundation,* and the *Key-bearer,* read Matthew 16, 13-19. Notice especially our Lord's closing words to Simon, whose name He had changed to Peter, a word meaning Rock: "I say to thee, thou art Peter, and upon this rock I will build My Church and the gates of hell shall not prevail against it. And I will give thee the keys of the kingdom of heaven. And whatever thou shalt bind on earth shall be bound in heaven, and whatever thou shalt loose on earth shall be loosed in heaven." Christ who is Rock and Key-bearer promises to make Peter the Rock, the Foundation, and to give him the keys. This

Giordoni Mallucci   *Courtesy of Nashville Register*

CHRIST'S CHURCH IS PAPAL

episode took place just before our Lord's Passion was
to begin.

Come now to the Last Supper. Our Lord is praying to
His Father and He says, with reference to the Apostles:
"While I was with them, I kept them in Thy name. Those
whom Thou hast given Me I guarded." John 17, 12. Now
read Luke 22, 24-32. An argument has arisen among the
Apostles, at the very table of the Last Supper, as to which
of them should be the greater. Our Lord settled it with
the words addressed to Simon Peter: "Simon, Simon, behold, Satan has desired to have you [the word 'you' is
plural, and it means the Apostles as a whole], that he
may sift you as wheat. But I have prayed for thee, that
thy faith may not fail; and do thou, when once thou hast
turned again, strengthen thy brethren." It has been our
Lord's special function to "keep" the brethren: He now
entrusts that task to Peter.

Our third episode occurs after our Lord's Resurrection.
Remember how He had said of Himself: "I am the Good
Shepherd." John 10, 14. Now read John 21, 9-17. Notice
especially the three injunctions our Lord gives to Peter:
Feed My lambs, feed My lambs, feed My sheep. The
Good Shepherd is giving over the lambs and the sheep
of the flock to be shepherded by Peter.

c) Powers Conferred on Peter by These Titles

In the three passages we have been considering, we
have so far noted only that our Lord is conferring His
own titles upon Peter. Let us now look more closely at
the powers He transfers along with the titles. In the passage from St. Matthew's Gospel, what is especially emphasized is Peter's *supremacy:* He is to have the Keys of
the Kingdom of Heaven, a phrase which means the
Church. What he binds or looses upon earth is bound or
loosed by the authority of God Himself.

What is especially emphasized in the passage from St.

Luke's Gospel is the *infallible teaching.* In order that
Satan's effort to scatter the Apostles may be frustrated,
our Lord prays that Peter's faith may not fail, that it may
be "unfailable," or *infallible.*

It would be impossible, in the time we now have, to
develop all the richness of the powers conferred upon
Peter in the passage from St. John's Gospel: for the word
used is *"feed,"* and all the food the spirit of man requires
is contained in it. Consider only two of the things our Lord
has to say about the food of man's spirit. After His forty
days' fast in the desert, He quotes the Old Testament
phrase: "Not by bread alone does man live, but by every
word that comes forth from the mouth of God." Matt. 4, 4.
Thus, since Peter is to feed our Lord's flock, He must feed
them with "every word that comes forth from the mouth
of God," and we of the flock know that we are getting
that true food from the shepherd appointed by the Good
Shepherd.

But there was another kind of food spoken of by our
Lord, the food of His own Body. It is to be the task of
Peter to ensure that with this sacramental food we also
shall be fed.

Upon Peter then as the first head, after Christ Himself,
of the Apostolic band which was to continue until the
end of time, our Lord confers supremacy and the infallible
guardianship of doctrine and sacraments.

4) Summary on Nature of Church Established by Christ

Let us now *summarize* what we have seen as to the
nature of the Church as stated by our Lord Himself. It
was to be one Church of all nations, possessing all power,
lasting for all ages, teaching all doctrines; it was to be
visibly united with a unity at once so evident and so overwhelming that men could argue from it to the Godhead
of its founder; it was to be constructed upon the Apostles

and their successors, ruled supremely and taught infallibly by the successors of St. Peter. The Catholic Church answers this description totally. It would be difficult to find any other church that would claim to answer *even one* element in it.

2. THE CHURCH CONTINUES CHRIST'S WORK ON EARTH

a. Channel of Christ's Truth and Life

But we are not simply concerned with a point by point demonstration. For our own understanding of the Church it is still more important that we should get a living picture of the Church as it continues our Lord's own mission among men. Of Himself, our Lord said: "I am the Way, and the Truth, and the Life." He is the Way, the Redeemer. As He says: "No one comes to the Father but through Me." But to find the Way is not enough, we need the Truth and the Life as well—the Truth that we may follow the Way with certainty and never err from it, the Life that we may have the strength to follow the Way to the goal which is the eternal vision of God. Our Lord, while He was upon earth gave men the Truth—the truth as to what men must know, the truth as to what men must do—and the life. Thus we see Him, over and above His function as Redeemer, carrying out the threefold function of Teacher and Law-Giver and Life-Giver.

But man's need of doctrine and of law and of life did not end when our Lord left this world. In the Church, we are still getting, and getting from Him, truth and law and life. We are still getting it, we insist, from Him, though through men. He sent the Church to teach and to administer Baptism, which is the gateway to all the sacra-

Philip Gendreau, N. Y.

ST. JOHN CAPISTRANO

This beautiful altar, built by the Franciscan missioners with the help of their Indian converts, proves how well the intrepid apologists for our faith convinced their savage pupils of the truth of Christianity and brought into their lives the graces of Christian living, cultural as well as spiritual.

519

ments: and the sacraments are life-giving. And to guarantee the truth and the life He promised that He would be with the Church all days, even to the consummation of the world.

b. We Go to the Church for God's Gifts

Thus while we go to the society of men with whom our Lord is, we go for the sake of our Lord's gifts and with the certainty that our Lord guarantees them. For, observe that in ensuring that we should get His gifts of truth and life, our Lord did all that was necessary, but not more than was necessary. The men who at any given moment are the officials of our Lord's Church may be and usually are very good men; yet they may be not very good men. But when they are good, their goodness adds nothing to our Lord's gifts; when they are bad, their badness takes nothing from our Lord's gifts. We belong to the Church not because priests and bishops and popes are good, *but because God's gifts are good*.

3. ERRORS UPON NECESSITY OF CHURCH AS CHANNEL OF GOD'S GIFTS

We have just seen that what our Lord established was the indispensable minimum. And it really is indispensable. Apart from the Church that our Lord founded, it is quite literally impossible for men to get all the gifts that our Lord gives through it. There are two errors upon this matter, the error which says that the Bible alone is sufficient, and the error which holds that within Christianity one religion is good as another.

a. The Bible Only

The first of the errors was very strong up to the beginning of this century. It has been gradually losing strength, and although one will find individual communities in which it flourishes as vigorously as ever, it no longer holds any great place in the Christian world as a whole. It has against it the double disadvantage that it is theoretically indefensible, and that it has shown itself in practice as utterly destructive of Christian unity: its effect has been to produce hundreds or thousands of different interpretations of our Lord's teachings.

We have seen the enormous importance that our Lord attached to His teaching. The question for us is how to be certain that we have His teaching. The New Testament will give us the actual words—not all of them, but a very rich treasury all the same. But more important than the words is *the meaning of the words*. Men have argued as to the meaning of every word our Lord ever spoke. When there is an argument about what words mean, the words themselves cannot settle the argument: for they are precisely what the argument is about.

While our Lord was still on earth, any doubt as to what He meant could be settled by asking Him, as Nicodemus did. John 3, 4. Now that our Lord is with His Father in heaven, doubts can still arise, and can be settled *by asking His Church*. If there is a *living teacher* in the world, guaranteed by Christ our Lord Himself, then it is possible for us to know with certainty the meaning of the things our Lord said. If there is no such living teacher guaranteed by Christ, then we can have the words plus our own guess at the meanings: but this is not at all the same thing as having the teachings of Christ. But there is such a living teacher, Christ's Church; and we can settle our doubts by asking this Church.

b. Indifferentism

The second error, which has gained the name of Indifferentism, is still very widely met. It takes the form either of saying that provided you are a Christian, it does not matter which of the various Christian bodies you belong to, or the slightly more extreme and on the whole more logical form of saying that provided you believe in Christ there is no necessity to belong to any Church at all.

Such views are possible only to one who has very little notion of who our Lord is and what our Lord did. Such a man is by way of admiring Christ our Lord but not thinking it important to find out what our Lord Himself wanted. He has no notion of the immensity of our Lord's gifts of truth and life, conveyed in doctrine and sacrament.

With regard to truth, he apparently holds that *any teaching will do,* since the churches which he classes as equally valuable give contradictory teachings. And of the life he has no views at all. Obviously a man who has so penurious a notion of what Christ our Lord came to give will not be likely to spend much time in making certain that a particular church can give it to him. Fundamentally he attaches no great importance to what the various churches have to give, because he attaches no great importance to what our Lord has to give.

4. THE CHURCH HERSELF—WHAT SHE IS

The student who has followed this course will probably be expecting what comes next. Upon the existence of God and again upon the divinity of Christ we saw that a contemplation of what God is and of what Christ is affects the mind more powerfully than the mere proofs that God exists and that Christ is God. The same principle applies to the Church.

A man who has really *seen* the Church will not be so much concerned as to whether he can find proof that she is divinely founded. She is like a tree that has stood so long,

→

Philip Gendreau, N. Y.

THE CROSS ACROSS THE WORLD

The shadow of Christ's Cross lies over the world—to help and bless, or to threaten and accuse. Apologetics is the science of helping people to see that the Cross which Christ's Church holds out to men is indeed the key to happiness, social as well as individual, temporal as well as eternal.

withstood so many storms, branched so widely, flowered
and fruited so richly, that it would require a very sus-
picious man indeed to wonder if her roots were sound.
One way to be satisfied about the roots is to study the tree.

Indeed there have always been men who argued, and
correctly so, from effect to cause, that is, *from the Church
to Christ* rather than from Christ to the Church. Such
men have been overwhelmed with the sheer marvelousness
of the Church: her unity so utterly beyond man's nature
to attain, her Catholicity throughout the ages and the
nations and all the varied types of men, her stability from
the time of Peter and the Apostles to the present Pope
and the bishops, her fruits of supernatural sanctity and
natural health.

And from all this they have been led to the certainty
that the Founder of a thing so marvelous must be God
Himself. And this line of argument was, as we have already noted, foreseen by our Lord Himself when He
prayed for those who should come to believe in Him: "that
they may be one, as Thou, Father, in Me, and I in Thee:
that they also may be one in Us: that the world may believe that Thou hast sent Me." The Unity of His Church
was to be a standing evidence that He, who had founded
it, was divine.

5. SUMMARY OF PROOFS THAT OUR LORD FOUNDED THE CATHOLIC CHURCH

Our Lord made many statements about the Church He
was founding which are true of the Catholic Church and
of no other.

    a. It should teach *all* nations, *all* doctrines, *all* days till
    the end of time and He would be with it in its teach-
    ing and baptizing. Matt. 28, 16-20.

    b. It should be *one* as He and His Father are one, and
    this unity should be both visible, so that the world
    could see it, and so remarkable that it would prove
    His Godhead. John 17, 20-21.

c. It should be founded *upon Peter* as

(1) Rock and Keybearer. Matt. 16, 13-19.

(2) Confirmer of the brethren. Luke 22, 24-32.

(3) Shepherd of the whole flock. John 21, 9-17.

REVIEW OF SECTION TWO-C.

POSTSCRIPT

You have now completed a first outline of apologetics. Do not think that by it you are equipped to meet any argument that can ever be leveled against the Church. Most of those who assail her teaching or her claims are not particularly learned. They can be handled easily enough. But you may also meet men armed with some of the best arguments that the Church's enemies have developed in the nineteen centuries of their assault upon her. These, too, can be answered, but not with what you have learned so far. You must continue to fit yourself for this essential soldiering. You are not yet fully trained. But you have made a beginning.

One final word upon the limits of apologetics. We have called it a statement of the case for the Church. But at best it is only part of the case, and not the strongest part: it is the statable part: the part that cannot be uttered is greater. The overwhelming case for the Church is *what life in the Church means* to those who live it; no one knows Christ our Lord as those know Him who have lived, or even tried to live, by His teachings and have been fed with the Eucharistic food.

The difference between living in the Church and merely hearing the arguments for the Church is like the difference between seeing the Grand Canyon and seeing a map of the Grand Canyon. Yet a right understanding of the arguments can accomplish great things, for others and for ourselves.

REVIEW OF UNIT FIVE

1. What is apologetics?
2. How can it be of value to you? to others?
3. What is "the whole case for the Church"?
4. Why is it necessary first to know what your opponent believes or accepts?
5. What is needed besides clever argumentation to bring faith to another?
6. What are the three main statements on which the case for the Church rests? Prove each to an imaginary objector specifying the position and education of your opponent.
7. How would you handle an atheist?
8. Formulate the argument for the existence of God from the order in the universe.
9. Answer the claim that the order in the universe is the product of chance.
10. What question would you ask the atheistic evolutionist?
11. How does the atheist try to bluff us?
12. Formulate the argument for the existence of God from contingency, i.e., argue from contingent beings to a necessary Being. Give an illustration.
13. What are some consequences that would follow if there were no God?
14. Prove in two ways that Jesus Christ is God.
15. Show how the willingness of the Apostles to undergo martyrdom proves the strength of their belief in the divinity of Christ.
16. Show that Christ acted as if He were God.
17. Show how Christ actually claimed to be God.
18. Was it Christ's intention that one religion be considered as good as another? Prove it.
19. What sort of a Church did Christ promise?
20. Show that Christ's Church was to be Catholic and externally visible and united.
21. How did Christ provide for the unity of His Church?
22. Prove that St. Peter and his successors were intended by Christ to be the head of His Church.

G. A. Douglas   ⟶   *From Gendreau, N. Y.*

ST. PATRICK'S CATHEDRAL, NEW YORK

This unusual view of St. Patrick's, shows clearly the cruciform construction used in most of the great cathedrals. Even in building her churches the Catholic Church reminds the world of Christ who redeemed the world on a Cross.

23. Why is it more important to know what God is than to be able to prove His existence? to know what Christ is than to prove His divinity? what the Church is than to prove Her founded by Christ?
24. How can we know what the Bible means in case of dispute?
25. What is indifferentism? Prove its fallacy.
26. Show how we can also argue from the Church to Christ's divinity, as well as from the divinity of Christ to that of the Church.

CONCLUSION OF THE YEAR AND THE SERIES— A RÉSUMÉ

Our story of *Our Quest for Happiness* is ended, but the quest still goes on. Four years ago we began this study of our holy religion and now we have reached the end. Let us take a quick look back and bring it all together one final time. We can do it best by following it once again on the chart at the front of the book on pages 11 and 12 and especially on page 13.

THE STORY OF DIVINE LOVE INVITING HUMAN LOVE

Our high school religion course has been a study of the story of how our great triune God has proved His infinite love for each and every member of the human race. It has also been a proof of the great debt of love we owe our triune God, and a presentation of the way in which God has enabled us to pay that debt of love and gain possession of Life eternally. It has shown us the Low Road of Love—the Road of the Commandments. It has shown us the Middle Road of Love—The Road of the Virtues. It has shown us the High Road of Love—The Road of the Counsels, The Road of the Gifts of the Holy Spirit.

AS FRESHMEN

As freshmen, we learned that the insatiable desire for happiness which springs eternal in the heart of man is really a desire for God, for He alone can satisfy it. We

learned that forgetfulness of self and unconditional service of God and of our neighbor can alone lead us to God.
We learned that reason and especially Faith guide us to
Him and to happiness. We saw that the main doctrines
of our holy Faith which we must believe and the main
duties we must perform are contained in the liturgical
year, which is only a method of living with Christ and
in Christ in His Mystical Body, the Church. Following
that, we studied the greatness and the goodness of God
in His Unity and Trinity, and then learned the limitless
extent of *The Creative Love of God the Father* and His
unending goodness as portrayed in Creation and especially
in the promise of a Redeemer, and in the gift of the sacraments, especially the first two, and in the guidance of the
commandments, especially the first three.

AS SOPHOMORES

Our sophomore year was a study of *The Redemptive
Love of God the Son;* His Incarnation for our salvation,
His early life, His obedience, His Public Life and all its
wonderful sequence of incidents. Then followed the Passion and Redemption, restoring Hope, and the continuation of that great act of divine love in the Mass, and
in the Holy Eucharist—the great challenge to our love
for God.

AS JUNIORS

Our third year found us peering into the mysterious
deeds of *The Sanctifying Love of the Holy Ghost,* first in
Himself, then in His spouse, the *Catholic Church,* then
in His operations in the Church, particularly in her history and in her power to forgive sins. Lastly, looking at
ourselves as temples of the Holy Ghost, we realized the
love which God manifested in His revelation to us of the
fifth and sixth commandments and we saw our obligation
to return that love in the practice of the virtues which
make up temperance.

AS SENIORS

Finally, this fourth and last year, we learned of the reward that awaits us—*The Beatifying Love of the Trinity.* We saw the glorious results of this Divine Love in the Blessed Virgin Mary, the warning it has given us in the knowledge of the Last Things and the encouragement it supplies in the realization that we can attain eternal blessedness. Then we looked at the three paths in which man seeks the happiness of serving God on earth and insures for himself the happiness of glorifying God in heaven for all eternity. We studied the final commandments, namely, those which prescribe the virtue of justice in deed and desire, and, just now, we have concluded by seeing how reasonable our holy religion actually is.

Our course is ended. From now on we go toward the Eternal Commencement without the loving care and protection of our Alma Mater. Now we must go into the wide world and lead it—with the gentle but powerful insistence of a life based on the seven virtues—lead it to God and to happiness.

GOD LOVES AND ASKS LOVE

God loves you! Every page of this course proves it. Every creature that is or ever was also proves it. *God loves you!* God loves all men! *All He wants is your love.* All He wants is your loving service of Him, in His Son, in His Church, in His images, your fellow men.

Do this and you will finally succeed in your Quest for Happiness. Do this and you will reach that Eternal Commencement which will never cease beginning for all

$\longrightarrow$

Philip Gendreau, N. Y.

TOWARD THE ETERNAL COMMENCEMENT

Our high school course is ended. Now we walk forth into the adult scene that is our modern world. God give us the grace always to be noble. God give us the grace to be proud of our faith, and to make our faith proud of us. God give us the grace ever to cling to our faith, and to serve our world in the humble imitation of Him who became Incarnate and died that He might show us how to die that we might truly live.

eternity. For there, as in the Preface of the Mass, every "Per omnia saecula saeculorum" is not an ending but a beginning of an Eternal Preface which knows no end.

It would be well if you would bring this last year of your high-school course to a conclusion with a special ceremony in which all first would adore their triune God and give thanks to Him for His many blessings, especially those of the past four years. Then could follow a pledge of undying fidelity to our holy Faith and all its precepts, together with a prayer for forgiveness, for grace and for final perseverance.

The pledge of fidelity could well be made by singing: "Faith of Our Fathers . . . we will be true to thee 'til death." It could be supplemented and made specific by an Act of Consecration to the Sacred Heart and to the Immaculate Heart, and the making of a solemn pledge to practice faithfully the matters included in the Plan of Life which you drew up at the end of Unit Two this year: Daily Prayer, Sunday Mass, Frequent Communion and Confession, the formation of the basic virtues, etc. The prayer for perseverance could be very appropriately, "Mother Dear, O Pray for Me," or "Hide Thou Me." The ceremony could end with benediction, if possible, and "Holy God We Praise Thy Name."

> Holy Father, Holy Son,
>   Holy Spirit, Three we name Thee,
> While in essence only one,
>   Undivided God we claim Thee;
> And adoring bend the knee
>   While we own the mystery.

A FINAL QUIZ TO ASSIST INTEGRATION OF WHAT HAS BEEN LEARNED

1. Give an outline of the four years of *Our Quest for Happiness.* Explain the work and units of each year and tell how each unit and each year is a logical step from the preceding unit and the preceding year.

2. Explain in detail the deeds of love which have been performed for us by God: Father, Son, and Holy Ghost, and which will yet be accomplished in us by the Blessed Trinity if we return God's love by using His grace to form in ourselves the virtues of Jesus Christ.

3. Look over Chart I on pages 10-11, especially the last column, and see if we have failed to mention anything listed there. If so, discuss it.

4. Give a detailed outline of the deeds, that is, the acts, the practices, the habits, the virtues, by means of which a person can effectively prove his appreciation of God's great love. Offer some practical suggestions for making these a part of daily living.

5. Give a detailed list of the obstacles in the way of performing those deeds, and also a list of the aids to assist us.

GENERAL INDEX
TO THE SERIES

Roman numerals indicate the volume; arabic numerals indicate the page.

Abortion,
definition of, III, 527
gravity of, III, 527
excommunication for, III, 528
IV, 282
Absolution,
sacramental, III, 479 ff
over remains, ceremonies of, IV, 151
Absolutism, State
danger of, III, 190
Abstinence,
as means of satisfaction, III, 468
days of, III, 469
obligation of, III, 469
total, III, 543, 545
Accident,
meaning of, in Eucharist, II, 590
calling priest for, IV, 135 f
supplying priest information, IV, 136
Acolyte, IV, 211
Acropolis, III, 142; IV, 477
Act,
good, elements of, I, 401-402
supernaturally good, elements of, I, 403
when supernatural, II, 113
of Consecration to Mary, IV, 67
Action, Catholic, III, 224 ff
Acts,
morally bad, I, 417
Acts of Apostles and Holy Spirit, III, 67
Adam,
creation of, I, 235
his body, I, 235
his soul, I, 236
fall of, I, 262 ff
fall of, I, 263
trial of, I, 262
seriousness of his sins, I, 264
Administration of sacraments, I, 318
Adoration,
and first commandment, I, 429
an act of religion, I, 429
an effect of the Mass, II, 492
Adultery, III, 594
a sin against conjugal fidelity, IV, 283
violates chastity and justice, IV, 283

Advent,
I, 114
feasts of season of, I, 115
spirit and color of, I, 115
Second, of Christ, IV, 176
Agility,
quality of glorified body, IV, 178
Agnostic,
in apologetics, IV, 462
Agnosticism, I, 201
Agony in Garden, I, 343
Aims,
of course, I, 23; II, 19; III, 19; IV, 17
of first year, I, 23
of second year, II, 23 f
of third year, III, 23
of fourth year, IV, 19 f
Alaric, III, 276
Albigensians, III, 319
Alcoholism,
and being truthful to self, IV, 391
Alexander VI, Pope,
accused by enemies, III, 336
Alexandria,
Catechetical school of, III, 261
Alexandrian Rite, II, 525
All Souls Day, IV, 166
Almsgiving,
as means of satisfying for sins, III, 464
Altar, II, 528
fixed and portable, II, 528
relics in, II, 529
furnishings of, II, 529
Ambition, rebuked by Christ, II, 298
Ambrosian rite, II, 526
Amendment,
firm purpose of,
included in true contrition, III, 429
part of contrition, III, 439
necessity, III, 439
nature of, III, 439
qualities of, III, 440
signs of good, III, 440
Angelico, Fra, IV, 80
Angels, I, 246 ff
creation of, I, 246
proof of existence of, I, 246

hierarchies, I, 249 ff
feasts of, I, 130
nine choirs, I, 249
their number, I, 253
attributes, I, 253
trial and fall, I, 259
gravity of sin of, I, 260
reward and punishment of, I, 261
guardian, I, 254
what they do for us, I, 255
our duties toward, I, 255
Angelus, the, II, 63
Anger,
and opposite virtues, I, 414
sinful and virtuous, III, 534
conquest of, III, 535
causes of, III, 535
Anglicanism, III, 345
Annas, II, 348
Annunciation, II, 54; IV, 36
Antiphons, Marian, IV, 75
Antiquity, Christian,
history of, III, 251 ff
Apologetics, IV, 447 ff
outline of steps in, IV, 449 ff
nature of, IV, 457 f
definition of, IV, 457
need of, IV, 458
technique of, IV, 458 f
approach in, IV, 459 ff
types of opponents in, IV, 461
need of facility in stating case for
Church in, IV, 462
treatment depends on ability of
apologist and opponents, IV, 463
use of arguments limited by ability
of participants, IV, 463
avoiding slick answers, IV, 465
what it can do, IV, 466
three key truths in, IV, 467
"Apologies," of St. Justin, III, 260
Apologists, I, 63; III, 258, 260
Apostasy,
defined, I, 69
Apostles,
the spread of the Faith and the, I,
95
of the Nations, I, 96
feasts of, I, 132
our duties as, I, 96
first, II, 207
twelve, II, 220
symbols of, II, 221
preaching of, II, 239
and Holy Spirit, III, 61
as original crew of Ark of New
Testament, III, 145
Apostolic Camera, III, 209
Apostolic Blessing of dying, IV, 131

Apostolic Fathers, I, 63; III, 258
Apostolic Visitors, III, 211
Apparitions, of our Lord, II, 396
Appropriation, of external works of
Trinity, I, 188
Arabs, III, 292
Archangels, three great, I, 248
Archbishop,
as head of province, III, 213
Arianism, I, 200; II, 93; III, 268 ff
spreads to barbarians, III, 269
Ark,
Church as, III, 129
(see Church, Catholic)
Armada, Spanish, III, 349
Arts, fostered by Church, III, 325
Ascension, II, 407
Asceticism, need of habit of, III, 573
Ash Wednesday, I, 124
Association,
of all labor management groups,
need of, IV, 439
Associations
economic, should handle matters of
less importance, IV, 419
Assumption of Mary, IV, 52
Astrology, I, 443
Atheism, I, 198
Atheist,
handling in apologetics, IV, 462
Atheists,
varieties of, IV, 462
as a freakish minority, IV, 468
tactics of, IV, 470
attempts to bluff us, IV, 476
Attila, III, 276
Attributes of Church, III, 168
relation to marks, III, 178
Attrition, III, 432
nature and effects, III, 432 f
for venial sins, III, 433
Authority,
defined II, 135
source, II, 135
in home, use of, II, 136 ff
in home, submission to, II, 159
Christ's submission to, II, 157
the Christian and, II, 158
in school, II, 169
at work, submission to, II, 170
civil, obligations of, II, 146
civil, duties to, II, 177
respect for, II, 177
divine, submission to, II, 183
ecclesiastical, exercise of, II, 149 ff
ecclesiastical, submission to, II, 179,
182
Authorized priest, III, 412, 443

Automobile,
danger of to morality, III, 603
Avignon, III, 329

Babylonian Captivity, III, 329 f
Backbiting, IV, 395
Bankruptcy, ease of declaring, a
cause of social disorder, IV, 423
Banns, IV, 315
Baptism,
and faith, I, 67
effects of, I, 326, 330, 333; II, 564
definition of, I, 327
outward sign of, I, 327
matter of, I, 327
conditional, I, 328
form of, I, 329
instituted by Christ, I, 330
kinds of, I, 331
of water, I, 331
of desire, I, 331
of blood, I, 332
remits sin and punishment, I, 333
confers divine life, I, 334
incorporates as with Christ, I, 337
character, I, 340
administration of, I, 342
who may administer, I, 342, 344
private, I, 344
who may receive, I, 344
of adults, I, 344
of minors, I, 346
of infants, I, 347
sponsors at, I, 347, 50
sponsors at, I, 347-50
conditional, I, 350
ceremonies of, I, 351 ff
practical reflection on, I, 360
first sign of union with God, II, 562
nature of, II, 562
necessity of, II, 565
See also Sacraments
Baptismal water, I, 329
Baptistery, I, 339
Barabbas, II, 360
Barbarian Invasions, III, 275 ff
Barbarossa, Frederick, III, 318
Bargaining, collective,
a means to social reconstruction,
IV, 437
Beatific vision
and sin, III, 377
essential joy of heaven, IV, 171
Beatitudes, I, 377-379
relation to Gifts, I, 379
as acts of perfect Christian, III, 88
nature of, III, 112

Beauty, God is, I, 160
Benedictine Order, III, 281 ff
Benediction, of Blessed Sacrament, II,
623
hymns used at, II, 624
Benedictus, II, 68
Berengarius and the Eucharist, II,
637; III, 314
Betrothal, IV, 315
Betting, IV, 366
Bible,
what it is, I, 81
official list of books of, I, 81, 82
inspiration of, I, 81
divisions of, I, 82-83
preservation of, I, 83
manuscripts of, I, 83-85
translations of, I, 85
interpretation of, I, 86
reading of, I, 87
how to use, I, 88
difficulties in (Genesis), I, 228
answers to difficulties, I, 233
use of, as a revealed book, IV, 452
how to prove it inspired, IV, 453
as sole source of religious truth, IV,
520
meaning of,
must be clarified by a living
teacher, IV, 521
See also Scripture, Sacred
Bibliography,
General Student, I, 25 ff; II, 25 ff;
III, 24 ff; IV, 20
(See, Readings, Related and
Parallel)
on converts and marks of the
Church, III, 232
Birth Control, III, 594; IV, 278
a sin against nature, III, 594
intrinsically evil, IV, 278
never permissible, IV, 280
excuse offered for, IV, 282
Bishop,
as voice of Teaching Church, I, 78
and diocese, III, 211
liturgical garb of, III, 212 f
Bishops,
infallibility of, III, 171
Black Death, III, 330
Blasphemy, I, 451
Blessed Sacrament,
Benediction of, II, 623
Visits to, II, 627
See Eucharist
Boastfulness, IV, 391
Bodies,
physical, moral, Mystical, III, 197

536

Body,
perfection of, as proof of its Creator, I, 35
as temple of Holy Spirit, III, 494 f
control of, III, 511
sanctity of, III, 518 ff
dissolution of, at death, IV, 113
of dead, Church's reverence for, IV, 152
glorified, IV, 172
resurrection of, IV, 176
eternal life of, after resurrection, IV, 176
qualities of glorified, IV, 177
Boleyn, Anne, III, 344
Bologna, university of, III, 317
Book of Common Prayer, III, 345
Books,
those on Index forbidden, I, 71
others also forbidden, I, 71
approved, how to recognize, I, 72
of the Bible, I, 81 ff, see Bible
impure, III, 586
Breviary, I, 133
Brotherhood, religious, IV, 217 ff
kinds of, IV, 217
need of vocations to, IV, 218
signs of vocation to, IV, 218
training for, IV, 219
Brotherhood of all men,
presupposes existence of Common Father, IV, 485
"brothers" of Christ, explained, IV, 51
Brothers of Christian Schools, III, 354
Burial,
Christian, IV, 152 ff
in consecrated ground, IV, 152
denial of, Christian, IV, 154
Business practices,
just and unjust, IV, 368
Business, condition of,
a factor in determining just wages, IV, 418
Byzantine Rites, II, 525

Caiphas, II, 348
Caliphs, III, 292
Calumny,
nature and gravity of, IV, 394
Calvary,
the perfect sacrifice, II, 453
source of grace, II, 456
and the Mass, II, 457
Calvin, errors of, III, 343
Candle, blessed,
in sick room, IV, 141

Candor, Christian,
need of, IV, 389
Canon, of the Bible,
See, Bible, Sacred Scripture
Canon of Mass, II, 480
Canon Law, codified, III, 361
Canossa, Henry IV at, III, 313
Capital, and labor,
principles regarding division of profits by, IV, 415
Capital, has appropriated too much of profits, IV, 415
Cappa Magna, of bishop, III, 212
Capuchins, III, 347
Cardinals, College of, III, 206
Career,
and marriage, IV, 239 ff
Careers, IV, 233
for men, IV, 234 ff
for women, IV, 238 ff
Carmelites,
reform of, III, 345
dedicated to Mary, IV, 99
Cassiodorus, III, 282
Catacombs, instruments of torture in, I, 67
Catacombs, I, 89
Catechumens, Mass of, II, 473
Cathari, III, 319
Cathedrals,
Gothic, III, 325
Marian, IV, 83
Catholic, meaning of, IV, 510
Catholic Action,
and Confirmation, III, 101
nature of, III, 224 ff
necessity of, III, 225
training leaders for, III, 225
steps in, III, 225
method of, III, 227
Catholic Church,
proving her the one true Church, IV, 510
Catholic Church, see, Church, Catholic; Faith
Catholic religion,
steps in proving, IV, 449
claims of, IV, 450
Catholicity of Church,
meaning of, III, 163 f
as mark of Church, III, 163
Catholicity,
carrying evidences of, IV, 136
Catholics,
what they can do in social reconstruction, IV, 441
should lead way in social reconstruction, IV, 441

how they should prepare for social leadership, IV, 441

Cemetery,
consecrated, IV, 152 f
soil of, consecrated, IV, 152
value of burial in, IV, 153
non Catholic, special permission for burial in, IV, 154

Censures, kinds of, III, 413

Centurion, II, 226

Ceremonies,
of sacraments, reasons for, I, 312
of Baptism, I, 351-59
of Confirmation, I, 382-86
necessity of, II, 523

Corinthians, III, 255

Chalcedon, Council of, III, 274

Chance, a poor explanation of the order in the universe, IV, 474

Chant, Plain, IV, 74

Character,
sacramental,
nature of, I, 316
purpose, I, 316-17
permanence of, I, 317
sacraments producing, I, 317
in Baptism, I, 340; II, 564
in Confirmation, I, 380
imprinted by three sacraments, II, 558
in Holy Orders, IV, 216

Charismata, III, 57

Charity,
importance of, I, 57
sins against, I, 440
and first commandment, I, 428
commanded by Christ, II, 267
objective of junior year, III, 20, 24
virtue of, III, 88 ff
nature of, III, 90
supernatural virtue, III, 90
confers power not facility, III, 90
an act of the will, III, 90
necessity of, III, 91
acts of,
internal and external, III, 91
sins against, III, 93
prescribed by fifth commandment, III, 524
in Mary, IV, 59 f
distinct from justice, IV, 340
not substitute for justice, IV, 342
and justice, IV, 382
plays leading role in social reconstruction, IV, 425

Charlemagne, III, 299 ff

Charles Martel, III, 292

Charter, given to Church, III, 148

Chartres, Notre Dame de, IV, 83

Chastity,
vow of, I, 450; IV, 223
in Mary, IV, 62
in marriage, IV, 321

Chateaubriand, III, 357

Cheating,
violation of justice, IV, 367
various forms of, IV, 367

Childhood, spiritual, III, 94

Children,
obligation of parents to, II, 138
training of, II, 139 f
moral and spiritual care of, II, 140 f
duties of, II, 159
duties to parents, II, 159
rights of parents to educate, a result of marriage contract, IV, 248
essential purpose of marriage, IV, 253
first blessing of marriage, IV, 270
management of, IV, 322

Children's Crusade, III, 322

Chivalry, III, 309

Chrism, I, 363

Christian life,
outline of, I, 405 ff

Christian living,
by means of the liturgy, I, 141 ff
Mass and Holy Communion in, I, 142

Christian, training of, I, 282

Christian antiquity,
history of, III, 251

Christianity, spread of, III, 256 ff

Christmas tide,
length, spirit, and color, feasts of, I, 116

Church,
support of, II, 180
teaches us about Holy Spirit, III, 43
and the Holy Spirit, III, 48, 130
characteristics of members of, III, 140
a supernatural organization, III, 168
third precept of, III, 483
social teaching of, a proof of God's love, IV, 403
true,
Catholic view on, IV, 507
Protestant view on, IV, 507 f
nature of, IV, 511
necessity of, challenged, IV, 520

Church and State,
  as perfect societies, III, 189 ff
  relation of, II, 324
  principles governing relations of, II, 148
  cooperation of, III, 297, 322
Church, Catholic,
  Living Voice of, as guide in faith, I, 77 ff
  Living Voice, and Sacred Scripture, I, 79
  our guide in moral matters, I, 398
  submitting to, II, 179 f
  power of, II, 256; III, 148
  names given to, III, 138 f
  definitions of, III, 139 ff
  origin of, III, 143
  conception of, III, 143
  proving Christ head of, III, 144
  St. Peter promised headship of, III, 146
  commandership conferred, III, 146
  launching of, III, 149
  a visible organization, III, 154 ff
  marks of, III, 156 ff
  identify true Church, III, 156 ff
  unity of, III, 158 ff
  social unity, III, 161
  holiness as mark of, III, 161 ff
  universality as mark of, III, 163 ff
  Apostolicity as mark of, III, 165 ff
  attributes of, III, 168 ff
  authority of, III, 168
  indefectibility or perpetuity of, III, 176 f
  purpose of, III, 179 ff
  powers of, III, 180 ff
  duty to submit to teaching of, III, 183
  governing powers of, III, 184 ff
  triple governing power of, III, 185
  source of powers of, III, 189 ff
  source of natural and supernatural rights of, III, 189 ff
  necessity of belonging to, III, 191
  organization of, III, 193 ff
  as Mystical Body, III, 193 ff
  (*see* Mystical Body)
  chief organs of, III, 200
  diplomatic service of, III, 209
  as a hierarchy, III, 215 ff
  hierarchical organization of, III, 215 ff
  as our Mother, III, 218 ff
  glory of marks of, III, 218
  a proof of God's love, III, 219
  her care of us, III, 220 ff

  our duties to, III, 223
  material support of, III, 228
  manifestations of divine life of, III, 246
  has power to forgive sins, III, 404
  value of membership in visible, III, 192
  sponsors social benefits, IV, 405
  right of, to speak on social problems vindicated, IV, 413
  principle enunciated, IV, 413
  case for, in apologetics, IV, 459
  claims to be true religion, IV, 490
  founder of, IV, 490 ff
  nature of, IV, 506
  as Church founded by Christ, IV, 506 ff
  objectors to, IV, 508
  purpose of, IV, 508
  intended by Christ to be united, IV, 513
  intended by Christ to be papal, IV, 513
  summary of nature of, IV, 517
  as channel of Christ's truth and life, IV, 518
  distributes Christ's gifts, IV, 520
  arguing from, to Christ, IV, 524
  summary of proofs of her founding by Christ, IV, 524
Church History,
  synopsis of, III, 253-367
  survey of, III, 235 ff
  nature of, III, 243
  key to understanding of, III, 246
  key to solving difficulties in, III, 247
  main divisions of, III, 249
  reasons for studying, III, 249 f
Church Militant, III, 198
  Suffering, III, 198
  Triumphant, III, 198
Church Year, *See,* Liturgical Year
Circumcision, II, 71
Circumstances,
  as affecting morality of act, I, 402
  influence of, on morality of act, II, 116 f
  in confessing sins, III, 448
  increasing gravity of sins against purity, III, 598
  as affecting stealing, IV, 358
Citizens, duties of, II, 176
City of God, of St. Augustine,
  a great work, III, 271, 276
  reason for writing of, IV, 459

Civil authorities, benefits of their work to improve social conditions, IV, 411

Clairvaux, monastery of, III, 317

Class warfare, an objective of Communism, IV, 422

Clergy, directed by Pope to train leaders for social reconstruction, IV, 426

Clotilda, wife of Clovis, III, 286

Clovis, III, 281, 286

Cluny, III, 408

Codices, of Bible, I, 84

Coercive power of Church, III, 185

Collectivism, rejected by popes, IV, 414

College of Cardinals, III, 206

Colors.
  liturgical, I, 115, 116, 118, 122, 125, 127, 139 ff; II, 532
  use and symbolism of, I, 140

Colosseum, I, 66

Columbus, Christopher, III, 338 ff

Commandments,
  relation to doctrines of Creed, I, 425
  Ten,
    first, I, 427 ff
    second, I, 445 ff
    third, I, 453 ff, II, 535 ff
    fourth, II, 134
    fifth, III, 516 ff
    sixth and ninth, III, 556 ff
    seventh and tenth, IV, 348 ff
    eighth, IV, 383 ff

Common welfare,
  limits rights of ownership, IV, 352
  wage levels should be adjusted to promote, IV, 418
  a concern of economic groups, IV, 419

Communion, of Mass, II, 484

Communion, Holy,
  best practice to develop all virtues, I, 58
  and control of concupiscence, I, 286
  effects of, II, 596
  who can receive, II, 605
  spiritual requirements, II, 604
  unworthy, II, 607
  first laws regarding, II, 608
  Easter, II, 610
  frequent, II, 610; III, 361
  necessity of, II, 612
  daily, II, 613
  history of frequent, II, 614

frequent, and Pius X, II, 615
  preparation for, II, 616
  thanksgiving after, II, 617

Communion of Saints, III, 198

Communism, III, 361
  false social principles of, II, 174
  objectives of, IV, 422
  program of, for solving evil economic conditions, IV, 432 f
  why its proposals are wrong, IV, 434
  advocates class warfare, IV, 434

Commutative justice, IV, 407

Company-keeping,
  with Catholics, I, 75
  allowed as preparation for choosing partner, III, 603
  dangers of, III, 603
  purpose of, IV, 308
  dangers of, IV, 308
  unjustified, IV, 308 f
  controlling dangers of, IV, 309
  length of, IV, 312

Competition, free,
  resulting in economic dictatorship, IV, 421
  needs control, IV, 439

Concentration of wealth,
  danger of, IV, 421

Conciliar, movement, III, 332

Concomitance, and Eucharist, II, 592

Concordat, with Napoleon, III, 357

Concupiscence, I, 270-72
  antidotes for, I, 286 ff
  lessened by Eucharist, II, 598
  a source of temptation, III, 388
  threefold, III, 389
  quieting of, a purpose of marriage, IV, 254

Confession,
  seal of, III, 417
  of sins,
    necessary and optional matter, III, 423

Confession, sacramental,
  nature of, III, 443
  necessity of, III, 443
  proved from Fathers, III, 445
  proved from Voice of Church, III, 446
  objection to, answered, III, 446
  qualities of, III, 446 ff
  kinds of, III, 452
  annual required, III, 485
  frequent, wish of Church regarding, III, 486
  a blessing, III, 490
  restores mental balance, III, 490

sincerity in, a means of preserving purity, III, 576
as preparation for death, IV, 122
integrity of, for dying, IV, 122
before marriage, IV, 316
seal of, IV, 400

Confessor,
duties of, III, 414
as Christ's representative, III, 415
as judge, III, 415
as physician of souls, III, 415
as teacher, III, 416
as father, III, 416
choosing, III, 454
gratitude to, III, 454
as guide in choosing vocation, IV, 198

Confessors, of the Faith, I, 65

Confidence, and prayer, I, 435

Confirmation,
definition of, I, 362
relation to Baptism, I, 362
essentials of, I, 363 ff
outward sign of, I, 363
matter of, I, 363
form of, I, 364
divine institution of, I, 364 ff
effects of, I, 366 ff; III, 100
and the beatitudes, I, 377 f
character, I, 380
necessity, I, 380
minister of, I, 381
administration of, I, 381
recipient, I, 381
sponsors in, I, 382
ceremonies of, I, 382 ff
practical reflection on, I, 386
review of, III, 99 ff

Congregations,
Roman, III, 207
religious, and organization of Church, III, 214

Conscience,
remorse of, proves supreme Law-giver, I, 35
a guide to morality, I, 398
nature of, I, 399; II, 130 ff
kinds of, I, 399
certain and doubtful, I, 399
true or false, I, 399
scrupulous, I, 399
examination of, III, 418

Consecration, of Mass, II, 481

Consecration,
Act of, to Mary, IV, 67

Consent,
in sin, I, 420
essential to contract, IV, 244

Consistory, Congregation of, III, 207

Constantinople, fall of, III, 335

Consummated marriage, IV, 250

Contemplation,
Mary's Prayer of, IV, 66

Contemplative orders, III, 215, 316, IV, 221

Contingency, argument from, proves existence of God, IV, 476

Contract,
nature of, IV, 243 ff
conditions for valid, IV, 244
matrimonial, nature of, IV, 243
matrimonial, effects of, IV, 248
non fulfillment of, a violation of justice, IV, 365

Contracts, fulfillment of by workers, II, 171

Contrition,
most important part of preparation for confession, III, 419
nature of, III, 425
and virtue of penance, III, 426
definition of, III, 428
an act of will, III, 428
includes hatred of sin, III, 428
includes sorrow for sin, III, 429
includes purpose of amendment, III, 429
necessity of, III, 430
qualities of, III, 430 ff
must be supernatural, III, 431
must be universal and sovereign, III, 431
kinds of, III, 432
motives of determine kind, III, 432
imperfect, III, 432
perfect, III, 435
effects of, III, 435
prevents loss of merits, III, 436
key to heaven in emergencies, III, 436
not difficult, III, 436
means of exciting, III, 437
act of,
must be made before being absolved, III, 438

Contumely, IV, 395 f

Conversions, in England, III, 288

Cooperation,
in another's sin
ways of sinning by, III, 93; III, 386
by all, required to reform social order, IV, 420

Corporations,
make possible injustice without accountability, IV, 429

easy bankruptcy of, a cause of so-
cial evils, IV, 423
Corpus Christi, II, 622
Council, Ecumenical,
Third, Ephesus, and Divine Mater-
nity, IV, 48
of Trent, III, 345
Councils,
plenary and provincial, III, 214
Church, III, 214
Counsel, Gift of, I, 371; III, 107
Counsels, evangelical, I, 450
Counter Reformation, III, 345
Country, defense of, obligation of, III,
532
Courts, papal ecclesiastical, III, 209
Courtship, IV, 309 ff
See, Company-keeping
Covetousness,
and opposite virtues, I, 412
vice of, IV, 375 ff
and desire to possess, IV, 377
danger of, IV, 377
effects of, IV, 378
opposite virtues, IV, 378 f
a main cause of modern social disorders, IV, 423
why men fall prey to, IV, 423
Crafts, fostered by Church, III, 325
Create, and make, I, 218
Created things,
purpose of, IV, 349 f
Creation,
fact of, I, 215
God's goodness, the cause of, I, 215
purpose of, God's glory, I ,216
meaning of, I, 217
of universe, I, 217
six days of, I, 219 ff
first day, I, 219
second day, I, 220
third day, I, 221
fourth day, I, 223
fifth day, I, 224
sixth day, I, 225
of Adam and Eve, I, 235 ff
of angels, I, 246
summary of, I, 256
Creator, God as, I, 157
Credit, control of, a danger, IV, 421
Creed,
Art. 1, I, 149-298
Art. 2-3, II, 29-95
Art. 4-7, II, 187-432
Art. 8, III, 27 ff
Art. 9, III, 129 ff
Art. 10, III, 369 ff
Art. 11-12, IV, 106 ff

Athanasian, I, 203
doctrines of, relation to command-
ments, I, 425
sequence of articles in, III, 130
doctrines of, relation of, III, 371
Cremation,
outrages Christian sensibilities, IV,
155
forbidden, IV, 155
Criteria,
for choosing vocation, IV, 195 ff
supreme, for choosing state, IV, 197
Criticizing, an offense against charity,
IV, 397
Cross,
Feasts of, I, 128
Way of, II, 365
Crucifix in sick room, IV, 141
Crucifixion, story of, II, 366 ff
Crusades, III, 316 ff; III, 321 f
Cult, disparity of, IV, 286
Czestochowa, shrine at, IV, 88
Curé of Ars, III, 360
Curia,
papal, III, 206 ff
officers of, III, 209
diocesan, III, 213
Cursing, I, 451
Cycles, of Liturgical Year, I, 111 ff

Dancing, Church's attitude toward,
III, 605
Dante and High Middle Ages, III,
328 f
Dataria, III, 209
Dating,
steady, when not permitted, IV
308
Day,
in the Liturgical Year, I, 133
as a miniature Church Year, I, 134
Days,
special dedications of, I, 138
Dead,
last rites for, IV, 147 ff
Memento of, IV, 151
Death, IV, 111 ff
importance of moment of, IV, 113
nature of, IV, 113
and the body, IV, 113
consequence of original sin, IV,
114 f
certainty and uncertainty of, IV,
116
preparation for happy, IV, 116
remote, IV, 117 ff
proximate, IV, 122 ff

prayer to Mary and, IV, 117
devotion to St. Joseph and, IV, 117
apparent, anointing after, IV, 138
marriage formalities in danger of,
IV, 263
of Christ, II, 373
Debts,
contracting large, IV, 366
Decalogue, I, 423
why observe, I, 423
how divided, I, 424
Decius, III, 262
Dedication,
of days of week, I, 138
of months of year, I, 139
Defender of Marriage Bond, III, 213
Deism, III, 354
Delegates, Apostolic, III, 211
Demons,
an obstacle in our quest, I, 276
their malice and hatred, I, 276
power of, I, 277
limitations of power, I, 277
See, Satan
Denominations, variety of, not intended by Christ, IV, 511
Desire to possess, purpose of, IV, 377
Desires, sinful, III, 597
Despair, I, 440; II, 427
causes of, II, 429
Detachment from created goods,
Christ recommends, II, 273
young rich man and, II, 294 ff
a needed virtue, IV, 380
the saints and, IV, 381
Detraction,
nature and seriousness of, IV, 395
reparation of, IV, 395
Devotions, Marian, IV, 89 ff
Diaconate,
powers of, IV, 213
Dictatorship,
economic, has replaced free compe-
tition, IV, 420
economic, needs to be controlled,
IV, 439
economic, *See,* Economic dictator-
ship
Dies Irae, explanation of, IV, 149
Dieting, and care of health, III, 551
Diocese, and bishop, III, 211
Diocesan priest, III, 213
Dioceses, division of Church into, III,
211
Diocletian, III, 264
Disciples, appointment of, II, 266
Discussion, cases for, I, 21
Disobedience, sinfulness of, II, 162

Disorder, social and economic,
Church shows way out of, IV, 403
Disparity of cult (or worship)
IV, 286
Dispensation,
for mixed marriage, when given, IV,
288
matrimonial, IV, 305
divine, can not be dispensed, IV,
305
ecclesiastical, may be dispensed,
IV, 305
Distribution of wealth,
inequality of, cause of encyclical,
IV, 409
of profits, correct principle regard-
ing, IV, 415
of riches, faulty, IV, 417
Distributive justice, IV, 407
Divine Comedy, III, 328
Divination, I, 443
Divine Office, I, 133
contents of, I, 134
divisions of, I, 134
Divinity of Christ, II, 349
gradually revealed, IV, 496
claim implicitly contained in ac-
tions, IV, 497
summary of proofs for, IV, 504
Divisions of the Liturgical Year, I,
132 ff
Divorce, IV, 291 ff
Church teaching on, IV, 291
Scripture on, IV, 292
Civil, IV, 293 f
Doctors of the Church, I, 64-65; III,
268 ff
Doctors Latin, III, 270
Doctrine,
apostolicity in, a mark of true
Church, III, 166
Doctrines of Creed, relation of, III,
371
Dominicans, III, 323
Domitian, III, 255
Donatism, III, 266
Dove, as symbol of Holy Ghost, III,
119
Dress, women's,
and modesty, III, 587
basic principles regarding, III, 589
Drinking, III, 543
and purity, III, 605
Driving, reckless, III, 546
Drunkenness,
a grave sin, III, 544
dangers of, III, 544
consequences of, III, 544 f

Dulia, I, 430
Duties to Church, III, 223
Dying,
  assisting the, IV, 140 ff
  sacramentals and, IV, 141

Easter duty, II, 610
Easter season, in Liturgical year, I, 120
Eastertide, length, spirit and color, feasts, I, 125
Ears, guarding of, III, 590
Ecclesiastical Year, *See* Liturgical Year
Economic agreements,
  need of international, IV, 440
Economic conferences,
  recommended by Pope, IV, 441
Economic dictatorship,
  has replaced free competition, IV, 420
  results of, IV, 421
  remedies for, IV, 421
  a result of free competition, IV, 421
  leads to struggle for control of State, IV, 421
  as successor of individualism, IV, 430
  as a false guide in economic life, evidences of, IV, 431
Economic institutions,
  reform of needed, IV, 418
Economic life,
  subjected to true guiding principle, IV, 420
  true guiding principles in, IV, 420
  results of deserting right principles in, IV, 423
  individualism no guide in, IV, 427
  right aims in, IV, 434 ff
  supreme purpose of, IV, 434
  how it can promote attainment of man's goals, IV, 435
  right methods of reconstructing, IV, 437
Economic power, despotic, a modern evil, IV, 420
Economic reform,
  requires cooperation of all, IV, 420
Economic system,
  ends of, IV, 420 f
  changes in, since 1890, IV, 420
Economics,
  wrong aims and methods in, IV, 427
  right aims in, IV, 434
  right methods in, IV, 437

free competition cannot be guiding principle in, IV, 420
Ecumenical Council,
  infallibility of, III, 171
  in governing Church, III, 214
Education,
  Christian, II, 143
  as activity of religious life, IV, 224
  pope warns against socialist program of, IV, 422
Effects,
  of Confirmation, I, 366-80
  of marriage contract, IV, 248
Egypt, flight to, II, 75
Elevation, of Mass, II, 483
Elizabeth, Queen, III, 345
Emancipation of woman, IV, 284
Ember days, I, 135
Empire, Holy Roman, III, 307
Employers,
  duties and rights, II, 143 f
  need of associations of, IV, 437
  should unite with employees in social reconstruction, IV, 439
Encyclical,
  meaning of, IV, 406
  on Holy Spirit, III, 43 ff
  on Church and State, III, 190
  on Marriage, Outline of, IV, 268 f
  on Christian Education, IV, 275
  Quadragesimo Anno (Reconstructing Social Order),
  Synopsis of, IV, 402 ff
  brief plan of, IV, 410
Encyclicals,
  of Leo XIII, III, 360
  and rights of workers, II, 173
  and the social problem, IV, 405 f
  subjects of some important, IV, 406
  three important social, IV, 406
Encyclopedists, III, 355
Enemies, love of, III, 93
Engagement, to marry, IV, 315
England, Church in, III, 293; III, 304, 314, 344, 358
Enlightenment, false ideas of the, III, 354
Envy,
  and related vices and virtues, I, 415; III, 538
Ephesus, Council of, defines Divine Maternity, IV, 48
Epiphany, feast of, I, 118
  time after, I, 118
Episcopacy,
  place of, in governing Church, III, 211
  as fulness of orders, IV, 215

Epistles, Trinity in, I, 181
Essence, definition of, II, 578
Eternal, God is, I, 164
Eucharist, Holy,
and union with God, II, 441
a bond of unity, II, 501
and Mystical Body, II, 503
and Transubstantiation, II, 587
and concomitance, II, 592
as sacrament, II, 546 ff
effects of, II, 504
defined, II, 578
outward sign of, II, 579
sign of passion, II, 580
of unity, II, 583
permanence of Christ in, II, 584
promise of, II, 245; II, 566; 570 ff
prototypes, II, 568
fulfillment, of promise, II, 576
as best means of preserving purity,
III, 575
adorableness of, II, 592
excellence of, II, 593
names of, II, 594
saints and, II, 595
remits venial sin, II, 600
minister of consecration, II, 603
of distribution, II, 604
liturgical devotions, II, 620
objections to, II, 635
Berengarius and, II, 637
and Protestantism, II, 637
as sacrifice, see Mass
Eucharistic Congresses, II, 628
Euthanasia, III, 528
Eutychianism, III, 274
Evangelists, II, 88
purpose of each, II, 88 f
Evasion, when permissible, IV, 389 f
Eve, creation of, I, 237
reasons for creation of, I, 237
Evil,
problem of, I, 232
inclination to, due to original sin,
I, 270
social,
roots and remedies of, IV, 423
Evolution,
problem of, I, 243
atheistic and theistic theories, I, 244
theory of, as regards world, life,
man, I, 244 ff
Evolution, of body, improbable, rash
to believe, I, 245
of soul an impossibility, I, 245
and what existed in beginning, IV,
473
poor basis for hope, IV, 485 f

mechanistic, III, 507
moral, III, 507, 509
Examination,
for marriage, who cares for, IV,
314 f
of conscience, III, 418
preparation for, III, 418
nature and length of, III, 420
plan to follow, III, 421
of conscience, daily, III, 424
Examen, particular, III, 424
Ex cathedra,
infallibility of utterances, III, 174
Excommunication, definition of, III,
413
Existence,
purpose of, I, 28; II, 443; IV, 17
accounting for,
key question in proving existence
of God, IV, 478
cause of, IV, 478
transmitters of, but not originators
of, IV, 478
God does not receive from another,
IV, 480
Exorcist, IV, 211
Extreme Unction, IV, 124 ff
definition of, IV, 124
outward sign of, IV, 124 f
divine institution of, IV, 127
effects of, IV, 127
minister of, IV, 130
who can receive, IV, 130
danger from internal cause, IV,
130
age of reason, IV, 130
danger of death, IV, 131
confession before, IV, 131
may be repeated, IV, 131
Eyes,
necessity of control of, I, 283
guarding, to protect purity, III, 585

Faculties, for confession, III, 412
Faith,
as a guide to happiness, I, 38 ff
natural and supernatural, I, 40-41
definition of supernatural, I, 41
basis of, I, 41-42
how saints practiced, I, 42
examples of lack of, I, 42-43
superior to reason, I, 44
and science, I, 44-46
qualities of, I, 46-47
as Master Guide, I, 52
necessity of, for salvation, I, 59

kinds of, I, 59
habitual and actual, I, 59
necessity of exercising, I, 59-60
truths to be believed by explicit, I, 61
profession of, public, I, 62
profession of, when required, I, 62
great teachers and champions of, I, 63 ff
the life of, I, 67 ff
sins against, I, 68 ff
how lost, I, 68 ff
doubts and, I, 69
how endangered, I, 70 ff
  harmed by immoral living, I, 70
  harmed by bad reading, I, 70
  sly efforts to undermine, I, 71
  harmed by mixed marriages, I, 72
how it is increased, I, 73 ff
fostered by the Christian home, I, 74
assisted by virtuous living, I, 74
practices which exercise and develop, I, 74
and prayer, I, 75
the sacramentals and, I, 75
and works of mercy, I, 76
and the sacraments, I, 76
the Rule of, I, 77 ff
and the Living Voice of the Church, I, 77
Living Voice as Rule of, I, 77 ff
Deposit of, as basis for Teaching Voice of Church, I, 78 ff
sources of, I, 79
mysteries of, I, 80
spreading the, I, 95
  how the Apostles, spread, I, 95
  spread by missionaries, I, 97
  spread by "Home" Missionaries, I, 97
  spreading by explaining, I, 98
spread of in Church History, III, 256
aids and obstacles in spread of, III, 256 f
spreads to America, III, 338
and happiness, I, 105
attacks on, I, 197
need to know, I, 197
and the first commandment, I, 428
and prayer, I, 435
sins against, I, 439
rule of, in morality, II, 130
Tridentine profession of, III, 349
challenge of, to us, III, 365
glorious unity of our, IV, 16

Mary's, IV, 60
and reason, compared, IV, 447
we must show the reasonableness of our, IV, 448
Fall,
of Adam, I, 258 ff; I, 263
of angels, I, 259
causes of, I, 264
effects of on our first parents, I, 265 ff
effects on us, I, 267
justice of God's punishment of, I, 268
Family,
honor of, II, 165
unit of society, II, 136
Farm, prices of,
must be adjusted to industrial wages, IV, 418
Farmers, organization of as result of *Rerum Novarum,* IV, 412
Fast days, III, 468
Fasting,
a means to control passions, I, 286
as means of,
  satisfying for sin, III, 464
opposes concupiscence, III, 464
prescribed by Church, III, 466
exemption from law of, III, 468
controlling bodily tendencies, III, 574
Father,
God as a, I, 155
the Unbegotten, I, 186
authority of, II, 136
wages of, should protect family, IV, 417
wages of, apportioned to needs, IV, 417
Fathers of the Church, I, 63; III, 268 ff
Fathers, Apostolic, III, 258, 260
Fathers, Greek or Eastern, I, 64
Fathers, Latin or Western, I, 65
Fatima, Our Lady of,
shrine of, IV, 88
devotion to, IV, 89
Fault, predominant, I, 416
Faults, revelation of grave, at times binds in conscience, IV, 399
Fear, Gift of, I, 373; III, 106
Feasts,
of Advent season, I, 115
of Christian reason, I, 116, 118
after Epiphany, I, 120
of Lenten season, I, 123
of Eastertide, I, 125

after Pentecost, I, 127
of Apostles, I, 132
of Saints, I, 131
living with Christ in the, I, 141 ff
Febronianism, III, 351
Federation, of labor-management associations needed, IV, 439
Feudalism, III, 301; III, 305
Fidelity,
conjugal,
obligation to, IV, 248
second blessing of marriage, IV, 270
nature of, IV, 270
to promises, IV, 386
Filioque, III, 55, 270, 304
Financial preparation for marriage, IV, 307
Finding,
as a means of acquiring ownership, IV, 356
Fire, tongues of, as symbol of Holy Ghost, III, 119
"firstborn" as referred to Christ, IV, 51
Flattery, IV, 390
Flesh, a source of temptation, III, 388
Florence, Council of, III, 334
Forgiveness of sins,
demands power of orders, III, 411
requirements in penitent for, III, 418
Form,
of sacraments, I, 309
of Penance, III, 479
in Extreme Unction, IV, 126
Formalities, for valid marriage, IV, 262
Fornication, III, 596
Fortitude,
definition of, I, 56
signs of, I, 56
signs of lack of, I, 56
Gift of, I, 371; III, 106
Fortune telling, I, 443
Forty Hours, II, 626
Franciscans, founding of, III, 323
in America, III, 354
Fraternal correction, Christ's advice on, II, 255
Free competition, cannot be directing principle in economics, IV, 420
Freemasonry, III, 355
Frederick Barbarossa, III, 318
Free will, responsibility, of, I, 258

Freedom,
a gift of God, I, 259
of angels and men, I, 259
and moral responsibility, I, 400
French Revolution, III, 356
Fruits of Holy Ghost, III, 111 ff
Fulda, founding of, III, 296

Galileo, III, 351
Gallican liturgy, II, 526
Gallican Rights, III, 351
Gallicanism, III, 351
Gambling, IV, 366
Generation of Word, as first procession in Trinity, III, 53
Genesis, problems in, I, 228
Gentiles, Christ reveals Himself to, II, 73
Ghibellines, III, 318
Ghost, Holy, *see,* Holy Spirit
Gifts of the Holy Ghost, I, 243, 367 ff
and supernatural organism, III, 86
Gifts,
of God to man,
natural, I, 240
preternatural, I, 240
supernatural, I, 242
natural, weakened by original sin, I, 267
loss of due to original sin, I, 269 ff
nature and value of, III, 104 ff
must be used, III, 105
order of, III, 105
Glory,
God's internal and external, I, 217
light of, in heaven, IV, 174
Gluttony,
and opposite virtues, I, 414
sinfulness of, III, 550
Gnosticism, I, 199; II, 92
God,
only source of happiness, I, 15
reason as a guide to, I, 21
faith as a guide to, I, 28; 28 ff
existence of proved by reason, I, 33 f
nature of, as known from reason, I, 36 ff
is Supreme Being, I, 36
is self-existent, I, 37
attributes of, from reason, I, 36 ff
glorified by liturgy, I, 108
who and what He is, I, 151 ff
value of knowledge about, I, 152
impossible for finite mind to comprehend nature of, I, 152

who He is, I, 153 ff
His nature, as revealed by Himself, I, 153 ff
His nature as taught by Church, I, 154
as Our Father, I, 155
what He is, I, 158 ff
a pure Spirit, I, 158
infinitely perfect, I, 159
unity of His perfections in Him, I, 159
perfections different from created perfections, I, 159
our ideas of, I, 162
has no defects, I, 162
attributes of, I, 156; I, 162-172
unity of, I, 156
summary of nature of, I, 172
unity in Trinity, I, 183
acts in us, I, 193
glory of, the purpose of creation, I, 216
gifts of, to man, I, 239
love for man, I, 297, 393
alone adored, I, 431
hearing word of, on Sunday, I, 455
goodness of, II, 42
love for man, II, 304 f, 309; IV, 15
union with, by Baptism, II, 562
union with, strengthened by Confirmation, II, 565
indwelling presence of, III, 49
mercy, wisdom and justice of, shown in forgiveness of sins, III, 393 ff
attributes of, an aid to purity, III, 568
presence of, in Mary, IV, 60
blessing of, needed to achieve a better social order, IV, 420
must be summit of society, IV, 440
proof of existence, first step in apologetics, IV, 449
a person, not a thing, IV, 449
existence of, proof of in apologetics, IV, 468
existence of, proof from universal agreement, IV, 468
value of argument, IV, 468 f
existence of, argument for, from order in universe, IV, 474
value of arguments for existence of, IV, 482 ff
existence of, summary of proofs of, IV, 487
existence of, makes religion necessary, IV, 489

as a personal being, IV, 473, 481
as originator of all else that exists, IV, 479 f
as being not receiving existence from another, IV, 480
primary distinction between, and other beings, IV, 481
must be infinite, IV, 481
as reason for existence of other beings, IV, 482
value of knowing who and what He is, IV, 484
Good, can it change to bad, II, 114 ff
Good name, sins against, IV, 394
Good Samaritan, I, 322 ff
Good Works,
Christ teaches need of, II, 275
Christ expects, II, 318
Goods,
lawful enjoyment of created, I, 17
uncontrolled desire for, root of social ills, IV, 423
Gospel,
meaning of, II, 87
Gospel teaching,
a return to life based on, required for social reconstruction, IV, 423
Gospels,
reveal the Trinity, I, 180 ff
as source of knowledge of Christ, IV, 492
authenticity of, IV, 494
Gossiping, IV, 395
Government, can help in social reconstruction, IV, 437
Grace, II, 411 ff
and the sacraments, I, 310
sacramental, I, 312
sanctifying, I, 242
sanctifying, produced by sacraments, I, 310
state of, needed for merit, I, 403
dangers of neglecting, II, 321
nature of, II, 411
kinds of, II, 412
actual, II, 412
habitual, II, 414
names of, II, 417
necessity of, II, 418
all receive sufficient, II, 419
state of, II, 420
means of, II, 421
attack on doctrine of, II, 422
sacraments as effective signs of, II, 557
principle of supernatural life of soul, III, 82 ff

as root-principle of supernatural "organism," III, 85
actual, III, 86
need of, and Pelagianism, III, 273
restored by perfect contrition, III, 435
restored by Penance, III, 482
sacramental, in Penance, III, 483
sanctifying conferred by Extreme Unction, IV, 127

Grande Chartreuse, III, 317
Gratitude, lesson in, II, 285 f
Greek Schism, III, 311 ff
causes of, III, 312
attempts to end, III, 334
Growth, spiritual, stages of, III, 94
Guadalupe,
feast of Our Lady of, IV, 45
story of apparition, IV, 45
Our Lady of, miraculous picture of, IV, 87
Guardian angels, I, 254
Guelphs, III, 318
Guidance, in selecting vocation, IV, 198
Guide to God,
reason as, I, 21
faith as, I, 28, 38 ff
Guilds, mediaeval, III, 328
elimination of, a result of individualism, IV, 429
destruction of, unnecessary, IV, 429
Gunpowder Plot, III, 350

Habit,
nature of, I, 48
value of, I, 48
Habits,
good, I, 48, 405 ff
bad, I, 48, 410 ff
bad, breaking, III, 599
duties of parents to form, IV, 273
must be started early, IV, 273
basic good, IV, 329
need of developing, IV, 329
good, *see* virtues
bad, *see* vices
Happiness,
universal desire for, I 14 ff; III, 19
perfect, must wait for heaven, I, 15
secret of, I, 16
desire of, proves existence of God, I, 33
and faith, I, 105

obstacles to, I 276
not essential purpose of marriage, IV, 258
in marriage, supernatural aids to, IV, 321
Harnack, as witness to date of Gospels, IV, 494
Hatred, worst sin against charity, III, 93
violates fifth commandment, III, 537
Health,
proper care of, III, 521
and intemperance, III, 541 ff
sometimes restored by Extreme Unction, IV, 129
Heathenism, defined, I, 68
Heaven,
our goal, I, 18
nature of, I, 19; IV, 168
soul and body in, I, 20
friends in, I, 20
two roads to, I, 405
goal of our quest, IV, 168 ff
existence and duration of, proved, IV, 168 f
getting an idea of, IV, 170
joys of, IV, 171
vision of God,
essential joy in, IV, 171
other joys of, IV, 174
companionship in, IV, 172
Hell,
meaning of, IV, 159
existence of, proved, IV, 159 f
externity of, proved, IV, 160
twofold pain of, IV, 162
Henry VIII, III, 344
Heresy,
definition of, I, 68
Heresies,
three groups of in early Church History, III, 266 f
Heretic, III, 141
Herod, II, 74
and Christ, II, 358
Heroic Act
in favor of Poor Souls, IV, 167
Heroism, of running away from temptations against purity, III, 579
Hierarchy, in organization of Church, chart of, III, 217
Hildebrand, III, 311 ff
History, Church, III, 235 ff
synopsis of, III, 235-367
as "log" of Ark, III, 236
Hobbes, III, 355

Holiness, of Church, III, 161
  influence on converts, III, 162
Holiness of God, I, 170
  an aid to purity, III, 568
Holocaust, II, 448, 460
Holy Eucharist, *see* Eucharist, Holy
Holy Ghost,
  Gifts of, I, 367 ff
  fruits of, I, 374-77
    in relation to self, I, 375
    in relation to equals, I, 376
    in relation to inferiors, I, 377
  see Holy Spirit
Holy House, of Loreto, IV, 45
Holy Office, Congregation of, duties,
  III, 207
Holy Orders, IV, 210 ff
  definition of, IV, 211
  steps in, IV, 211 ff
  outward sign of, IV, 215
  minister of, IV, 215 f
  who may receive, IV, 216
  effects of, IV, 216
Holy Roman Empire, III, 307
Holy Saturday, I, 124·
Holy Spirit, III, 27-128
  Baptism makes us temples of, I, 339
  in Old Testament, III, 33 ff
  possesses divine powers, III, 33, 38
  is Giver of Gifts, III, 35
  announced by prophets, III, 36
  revealed in New Testament, III, 37
  is God, III, 37
  inspired prophets and Scripture, III,
    38
  and Incarnation, III, 38
  equal to Father and Son, III, 39
    but distinct, III, 39
  proceeds from Father and Son, III,
    40
  coming of, announced by Christ,
    III, 41
  coming of, III, 42
  and the Incarnation, III, 47
  and Church, III, 48
  twofold external mission of, III, 48
  in souls of just, III, 48
  Indwelling attributed to, III, 49
  blessing conferred by, III, 51
  our duties to, III, 52
  procession of, III, 54
  proceeds as from single principle,
    III, 54
  procession of, defined, III, 55
  Temporal Missions of, III, 57
  purposes of mission of, III, 57
  names of, III, 58

  and the Apostles, III, 61 ff
  and Acts of Apostles, III, 67
  in lives of martyrs, III, 70
  and the persecutions, III, 70
  Trainer of souls, III, 81
  gifts of, III, 102 ff
  gifts of, and supernatural "organ-
    ism," III, 86
  fruits of, III, 111
  fruits of, produced by virtues, III,
    88
  means of sanctification used by, III,
    95
  in Divine Office, III, 117
  in Holy Sacrifice and ritual, III, 118
  in symbols, III, 119
  our duties to, III, 121 ff
  as soul of Mystical Body, III, 196
  as guide of Church, III, 236, 243 ff
Holy Water, in sick room, IV, 141
Holy Week, I, 124
Holydays of Obligation, I, 137-38; II,
  536
Home life,
  and faith, I, 74
  and the liturgy, I, 144
Home, sacramentals in, I, 145
Homicide, III, 525
Hope,
  and the first commandment, I, **428**
  virtue of, II, 424 ff
  nature of, II, 424
  necessity of, II, 426
  sins against, I, 440; II, 427
  Christ our, II, 431
  virtue of in Mary, IV, 60
  impossible without a God, IV, **485 f**
Host, oblation, of, II, 477
Housing, proper, required by **justice,**
  IV, 436
Huguenots, III, 349
Human race, unity of, I, 238
Human respect, resistance to, III, **606**
Human tendencies, III, 499 ff
Humanism,
  pagan and Christian, III, 335
Humanitarianism, III, 354
Hume, III, 355
Humility,
  basic virtue, I, 53
  mistaken ideas about, I, 53
  true nature, I, 53-54; IV, 57
  opposed to pride, I, 412
  and prayer, I, 435
  of John Baptist, II, 203
  recommended by Christ, II, **254,**
    280
  of Mary, IV, 57

Hundred Years War, III, 330
Huns, III, 276
Huss, John, III, 332 f
Hymns,
Eucharistic, II, 630
in honor of Mary, IV, 77
Hyperdulia, I, 430
Hypocrisy,
Christ warns against, II, 328
and truthfulness, IV, 390
Hypocrites, II, 326
Hypostatic union, II, 55

Iconoclasts, III, 293; IV, 80
Idleness,
a cause of temptation, III, 390, 574
Idolatry, I, 442
Image Breakers, III, 293
Imagination,
necessity of guarding, III, 584
Immaculate Conception,
an exception to original sin, I, 274
promise of, I, 274
meaning of, I, 274
first privilege of Mary, IV, 29, 50 f
meaning of, IV, 29
defined by Church, IV, 30
proclaimed at Lourdes, IV, 30
in art, IV, 32
patronal feast of U. S., IV, 32
Immorality and faith, I, 70
Immortality of soul, IV, 114
Impassibility of glorified body, IV, 178
Impediments, matrimonial, IV, 301 ff
definition, IV, 301
kinds, IV, 302
diriment, defined, enumerated and explained, IV, 302
prohibiting, defined, enumerated, explained, IV, 304
Imperfections, III, 385
moral, I, 422
not in themselves matter for confession, III, 424
Imperialism,
economic, a cause of war, III, 530
international, IV, 421
Impure actions,
are grievous matters, III, 596
Impurity,
foulness of, III, 566
scriptural passages on, III, 569
evil effects of, III, 570 f
Incarnation,
and Liturgical Year, I, 113
promise fulfilled in, I, 296

center of history, II, 42; III, 244 f
meaning of, II, 54 f
importance, II, 55
Redemption and, II, 56
a mystery, II, 57
lessons of, II, 57 ff
confers dignity on us, II, 60
and Blessed Virgin, II, 61
a work of the Holy Spirit, III, 38
and Holy Spirit, III, 47
greatest external operation of Holy Spirit, III, 47
results of, III, 47
and Nestorianism, III, 273
Inclinations of man,
good in themselves, I, 271
Income, superfluous, obligations of, IV, 414
Incompatibility, in marriage, IV, 285
Indefectibility, of Church, III, 176
Index of Forbidden Books, I, 71; III, 349
Indifference, religious,
a danger to faith, I, 73
forms of, IV, 521
and attendance at non Catholic school, I, 73
Indissolubility,
as quality of marriage, IV, 250 ff
Individualism,
rejected by pope, IV, 413
results in economic dictatorship, IV, 421
results of, IV, 429
as a false guide in economic life, evidences of, IV, 431
no guide for economic life, IV, 427
Indulgence,
a means of satisfying for temporal punishment due for sin, III, 470 f
power to grant given to Church, III, 470
and treasury of Church, III, 471
definition of, III, 471
plenary, III, 472
partial, III, 473
time periods in, III, 473
conditions for gaining, III, 475
advantage of, III, 476
of Rosary, IV, 93
at moment of death, IV, 133
plenary, attached to Funeral Mass, IV, 155
Third, Seventh, and Thirtieth Day (Months Mind) Mass, IV, 155
toties quoties, IV, 166
applicable to Poor Souls, IV, 167

Indwelling, Divine, III, 49; 76 ff
 results of, III, 51
 duties as result of, I, 194
 nature of, III, 78
Indwelling of Trinity, I, 191; III, 76
Infallibility,
 of Church, III, 169 ff
  nature of, III, 169
  necessity and fact of, III, 169
  proof of, III, 170 ff
  when exercised, III, 171
 of pope, III, 173 ff
 summary of, III, 175
Infidel, III, 141
Infidelity, I, 68
Infinity,
 of God, I, 162; IV, 481
Inheritance,
 as means of acquiring ownership,
  IV, 356
Injuries, Christ commands we forgive, II, 258
Innocence,
 and modesty, III, 591
 meaning of, III, 591
 value of, III, 591
Innocent III, III, 323
Inquiry, as method in Catholic Action,
  III, 227
Inquisition, III, 320
 Spanish, III, 338
Insecurity, a cause of
 social disorders, IV, 423
Insignia, papal, III, 203 ff
Inspiration of Sacred Scripture,
 meaning of, I, 81
Institutions, social, and economic, reform of, needed, IV, 418
Instruction, religious, need of, I, 73
Instruction of faithful, a purpose of
  the liturgy, I, 109
Integrity,
 gift of, 241
 loss of, I, 266
 effects of loss of gift of, III, 389, 573
Intellect,
 infused knowledge of, I, 241
 loss of preternatural knowledge, I,
  266
 possessed by original being, IV, 473
 existence of, presupposed by order
  in universe, IV, 474
Intemperance, III, 543
 consequence of, III, 544
Intention,
 to receive, necessary in Baptism of
  adults, I, 344

necessary in Confirmation of adults,
  I, 382
needed to gain indulgence, III, 475
proper, in Mary, IV, 39
Interdict, definition of, III, 413
Interior worship, not sufficient, III,
  155
Internationalism, economic, IV, 421
Invasions, Barbarian, III, 275
Investiture, lay, III, 305 ff
Iron Crown of Lombardy, III, 290

Jansenism, III, 351
 and frequent Communion, II, 615
 last traces of, opposed, III, 361
Jerusalem,
 Council of, III, 254
 siege of, III, 255
 view of, II, 53
Jesuits,
 founding of, III, 347
 suppression of, III, 356
Jesus Christ,
 cause of grace of the sacraments,
  I, 110
 living with, in the Liturgical Year,
  I, 113 ff; 141
 only begotten Son, I, 186
 founder of the sacraments, I, 312
 as minister of sacraments, I, 318
 charts of events of life of;
  preparation, II, 193 ff
  first year, II, 199 ff
  second year, II, 214 ff
  third year, II; 247 ff; 259 ff; 265
   ff; 278 ff; 289 ff
  Holy Week, II, 310 ff; 337 ff; 353
   ff; 382 ff; 389 ff
 fulfills prophecies, II, 50
 birth of, II, 69 ff
 reveals presence on earth, II, 69
 presentation of, II, 72
 hidden life of, II, 76 ff
 proving divinity of, II, 89 ff; IV,
  495 ff
 attacks on divinity and humanity of,
  II, 92 ff
 model of obedience, II, 157
 public life of, II, 191 ff
 "baptism" of, II, 195
 forty days fast, II, 196
 first disciples, II, 196
 marriage at Cana, II, 199
 cleansing temple, II, 201
 Samaritan woman at well, II, 203
 official's son, II, 205
 forgives sin, II, 211
 virtues of, II, 213

affirms divinity, II, 215
Sermon on Mount, II, 222 ff
appearance of, II, 225
sympathy of, II, 226
forgives woman, II, 228
parables of, II, 230 ff
power over nature, II, 236
Jairus' daughter, II, 238
multiplication of loaves, II, 241
promises of Eucharist, II, 245
rebukes Pharisees, II, 248
predicts Passion, II, 250; 254
Transfiguration, II, 251
advice on fraternal correction, II, 255
confers power on Church, II, 256
commands forgiveness of injuries, II, 258
and woman taken in adultery, I, 260
and blind man in Temple, II, 262
Good Shepherd, II, 263
sends out disciples, II, 266
commands charity, II, 267
Good Samaritan, II, 267
at Bethany, II, 268
teaches Our Father, II, 269
sign of Jonas, II, 270
teaches need of good works, II, 275
eats with sinners, II, 280
recommends humility, etc., II, 280
calls for sacrifice, II, 282
danger of riches, II, 284
on scandal, II, 284
unprofitable servants, II, 285
teaches qualities of prayer, II, 287
raises Lazarus, II, 289
divinity of, shown, II, 291
legislates on unity and indissolubility of marriage, II, 292
and rich young man, II, 294
predicts Passion again, II, 298
rebukes ambition, II, 298
virtues of, II, 301
is anointed, II, 312
triumphal entry, II, 314
demands good works, II, 318
endeavors to win Pharisees, II, 320
commands obedience to state, II, 323
warns Pharisees, II, 328
tells of end of world, II, 331
recommends vigilance, II, 332
use of talents, II, 333
describes Last Judgment, II, 333
at Last Supper, II, 337 ff
institutes Holy Eucharist and Holy Orders, II, 341

last words to Apostles, II, 341
prayer at Last Supper, II, 342
Passion of, II, 343 ff
before Annas and Caiphas, II, 348
patience of, II, 350
and Pilate, 356 ff
and Herod, II, 358
is scourged, II, 362
Crucifixion of, II, 366
Last Words, II, 368 ff
death of, II, 373
burial of, II, 378
Resurrection of, II, 389 ff
apparitions of, II, 396
confers power to forgive sins, II, 402
makes Peter head of Church, II, 406
sends Apostles to teach world, II, 407
Ascension of, II, 407
as sacramental sign of salvation, II, 561
purpose of Mission of, III, 45
founder of Church, III, 143
as head of Mystical Body, III, 194
center of history, III, 244
and Monophysitism, III, 274
Second coming of, IV, 175
as key topic in Apologetics, IV, 488
life of, recorded in New Testament, IV, 491
prophecies verified in, IV, 491
claim to be God, IV, 491
sources of knowledge about, IV, 491 ff
Gospels as source of knowledge of, IV, 492
St. Paul's epistles as source of knowledge of, IV, 492 f
wealth of material about, IV, 495
claims to be God, IV, 495
reveals His divinity gradually, IV, 496 ff
acts and speaks as God, IV, 498
explicit claim to be God, IV, 502
value of knowing what Christ is, IV, 504
divinity of, summary of proofs for, IV, 504
divinity of, proved from nature of Church, IV, 524
Jobs, types of available, IV, 234
finding the right, IV, 236
Jocist Movement, III, 227
Jonas, sign of, II, 270

Judas,
  arranges betrayal, II, 335
  at Last Supper, II, 340
  kills self, II, 354
Judgment,
  Last, IV, 180 ff
    circumstances, IV, 180
    sentence, IV, 181
  Particular, IV, 156
    when, IV, 156
    how and by whom, IV, 156
  necessity of, IV, 158
Judgment, rash, IV, 397
Judicial power of Church, III, 185
Julian the Apostate, III, 269
Juppiter, temple of, IV, 477
Jurisdiction,
  of Church, III, 168, 181
  pope's primacy of, III, 201
  ecclesiastical, hierarchical organiza-
    tion of, III, 215
  power of,
    necessary for forgiving sins, III,
      412
    who possesses, for absolving, III,
      412
Justice,
  of God, I, 170
  of God, and forgiveness of sins, III,
    396
  of God, thought of, an aid to purity,
    III, 568
Justice, virtue of,
  and virtue of penance, III, 428
  nature of, IV, 335
  definition of, IV, 337
  natural and supernatural, IV, 337 f
  a social virtue, IV, 338
  a virtue of the will, IV, 338 f
  divisions of, IV, 339
  legal, IV, 339
  distributive, IV, 339
  commutative, IV, 339
  social, IV, 340
  and related virtues, IV, 340
  distinct from charity, IV, 340
  and Ten Commandments, IV, 342 ff
  and virtue of religion, IV, 342
  and filial piety, IV, 343
  and chastity, IV, 345
  social importance of, IV, 346
  preaching, by example, IV, 348
  kinds of,
    defined, IV, 407
  social, a guiding principle in eco-
    nomic life, IV, 420
  needs charity for social reconstruc-
    tion, IV, 425

  commutative, goals in economic re-
    quired by, IV, 435
  social economic goals required by,
    IV, 435
Justice of the Peace,
  cannot marry Catholic, IV, 263
Justification, III, 82
Justinian, III, 285

Keel, Mystical, of Church
  Christ as, III, 145
Keys, power of,
  promised to St. Peter, III, 405
  to all the Apostles, III, 407
  promise of, fulfilled, III, 407
  a permanent power, III, 409
  extent of, III, 410
Killing,
  accidental, III, 525
  of spiritual life, III, 552
Kissing, morality of, III, 602
King James Version, I, 85
Knowledge,
  God's, I, 168
  and moral responsibility, I, 401
  needed for sin, I, 420
  Gift of, I, 372; III, 109
  of Holy Spirit, necessity of, III, 123
Knights,
  of St. John, III, 321
  Templars, III, 321
  Teutonic, III, 321
Knox, John, III, 344
Koran, III, 291
Kulturkampf, III, 360

Labor,
  manual, dignity of, II, 78
Laboring man,
  pope recommends
    retreats for, IV, 426
Language,
  purpose of power of, IV, 383
Languages, variety of, I, 238
Last Blessing, of dying, IV, 131
Last Judgment, II, 333; IV, 180
  and works of mercy, IV, 143
Last Supper, II, 337 ff
Last Things, IV, 106 ff
Latin, why used in Mass, II, 527
Lateran Palace, III, 266
latria, I, 430
Lauda Sion, II, 630 ff

Law,
physical and moral, I, 230
moral, I, 395 ff; II, 108 ff
  divisions of, I, 396 ff; II, 109 ff
  basic principles, II, 108 ff
natural, I, 396
revealed or positive, I, 396
divine and human, I, 397
human,
  civil and ecclesiastical, I, 398
divine, cannot be changed by man,
  I, 398
Lay investiture, III, 306 ff, 318
Lazarus and Dives, II, 283
Lazarus,
raising of, II, 289
Leadership,
fields for, II, 151
requirements for good, II, 152
obedience and, II, 153
of workingman, II, 171
Catholic, and our high school students, IV, 237 f
need of, IV, 328
how Catholics should prepare to exert, IV, 441
Legates, papal, III, 210
Legislative power of Church, III, 185
Legitimate marriage, IV, 250
Lent, I, 121
spirit and color of, I, 122
Leo XIII, Pope, and *Rerum Novarum,*
  IV, 409
Leonardo da Vinci, III, 340
Lepanto, III, 349; IV, 91
Liberalism, false principles of, followed by capital, IV, 415
Liberality, virtue of, IV, 380
Liberian Basilica, IV, 83
Liberty and Law, II, 111
Lie, definition of, IV, 387
Lies,
"white," IV, 390
Life, Public, of Jesus Christ,
see, Jesus Christ
Life,
virtuous, an aid to faith, I, 174
God is, I, 160
levels of, I, 161
outline of good Christian, I, 405 ff
supernatural, of soul, II, 416
natural and supernatural spiritual,
  III, 82
supernatural, a gift of God, III, 84
supernatural sources and fruits of,
  III, 87
supernatural,
  Church as Mother of, III, 220

of Church,
  manifestations of divinity of, III, 246
divine and human element, III, 246 f
physical protection of, III, 518
care of, III, 522
violations of proper care of, III, 522
justifiable risk of, III, 523
taking human, III, 525
  State may take for crime, III, 529
killing of supernatural, III, 552 f
plan of, mapping a, IV, 182
purpose of, IV, 185
state in,
  choice of, IV, 194 ff
  importance of, IV, 194
  three choices of, IV, 194
  criteria for choosing, IV, 195 ff
  aids in choosing, IV, 197 ff
Christian,
  a return to, necessary for reconstructing social order, IV, 423
economic, *See,* Economic life
purposelessness of, without a God,
  IV, 486
Church, as channel of, IV, 518
religious,
  active and contemplative, IV, 221 ff
Light of glory, in heaven, IV, 174
Limb, proper care of, III, 522
Limbo, IV, 163
of Infants, IV, 163
Literature,
Catholic, as a means to spread the Faith, I, 98
in the Middle Ages, III, 328
Mary and, IV, 70 ff
Liturgical Year,
meaning of, I, 107 ff
purpose of, I, 108 ff
presents Christ as our model, I, 110
how divided, I, 111
living with Christ in seasons and feasts of, I, 141 ff
summary of, I, 145
Liturgies, II, 523
the four great, II, 525
Liturgy,
meaning of, I, 108
living in the spirit of, I, 141
practical hints for living, I, 144
and home life, I, 144
Gallican, II, 526
Roman, II, 527
and Mystical Body, III, 197
Holy Spirit in, III, 113 ff

555

Little Flower, III, 360
Living Voice of Teaching Church,
see, Church, Faith
Living wage,
demanded by commutative justice,
IV, 435
Lollards, III, 332
Lombard League, III, 318
Lombards, III, 286
Loneliness, in unmarried state, IV, 233
Loreto, Holy House of, IV, 45
Loss, pain of, in hell, IV, 162
Lourdes, IV, 30
shrine of B.V.M., IV, 86
Love,
law of,
Christ's statement, of, I, 406
the great commandment, II, 326
326
of God, for us, II, 29 f; IV, 15
of God, revealed in Eucharist, II,
547
of self, III, 91 f
a basic tendency, III, 504
our duty of, to Holy Spirit, III, 124
Church as proof of God's, III, 219
of fellow men, a basic tendency, III,
504
identified with sacrifice, IV, 258
See, Charity
Lust,
and opposite virtues, I, 413
vice of, III, 599
breaking bad habits of, III, 599
Luther, Martin, III, 342
errors of, III, 340
Lying, IV, 387 f
by signs other than speech, IV, 387
gravity of sins of, IV, 393

Macedonianism, I, 200
Madonnas, III, 340; IV, 82
Man, purpose of, depends on man's
Creator, IV, 486
Magi, II, 74
Magic, black, I, 444
Magnificat, II, 67
Magyars, III, 302
Man,
creation of, I, 235
gifts from God, I, 239
loses preternatural gifts, I, 265 ff
needs of natural and supernatural
life compared, I, 314-16
social obligations to God, I, 453
Manichaeism, I, 199; III, 262

Manna, figure of Eucharist, II, 569
Manuscripts of Bible, I, 83 ff
Maps,
Galilee, II, 218
Palestine, II, 209
Jerusalem, II, 388
Marcus Aurelius, III, 261
Marianists, IV, 99
Marists, IV, 99
Marks of Church, III, 156 ff
and converts, III, 167 f
Marks, relation to attributes, III, 178
Marriage Bond, Defender of, III, 213
Marriage,
and a career, IV, 239 f
nature of, IV, 243 ff
is sacred, IV, 245
for Christians, a sacrament, IV, 245
essential nature, IV, 246
set by God, IV, 246
not subject to will of parties, IV,
246
requisites for valid, IV, 247
contract,
effects of, IV, 248
chief qualities of, II, 292; IV, 240
sacramental consummated,
indissoluble by any power on
earth, IV, 252
essential purpose of, IV, 253 f
essential secondary purposes, IV,
254
other purposes of, IV, 256 f
false modern ideas on purpose of,
IV, 256 f
a remedy for concupiscence, IV,
254
source of false ideas on, IV, 258
before justice of peace, not valid,
IV, 263
before non Catholic clergyman,
brings excommunication, IV,
264
obligations of, IV, 272
not a completely civil function, IV,
285
a sacred act, IV, 286
mixed, IV, 286 ff
kinds of, IV, 286
forbidden by Church, IV, 286
reason for forbidding, IV, 287
promises broken, IV, 287
endanger faith, IV, 287
conditions for permitting, IV,
288
how it endangers faith, I, 72
promises in, IV, 288
declaration of nullity of, IV, 295

556

and proper economic conditions, IV, 301
building a successful, IV, 306 ff
  remote preparation, IV, 307
  proximate preparation, IV, 308
  immediate preparation, IV, 314
dangers of hasty, IV, 312
time and place of, IV, 316
ceremony, IV, 317
having Christ at your, IV, 318
love and sacrifice in, IV, 319
and dedication to Sacred Heart, IV, 323
See also, Matrimony, Sacraments
Martha, and Mary, II, 268
Martyr, meaning of, I, 65
Martyrdom, I, 332
Martyrs, I, 65; III, 254, 257, 261, 262, 262 et passim
Martyrs, Holy Ghost in lives of, III, 70
Marx, Karl, III, 361
Mary, Blessed Virgin,
faith of, I, 42
devotion to control concupiscence, I, 287
and the Incarnation, II, 61
and Visitation, II, 64
beneath Cross, II, 371
value of intercession of, III, 127
and Nestorianism, III, 273
Rosary of, and Lepanto, III, 349
devotion to, as means to preserve purity, III, 578
unselfishness of, IV, 27
early life of, IV, 28
parents of, IV, 28
nativity of, IV, 32
presentation of, IV, 33
virginity of, IV, 33
espoused to St. Joseph, IV, 34
in Gospels, IV, 36 ff
visitation of, IV, 37
in Nazareth, IV, 37
place in heaven, IV, 38
humble tasks performed by, IV, 39
during Public Life, IV, 39
requests first miracle, IV, 39
on Calvary, IV, 39 f
after the Resurrection, IV, 41
at Ephesus, IV, 42
death of, IV, 42
Assumption of, IV, 42
simple life of, IV, 42 f
feasts of, IV, 44; I, 129
how her clients honor, IV, 46
devotion to, necessary to salvation, IV, 53

privileges of, IV, 47 ff
  greatest, Divine Motherhood, IV, 48
  other great privileges, IV, 50
  Immaculate Conception, IV, 50
  perpetual virginity, IV, 51
  sinlessness, IV, 51
  preservation from corruption, IV, 52
  full of grace, IV, 52
  Mediatrix, IV, 52
  Spiritual motherhood of all men, IV, 53
  Queen of angels and men, IV, 55
  mother of real and Mystical Body of Christ, IV, 53
virtues of, IV, 36, 56 ff
  perfect in all virtues, IV, 57
  St. Alphonsus on, IV, 57
  St. Thomas on, IV, 57
  theological, in, IV, 59
  moral, in, IV, 62
and the arts, IV, 69 ff
  and art of Christian living, IV, 69
  literature, IV, 70 ff
  music, IV, 74 ff
  painting, IV, 79 ff
  oldest portrait of, IV, 79
  symbols of, IV, 82
shrines and pilgrimages of, IV, 86 ff
devotions to, IV, 89 ff
  our need of, IV, 89
  Albigensianism and, IV, 89
  saints devoted to, IV, 90
  May devotions to, IV, 91
  October devotions to, IV, 91
  and Saturday, IV, 92
  Little Office of, IV, 92, 97
  Seven Sorrows of, IV, 97
  devout practices to honor, IV, 96
  prayers to, IV, 92 ff
  and sacramentals, IV, 96
  using images of, IV, 96
  societies devoted to, IV, 97 f
  confraternities and sodalities of, IV, 99 f
  resolutions in honor of, IV, 101
  final program in honor of, IV, 102
  and prayer for happy death, IV, 117
Mary Magdalen, II, 397
Maryknoll, IV, 99
Masonry, III, 355
Masons,
denied Christian burial, IV, 154
Mass, II, 435-551
attendance at, a means to virtue, I, 58

Sunday, in the liturgy, I, 142
weekday, I, 142
Ordinary of, I, 143; II, 530
supreme act of virtue of religion, I,
433
and Calvary, II, 457
same in essence, II, 458
Calvary reenacted, II, 459
a true sacrifice, II, 462
essentials of, II, 462
an unbloody sacrifice, II, 463
structure and division of, II, 470
of Catechumens, II, 473
of Faithful, II, 476
Offertory, II, 476
Preface, II, 479
Canon, II, 480
Consecration, II, 481
fruits of, II, 491
general fruits of, II, 495
special fruits, II, 497
social importance of, II, 497
and forgiveness of sin, II, 494
and the saints, II, 504
source of courage, II, 509
and St. Thomas Aquinas, II, 507
and St. Thomas More, II, 509
Pontifical, II, 513
Solemn, II, 516
High, II, 516
Low, II, 517
and Music, II, 516
parochial, II, 518
of feasts, II, 519
ferial, II, 520
votive, II, 520
requiem, II, 521; IV, 155
nuptial, II, 521
time and place of, II, 522
essentials of liturgy of, II, 524
obligation to hear, II, 535
must hear an entire, II, 537
proper attention at, II, 538
when excused from, II, 539
the Holy Spirit in the liturgy of,
III, 118
Funeral, IV, 147 ff
a consolation, IV, 147
when and where offered, IV, 147
Masses,
Kinds of, II, 513
Maternity, Divine,
of Mary, IV, 48
in Scriptures, IV, 48
defined at Ephesus, IV, 48
in liturgy, IV, 50
feast of, IV, 50

Matrimony, IV, 242 ff
nature of, IV, 243
divisions of, IV, 250
as a sacrament, IV, 260 ff
and essentials of sacrament, IV,
260 ff
outward sign of, IV, 261
prescribed formalities, IV, 262
effects of sacrament of, IV, 266
sacramental graces of, IV, 267
blessings of, IV, 270
errors concerning, IV, 275 ff
basic answer to errors, IV, 275
basic false principle, marriage a
human institution, IV, 277
remedies for abuses and errors
about, IV, 298 ff
basic remedy, IV, 299
means thereto, IV, 299 f
Matter
of sacramental signs, I, 309
Matter, grave, in mortal sin, I, 419
in Extreme Unction, IV, 126
Maturity, spiritual, III, 94
Mechanistic Evolution, III, 507
answered, III, 509
Mediatrix, Mary as, IV, 52
Meditation, II, 84 ff
method of, II, 85
as aid in learning, III, 32
Meekness, III, 536
Memento,
of the Dead, IV, 141
Mendicant Orders, III, 323
Mercedarian Fathers, with Columbus,
III, 339
Mercy, works of,
and faith, I, 76
basis of Last Judgment, II, 333
and the dying, IV, 142 f
corporal, 143; spiritual, 146
Mercy, of God, I, 171
shown in forgiveness of sins, III,
395
"Mercy" Killing, III, 528
Meritorious act, see, act
Merits, past
restored by sacrament of Penance,
III, 482
Messias,
types and figures of, I, 291
figures of, II, 46 ff
in prophecy, I, 291
preparation of world for, I, 293
Christ proves self to be, IV, 491
Metropolitan, archbishop as, III, 213,
217
Michael Caerularius, III, 311

Michaelangelo, III, 340
Middle Ages, history of, III, 317 ff
Migration of Nations, III, 275
Milan, edict of, III, 265
Mind, existence of divine, proved by
order in world, IV, 476
Minor Orders, IV, 211 f
Minors, baptism of, I, 346
Miracles, II, 200
of Christ, II, 219, 317, 395
as guarantee of Christ's claims, IV,
495
number of, II, 237
Miraculous Medal, IV, 96
Missal,
how to use, I, 143 f
and assistance at Mass, II, 468
Mission activities,
in twentieth Century, III, 363
Missionaries,
and the spread of the Faith, I, 97
"Home," I, 97
Missions,
spreading Faith by helping, I, 98
Internal, of Trinity, III, 53 sqq
Temporal, of Holy Ghost, III, 56 ff
Mixed marriage, IV, 286 ff
two kinds, IV, 286
forbidden by Church, IV, 286
how to avoid, IV, 290
company keeping with non Catholics leads to, IV, 290
Moderation, Church as
champion of, III, 386
Modesty,
virtue of, III, 583 ff
relation to purity, III, 583
nature of, III, 583 f
kinds of, III, 584
importance of early training in, III,
590
and innocence, III, 591
sins against, III, 597
gravity of sins against, III, 598
Mohammed, III, 290
Mohammedanism, III, 290 ff
Monasticism,
in East, III, 263
in West, III, 281 ff
spread of, III, 283
influence of, III, 283
Irish, III, 284
Money,
avoiding quarrels over, IV, 322
Monks, Irish
on continent, III, 289
Monogamy,
reinstated by Christ, IV, 251

Monophysitism, II, 93; III, 274
Monothelitism, II, 94; III, 290
Montanism, III, 262
Monte Cassino, III, 281
Months, dedications of, I, 139
Moors, III, 282
Moral act, good,
elements of, I, 401 f
Moral law,
breaking of, II, 118
handicaps in observing, II, 122
Moral laws, revealed, I, 80
Moral principles,
economic result of deserting, IV,
423
Morality,
guides in, I, 395 ff; II, 129 ff
basic rules of, I, 401-404
basis of, II, 105 ff
natural and supernatural, II, 112 ff
basic principles of, II, 112
Living Voice in, II, 130
and conscience, II, 130 ff
power of Church to guide, III, 148 f
erroneous modern views on, III, 507
reform of, required for reconstruction of social order, IV, 420
Morals,
reform of, a requisite of social reconstruction, IV, 440
Mortification,
to control temptation, III, 391
Mary's practice of, IV, 66
Moslems, III, 292
Mother,
authority of, II, 136
Church as, III, 218 ff
Christian, greatest career, IV, 238
Motherhood, spiritual, of Mary, IV,
53
Motive, supernatural,
and goodness of an act, I, 404
Movies, modesty and, III, 587
Mozarabic rite, II, 526
Multiplication of loaves, first, II, 241
second, II, 249
Murder,
definition of, III, 527
Murder,
lesser sins leading toward. III, 533
Murillo, IV, 32, 82
Music and the Mass, II, 516
Mystery, nature of, I, 175
Mysteries, in nature, I, 178
Mystical Body,
Baptism incorporates us in, I, 337
doctrine of, III, 193 ff
Christ as Head of, III, 194

Holy Spirit as Soul of, III, 196
members of, III, 196
and Liturgy, III, 197
three sections of, III, 198
defends itself against heresy, III, 265 ff
sin and membership in, III, 370
and indulgences, III, 471, 476
influence of doctrine of, in social reconstruction, IV, 441

Name, good,
sins against, IV, 394
Name day, I, 145
Names, of Holy Spirit, III, 58
Nantes,
Edict of Religious Toleration of, III, 350
Napoleon, III, 357
Narcotics, use of
morality of, III, 546
dangers of, III, 548
Nationalism,
excessive, a cause of war, III, 530
of Richelieu, III, 350
in France, III, 351
Nativity, II, 69 ff
Natural rights of Church, III, 189
Naturalism, I, 272, 423; III, 355
compared with supernaturalism, I, 273
fosters worldliness, I, 280
Nature,
defined, I, 183; 578
Nazareth,
Christ's thirty years at, I, 76
Necessity, grave,
and stealing, IV, 360
Neighbor, love of, III, 92
Nepotism, III, 306, 336
Nestorianism, I, 93; III, 273
Nervous breakdown, and unwillingness to face facts, IV, 393
New Testament, I, 82 f
when written, III, 257
Newman, Cardinal, III, 358
News, falsification of,
a sin against truth, IV, 397
Nice, Ecumenical Council of, III, 268
Nicodemus, I, 202, 387
Nicolaitism, III, 306
Nocturnal Adoration, I, 629
Non Catholics,
assisting dying, IV, 142
marriages of, not bound by form, IV, 264

Non Christians,
approach to, in apologetics, IV, 461
November, Month of Poor Souls, IV, 167
Novena,
of Pentecost, III, 116
Novitiate, IV, 205
for brotherhoods, IV, 219
Nullity, declaration of, IV, 295
not a divorce, IV, 295
who can issue, IV, 295 f
Nunc Dimittis, II, 73
Nuptial Blessing, IV, 316, 318
Nuptial Mass, IV, 318

Oath of Supremacy, III, 344
Oaths, I, 447 ff
kinds of, I, 448
when lawful, I, 448
sinful, I, 452
Obedience, II, 82 •
and peace, II, 105
and order, II, 105
and justice, II, 155
Christ, model of, II, 157
of children, II, 162
limitations and exceptions, II, 163
of Mary, IV, 63
vow of, I, 450; IV, 223
Objectives of entire course, I, 23; 392; III, 20, IV, 18
of first year, I, 23 f
of sophomore year, II, 24
for junior year, III, 23
for senior year, IV, 20
Objectives,
of Book Four,
Unit One, IV, 23
Unit Two, IV, 107
Unit Three, IV, 186
Unit Four, IV, 330
Unit Five, IV, 4
Objectives of Communism, IV, 422
Oblates of Mary Immaculate, IV, 99
Obsession, diabolical, I, 279
Obstacle to happiness,
the world as an, I, 280
the flesh as, I, 281
Obstacles, to eternal happiness, I, 276 ff
Occasions of sin,
proximate, avoidance of, a sign of firm purpose of amendment, III, 441
avoiding, to preserve purity, III, 529

Occupations,
  balance of wage scales in various, needed, IV, 418
Octaves, I, 136
Odoacer, III, 278
Offertory of Mass, II, 476
Office, Divine, *See,* Divine office
Officialis, III, 213
Offspring,
  purpose of marriage, IV, 253
  first blessing of marriage, IV, 270
Oil,
  a symbol of Holy Spirit, III, 120
  of the sick, IV, 26
Old Testament, I, 82
Oleum Infirmorum, IV, 126
Omnipresence, of God, I, 166
Oneness of God, I, 156
Oratorians, III, 347
Order in Universe,
  as proof of God's existence, IV, 474 f
  conclusion from, IV, 475
Orders, power of, III, 181; III, 185 ff
  hierarchical organization of, III, 215 ff
  needed for forgiving sins, III, 411
Orders,
  Major, IV, 213
  Minor, IV, 211 f
Orders, religious,
  and organization of Church, III, 214
  exempt and non exempt, III, 214
  chief purpose of members of, III, 214
  contemplative and active, III, 215
  and Mary, IV, 99
Ordinary of the Mass, I, 143
"Organism," supernatural, and grace, III, 84 ff
Organization, of Church, III, 200 ff
  hierarchical, III, 217
Origen, I, 64; III, 261
Original sin, I 262 ff, 267
  its nature, I, 268
  effects on us, I, 269
  and guarding of purity, III, 584
  See, Sin
O Sacrum Convivium, II, 634
O Salutaris Hostia, II, 625
Outward sign,
  of sacraments, I, 309
  of Baptism, I, 327
  of Confirmation, I, 363
Ownership, recommended, II, 139
  right of, and limitations on, IV, 352
  nature of, IV, 353 f
  kinds of, IV, 355
  ways of acquiring, IV, 355

Ownership,
  vices and sins violating, IV, 357
  right of, defended by Leo XIII, IV, 413
  methods of acquiring, encyclicals on, IV, 414 f
  private, necessity of, IV, 357
  private, abolition of, an objective of Communism, IV, 422
  private, natural need for, violated by Communism, IV, 434
  public, some recommended, IV, 436
Oxford Movement, III, 358

Pain,
  in hell,
    of sense, IV, 162
    of loss, IV, 162
Painting, IV, 79 ff
Palaeologus, III, 334
Palestrina, III, 340; IV, 75, 78
Pallium, III, 204
Pantheism, I, 199
Pantheon, III, 143
Papacy,
  in organization of Church, III, 201
  temporal power of, III, 285
  alliance with Franks, III, 297
Papal assistants, III, 206
Papal States, seizure of, III, 358
Parables, II, 230 ff
  purposes of, II, 231
  list of, II, 232-3
  of Kingdom, II, 235, 275; 282; 321
Paraclete, III, 60
Parallel Readings, *See,* Readings
Parents,
  relations of, II, 138
  duties of children, II, 138 f; IV, 272
  duties to, II, 159
  duties to one another, IV, 272
  right to educate children, IV, 273
  as proximate principle of being of their children, IV, 343
Parish,
  as unit in governing Church, III, 213
  membership in, determined by residence, III, 213
Paris, University of, III, 317
Parking, III, 603
Parthenon, III, 142
Partnership, of capital and labor, recommended by Pius XI, IV, 417
Paschal Lamb,
  figure of Eucharist, II, 568

Passion,
first prediction of, by Christ, II, 250
second prediction of, II, 254
third prediction of, II, 298
Passions,
good when controlled, I, 281
first movement not voluntary, III,
602
See, Original Sin
Passiontide, I, 122
Pastor,
as representative of Teaching
Church, I, 78
gratitude due to, II, 518
in government of Church, III, 213
to be summoned on sick calls, IV;
134
should be notified of sickness, etc.,
IV, 134
authorized,
as necessary witness of marriage,
IV, 262
visit to, before marriage, IV, 314
which can assist at marriage, IV,
314
Pastoral Rule, of St. Gregory the
Great, III, 288
Patience, of Mary, IV, 65
Patriarch, III, 217
Patriotism,
duty of citizen, II, 176
Pauline Privilege, explained, IV, 252
Pax, II, 407
Peace offerings, II, 448
and Mass, II, 485
Pelagianism, III, 273
Penance,
Ember days and, I, 136
as plank after shipwreck, III, 370
sacrament of, III, 401 ff
definition, III, 401 f
divinely instituted, III, 402
outward sign of, III, 402
matter, III, 402
form, III, 403
power to confer grace, III, 403
effects of, III, 481
what it should mean to us, III,
486
gift of God, III, 487
a life raft, III, 487
source of Christ-life, III, 489
gives self-knowledge, III, 489
gives guidance, III, 490
sacramental,
value of, III, 457
in Early Church, III, 458 f
duty to perform, III, 459

omission of, III, 460
time and manner of performing,
III, 460
virtue of, III, 426; III, 462
prayer, fasting, almsgiving, III,
464
value of, voluntary, III, 465
Mary's practice of, IV, 66
Penances,
prescribed by Church, III, 466
negative, best and safest, III, 465
Penitentiary, Sacred, III, 209
Penitents,
types of, III, 453
Pentecost,
novena, III, 116
period after, III, 117
Pepin, III, 297
Perfect contrition,
helping dying to elicit, IV, 142
See, Contrition
Perfections,
of God, I, 159
God possesses all, I, 167
Perjury, I, 452
nature and malice of, IV, 396
Persecution of Church,
history of early, III, 252 ff
in twentieth century, III, 361
Persecutions, The Great, III, 70,
254 ff
Person,
defined, I, 183
Persons, Divine,
in the Trinity, I, 185
Peter the Hermit, III, 316
Petition, an effect of the Mass, II, 493
Pharisees, II, 217
rebuked, II, 248
Christ endeavors to win, II, 320
Photius, III, 303 f
Piety,
Gift of, I, 372; III, 107
Pieta, of Michelangelo, IV, 125
Pilate, and Christ, II, 356
Pius X, and Frequent Communion,
II, 615
Pius XI, IV, 405
Plain Chant, IV, 74
Plan of course, I, 13, 21 f.
Pleasure,
not the goal of human life, III, 514
love of, causes loss of vocation, IV,
204
Plenary council, nature of, III, 214
Poems, in honor of Mary, IV, 72 f
Poetry, Marian, IV, 70 ff
Poland, conversion of, III, 309

Political Popes, III, 336
Polytheism, I, 198
Pontiff, Supreme, as title of pope, III, 202
Pontifex, III, 202
Poor Clares, III, 325
Poor Souls,
  and spiritual works of mercy, IV, 146
  devotion to, IV, 166
  Month of, IV, 167
Pope,
  as voice of Teaching Church, I, 79
  as successor of St. Peter in primacy, III, 153
  infallibility of, III, 173
  head of Church Militant, III, 201
  titles of, III, 202
  insignia of, III, 203 ff
  election of, III, 205
  informal and liturgical garb of, III, 203 ff
  St. Gregory VII, III, 311
  Leo XIII, III, 360
    encyclical of on Holy Spirit, III, 43
  Pius IX, III, 358
  Pius X, III, 361
Popes,
  Renaissance, III, 336
  defend right to private property, IV, 414
Port Royal, III, 351
Porter, IV, 211
Possession,
  by devil, I, 279
  why permitted, I, 279
Possessions,
  desire for, a basic tendency, III, 502
Postulancy,
  for brotherhoods, IV, 219
Poverty,
  vow of, I, 450, 223
  of Mary, IV, 63
Power of God, I, 169
Power of Church to govern, III, 184
Power of jurisdiction, III, 168
Power of Keys,
  proved from history of Church, III, 409
  defined by Council of Trent, III, 410
Power of Orders, III, 181 ff; 215 ff; 411

Pragmatism, III, 507 f
Praise, honest, need of, IV, 390 f
Prayer,
  and faith, I, 75
  public and private, I, 75
  a means to secure control of senses, I, 286
  act of virtue of religion, I, 433
  necessary for salvation, I, 434
  qualities of, I, 435
  kinds and types of, I, 436 ff
  mental, I, 437
  purpose of, I, 437 f
  public, I, 438
  liturgical, I, 438
  group, value of, II, 258
  Christ teaches, II, 269
  qualities of, II, 287
  perseverance in, II, 287
  humility in, II, 288
  and control of temptation, III, 392
  as means of,
    satisfying for sin, III, 464
  opposes pride, III, 464
  Mary's practice of, IV, 66
  as aid in choosing vocation, IV, 194
  for choosing vocation, IV, 221
Prayers,
  lists of, I, 8, 463; II, 13 f; III, 8; IV, 8-9
  to Mary, IV, 92 ff
  for the dying, IV, 141
Precept, of Church,
  First, II, 535 ff
  Second, III, 466 ff
  Third, III, 483
  Fourth, II, 610
  Fifth, III, 228 ff
  Sixth, IV, 286 ff; 302-4; 316
Predominant fault, I, 416
Preface,
  of Mass, II, 479
  of the Dead, IV, 150
Premonstratensians, III, 317 f
Presbyterianism, III, 344
Presence of God,
  practice of, I, 194
  in Mary, IV, 60
Presentation, II, 72
  of Blessed Virgin, IV, 33
  ceremony of, IV, 33
Preservation of Universe and Divine Providence, I, 229
Presumption, I, 440; II, 430
  cause, II, 431
Prices, balance between, required for prosperity, IV, 436

Pride,
and faith, I, 70
source of concupiscence, I, 271
the fall and, I, 297
sins springing from, I, 410
virtues opposed to, I, 410
Priest,
as voice of Teaching Church, **I, 78**
Priesthood, IV, 206 ff
diocesan, III, 152; IV, 206 f
regular, IV, 206 f
duties of, IV, 210
dignity and responsibility of, **IV,**
210
steps to, IV, 211
powers conferred by, IV, 213
ceremonies of ordination to, IV, 213
Priests, diocesan, III, 213; IV, 206 f
Primacy,
of St. Peter, III, 150 ff
foreshadowed, III, 152
of Pope, III, 153
of jurisdiction,
extent of, III, 201 f
of honor, III, 202
Primate, III, 217
Principle,
basic,
for remedying abuses of marriage,
IV, 299
correct,
governing division of profits, IV,
415
Privileges, of Blessed Virgin, **IV, 29**
Problems, scriptural,
answers to, I, 233
Processions, Divine,
meaning of, III, 53
Procreation,
essential primary purpose of marriage, IV, 253
Profanity, I, 451
Professors, non-Catholic,
shattering faith, IV, 449
Profits,
distribution of, correct principle
governing, IV, 415
Proletariat, improving condition of,
IV, 415
Promises,
of a Redeemer, I, 288 ff; II, 43 ff
fulfilled, I, 295; II, 52 ff; III, 394
in mixed marriages, IV, 288
fidelity to, necessity of, IV 386
Propaganda, Congregation of, III, 208
Proper of the Saints, I, 143
See, Sanctoral Cycle

Proper of the Season, I, 143
See, Temporal Cycle
Property, Church,
confiscated in England, III, **344**
in France, III, 356
Property,
natural right to own, IV, 352
individual and social rights of, **IV,**
352
right to own, entails obligations, **IV,**
352
danger of socializing, IV, 357
unlawful keeping of, IV, 360
interfering with use of, IV, 361 f
unjust strikes end, IV, 361 f
damaging, IV, 364
various ways of injuring right **to,**
IV, 370
individual and social aspect of, **IV,**
413
private, right of,
defended by popes, IV, 413
private,
state control of, IV, 414
Propertyless, excessive numbers of,
must be remedied, IV, 415
Prophecies,
concerning Redeemer, I, 288 ff; **II,**
43 ff
fulfilled in Christ, I, 295; II, 50
fulfilled in Resurrection, II, 394
Protestant Revolt, III, 342 ff
spread of, III, 343
Protestantism, I, 201
and the Eucharist, II, 637·
Prototypes, of Saviour, II, 46 ff
Providence, Divine, I, 229
and physical and moral law, I, **230**
characteristics of, I, 231
our response to, I, 232
Christ reminds us of, II, 271
Province,
and archbishop, III, 213
as administrative subdivision **of**
Church, III, 213
Provincial Council, III, **214**
Prudence,
nature of, I, 54
signs of, I, 55
signs of lack of, **I, 55**
and desire to possess property, **IV,**
380
Punishment,
temporal and the Mass, II, 494
eternal and temporal, subject **to**
power of keys, III, 410
eternal and perfect contrition, **III,**
435

eternal, and absolution, III, 456
temporal, removed in proportion to intensity of contrition, III, 435
remission of, in Penance, III, 482
for sin, remitted by Extreme Unction, 127
Pupils,
duties of, II, 169
Purchase,
as a means of acquiring ownership, IV, 356
Purchasing power,·
just use of, IV, 368
Purgatory,
nature and duration of, IV, 163
existence of, proved, IV, 164
nature of punishment in, IV, 164
Purification, II, 72
Purity,
virtue of, III, 562 ff
definition of, III, 562
blessings of, III, 562 f
on individual, III, 563
social, III, 565
rewards of, III, 565
aids to,
intellectual, III, 566 ff
physical, III, 573 f
supernatural, III, 575 ff
Holy Eucharist, III, 575
Confession, III, 575
prayer, III, 578
false ideas on training to, III, 581
gravity of sins against, III, 598
of Mary, IV, 62
virginal, necessity in unmarried state, IV, 231
Purpose,
as affecting morality of act, I, 402
influence of, on morality of act, II, 117

Quadragesimo Anno,
synopsis of, 402, 409 ff
brief outline of, 410
Qualities, of marriage, IV, 250 ff
Quarrelling, III, 539
Quest for Happiness,
summary of, IV, 528 ff
Quest,
rules for a successful, I, 392 ff

Raccolta, indulgences in, III, 473
Raphael, III, 340; IV, 82
Rash judgment, nature and gravity of, IV, 397

Ratified marriage, IV, 250
Rationalism, III, 355
definition of, I, 68
Reader, IV, 211
Reading and Faith, I, 70
Reading and purity, III, 586
Readings, Parallel,
Unit One, IV, 26
Unit Two, IV, 110
Unit Three, IV, 192
Unit Four, IV, 334
Readings, Related,
Unit One, IV, 25
Unit Two, IV, 110
Unit Three, IV, 190
Unit Four, IV, 333 f
Reason,
a natural guide, I, 32 ff
its nature, I, 32
power of, I, 33 ff
tells us about God, I, 36 ff
tells us some of our duties to God, I, 37
reliability of, I, 38
as a guide to happiness, I, 28, 38
inferior to faith, I, 44
ability of, I, 45
use of,
required for contract, IV, 244
required for marriage contract, IV, 244
and faith,
compared, IV, 447
Real Presence,
doctrine of, II, 585
Rebirth, spiritual, need of, II, 202
Reccared, III, 287
Reception of sacraments, I, 320
Reconstruction, social,
not an easy task, IV, 425
complete plan for, IV, 439
Recreation, moderate,
value of, III, 391
Redeemer,
promise of, I, 288; II, 43 ff; IV, 490
pointed out and described, I, 291
prophecies concerning, II, 49 ff
Redemption,
and the Incarnation, II, 55
the Liturgical Year and, I, 120 ff
liturgical drama of, III, 115
Reforms, social, required, IV, 421
Relationship, spiritual,
from Baptism, I, 348
an impediment to marriage, I, 348
Relics,
use of, I, 431
on altar, II, 529

Religion,
virtue of,
and sacrifice, I, 432
and prayer, I, 433
sins against, I, 441
in Mary, IV, 66
and justice, IV, 342
vows of, I, 449
unity of our, II, 21; III, 21
value of realizing unity of, III, 22
Catholic, unity of, IV, 16
carrying evidences of, IV, 136
Catholic, steps in proving, IV, 449
necessity of, derived from nature of
God and man, IV, 450
necessity of, follows from existence
of God, IV, 489
true,
claim of Catholic Church to be,
IV, 490
necessity of finding, IV, 489
nature of, IV, 489
Religious life, in general, IV, 198 ff
correct idea of, IV, 226
pros and cons of, IV, 229
Religious Orders,
and organization of Church, III,
214
Remains of sin,
removed by Extreme Unction, IV,
128
Remarriage,
forbidden during life of spouse, IV,
251
Remedy, main,
for social evils, reform of morals as,
IV, 420
Remedies, for social evils, IV, 421
Remorse of conscience,
a result of impurity, III, 572
Renaissance,
pagan and Christian, III, 335
Popes, III, 336
and arts, III, 340
Reparation, and the,
Mystical Body, III, 476
and contemplative orders, III, 477
at Mass, III, 477
Repentance,
need of, II, 274
Reputation,
sins against, IV, 394 ff
right to, IV, 394
revealing sins of others to protect,
IV, 400
Rerum Novarum and *Quadragesimo
Anno,* IV, 409
Rerum Novarum,
good resulting from, IV, 409 ff

Reservation of sins,
reasons for, III, 413
Responsibility, moral,
conditions for, I, 400 ff
degrees of, in taking life, III, 525
Restitution, IV, 371 ff
included in satisfaction, III, 459
defined, IV, 371
when required, IV, 371
for damage, IV, 374
and cooperation, IV, 374
gravity of obligation, IV, 375
to whom? IV, 375
and possession,
in good faith, IV, 372
in bad faith, IV, 372
Resurrection,
and the Saducees, II, 325
of body,
an effect of the Eucharist, II, 602
at Last Judgment, IV, 172, 176 f
Revelation,
meaning of, I, 79
periods of, I, 79 f
pre-Christian, I, 80
Christian, I, 80
content of, I, 80
and natural truths, I, 80
and moral precepts, I, 80
proving possibility of, a step in
apologetics, IV, 450
see also Faith; Living Voice; Church,
Catholic; Scripture, Sacred, etc.
Reverence,
for God and holy things, I, 445
for parents, II, 161
Church's, for bodies of dead, IV,
152
Revenge, III, 538
Revolution, French, causes and results,
III, 356
Rheims, cathedral, IV, 85
Richelieu, Cardinal, III, 350
Riches,
dangers of, II, 284; 294
not properly distributed, IV, 417
Right,
of Church to teach, III, 182
nature of a, IV, 335
natural, to own property, IV, 350
Rights,
inalienable, II, 176
of Church,
natural and supernatural, III, 189
basic, belong to all human beings,
IV, 335
cannot be abolished, IV, 335
Rings, papal, III, 205

Rites, Last, IV, 147 ff
Robber Synod of Ephesus, III, 274
Robbery, IV, 357
Rochet, bishop's, III, 212
Rock, St. Peter as, IV, 514 ff
Rogation days, I, 136
Roger Bacon, III, 327
Roman Catechism, III, 349
Roman Congregations, III, 207 f
Roman Curia, III, 207 ff
Rosary,
  joyful mysteries of, II, 83
  and Lepanto, IV, 89
  as Marian devotion, IV, 92
  mysteries of, IV, 92 f
  how to say, IV, 93
  indulgences of, IV, 93
Rota, Roman, III, 209
Rousseau, III, 355
Rubrics, II, 530
Rule of Faith,
  Scripture as, I, 86
  Living Voice as, I, 77 f

Sabbath, I, 454
Sacramental graces of Matrimony, IV, 267
Sacramental principle, II, 555
Sacramentality,
  third blessing of matrimony, IV, 270
Sacramentals, II, 555
  an aid to faith, I, 75
  in home, I, 145
  not charms, I, 445
  and the dying, IV, 141
  Marian, IV, 96
Sacrament,
  definition of, I, 308
  essentials of, I, 308 ff
  outward sign of, I, 309
Sacraments,
  in general, I, 307-326
  Baptism, I, 302 ff; II, 562 ff
  Confirmation, I, 361 ff; III, 98 ff
  Holy Eucharist, II, 546
  Penance, III, 401 ff
  Extreme Unction, IV, 124 ff
  Holy Orders, III, 193; IV, 210 ff
  Matrimony, IV, 242 ff
  and faith, I, 76
  matter of, I, 309
  signs and effects of, I, 311
  divine institution of, I, 312
  number of, I, 313

proof of number, I, 313
why only seven, I, 314
producing character, I, 317
minister of, I, 318
administration of, I, 318 ff
conditions for valid administration of, I, 318
validity not dependent on faith or holiness of minister, I, 319
reception of, I, 320 ff
valid reception of, I, 320
worthy reception of, I, 320-21
dignity of, I, 322
source of grace, II, 552
the great signs, II, 557
supply seven spiritual needs, II, 557
what they do for us, II, 558
elements of, II, 558
confer grace, II, 559
how they produce their effects, II, 560
review of, III, 400
as Church's means of sanctification, III, 186
Last, IV, 122
  administration of, IV, 139
See also under separate sacraments
Sacred Heart, devotion to, III, 353
Sacred Penitentiary, III, 209
Sacred Scripture,
  and St. Jerome, III, 272
  See Bible, Scripture, Revelation
Sacrifice,
  an act of religion, I, 432
  Christ calls for, II, 282
  prelude to divine union, II, 444
  universality of, II, 444
  in Old Law, II, 445
  Mosaic sacrifices, II, 447
  nature of, II, 449
  purpose of, II, 449
  necessity of, II, 452
  Calvary the perfect sacrifice, II, 453
  interior and exterior, II, 464
Sacrilege, I, 441
Saducees, II, 325
St. Agatha, III, 262
St. Agnes, I, 66
St. Albert the Great, III, 327
St. Alphonsus, and Mary, IV, 57
St. Ambrose, III, 271
St. Angela Merici, III, 347
St. Anne, IV, 28
St. Ansgar, III, 302
St. Anthony, first abbot, III, 263
St. Athanasius, III, 268
St. Augustine, III, 271

St. Augustine, Apostle of England, III, 288
St. Bartholomew's Day, III, 349
St. Basil, III, 268
  and monasticism, III, 264
St. Bede, III, 295
St. Benedict of Nursia, III, 281
  Medal of, I, 445
  Rule of, III, 282
St. Bernadette Soubirous, III, 361; IV, 86
St. Bernard, III, 317
St. Boniface, III, 295 ff
St. Catherine of Sienna, III, 331
St. Cecelia, I, 43
  crypt of, I, 89
St. Charles Borromaeo, III, 347
St. Clement of Rome, I, 63; III, 260
St. Columba, III, 284
St. Columbanus, III, 284
St. Clare, III, 325
St. Cyril and Methodius, III, 303
St. Felicitas, III, 261
  martyrdom of, III, 72
St. Francis of Assisi, III, 323
St. Frances de Sales, III, 353
St. Gall, III, 284
St. Genevieve, III, 276
St. Gregory, I, the Great, III, 287
St. Gregory,
  Nazianzen, III, 269
  of Nyssa, III, 269
St. Hilarion, III, 264
St. Ignatius of Antioch, I, 63
  martyrdom of, III, 72
St. Ignatius Loyola, III, 347
St. Irenaeus, I, 63; III, 260
St. Isaac Jogues, III, 354
St. Jerome, III, 271
St. Joachim, IV, 28
St. Joan of Arc, III, 335
St. John Baptist, I, 131; II, 67, 193
  death of, II, 240
St. John Baptist de la Salle, III, 353
St. John Bosco, III, 361
St. John Chrysostom, III, 270
St. John of the Cross, III, 345
St. John Damascene, III, 293
St. John Fisher, III, 344
St. John Nepomucene,
  martyr of Seal of confession, III, 417
St. John Vianney, III, 360
St. Joseph,
  Devotion to, and happy death, IV, 117
  life of, IV, 117 ff
  virtues of, IV, 119

death of, IV, 119 f
patron of happy death, IV, 121
a just man, IV, 121
feasts of, IV, 121 f
St. Justin, Martyr, Apologies of, I, 63
St. Leo, the Great, and Attila, III, 277
St. Louis, III, 322
St. Margaret Mary, III, 353
St. Mary Major, Church of, IV, 83
St. Mary of the Snows, Church of, IV, 83 f
St. Pachomius, III, 263
St. Patrick, III, 278
St. Paul, III, 252, 254
St. Paul the Hermit, III, 263
St. Perpetua, III, 261
  martyrdom of, III, 73
St. Peter,
  confession of faith, II, 249
  at Transfiguration, II, 253
  denies Christ, II, 350 ff
  made head of Church, II, 406
  first sermon of, III, 68
  promised captaincy of Church, III, 146
  as pilot of Ark of New Testament, III, 158
  primacy of, II, 150 ff
  after Pentecost, III, 252
  martyrdom of, III, 254
  promised Power of Keys, II, 405
  as Christ's representative, IV, 513
  receives Christ's titles, IV, 514
  power received by, IV, 516
  supremacy of, IV, 516
St. Peter Canisius, III, 347
St. Philip Neri, III, 347
St. Polycarp, I, 63; III, 260
St. Rose of Lima, III, 354
St. Scholastica, III, 282
St. Simon Stock, and scapular, IV, 96
St. Stephen, Martyr, I, 66
St. Teresa of Avila, III, 345
St. Therese of Child Jesus, III, 360
St. Thomas, II, 404
St. Thomas Aquinas, III, 327
  and the Mass, II, 507
  on Mary's virtues, IV, 57
St. Thomas à Becket, III, 319
St. Thomas More,
  and the Mass, II, 509
  and Henry VIII, III, 344
St. Vincent de Paul, III, 353
Saints,
  Communion of, III, 198
  and detachment, IV, 381
  and Eucharist, II, 595
  and Faith, I, 42

feasts of, I, 131
and Mary, IV, 90
as models, I, 129
proper of, I, 143, *See* Sanctoral
Cycle
and self denial, I, 285
value of reading the lives of, I, 58
Salerno, university of, III, 317
Samaritan, Good, Parable of, II, 267
Sanctification,
of Faithful, a purpose of the Liturgical Year, I, 109
Church's power of, III, 185 ff
Sanctifying grace, II, 411 ff
and the indwelling of the Trinity, I, 192
where obtained, I, 304
in Confirmation, I, 366
an effect of the sacrament of Matrimony, IV, 266
See Grace, sanctifying
Sanctoral Cycle, I, 111, 129
Sanhedrin,
condemns Christ, II, 354
Santa Casa, IV, 45
Saracens, III, 292, 301
Satan,
temptations from, I, 278
characteristics of, I, 278
special tactics of, I, 278 f
See also Demons
Satisfaction,
an effect of the Mass, II, 493
for sin, III, 455
sacramental, III, 455
as to eternal and temporal punishment, III, 456
nature of, III, 456
intention to perform penance essential, III, 457
special value of, III, 457
antidote to remains of sin, III, 457
in Early Church, III, 457 f
extra-sacramental,
need of, III, 461
virtue of penance, III, 461
means of exercising, III, 464
value of voluntary, III, 465
indulgences, III, 470
fruits of, III, 477
Saturday, Mary's day, IV, 92
Saviour, *see* Redeemer
Savonarola, III, 336
Scandal, III, 552 ff
of children, II, 255
Christ's teaching on, II, 284
defined, III, 553

gravity of, III, 553
how given, III, 553
by deed, and omission, III, 555
obligation to repair, III, 556
in sins,
of impurity, III, 598
Scapular,
of Mt. Carmel, IV, 96
on sick person, IV, 141 f
Schism,
defined, I, 69
Great Western, III, 331
Schismatic, III, 141
Scholasticism, III, 327
School,
Church and, II, 169
non-Catholic, harmful influence on faith, I, 73
attendance at non-Catholic forbidden, I, 73
Schoolmen, Great, III, 327
Sciences,
fostered by Church, III, 325
Scientific experiments endangering life or health, III, 549
Scourging, of Christ, II, 362
Science,
and Faith, I, 44 ff
Catholic Church and, I, 46
Scripture, Sacred,
as source of Deposit of Faith, I, 79
first source of revelation, I, 80
See also, Bible; Revelation
Seal of Confession, IV, 400
Season, Proper of, I, 143
See, Temporal Cycle
Secret,
keeping a, obligation of, IV, 400 f
professional, obligation of observing, IV, 389, 400
Secret societies, III, 355
Secretary of State, papal, III, 209
Sectional Outlines (for page references to, see Table of Contents in each volume)
Sects, religious, variety of, not intended by Christ, IV, 511
Sedia Gestatoria, III, 205
Self control, III, 516
necessity of, I, 281; III, 573
nobility of, I, 282
Self defense,
in taking life, III, 528
Self denial,
as a means of spreading the Faith, I, 99
need of, II, 251
Self-esteem,
a basic tendency, III, 500

Self sacrifice,
and love in marriage, IV, 319
Seminary, IV, 205, 212
Seniors, foreword to, IV, 15
Sense, pain of,
in hell, IV, 162
in purgatory, IV, 164
Senses,
custody of, I, 283
need of controlling, III, 574, 584
Separation, ecclesiastical, IV, 294
Septuagesima, I, 121
Septuagint, I, 85, 88
Sequence,
of subject-matter, charts showing,
IV, 10-12
Sequence of the dead, IV, 149
Sermon,
St. Peter's first, III, 68
Servile work,
defined, I, 456
when permitted, I, 456
why we abstain, I, 457
Servites, IV, 99
Seventh Commandment,
purpose of, IV, 353
Sex,
instruction,
danger of unwise, III, 581; IV,
301
detailed, unnecessary, III, 582
to be given privately, III, 582
will training more important
than, III, 582
power
sinfulness of misuse of, III, 593
tendency, III, 558; IV, 254
purpose and necessity, III, 558
not evil in itself, III, 558
God helps us to control, III, 558 f
Shepherd, Good, II, 263
Sick,
should know seriousness of their
condition, IV, 135
visiting, a work of mercy, IV, 144
Sick call,
who is to be summoned for, IV, 134
receiving priest, IV, 139
Sick room,
preparing, IV, 138
Signatura, Apostolic, III, 209
Signs,
and the sacraments, I, 309 ff
sacramental,
reasons for use of, I, 310
in life, II, 553
natural and arbitrary, II, 554

Simeon, II, 72
Simonians, III, 255
Simony, I, 442
Simple, God is, I, 162
Sin,
definition of, I, 417; II, 118; III,
378
kinds of, I, 418; II, 119; II, 378
original, I, 418
actual sin, I, 418; III, 378
kinds of, I, 419
as to degrees of guilt, I, 419
mortal, I, 419
conditions for, I, 419; II, 120 f;
III, 380
malice of, I, 420
venial, I, 421; III, 382
evils of, I, 421; III, 383
semideliberate, I, 422
Christ forgives, II, 211
power to forgive, II, 256
avoidance of, a duty to Holy
Spirit, III, 124
and Indwelling Spirit, III, 369
and membership in Mystical Body,
III, 370
one great evil in life, III, 377
degrees of gravity in, III, 384
habitual, III, 385
forgiveness of and God's perfections,
III, 393 ff
venial, how forgiven, III, 397
forgiven by sacraments, III, 397
forgiven by perfect charity and contrition, III, 397
mortal,
concealing in confession, III, 450
satisfaction for, III, 455
See, Satisfaction for sin
remitted by Extreme Unction, IV,
127
offering, II, 460
Sins,
capital, I, 410 ff
Christ gives Apostles power to forgive, II, 402
circumstances of, to be confessed if
necessary, III, 423
crying to heaven for vengeance, III,
384
against Holy Ghost, III, 384
doubtful, obligation to confess, III,
450
forgotten, III, 450
mortal,
if unconfessed are necessary matter for confession, III, 423

forgiveness of,
  Church has power of, III, 404
  scriptural proof of Christ's power
    of, III, 404
  power of promised to Apostles,
    III, 405 f
  power conferred, III, 407
  passed on to successors of Apos-
    tles, III, 407 f
  See, forgiveness of sins
  remission of, an effect of Penance,
    III, 481
  reserved, III, 412
Sincerity,
  necessary in confession, III, 447
Single, state in world, IV, 230 ff
Sisters,
  fields of activity of, IV, 224
  of Charity, III, 353
Slander,
  nature and gravity, IV, 394
  reparation of, IV, 395
Slavs,
  conversion of, III, 303
Sloth,
  and related vices and virtues, I,
    415-16
Smoking,
  morality of, III, 549
Social importance of Mass, II, 497
Social apostles,
  lay should be prepared, IV, 441
Social conditions,
  improvement of, by civil
    authorities, IV, 411
Social evils,
  traceable to covetousness, IV, 423
Social institutions,
  reform of, needed, IV, 418
Social justice,
  defined, IV, 407 f
  a guiding principle in economic
    life, IV, 420
Social order,
  reforms needed in, IV, 418
    require cooperation of all, IV, 420
    require reform of morals, IV, 420
Social pressure,
  exerting, to oppose errors on mar-
    riage, IV, 300
Social problem,
  and the encyclicals, IV, 405
Social Reconstruction,
  Pius XI's encyclical on, IV, 402 ff
  requires return to Gospel living, IV,
    IV, 423
  not an easy task, IV, 425

plan of procedure in, IV, 425 f
demands return to Christian living
  and institutions, IV, 423
complete plan for, IV, 439 f
Social reforms, required, IV, 421
Social teaching of Church,
  proof of God's love, IV, 403
Social unity, of Church, III, 161
Socialism,
  dangerous error, IV, 415
  two camps of, IV, 422
  contrary to Christian truth, IV, 422
  proposals of, IV, 434
  why opposed to Catholic teachings,
    IV, 434
Socialist,
  good Catholic cannot be a, IV, 422
Society, perfect,
  Church as a, III, 168; 189 ff
Society of Jesus, III, 347
Societies, Marian, IV, 97
Soul,
  in heaven, I, 20
  a spiritual being, I, 236
  immortal, I, 236; IV, 114
  separation of, from body, IV, 113
  death and, IV, 114
    nature of, IV, 114
  natural and supernatural life of, IV,
    114
  strengthened by Extreme Unction,
    IV, 129
Souls,
  in Purgatory, and the Mass, II, 495
  sanctity of, III, 520
  protecting supernatural life of, III,
    523
Source, God as our, I, 152 ff
Spanish Armada, III, 349
Speech,
  purpose of power of, IV, 383
Speeding, III, 546
Spendthrift habits,
  endanger happy marriage, IV, 308
Spiration,
  as second procession, III, 54
Spirit,
  God as a, I, 36, 158
Spirit, Holy (*See,* Holy Spirit)
Spirit, pure, nature of, I, 158
Spirituality,
  of glorified body, IV, 178
Sponsors,
  for Baptism, I, 347
    necessity and duties of, I, 348
    qualifications of, I, 349
  in Confirmation, I, 382

571

Spouses, duties of, IV, 272
Stabat Mater, IV, 78
Star, as symbol of Holy Spirit, III, 120
State,
 purpose of, II, 174
 source of authority, II, 175
 exists for people, II, 175
 obedience to, commanded by Christ, II, 323
 and Church, principles governing relations of, II, 148; III, 189
 Christ's answer on relations of, II, 324
 as perfect society, III, 189
 and Church, III, 329
 absolutism, danger of, III, 190
 should promote organizations of members of industry or profession, IV, 419
 struggles for control of, a result of economic dictatorship, IV, 421
 must control free competition, IV, 421
State of life,
 freedom of choice of, II, 164; IV, 194 ff
 prayer for choosing, IV, 221
 unmarried, IV, 230 ff
Stations of Cross, II, 366
"Steady" company,
 morality of keeping, III, 603
Stealing, IV, 357
 grave amount in, IV, 358
 by cooperation, IV, 358
 an exception, grave necessity, IV, 360
Sterilization, IV, 283
Stinginess,
 to be avoided, IV, 380
Stipend, II, 533
Strength, Confirmation and, III, 101
Strike,
 just and unjust, IV, 361
 condition for just, IV, 362
 as last resort, IV, 363
Study circles,
 recommended by pope, IV, 441
Subdiaconate,
 powers of, IV, 213
Subject matter,
 chart showing division of, for four years, I-IV, 10-11
 survey of four years of course in, II, 17
 sectional outlines of, *see,* Table of Contents, for page references

where to locate major subdivisions, I-IV, 10-11, II, 28
location of major areas, III, 26
for senior year, outline of, IV, 18
Substance,
 meaning of, II, 589
 change of, II, 589
Suffering,
 as point of departure in apologetics, IV, 486
Suicide, III, 539 ff
 gravity of, III, 539
 causes of, III, 540
 guards against, III, 541
 slow, III, 541
Summary,
 of four years, III, 17-19
Sunday,
 in Liturgical Year, I, 133
 and prayer, I, 455
 sanctification of, I, 454 ff; III, 535 ff
Superstition, I, 444
Supremacy, Oath of, III, 344
Supernatural rights of Church, III, 189
Suspension,
 definition of, III, 413
Suspicion, unfounded,
 violates neighbor's rights, IV, 399
Syllabus of Errors, of Pius IX, III, 358
Symbolism,
 of ceremonies of Baptism, I, 352-59
 of ceremonies of Confirmation, I, 382-86
Symbols,
 of Trinity, I, 196 ff
 of Holy Spirit, III, 119 ff
Synod, diocesan, III, 214

Tale bearing, IV, 399
Tantum Ergo, II, 625
Tattle-tales,
 ignobility of, IV, 399
Teacher,
 source of authority, II, 169
 duties of, II, 142
Teaching,
 unity in, a mark of true Church, III, 158
 power of Church, III, 181 ff
 social, of Church, a proof of God's love, IV, 403
Temperance, III, 386
 virtue for junior year, III, 24; 511 ff
 definition of, III, 513
 in relation to other virtues, III, 514

natural tendency toward, III, 514
virtues allied to, III, 515
vices opposed to, III, 515
Temporal Cycle,
divisions of, I, 111 f
Christmas season of, I, 113 ff
Paschal or Easter season of, I,
120 ff
Temporal Missions, of Holy Spirit,
III, 57
Temporal Power, of Pope, III, 297-9
Temporal Welfare,
purpose of State, II, 174
Church's concern for, IV, 403
Temptation,
Eucharist strengthens against, II,
600
nature of, III, 387
reacting to, III, 388
dallying with, III, 388
sources of, III, 388
means of avoiding, III, 390
why permitted by God, III, 390
is not sin, III, 600
how to handle, III, 392
Temptations, and the Gifts of the Holy
Ghost, I, 368
Tendencies,
basic human, II, 124; III, 499 ff
form virtues when properly directed,
III, 500
list of, III, 501
purpose of, III, 501
virtues and vices arising from, III,
501
bodily, III, 511, 513
and their control, III, 511 f
basic rule regarding, III, 513
Tendency,
basic human attracting man to
woman, III, 558
Tertullian, I, 64; IV, 261 f
Tetzel, III, 342
Teutonic tribes,
Conversion of, III, 295 ff
Thanksgiving,
an effect of the Mass, II, 492
Theatines, III, 347
Theme,
central
for four years, I, 22; II, 118; III,
19; IV, 17
for freshman year, I, 23
for sophomore year, II, 23
of junior year, III, 20
for senior year, IV, 19
Theodosius, III, 270

Theological,
definition of, I, 41
Thief,
Good, II, 369
Thirty Years War, III, 350
Thoughts, sinful, III, 597
Tiara, papal, III, 203 f
Tierce, and Holy Spirit, III, 117
Titles, of Pope, III, 202
Time,
proper of, *see,* Season
Tolerance, III, 354
Tongue,
guarding modesty of, III, 590
Tonsure, IV, 211
Total abstinence, III, 543, 545
Totila, III, 285
Tours, Battle of, III, 292
Tradition,
as basis of Deposit of Faith, I, 79 ff
and the Living Voice, I, 79 ff
second source of revelation, I, 89
meaning of, I, 91
value of, I, 93
where recorded, I, 94
and the Trinity, I, 181
Trajan, III, 255
Transfiguration, II, 251
Transubstantiation, II, 587
explained, II, 590
errors on, II, 591
Trent, Council of, III, 345, 347
Trinity, Holy,
mystery of mysteries, I, 175
Keystone of our Faith, I, 175
benefits of knowing, I, 178
revelation of, I, 179
foreshadowed in Old Testament, I,
179
clearly revealed in New Testament,
I, 180
in tradition, I, 181
what we can know about it, I, 182 ff
taught by Church, I, 182
wherein mystery lies, I, 184
not contrary to reason, I, 185
eternity and equality of Persons in,
I, 187
reflections in nature of, I, 189
in man, I, 190
mystery of, above all creatures, I,
176
Indwelling of, I, 191
in the soul, I, 192
in Liturgy, I, 195 ff
key position of, I, 198
attacks on, I, 198 ff

and unity of God, III, 46
Indwelling of, III, 79
Truce of God, III, 309
Truth,
God is, I, 160
man has right to, IV, 384
vices opposed to, IV, 387 ff
Church as channel of, IV, 518
Truthfulness, IV, 383 ff
necessity of, IV, 384
practice of, in imitation of divine
perfections, IV, 401
Turks, III, 292

Understanding,
Gift of, I, 370; III, 110
Unemployment,
a sequel of unbalanced wage scales,
IV, 418
Ungunda, wife of Hermenegild, III,
286
Unhappiness, source of, I, 17
Union,
with God,
the Eucharist and, II, 441
with Christ,
an effect of the Eucharist, II, 597
Unions,
Catholic preferred, IV, 437
industry-wide, need of, IV, 439
Unitarianism, I, 200
Units,
sequence of, for four years, I-IV, 12
Unity,
an objective of the liturgy, I, 110
as mark of Church, III, 158 ff; IV,
512
social, of Church, III, 161
of our Faith, IV, 16
as a quality of marriage, IV, 250 ff
difficulty of maintaining, IV, 514
Universality,
as mark of Church, III, 163 f
Universe,
planning in, proves existence of
God, I, 33
creation of, I, 217
and Divine Providence, I, 229
existence of,
not taken into account in theories
of atheists, IV, 472
complexity of, proves intellect ordering it, IV, 475
Universities,
mediaeval, III, 317
and scholasticism, III, 327

Unions,
federation of, need of, IV, 439
Unmarried state, IV, 230 ff
advisability of, IV, 230
motives for choosing, IV, 230 f
difficulties of, IV, 231
Unrest, social
traceable to violations of marriage,
IV, 243
Untruthfulness,
sinfulness of, IV, 393
Usury, IV, 370
Utilitarianism, III, 507
answered, III, 508

Validity of marriage,
famous declarations of, IV, 296
requirements for, IV, 242 ff, 262 ff
Vandals, III, 278
Vatican Council, III, 358
on papal infallibility, III, 174
Veneration and adoration, I, 430
Veracity, See, Truthfulness
Vestments, of Mass, II, 531
Viaticum, II, 611; IV, 122
obligation to receive, IV, 123
and eucharistic fast, IV, 123
administration of, IV, 139
Vicar General, III, 213·
Vice,
and habitual sin, III, 385
and virtue, III, 386
Vices, I, 410-417; II, 122
basic, II, 124
opposed to Christian marriage, IV,
277
opposed to blessing of children, IV,
277
opposed to conjugal fidelity, IV, 283
Vigils, I, 136
Vikings, III, 301 f
Virginity,
virtue of, III, 592
a supernatural virtue, III, 592
perpetual of Blessed Virgin, IV, 33,
51
Virtue, I, 41
definition of, I, 48
aids to practice of, I, 58
planned practices of, I, 57-59
practice of, a duty to Holy Spirit,
III, 125
social importance of, IV, 329
giving example of, IV, 330
of religion, I, 429
and vice, III, 386

574

Virtues,
infused, I, 41 ff
as habits, I, 48 ff; 407 ff
infused supernatural, I, 243
theological, I, 13, 23, 24, 49, 51, 57,
  59 ff, 239, 335, 407-409; II,
  128
  needed in quest, I, 392
  practice of prescribed by first
    commandment, I, 428
  sins against, I, 439 ff
natural, I, 49; II, 127
supernatural, definition of, I, 49-50
natural and supernatural compared,
  I, 50; II, 127
cardinal, I, 24, 51, 54 f, 239, 335,
  407-409; II, 129
how they grow, II, 182
necessity of practice, II, 129
taught by Christ, II, 301
  See also, I, 48 ff, 407 ff
seven basic, I, 52; 407 ff; IV, 67
Christ and the basic, II, 81
of Mary, IV, 56 ff
  theological in Mary, IV, 59 ff
  moral, in Mary, IV, 62 ff
  chastity, IV, 62
  poverty, IV, 63
  obedience, IV, 63 f
  patience, IV, 65
  religion, IV, 66
opposed to capital sins, I, 410-416
opposed to covetousness, IV, 380
theological and moral, and supernatural organism, III, 85
for freshman year, I, 52
for sophomore year, II, 82
for junior year, III, 24
for senior year, IV, 20
Visibility, of Church, III, 154 ff
Vision, Beatific,
essential joy of heaven, IV, 171
nature of, IV, 172
Visitation, II, 64
Vocation,
in life,
  choosing of, IV, 194 ff
Vocation, religious,
grandeur of, IV, 199
signs of, IV, 199 ff
nature of, IV, 201
motives for choosing, IV, 202
impediments to, IV, 203
neglect of, IV, 203
love of pleasure leads to loss of, IV,
  204
testing, IV, 204, 228
for women,
  reasons for neglect of, IV, 228

Vocations,
to the work of the missions, I, 97
religious,
  of women, need of, IV, 226 f
Voltaire, III, 355
Vows, I, 448 ff
conditions for, I, 449
of religion, I, 449
merit of, I, 450
of religious priest, IV, 206, 208
of religion, IV, 223
  and evangelical counsels, IV, 223
  simple and solemn, IV, 223
  effects of, IV, 223
opposed of marriage, IV, 304
Vulgate, I, 85; III, 272

Wage contract, not unjust, IV, 417
Wage, family,
nature of, IV, 417
must be paid, IV, 441
Wages,
proper,
  needed to achieve security for
    poor, IV, 417
  factors governing, IV, 417
  balance between various, needed,
    IV, 418
Wake,
attending a, IV, 144
Waldensians, III, 319
War,
causes of, III, 350
when permitted, III, 530
Warfare, class,
an objective of Communism, IV,
  422
Water,
matter of Baptism, I, 329
baptismal, I, 329
appropriateness as sign of Baptism,
  I, 329
as symbol of Holy Spirit, III, 120
Waterpipes, system of,
as simile in illustrating argument
  from contingency, IV, 481
Wealth,
poor distribution of, a cause of issuing *Rerum Novarum,* IV, 409
concentration of, a danger, IV, 417,
  421
Wedding, oriental, IV, 36
Week, in Liturgical Year, I, 132 ff
Welfare,
common,
  duties of capital and labor to, II,
    145

restricts rights of ownership, IV, 352

temporal,
of men, Church's concern for, IV, 403
relation to spiritual, IV, 403

Western Schism, III, 331 ff

Will,
sin an act of the, I, 417
free, and merit, III, 87
training of,
importance of, in purity, III, 582

Wisdom,
of God, I, 168
shown in forgiveness of sins, III, 395
Gift of, I, 369
highest of gifts, III, 110

Witchcraft, I, 444

Witnesses,
needed for valid marriage, IV, 263

Woman, dress of,
and modesty, III, 587
Christian ideal in, III, 587

Woman, false emancipation of, IV, 284

Women,
religious life for, IV, 219 ff
aids in deciding on choosing, IV, 224 f
need of, IV, 226
careers for, IV, 238 ff
the highest, the Christian artist-mother, IV, 238
workers,
protection of, necessary, IV, 436

Work,
servile, I, 456
nature of, II, 540
when permitted, II, 540
important means of acquiring ownership, IV, 356

Workers,
just wages for, principles governing, IV, 417
associations of, reform of needed, IV, 418
State should promote organizations of, IV, 419

Working conditions,
dangerous, III, 551
healthful, required by justice, IV, 436

Workingman,
encyclical on rights of, II, 173; IV, 406, 409 ff
leadership of, II, 171

World,
an obstacle to happiness, I, 280
tactics of, I, 280
spirit of, I, 280
as source of temptations, III, 389
end of, IV, 175
signs of, IV, 175

Worship,
disparity of, IV, 286
an obligation of nature, II, 536
interior not enough, III, 155
unity of,
a mark of true Church, III, 160

Wyclif, III, 332

Ximines, Cardinal, III, 345

Year, Liturgical, *see,* Liturgical Year

Youth,
spiritual, III, 94
special problems of, III, 602

Zwingli, III, 343